God-Centered Business: A Foundational Framework to Grow with Resilience

Stan Washington

God-Centered Business: A Foundational Framework to Grow with Resilience

Copyright © 2020 Stan Washington

Interior illustrations copyright © 2020 Stan Washington

All rights reserved. This book or any portion thereof may not be reproduced or used in any manner whatsoever without the express written permission of the publisher except for the use of brief quotations in a book review.

Scripture taken from the New King James Version. Copyright © 1982 by Thomas Nelson, Inc. Used by permission. All rights reserved.

Scripture quotations marked (CEV) are from the Contemporary English Version Copyright © 1991, 1992, 1995 by American Bible Society, Used by Permission.

Scripture quotations marked (NIV) are taken from the Holy Bible, New International Version®, NIV®. Copyright © 1973, 1978, 1984, 2011 by Biblica, Inc.™ Used by permission of Zondervan. All rights reserved worldwide. www.zondervan.comThe "NIV" and "New International Version" are trademarks registered in the United States Patent and Trademark Office by Biblica, Inc.™

Scriptures marked as "(GNT)" are taken from the Good News Translation - Second Edition © 1992 by American Bible Society. Used by permission.

Scripture quotations marked (NLT) are taken from the Holy Bible, New Living Translation, copyright © 1996, 2004, 2007, 2013, 2015 by Tyndale House Foundation. Used by permission of Tyndale House Publishers, Inc., Carol Stream, Illinois 60188. All rights reserved.

Scripture quotations are from the ESV® Bible (The Holy Bible, English Standard Version®), copyright © 2001 by Crossway, a publishing ministry of Good News Publishers. Used by permission. All rights reserved.

The Holy Bible, Berean Study Bible, BSB, BLB
Copyright ©2016, 2018 by Bible Hub
Used by Permission. All Rights Reserved Worldwide.

Scripture taken from the NEW AMERICAN STANDARD BIBLE®, Copyright © 1960, 1962, 1963, 1968, 1971, 1972, 1973, 1975, 1977, 1995 by The Lockman Foundation. Used by permission.

Scriptures marked (WNT) are from the Weymouth New Testament. The Weymouth New Testament, otherwise known as *The New Testament in Modern Speech* or *The Modern Speech New Testament*, is a translation of the New Testament into nineteenth century English by Richard Francis Weymouth. Third Edition 1913 Public Domain. These files were produced by keying for use in the Online Bible. Proofreading was performed by Earl Melton. The printed edition used in creating this etext was the Kregal reprint of the Ernest Hampden-Cook (1912) Third Edition, of the edition first published in 1909 by J. Clarke, London. Kregal edition ISBN 0-8254-4025-4..

Printed in the United States of America

First Printing, 2020

ISBN: 978-0-9909831-6-3

DEDICATION

This book is dedicated to those GOD has called to be an entrepreneur and to those HE has called to teach, who have a heart filled with HIS grace and are willing to patiently grow HIS flock through imparting business concepts to many.

This book is also dedicated to those who have been silenced, devalued, and marginalized. GOD says you are very valuable to HIM and you have unique talents no one else has.

Contents

It Starts with You

Many people spend wasteful time trying to be someone else. I know I did. I did not like my body, hair, name, or bank account amount. I felt GOD had made a mistake or was punishing me for being alive. I could not be further from the truth. It wasn't until I realized that GOD made me special and that I am the only one who can reach certain people, that I started to be successful.

Why this is important

Quite honestly, something snapped when I was on a short term missions trip in Harare, Zimbabwe. We drove past the president's palace at 50 miles per hour for at least a half-hour. When we finally reached our destination, a ragtag bunch of pastors, brave enough to preach and teach, got out of the van and spoke about JESUS. Many people who had huts outside of the palace gave their lives to be saved. They received hope they never had before.

Like clockwork the mountain top experience wore off when I returned to the states and I went back to ignoring the poor and homeless. It was easy to do because the homeless were invisible people. But GOD kept summoning me to serve this community every now and then. I would serve at a shelter and go on short term missions trips to Wu Jiang China and Rosarito Mexico, where I saw entire families living on the street. After I gave my Yuan and a few Pesos as a temporary solution to whoever was in front of me at that time, I tried to make a difference, so I told people about JESUS and that became the eternal difference maker. I am not alone as many people want to make a difference and are doing it in their own way.

From saving animals, to buildings, to old traditions, there are many voices calling over each other, trying to advocate for their cause. However, it has become increasingly clear that while advocacy is great, it should not be the finish line. GOD wants a simple message. "Believe in MY SON."

GOD has blessed many entrepreneurs with a talent unique to only her or him. Some are gifted in hospitality, others in art, others in something they consult with people as a service. All GOD wants is a mention of HIS gift, namely JESUS. But some entrepreneurs are too hurt to mention JESUS.

The hurt entrepreneurs are feeling is quite devastating. Many entrepreneurs have lost their businesses over the past 20 months due to financial woes or a well-known pandemic problem and some have lost hope. They need guidance and are now willing to listen to GOD. A focused effort is needed to guide business owners in solid business practices, while enabling creativity in sharing the love of CHRIST.

The primary goal

Many business owners who crave "success' and exposure will shout about their business more than they speak about JESUS. This framework will help you identify your GOD given talent, vision and audience. The goal of this class is to create a community of mature followers of CHRIST who are not only **successful business owners** but GOD-centered business owners who seek growing HIS kingdom.

Introduction

Has GOD given you a desire to go into business, but you feel conflicted because of the many lessons you've read or heard from those who place money and power over GOD? It is difficult to navigate literature that sometimes goes against the person GOD created you to be.

About the Author

As I sat in the expensive executive company car given to me to drive as I pleased, I could not convince myself to leave my true identity in the car any longer. Everything within me said I was living a lie when it came to serving GOD by serving those who craved money over people.

When requested to lead a daily message of godly encouragement to employees, I declined. I did not want my relationship with JESUS known at work because I was afraid I would offend someone. GOD took care of that.

When I left my previous company after being down-sized, I worried about getting another position of power and wealth. I searched day and night with fear and anxiety. Many rejections came. Finally, I received a couple of offers. Something was wrong. One offer, while powerful and lucrative, seemed the same as the job I left. The other was from a hotel chain. Strange words were mentioned in the interview.

"We are in charge of the porn shown in the guest rooms," the interviewer said.

Should I overlook this and get the money? I considered.

But GOD said, "Make a choice." I turned the positions down with no other offers in sight. I felt broken.

A friend said, "You have to do something." So I started a business. Having good intentions, I became a career coach. It was a safe choice and easy to start. I took online classes on starting a business, even though I had helped small business owners for years to reach millions in sales. Yet I felt more prepared because I had led a large organization within the world's largest quick service restaurant.

After mediocre success with my startup, my money was getting low.

"LORD, what is going on?" I asked in prayer, feeling dejected.

HE gave me a vision to use the skills I learned being a leader, mixed with running technology-focused efforts. For years afterwards, I and others had toiled over building a technology platform that would be affordable and rival other platforms. We prayed for triumph daily.

> Money was coming in, but my heart was empty.

I started seeing some success, but that was not the complete vision. Money was coming in, but my heart was empty. The model was working, but something was still wrong.

Restless one night, I fought for sleep.

"Whose business is this?" I felt the inquiry in my spirit.

"YOURS," I said in response to GOD. I mean, the answer had to be "YOURS" when the voice I heard came from GOD. Unlike the encounter Peter had when he denied CHRIST three times and was questioned three times by JESUS for restoration, I was questioned several times. Exhausted, I answered, "YOURS," this time with humility, not knowing what was to come.

GOD then said, "Then give ME 100% of the company."

"What does that mean?" I asked.

His reply did not feel good. "Let go of the customers who have been paying but not using the service." That was a scary statement.

He then said, "Change the method in which you do business. Write this method down and help people see Me."

After taking a deep breath, I realized HE was serious. I sent messages to all the customers HE told me to, and stopped writing the wealth-driven methodology I had started. I quieted down to listen to GOD. "Now what?" I asked.

"Feed MY sheep," HE answered.

"What? Am I supposed to become a pastor or something?"

"No," HE answered. "Just show them how to make ME the center of their lives and businesses. Let ME provide the increase to those who are truly seeking ME."

About the Methodology

The methodology you will find in this book was written for those who want to be successful in their business and serve GOD through their business. From raking leaves to selling a product or service, they want GOD to be shown through their service to others. GOD can be the center of your business, enabling more people to see HIM and come to HIM as their Savior.

Who is this book for?

For Entrepreneurs (Learn by Teaching)

If you are a business owner who is curious about the principles of a GOD-centered business and how to share these principles with others, wonderful choice! Incorporating GOD into your business is exactly the purpose of this methodology. One leadership quality GOD desires is that we make disciples for HIM. Teach the framework to enable your staff or fellow business owners to discover answers and grow in their faith in JESUS.

GOD will expand your territory as you show that you truly seek HIM as you run your business.

For Organization Leaders (Administrators, Executive Leaders, and Pastors)

Thank you for being a transformation leader!

The GOD-Centered Business is a transformational methodology that challenges business owners to fully give their lives to JESUS and make Him known through a renewed look at their approach to operating their business.

GOD provides the vision.
GOD grows the business leader to grow people.
GOD increases the business in unexpected ways.

Build a community where entrepreneurs can come together to solve problems while surrendering their lives to GOD to be used for His purpose. This guide has tips to help you provide atmosphere of accountability so people will not slip through the cracks. Be successful together.

For Instructors (Volunteers, Group Leaders, Facilitators)

Congratulations for being chosen to lead a flock of business owners in the direction of GOD's purposes for their lives. Your role is key to the success of many. Teaching the GOD-Centered Business methodology is your chance to plant the seeds of encouragement that will be passed on to the business owner's customers. In turn their customers may be added to your flock to be prayed for and nurtured.

What will a successful program look like?

Teach the framework versus trying to answer all the questions. You will be successful if you can be transparent about mistakes, times when you lacked knowledge, and any struggles you have as a human that are appropriate to reveal within a class period. Let your class know you are a guide and will provide them with a framework where they can follow GOD for their answers. As an instructor, your goal is to get the class to think rather than trying to have the information fully understood and adopted right in front of you.

What is the purpose of this book?

Self-study or group study. The goal is to build a local community where business leaders can learn to **be successful *in*** business and serve GOD ***through*** their business. This book is designed to guide participants in a course of study called the GOD-Centered Business. Throughout this course there are exercises that will serve as tools to help entrepreneurs think. Each image and accompanying exercise has been carefully cultivated to broaden the participant's thinking.

The information, while presented in a linear fashion, is to be used over and over. The more you follow the principles and guidelines, the better you will become at using the principles. One cycle through all of the information is known as an iteration. Be careful about teaching bits and pieces of the information outside of the suggested structure of the class as each chapter builds upon the last and assumes the you have completed exercises from the previous chapter.

If you are doing a self-study, then you can skip the section on setting up a class and go to "**Questions You May Have**" found after the Checklist for Groups or Classes. My prayer, however, is that you stop working alone. If you are not part of a community, then prayerfully form one.

Action Steps to Get Started

1. Start with a group of business people who need to talk.

What is success to GOD?

Remember those who are hurting.

According to the Small Business Administration, in 2018 there were 30.2 million small businesses in the United States. According to CNBC, in 2020 7.5 Million small businesses were at risk of going out of business permanently.

Many entrepreneurs have fallen on hard times and are possibly ready to turn their hearts to GOD, but with such overwhelming numbers, the laborers are few. Also, many who have lost their jobs are considering starting a business, but do not know how. Some who are widowed, single parents, divorced, mature, or medically challenged, feel forgotten as they take on the challenge of a business, seemingly, by themselves. Tell them they are remembered.

Instead of having the business owner search the internet or get advice that may be contrary to your faith teaching, why not incorporate the GOD-centered business curriculum into your overall ministry or business strategy. The purpose of forming a group of business leaders is to provide support and love for those who feel isolated.

2. Present the framework

The GOD-centered business owner dreams bigger than herself or himself. Your business is about people. GOD guides the business and guides the business owner to the people to serve. You can come alongside by presenting this curriculum to your congregation or to the local business owners GOD sends your way.

If you are teaching a class, here is the suggested schedule:
Week 1: Dream Bigger—Allowing GOD to stretch you to achieve HIS vision for your business.
Week 2: Remove the Trash—Modifying your leadership style to align to GOD's passion.
Week 3: Seek Wisdom—Depending on GOD to identify and fill gaps in resources and skills.
Week 4: Go to the Desert—Breaking GOD's vision into small pieces to plan and prepare for resilience.
Week 5: Emerge Different—Being led by GOD to price and market your expertise in your industry.
Week 6: Kingdom-First Mindset—Gaining confidence from GOD to tell versus sell.
Week 7: Lead to Promises—Living GOD's promises through outstanding customer service.

If you are delivering this in a class, this book is designed to help the presenter as well as the recipient learn about GOD and follow HIM. If you are doing a self-study, then you will be fully satisfied with the content, but I urge you to get with a group to discuss. This structured method is flexible for all business types. It is meant for business owners to work together with their customers to discover gaps in their business strategy versus guessing at blind spots. It can be used as a one-time seven-week class or an ongoing group that goes through the information in ten-week increments, with classes three or four hours per week.

Through this class, business owners will learn how to retrofit or create a resilient business that withstands life's obstacles and grows with purpose. As you walk with them during this class, you can remind them that they are called to an incredible work. You're here to walk alongside them just as CHRIST does.

3. Select instructors. (If you are organizing a class)

The best instructors have T.I.M.E.

Teachable: The willingness to learn something new is highly important.

Innovative: 1. Very creative people or 2. GOD has given them a business idea, but maybe they don't know how to get going with it.

Motivated: Dependable and available to teach consistently for 10 weeks (three weeks of preparation time; seven weeks of instruction). One to two hours of preparation time is also needed each week.

Excited: Holding attention takes enthusiasm and excitement. A passion for making CHRIST known is required.

Imperfect people are required.

The best instructors also know they aren't perfect. People with rough edges are those who feel they do not have themselves together. Encourage this group that imperfect people are required. Explain to the reluctant that even if they aren't good at speaking, have failed over and over, or have some other barrier but still have a passion for making Jesus known as the only answer to salvation and earthly problems, then they are great candidates to lead a group through the GOD-centered business class.

4. Pray, prepare, practice and produce.

Pray. Encouragement is desperately needed. Please pray for the business leaders in your congregation or community. Some work so hard, they have no time for anything else. Transformation is needed from a business-centered life to a GOD-centered business that gives life.

Prayer for the GOD-Centered Business Community

Dear LORD, please bless this community with YOUR wisdom. Fill this group with YOUR HOLY SPIRIT, making the experience special and filled with power. Amen.

Prepare. Here the instructor accepts the "Prepare with a Promise" and "Prepare by Accepting God's Call" terms, and does the required exercises in the first week of the ten-week program.

Prepare with a promise. Groups need structure, especially busy people. Committed instructors are necessary for true transformation. Cancellations happen, but too many cancellations destroy a group. The following promise is taken by the instructor.

I promise, to the best of my ability, to be prayerful, patient, prepared and punctual during the teaching sessions.

Prepare by accepting GOD'S call. Throughout the book I will sometimes call the instructor a teacher. In Ephesians 4:11, teaching is listed as one of the gifts of the Spirit, and therefore is a calling. It is more than volunteering. Called people consider the work GOD has given them to do to be a very high priority in their lives. The assumption is that each teacher would be serious, but a calling is a promise to GOD that you outwardly accept the responsibility for guiding a vulnerable flock.

People are vulnerable and need to talk to others who are trustworthy. Realize that many who are hurt, may not trust those who sound like they are helping but seem to be insincere. That is why it is important to take the teaching position seriously. James writes about it: "My brethren, let not many of you become teachers, knowing that we shall receive a stricter judgment" (James 3:1).

GOD takes the role of the teacher seriously. HE will bless those who are open and honest. If you chose to be a teacher, be honest and admit that you don't have all of the answers. (But have a plan in place to seek more information.)

I promise sincerity in presenting GOD's word, I promise to the best of my ability to teach with gentleness and patience, I also promise to the best of my ability to be open, honest and transparent when teaching this class and any class related to GOD's word.

Prepare by understanding the exercises before teaching. Part of the journey is discovery versus knowing all of the answers. Everyone involved with presenting the information should become familiar with the content of the GOD-Centered Business methodology. Even if you are not presenting but instead are supporting the class, you should be familiar with the methodology. Identify areas where there are gaps in understanding and discuss them with the team involved in the class before presenting the material to participants.

Before teaching, it is important to check your own motives and possible blind spots that can hinder the success of the participants absorbing the information.

The following exercises from chapter 2 can aid in self-examination:

Exercise 2—**Identify the Root to Remove** can help you self-examine behaviors that may block success.
Exercise 3—**Stabilize Your Leadership Style by Filling the Heart** is a leadership adjustment exercise that can help you change the blocking behaviors.

Exercise 8—**Plan to Address Internal Issues** is a problem identification exercise usually performed by business owners to list issues to address.
Exercise 11—**Forgiveness** is an overview on how to forgive
Exercise 12—**Forgive Them** is an exercise to forgive people and be a better leader.
Exercise 13—**Seek Forgiveness** is an exercise to ask for forgiveness and be a

stronger leader.

Some people like to do in-depth study of all the information as part of their preparation. Others like to prepare just before presenting. Whatever your style, being prepared is important to keep the group engaged.

Before teaching the class do Exercises 2, 3, 8, 11, 12 and 13 of "Remove the Trash." Also, review all class materials.

Practice. Perfection is not required— this could not be stressed enough. Practice, however, enables the instructor to become familiar with the information. The instructor can hold a practice session with your staff or he can practice at home by himself.

In either case, jot down notes to give feedback or provide suggestions. Practice time doesn't take seven weeks; rather, it is to be used to discuss how to present the information and to answer questions that may arise.

Produce. Ready to begin the journey? This is a continuous improvement program. The more you do it, the better you will become. Produce the fruit of the Spirit and your efforts will return to you with abundance.

Checklist for Groups or Classes

Preparing for the class is important. To ensure things go as smoothly as possible, pray about the location and obtain it before scheduling the class. This class can be taught in person or online. Also, pray about whether or not you should charging for the class and whether to offer food, certificates, handouts, and other extras.

Some organizations might choose to use this class as a fundraiser. Other organizations may have the funds to pay for everything, including the books. The main thing is to be led by GOD and be honest about where you are financially.

Here is a **suggested template** for preparing for and communicating the class.

45 Days Out

☐	Identify team for registration and instruction. Open registration begins.
☐	Post on social media that registration is open.
☐	Post on your website the date, time, and location of the event and add any special instructions.
☐	Write GOD's vision for the class and have a written copy available to anyone involved in the program.
☐	Review each exercise.
☐	Choose if the class session will be a half-day, whole day or will run for several weeks (**recommended**).

30 Days Out

☐	Send reminders to current registrants.
☐	Post a "save the date" message on social media and your website providing the number of days left to register.
☐	Pray for current registrants, that their hearts be opened to the LORD's leading.
☐	Send the link to download the first exercise to the participants.

15 Days Out

☐	Send reminders to current registrants.
☐	Obtain final registrants.
☐	Post this message on social media and your website: *Registration will close in 7 days.*
☐	Send the link to download the first exercise to the participants.

7 Days Out

☐	Post this message on social media: *Registration is closed.*
☐	Send a reminder to current registrants that the class is a week away
☐	Send the link to all participants to download the first exercise
☐	Ask for prayer requests from registrants.
☐	Pray for a successful class and that many will come to know GOD closely through the process.
☐	Post on social media that class starts next week.
☐	Verify the attendance of any volunteers.

1 Day Out

☐	Send reminder to current registrants that class is tomorrow
☐	Send any last minute special instructions to registrants
☐	Verify the attendance of any volunteers.
☐	For Instructors: Pray that GOD gives you the right words.

Day Of

☐	For instructors: Pray for the HOLY SPIRIT to be poured out on t and the class.
☐	Arrive early to set up the room if meeting in person. (Registration table near the entrance, food table, name tags and handouts.)
☐	Set up and test audiovisual equipment
☐	For a virtual meeting: Start the virtual meeting application 15 minutes before start time.
☐	Ask the class for a team name. This will come in handy as the participants build a community.

Optional Graduation

☐	*Host a graduation for the class.
☐	Set up dates to follow-up with class members to see how they are doing.

*The GOD-Centered Framework is a methodology that will be done over and over. Recognition for understanding the content and completing the exercises is welcome by many. If you or your organization chooses to host a graduation, then print out certificates with the student's name, the name of the class and the name of the organization hosting the class. Be sure to date and sign the certificate.

About the Instructor (Teacher)

This leader is to be used as a guide for you, to teach GOD-centered business principles. Adjust the time it will take to teach the class for larger group sizes. Also, if you are teaching this class online, add frequent breaks and question/answer sessions. This book should be used with the "GOD-Centered Business Presentation." Visit www.honorservicesoffice.com to download a copy of the presentation.

The personal journal can be instructor led or you can recommended that the class do it on their own.

Please make yourself familiar with the following images:

Instructor-Led Exercises

In this section, there will be an exercise to further demonstrate the topic. You will guide the class through the exercise and materials needed.

New Business Exercises

Some exercises are made specifically for those who are starting a new business. Existing business owners can choose to do them as a way to review aspects of their business that may need a bit of attention.

Existing Business Exercises

Other exercises are made specifically for those who have been in business. New business owners can choose to do them as a way to review aspects of their business that may need a bit of attention.

Prayer

Throughout the book, you will be prompted to pray. Take this time to ask GOD questions and give Him any worry or praise. You will lead the group to write a **lot** of prayers. Prayer is a primary component of the GOD-Centered Business Framework. Encourage the class to make this a habit to rely on.

Before you begin, please remember your role is to present GOD as the center of any business venture. Some people may gain monetarily, others may not; however, all who follow GOD will become eternally wealthy. Encourage participants to grow, and be patient when they resist a concept. Be transparent, showing people they do not have to be perfect.

Questions You May Have

Many business owners work from their gut. In other words they use their instincts to make vital business decisions, many times without consulting God. But the God-centered business owner follows his or her faith in God and places all decisions before Him. So what does this mean? The following are questions you might be asking.

"Will I need to become the expert and lead people?"

Yes.

"Do I have to become a preacher?" No, unless God has called you to do so. God wants people in every industry to reach people for Him.

"Do I have to speak about God all the time?" Not always with words, but always with the heart.

"Should I start selling in the church?" Be careful is the only advice I can offer. The gathering of God's people is meant for worshiping Him. Attention away from Him onto your business may cause harm or unanticipated consequences.

"Should I serve people who do not believe in Jesus or God in general?" Absolutely! God sent you into the world to tell people of the great news about Jesus.

"Will I need to become the expert and lead people?" Yes. The whole purpose of the methodology is to prepare you before preparing your business.

Warning

This symbol is used to provide warnings and potential barriers.

The first warning is for the instructor. This class is not built on the normal business classes you may have learned.

Many of the principles are focused on foundational beliefs in GOD and JESUS being the Savior of humanity. Clear your mind of any assumptions or learnings from other business classes you may have seen. This class will teach concepts like caring for customers who may or may not buy the business owner's product or service. The world's business class may teach a concept of moving on from those who do not buy from you.

This is a GOD-Centered Business Framework that helps the business owners grow a large audience to follow GOD while growing their business, without being in conflict with HIM.

Overview and Definitions

Material Overview

Introduce the PowerPoint presentation and any handouts.

Welcome and Introductions

Welcome! Let me start out by saying you are not alone on your business journey.

If you are studying this book together, introduce yourselves, providing the name of your company or industry, whether or not you are a first-time entrepreneur, and any expectations you might have about the class.

Then have everyone state for one unique thing about himself or herself.

Ask who would like to go first, otherwise go alphabetically.

(Optional) Ask for a group name. Have the participants write a name and vote on the name. This is not a contest. If no name can be agreed to, then name the class by the dates you are presenting.

Example: This is our August through November 2022 class.

Remember, the purpose is to build a community.

Walkthrough the Agenda / Break Schedule

Dream Bigger	*(9 Vision Exercises – 4 Leadership Exercises)*
Remove the Trash	*(13 Leadership Exercises)*
Seek Wisdom	*(6 Skills / Capabilities Exercises)*
Go to the Desert	*(12 Business Builder / Testing Exercises – 1 Case Study)*
Emerge Different	*(10 Marketing / Pricing Exercises)*
Kingdom-First Mindset	*(4 Sales Exercises)*
Lead to Promises	*(4 Customer Service / Referral Exercises)*

Note: If teaching in person, the recommended break schedule is once per hour; online—every 30 minutes.

Ask the class to name the group.
"This is the beginning of your crowd or community."

Class Timeline

Note: This will depend on how long you will teach the class. Will you teach it in a half-day session? One full day? Over several weeks? The times are based on teaching for several weeks.

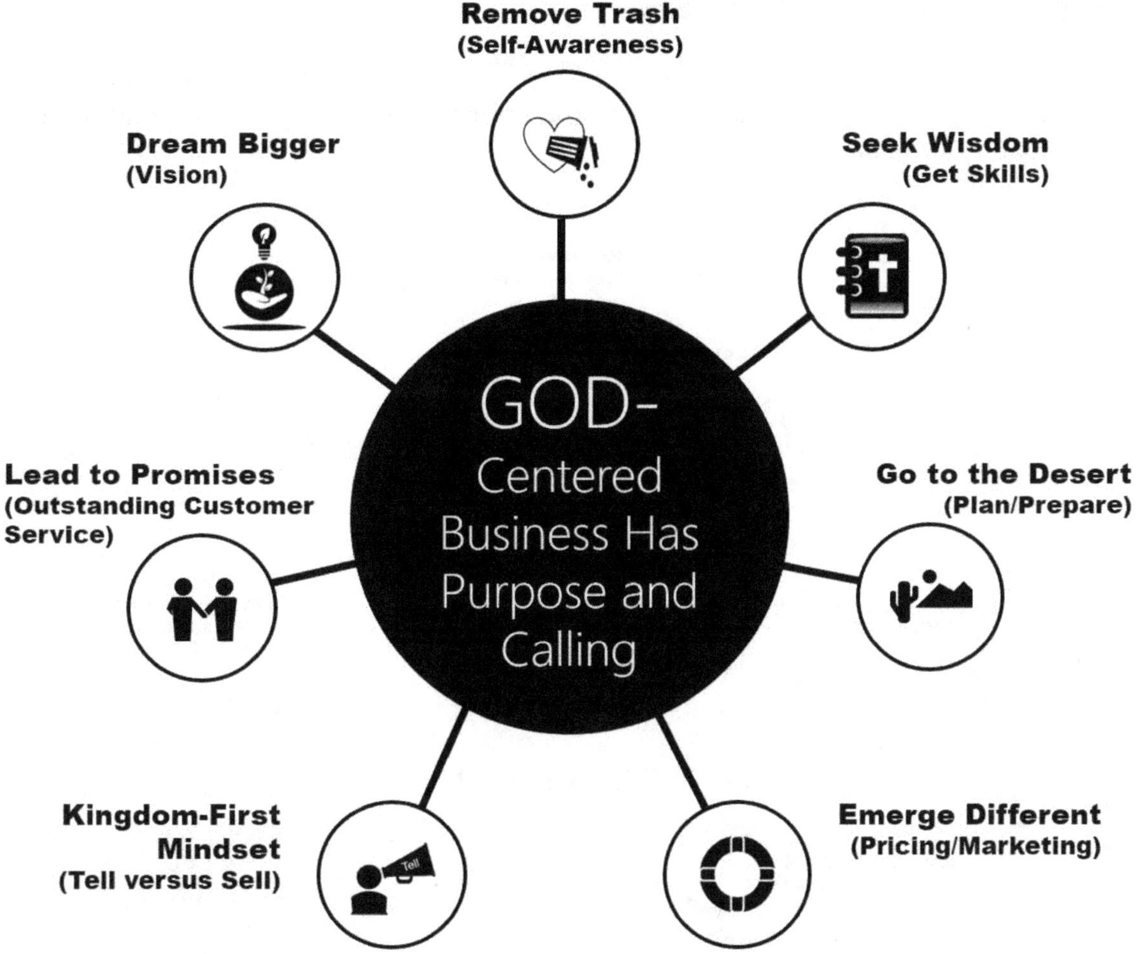

Methodology Overview

The purpose of using a methodology is to adjust your mindset. It can help you divide a larger task into smaller, more manageable tasks. GOD provides the vision and you break it apart, build it, test it and ensure you have quality. You keep progressing towards perfection versus thinking you have to be perfect right away. If this image is overwhelming to you, don't worry. I am here to guide you.

This is a methodology for developing and growing your business to be successful. This framework will enable you to take an idea to an operating business. It will also guide you in adjusting your existing business.

You get your vision from GOD, adjust your leadership style, seek the right skills or help, prepare to be ready, develop the right pricing and marketing, tell people about your product or service, and provide outstanding customer service.

The colors are divisions of interactions that will be explained on the next image.

Methodology People Overview

The other purpose of the methodology is to address how you, the GOD-centered business owner interacts with people. You are a **leader** who will **partner** with your customers, building solid **relationships** for GOD's purpose.

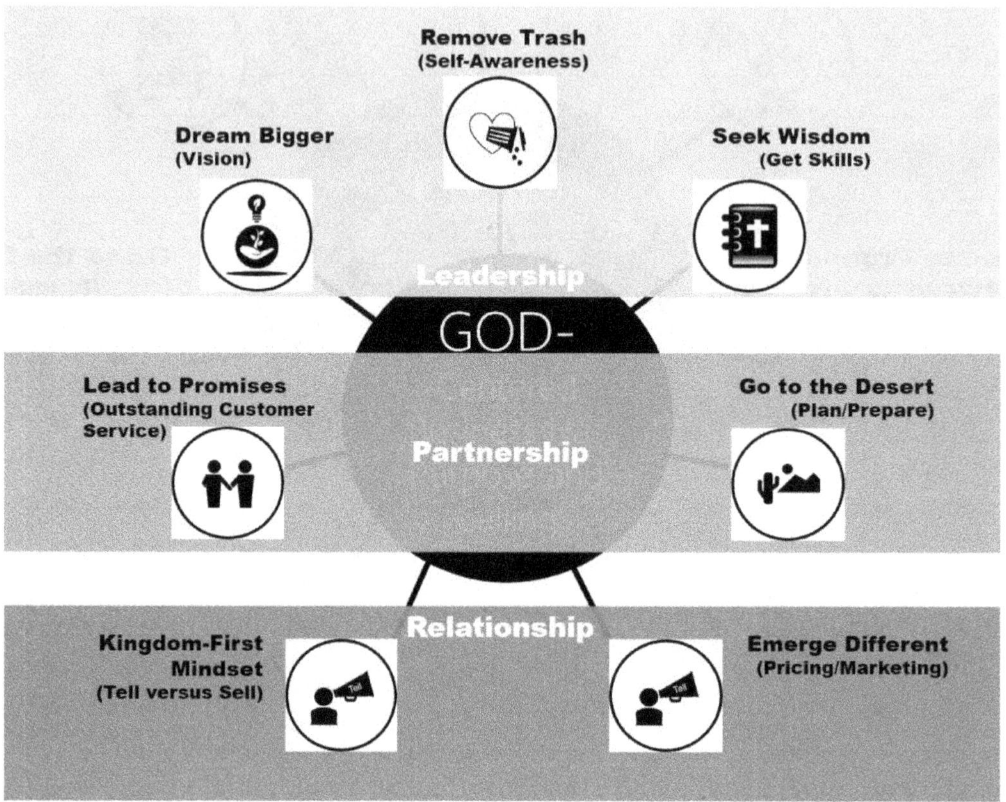

How your business interacts with people will make or break your achieving GOD's success.

Leadership

It takes a strong leader to slow down and get quiet enough to hear GOD. GOD-centered leadership means being prepared to guide people to achieve GOD's purpose. You'll find out more about that in the pages ahead.

Partnership

GOD wants us to assemble with other people to grow one another. Seek people to guide or receive guidance from those who will provide you with valuable information. More on that later in the book.

Relationship

As you develop your business, your purpose also is to build relationships so people will see GOD. The stronger your relationships, the more people will follow you. Will you give these relationships to GOD as a gift back to HIM? (More on this topic later.)

The first three chapters also provide guidance in your leadership style.

The fourth and seventh chapters deal with how you partner with your customers to develop and implement solutions. In chapter four I will assign you to a thought group to work with each other on your business ideas and get feedback.

The fifth and sixth chapters deal with how you develop and maintain relationships.

Now let's discuss the problems we will address during the class.

Customer Expectations

Note: There are two images and three topics.

Some businesses are not meeting customers expectations.

Expectation	Customer Response
More Than Exceeded Expectations	Will refer and try to exclude
Exceeded Expectations	Will refer
Met Expectations	Will return
Low Severity Problems	May return but will look for other problems
Medium Severity Problems	Will not return and will only tell a few people
High Severity Problems	Will not return, will tell lots of people and may try to have you close

New customers have expectations. If you "more than exceed" those expectations, customers will try to keep you from other customers by paying extra. They will also try to keep you in an exclusive group, serving only their network.

1. Meet a Customer's Expectations

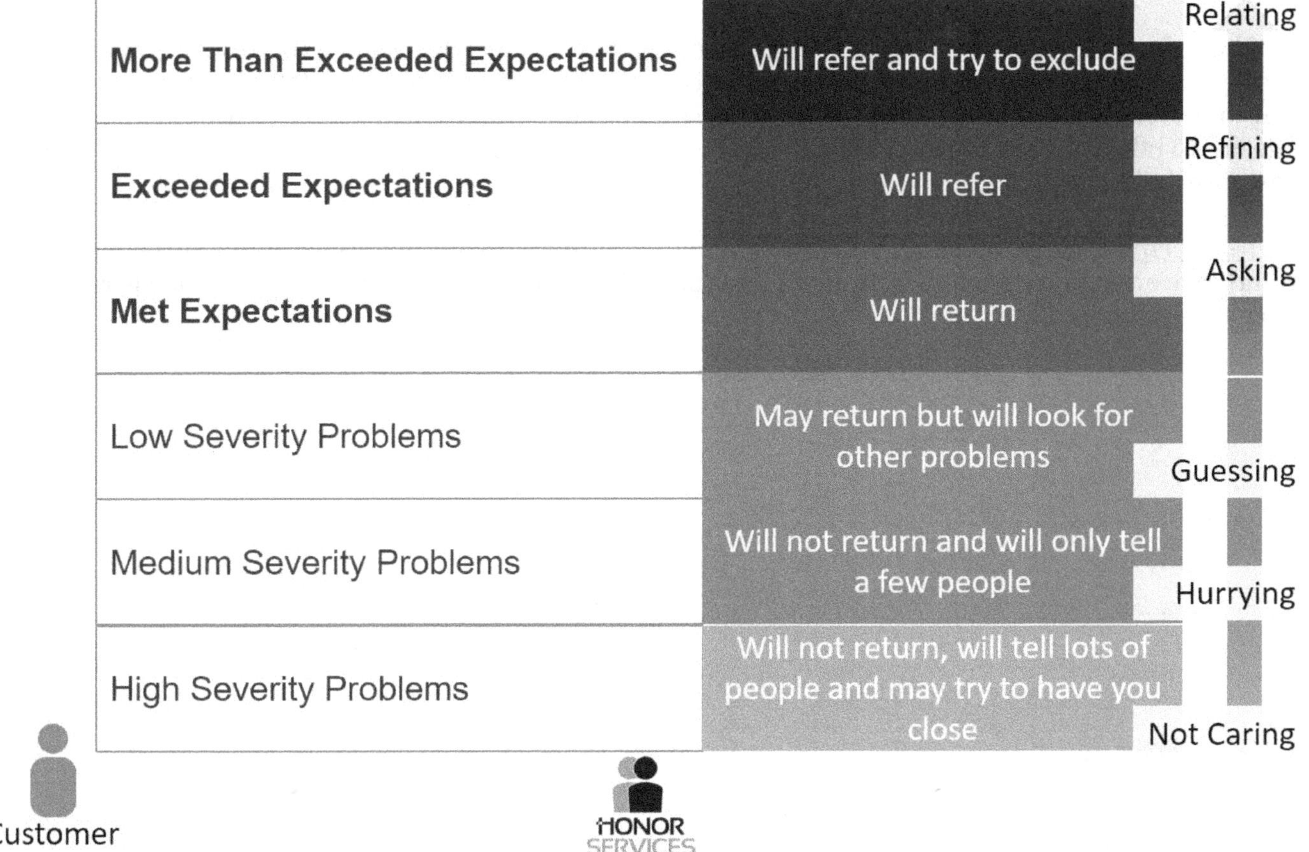

The purpose for being in business is to profitably solve your customer's problem or meet her needs." Failure to meet or exceed the customer's expectations can be harmful to the business.

2. Listen to the Customer

Working in the dark or in a vacuum means you thought of an idea and went ahead and started a business without consulting your potential customer. This is extremely detrimental to your business. Before going out of business, you will spend most of the time guessing and missing your customer's expectations.

Have you ever noticed a new business appear in your community that provided a product or service that doesn't fit the needs of your community? Has anyone tried to sell you something that you did not need or you had no use for?

Ask your customer what he wants, needs, and how he wants it.

3. Refine the original Idea

Many people make huge investments in things that may not be the right idea.

Relate to your best customers. This will cause them to want to pay for you to only deal with them. Has anyone experienced this?

On the downside, some entrepreneurs jump into business, *guessing* their next steps. They do not know how to correct problems that arise, let alone identify them.

Hurrying is the next problem. Self-imposed timelines creates false adversity towards testing and refining the business based on the customer's needs. "I don't have time" or "I'll fix it later" or "I don't want to perfect because it will take too long" are excuses for shortcuts and are a refusal to admit a lack of desire to take the time to provide quality. This course will help you create business features that are constantly being improved.

Not caring means you should not be in business. If there are glaring issues with your business, you should care enough to listen to customers and fix problems before your product or service is ready for the customer's use.

Seven Important Definitions

Take a moment to read through the definitions . Many people say, “I am going into business.” But really, they should be saying “I am operating a business.” Have you ever said that?

Proven Business – Demonstrated by evidence or argument to be true or existing.
(of a new method, system, or treatment) **tried and tested.**

Business Operations – Repeatable and **consistent** delivery of a quality product or service using structured methods to address ideas, problems and innovations.

Business Marketing - The action or business of promoting, **creating awareness** and selling products or services, including market research and advertising.

Business Accounting – The action or process of keeping financial accounts to **identify and control** spending of income.

Business Sales – The process of understanding and meeting the needs of customers with the business product or services, guiding them through the purchase and delivery phase.

Business Structure – A structure for filing taxes, protecting assets and categorization **for legally operating** a business. Most common are LLC, Inc., Sole Proprietor.

Business Customer Service – The **assistance and advice** provided by a company to those people who buy or use its products or services.

Here is something else to consider...

Is the **business** proven or **have you proven** you can handle the business? Are you doing the business versus operating the business? Do you have a prepared marketing strategy? Do you have a sales process? And lastly, do you know how to handle problems with your product or service? Skipping any of these important business areas is detrimental to the business. 85%—90% of small businesses fail, according to Forbes.

GOD-centered businesses will be sustained by GOD. This class is to keep you focused on HIS vision and the steps to reach HIS purpose for your business.

https://www.forbes.com/sites/neilpatel/2015/01/16/90-of-startups-will-fail-heres-what-you-need-to-know-about-the-10/#42e3e0e06679

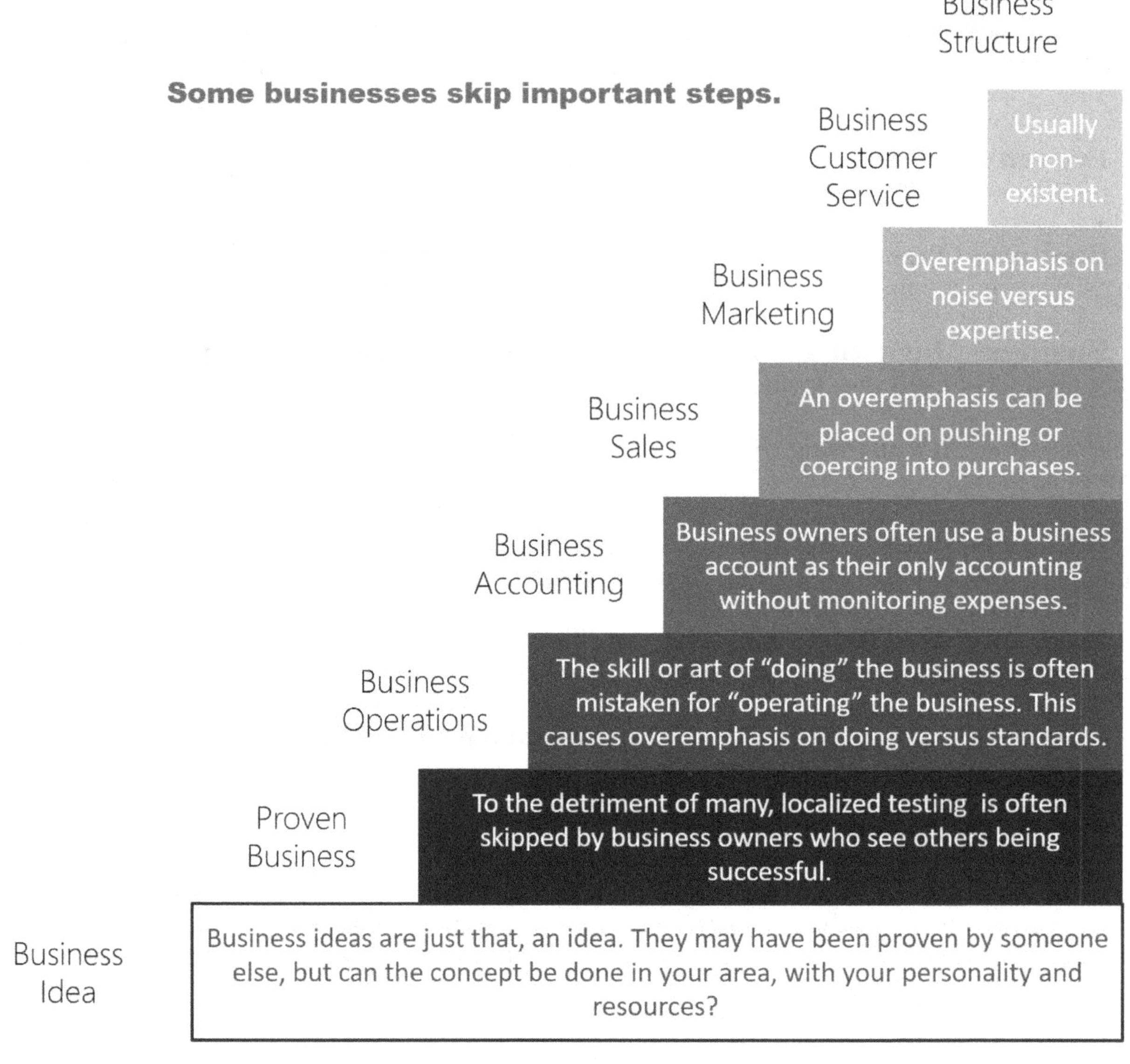

View this image. Which step would you or did you skip? Why?

Most people start with an idea, skip over the vital parts of **operating** the business and start **doing** the business with a business structure.

By skipping this step if you have a proven business, even if you can execute this type of business, you will miss out on vital feedback you need to make the concept successful. By simply doing the business versus operating the business, you will miss out on quality and not have repeatable processes which inhibits growth.

Remember, the last image says Business Operations is repeatable and consistent processes. By not having accounting practices, you will not be able to identify which expenses to control to increase profits. The lack of a sales process means you will miss out on solid relationships and leads. Without a marketing strategy, your customers will not understand who you are or what you do or why they should use your product or service. Without a customer service model, complaints will become the norm, rather than problems corrected.

Some businesses are really Hobbies or "Hustles."

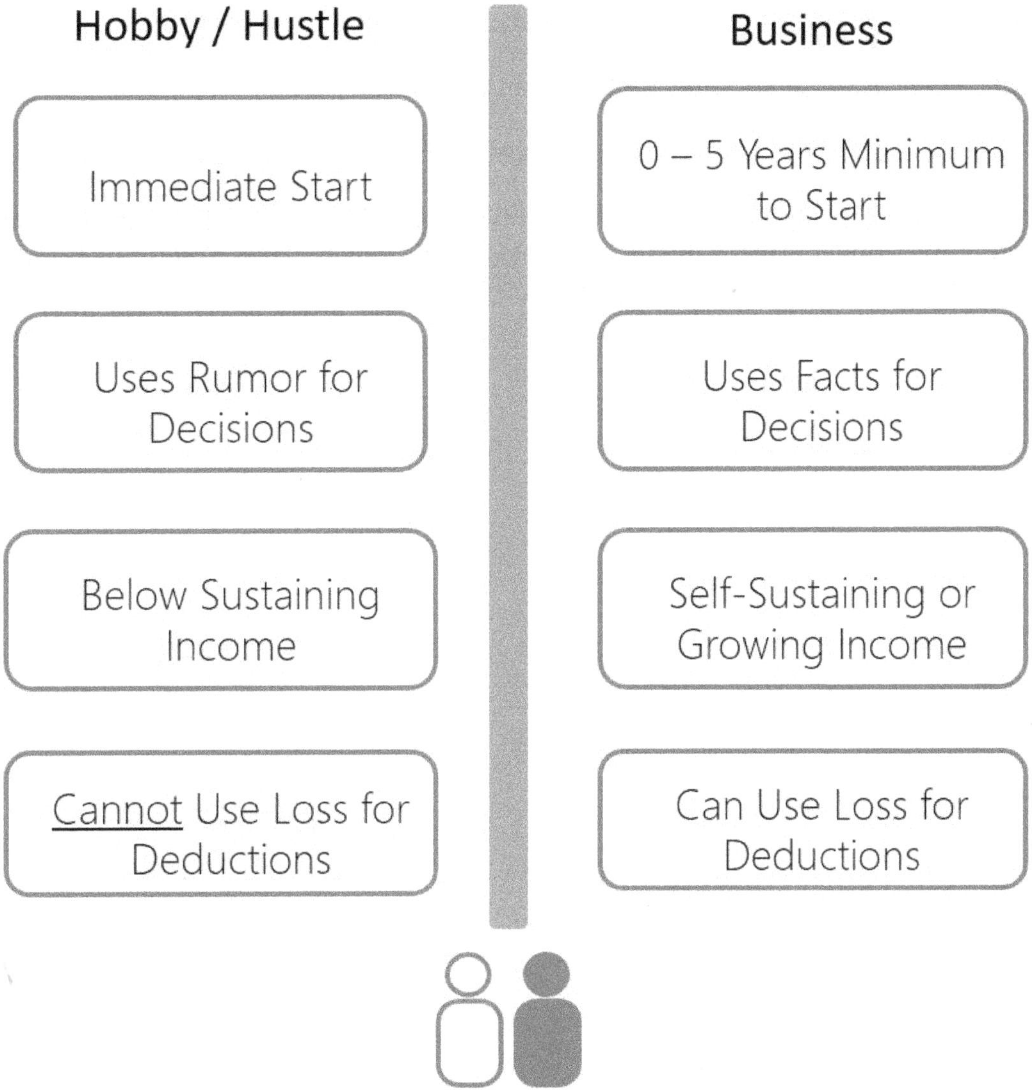

Hobby / Hustle	Business
Immediate Start	0 – 5 Years Minimum to Start
Uses Rumor for Decisions	Uses Facts for Decisions
Below Sustaining Income	Self-Sustaining or Growing Income
Cannot Use Loss for Deductions	Can Use Loss for Deductions

One final concept before we get started with the framework is knowing the difference between a hobby versus a business. They look and act the same. Both make money. Both involve selling a product or service. But many people who say they are in business are really performing a hobby or hustle. The difference is in loss calculation.

What is a loss you may ask? A loss is when your allowable business tax deductions are greater than your business net income.

Is it a business or a hobby? A key feature of a business is that people do it to make a profit. People engage in a hobby for sport or recreation, not necessarily to make a profit. A hobby can have a loss equal to its income. The business owner cannot use the loss of a hobby as a deduction on income taxes.

If the business sustains loss for too long, it may be reclassified as a hobby which will cause the business owner to not be able to deduct a loss on taxes.

Since I am not an expert on taxation, I recommend you see an accountant to understand the structure of your business after you complete all the steps to develop your business.

Consider the following questions:

Are you trying to make money quickly?
Are you trying to easily set up your business, let's say, within a few months or so?
Are you trying to use a skill to make a product or service but are not planning to spend at least half your time doing operations, sales, marketing, and accounting?

If these questions resonate with you, then please consider resetting your expectations.

This class will help you build the vision GOD will give you for your business through interaction with your customers. You will then validate every aspect before you market, sell to, and serve your customer in hopes that she will have an everlasting relationship with HIM. We are your community!

Chapter 1 – Dream Bigger: Developing the Vision for Your Business

"What does success look like to you?"

"What does success look like to GOD?"

"Do you like you?"

Dream Bigger preparation (Week 1)

For best results, do this exercise before arriving as a group. If you do this in class, then separate into a quiet location and instruct everyone to turn off phones. For sake of time, make sure the class understands the exercises in the chapter and have them complete them over the next week if they have not done so already.

Introduce the Dream Bigger Chapter

This chapter will be used to get or revise the vision for the business. We will walk through the leadership style needed to be successful in making this vision come to life. There are nine vision exercises and four leadership exercises. Be prepared to be stretched by GOD.

Dream Bigger Objective

You will learn the GOD-centered vision process, why you need customer input, and GOD-centered leadership for success.

Dream Bigger Prayer

Pray that:
The LORD guides the class during this quiet time.
The class be decreased and GOD be increased.
The class be sent to the group HE wants them to go to.
GOD will provide a breakthrough, enabling someone to admit any fear and doubt.

Warning

Stay encouraged. Arguments or debates are not what the class is designed for. Expect disruptions and handle each peacefully.

The GOD-Centered Methodology

Objective: To understand the importance of revising. If the product or service has not been scrutinized, has not failed or has not been revised, it may not be ready.

The methodology you will be using is Agile Adopted for Business (AFB). This is an iterative method that you will repeat over and over, delivering value during each cycle. Since business changes rapidly and often, this is a method of continuously improving business features rather than a onetime planning exercise.

Iterative Approach

Revision Thinking

1. Listen to GOD to get the vision.

Prepare Yourself

2. Refine your leadership style, removing blockers to success.

Get others involved

3. Seek expert wisdom.

Get feedback and build.

4. Get prepared and plan what you will deliver.

Refine vision from test results.

5. Develop an expertise message.

Execute marketing plan.

6. Tell about product or service.

Use CRM.

7. Perform outstanding customer service.

Repeat.

HONOR SERVICES OFFICE

HONOR SERVICES OFFICE

Iterative Approach.

Iterative means "a repeating cycle." This approach means you are never totally "done," but bits and pieces are. From vision to building parts of the business, think revision and test to revise. If you don't want it to take four times as long and cost ten times as much, then test to revise until you get the Minimal Viable Product (MVP). This term will be discussed later.

First, you will quiet down to listen to GOD to get the vision for your business or to get new ideas or modify your existing business.

Second, you will look introspectively to adjust your leadership style.
Third, you will look for the expertise needed to meet the vision.
Fourth, you will meet with people, understand their needs, build with quality, and test to refine.
Fifth, you will develop messages showing you as the expert to be used in marketing.
Sixth, you will develop your sales approach with confidence provided by GOD.
And seventh, you will perform outstanding customer service that includes the love of GOD.
This is the method you will do over and over, revising, refining, constantly making things better.

Motive for Being in Business

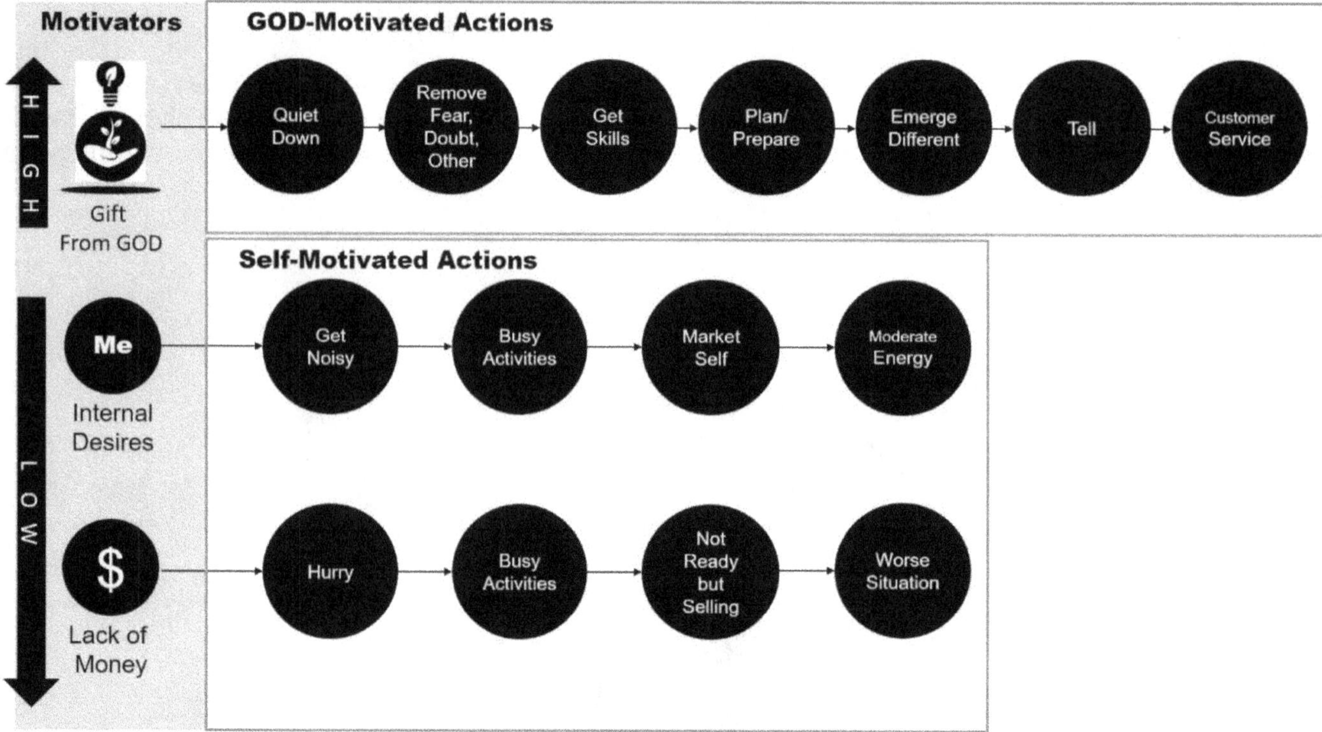

What motivated you to go into business?
Let's look at three reasons people go into business.
One: Lack of money.
Two: Some internal desire. Both will result in low to moderate results.
But the third is motivated by GOD which produces high results.

GOD wants the GOD-centered business owner to be true to HIS purpose.

If done in a class setting, ask if anyone would like to share his or her motives. (Limit this to 2–3 people)

Write out the following statement:
The reason I went into business is because: (finish the sentence)

NOTE: This will be used in the "Hidden Motives" exercise in the Remove the Trash chapter.

Admiration is a Foundation

Objective: Address the **influencer** soft-skill needed in business.

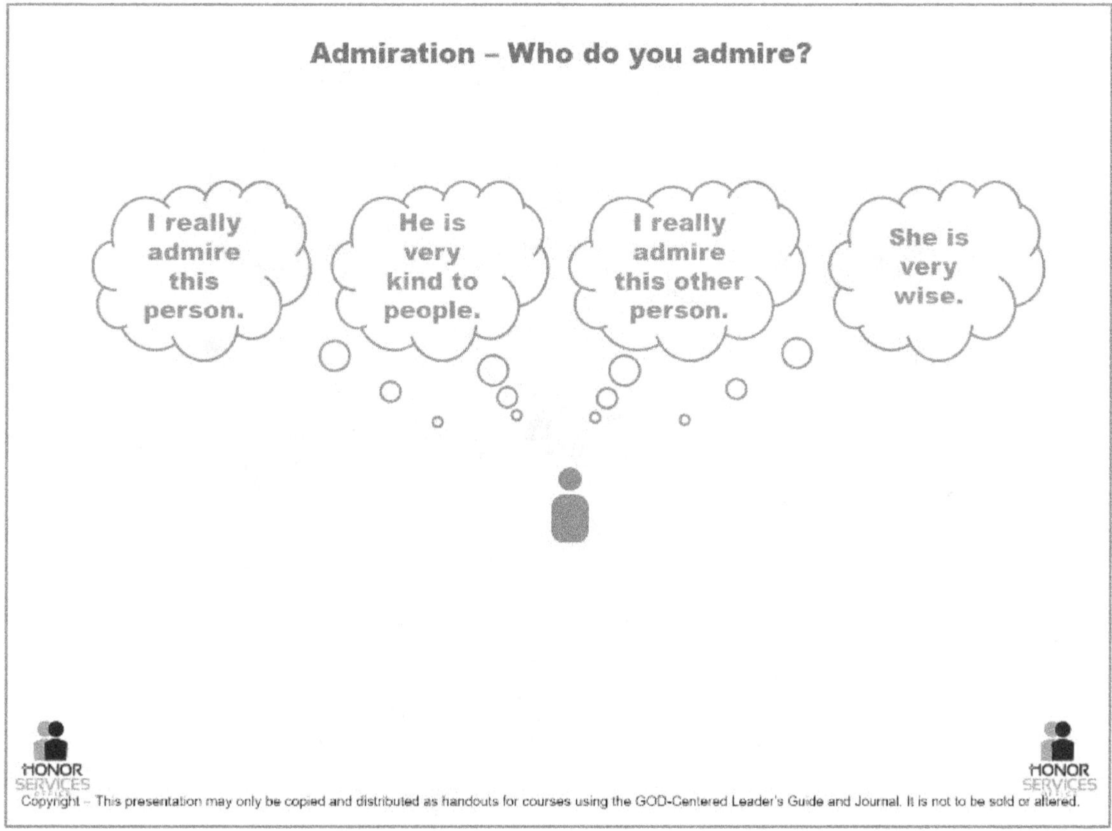

Who do you admire? What qualities do you remember about that person? Admiration is a great quality and should be used generously by the GOD-centered business owner. But pointing people to GOD enables your customers to admire GOD through your actions.

Recognize Influences

The person or people who most influenced me to go into business is/are... (finish the sentence)

Recognize Qualities

The qualities I like most about the individual or people listed previously are... (finish the sentence)

Whether you like it or not, you are being watched. Your actions and lifestyle influence people. You can be an influencer who points people to GOD.

Schedule time to reach out to the people you admire and thank them specifically for the qualities you listed. Thankfulness will be discussed in upcoming exercises. Depending on the amount of time you allotted for this class session, you might elect to end your class time here.

Principles of the GOD-Centered Business

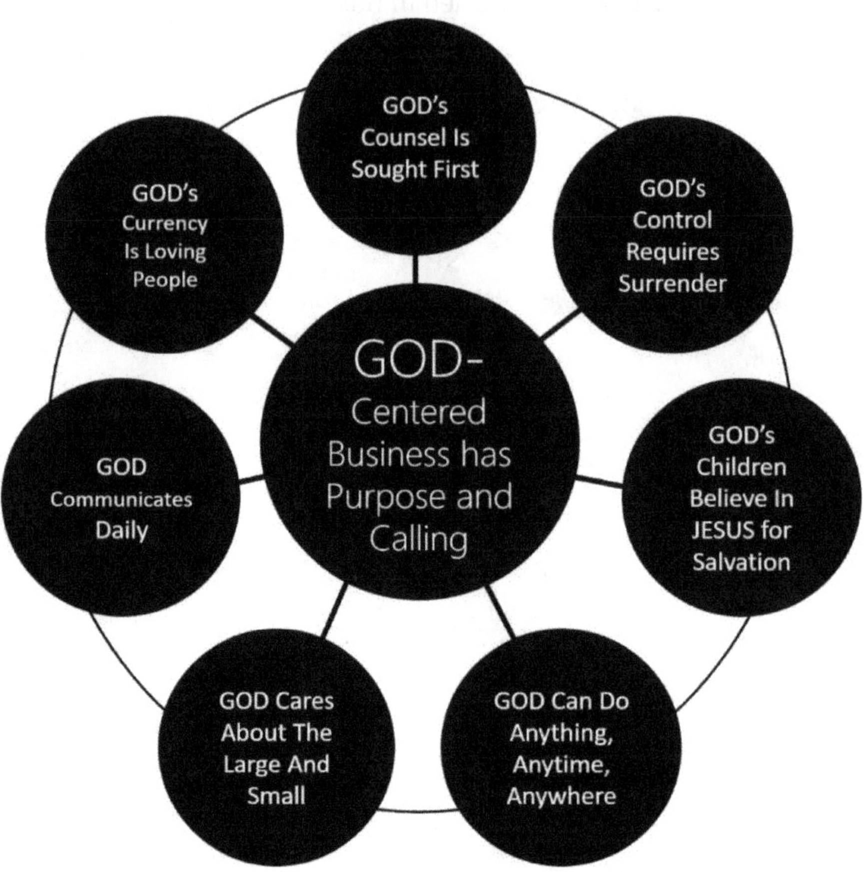

GOD's currency is loving people. "For God so loved the world that He gave His only begotten Son, that whoever believes in Him should not perish but have everlasting life " (John 3:16.)

GOD's counsel is sought first. "First seek the counsel of the LORD" (1 Kings 22:5 NIV)

GOD's control requires surrender. "Surrender your heart to God, turn to him in prayer, and give up your sins—even those you do in secret. Then you won't be ashamed; you will be confident and fearless" (Job 11:13-15 CEV).

GOD's children believe in JESUS for salvation. "But as many received Him, to them He gave the right to become children of God, even to those who believe in His name" (John 1:12 NASB)

GOD can do anything, anytime, anywhere. "For with God nothing will be impossible" (Luke 1:37)

GOD cares about the large and small. "Look at the birds of the air that they do not sow, nor reap nor gather into barns, and yet your heavenly Father feeds them. Are you not worth much more than they?" (Matthew 6:26 NASB)

GOD communicates daily. "All scripture is God breathed and is useful for teaching, rebuking, correcting and training in righteousness, so that the servant of God may be thoroughly equipped for every good work" (2 Timothy 3:16-17 NIV)

One last word before you begin the journey: Your goal is different. Your business is made to make profits, but GOD makes business owners *prophets* for HIS purpose. HE wants more servants just like you.

Group discussion

GOD's Counsel Is Sought First

What's usually your first response when you have a need? Why? (Be honest.)

- I pray and ask GOD
- I try to figure things out on my own.
- I ask others for their help.

When you need wisdom from GOD, where do you go?

- The Bible
- A pastor
- A spouse who is a believer
- A praying friend who shares Scripture
- My small group
- All of the above

In what way have you benefited from the wisdom of GOD in the past? Why is it important to seek wisdom from GOD?

In what way have you benefited from the wisdom of GOD in the past? Why is it important to seek wisdom from GOD?

Currently, what is your biggest concern? This can be business or personal.

Write a prayer about this concern (optional). What Bible verses, if any, come to mind that remind you of the resources of GOD? Why? Add a calendar item on your smartphone to revisit this next year on this date.

GOD's Control Requires Surrender

What parts of the business or your life are you trying to control?

What is GOD telling you to let go of?

GOD's Children Believe in JESUS for Salvation

Have you surrendered your life to JESUS?

☐ Yes

☐ No

☐ I don't know how.

Do you believe that JESUS, being GOD, became a human to die for the sins of mankind and is now alive with all power?

☐ Yes

☐ No

☐ I don't understand this.

GOD Can Do Anything, Anytime, Anywhere

When have you or someone you know experienced GOD's help? What was the result?

What current concerns do you have for your business?

How do you think GOD's statement to Abraham can help you in your business concerns?

GOD told Abraham, "Is anything too hard for the LORD?" (Genesis 18:14). What is your honest response to this statement:

I believe it wholeheartedly.
I sort of believe it.
I have yet to see evidence of this.

Are you willing to let GOD guide you and grow you before HE gives you an answer?

- ☐ Yes
- ☐ No
- ☐ I have to think about this.

GOD Cares About the Large and Small

For what big thing will you ask GOD? Write a prayer. Why is this important to you?

For what small thing will you ask GOD? Write a prayer. Why is this important to you?

Do you believe GOD can handle the situations you just wrote about? Why or why not? If you answered no, what do you think it will take for you to believe? Ask GOD to help you prayerfully consider.

GOD Communicates Daily

Do you believe that GOD wants to communicate with you every day? Why or why not?

What do you think it means to apply GOD's word to your life daily? How will you apply GOD's word to a situation you're currently facing?

When do you communicate with GOD?

Every day
Twice or more weekly
Maybe once a month

Are you willing to ask GOD for direction daily? Write your commitment to seeking GOD's direction here.

On a scale of 1 to 10, with 1 being a priority, where does reading the Bible fit in your daily schedule? Why?

How would you describe your commitment to learning about GOD?

I'm fully committed.
I'm not sure.

GOD's Currency is Loving People

While this is the first principle, I saved it for the last discussion.

Write out a prayer for the person or persons you listed above.

What do you believe about GOD's love for you?

Take a moment to list a person or people with whom you are in conflict or have been in conflict in the past. In a few words, how would you describe that person? How do you think GOD sees that person/these individuals? Why?

Now that we have the guiding principles, let's use them to set our goals and find our direction.

GOD-Centered Positioning System (GCPS)

Knowing where you are in the journey is important. The GCPS is your guide to take you step by step on your journey. While the path looks like a one way route, you will find yourself going back and forth between sections to build a firm foundation.

The GOD-centered positioning system is like a GPS for life.

GOD wants to guide you on your journey. Although we don't understand right away every detail of

GOD's plan for us, we can know that HE guides us step by step.

Look at the illustration above. Where do you think you are in your journey? Why? Are you willing to surrender your journey to GOD? Why or why not? What do you think it will take for you to surrender?

Assess Gifts and Talents

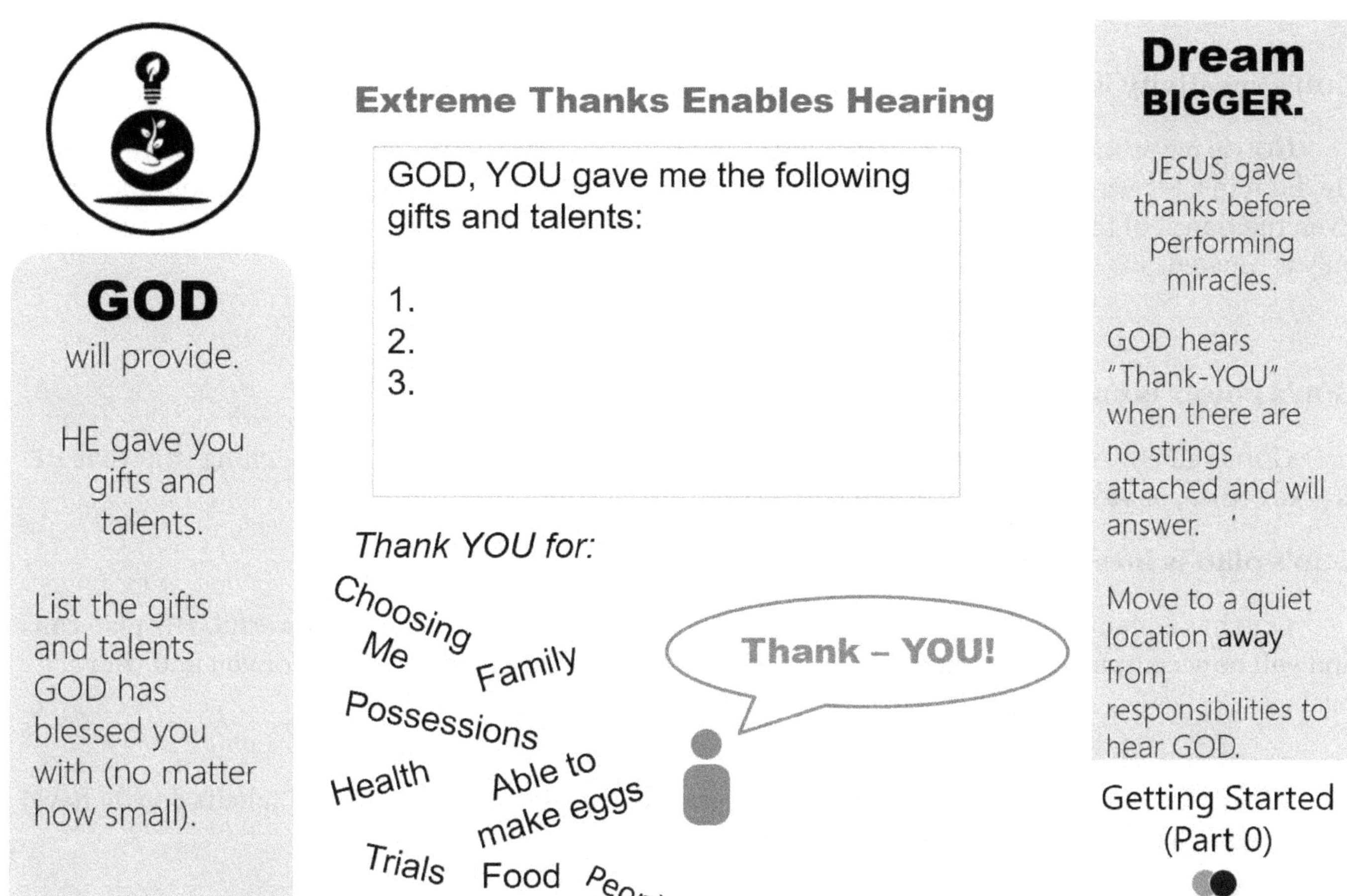

GOD given vision versus human.

I have a few questions for you. **"What does success look like to you?"** Better question to ask is **"What does success look like to GOD?"** Does HE want you to have broken relationships, angry customers and poor health due to stress and worry? No. Unfortunately I had to say "No" to some of you because you may have been chasing monetary success for so long that you may have forgotten what is important to GOD, namely the people HE placed in your life.

Second question, **"Do you like you?"** I mean, when I was a janitor I hated myself. I did not like the job, and I felt ashamed. Years later I still use the lessons I learned from being a janitor. I wish I could go back and learn more. I did not value where I was and who I was and how carefully GOD made me.

Lastly, after facing the reality of becoming a business owner, ask yourself the third question, **"What do I own and what does GOD own?"** This question is extremely important as it will set the direction of your business.

For many micro-businesses, the owner thinks of an idea, looks at his or her skills, time, and personality to determine what type of business he or she should be in. The problem with this approach, while sound, is the limits the business owner puts in place by looking at himself/herself for all the answers and energy. Keep in mind:

GOD's creativity is limitless.

GOD is never limited by the vision you came up with. When GOD created the heaven and the earth, He did it in a big way. Nothing was done on a small scale; however GOD was concerned about the small. Even the tiniest of things, like atoms in a human, exist on such a large scale, they can never be counted, only estimated.

GOD's power is endless.

GOD is all powerful and cannot be stopped. When HE gives you a vision, HE is telling you what HE is going to do, or already has done with HIS power.

GOD's plan is incredible.

GOD has a plan that includes your future. Since HE is not limited and is all powerful, HIS plan can and will be accomplished. HE has already seen into the future and made HIS plan for you and your business.

What aspects of your life usually merit your gratitude to GOD? What gifts and talents do you have? Take time to list those gifts and talents, no matter how small.

Read the list to your community and thank GOD for what HE has given you. Revisit these daily and thank GOD for what HE is doing in your life. Do this without expecting GOD to do something for you.

Practicing thanks to GOD builds resilience and keeps our ears open to HIS leading. We learn to see many different circumstances as worthy of giving HIM praise. Open your eyes to gifts and talents you may be overlooking or discrediting.

Open your eyes to gifts and talents you may be overlooking or discrediting.

Now let's get started with the vision. Many people think strategy has to be something lofty or unattainable. Think of a **strategy** simply as a destination and the steps to get there. Some people do lofty strategic plans that are the equivalent of saying something like "I'm going on vacation." There is no destination declared, nor steps to accomplish this. It would be better to say "I am going on vacation on a specific island on a specific date."

Excited about being in business? You should be. New ideas can translate to you selling a product or service which, in turn, can enable you to earn money. But is that where you should end? GOD wants you to dream bigger than profits.

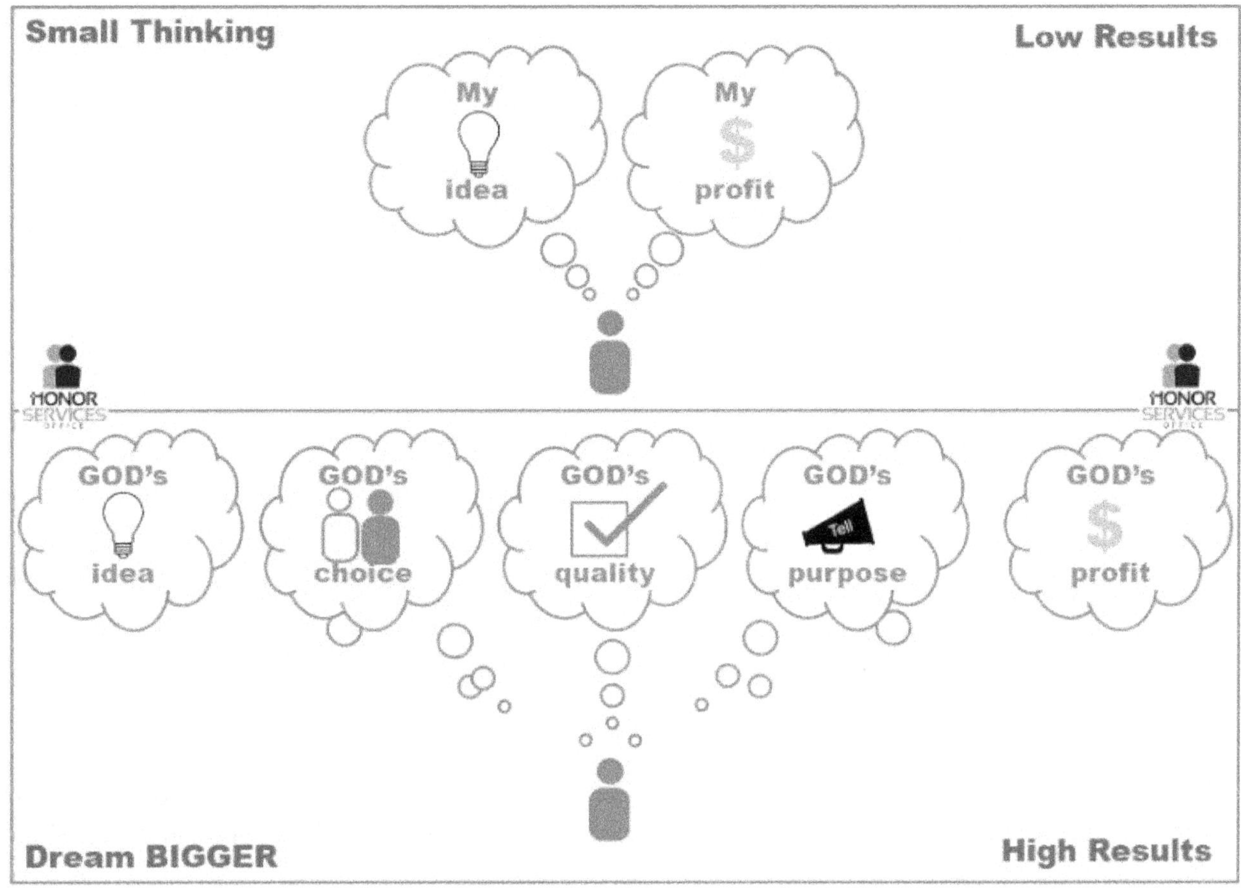

What was your first thought as you considered operating a business? Do you honestly relate to the image at the top? To encourage your class members, you might admit to having this thought yourself.

Your attitude contributes to the success of your business. The GOD-centered business owner finds success in pleasing GOD by serving HIS people.

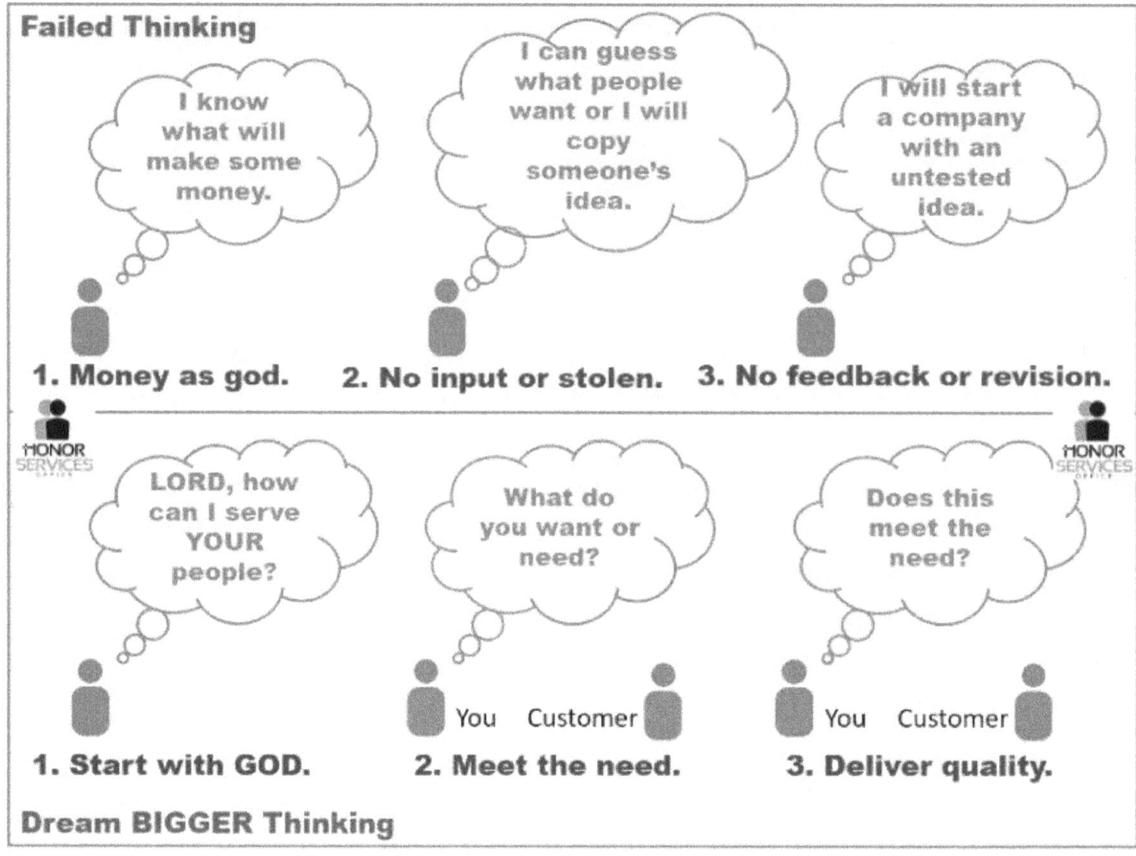

When have you ever been tempted to take a shortcut on something? Maybe you thought you didn't have enough time to revise something or you were in a hurry and just wanted a project done. What was the result?

Proverbs 14:12 (ESV): *There is a way that seems right to a man, but its end is the way of death.*

When we decide to implement ideas we came up with without consulting GOD, more than likely we won't succeed the way GOD would have us to do.

You've heard the old saying, "Imitation is the sincerest form of flattery", haven't you? Have you ever wished you could copy the success of another company? Why or why not?

In our success-driven society, we try to come as close to what is deemed a success as possible. Or, we rush out with an idea without praying about it out of fear that if we wait on GOD to answer, wait to test the idea, or take the time to ask for feedback, too much time will elapse and we'll miss out on valuable sales or building a solid customer base. But the avoidance of soliciting feedback could lead to the exact opposite of what we want: the cancellation of sales and bad word of mouth.

If you started your business already, it is not too late to make it GOD-Centered. In this class, you will learn to listen to GOD first, and then listen to your customer before wasting a lot of time and money.

Exercise 1—Vision or "Re-vision" Leadership Development

Objective: Seek businesses that solve problems and ask GOD for creative solutions to your customer's problems.

Epic. The vision GOD gives you is called an Epic. Think of a major story that has multiple movies associated with it. The overarching umbrella is the epic and each movie is a "feature" film. This big vision can be broken into multiple visions or "epics."

Prayerfully answer the following questions about your business.

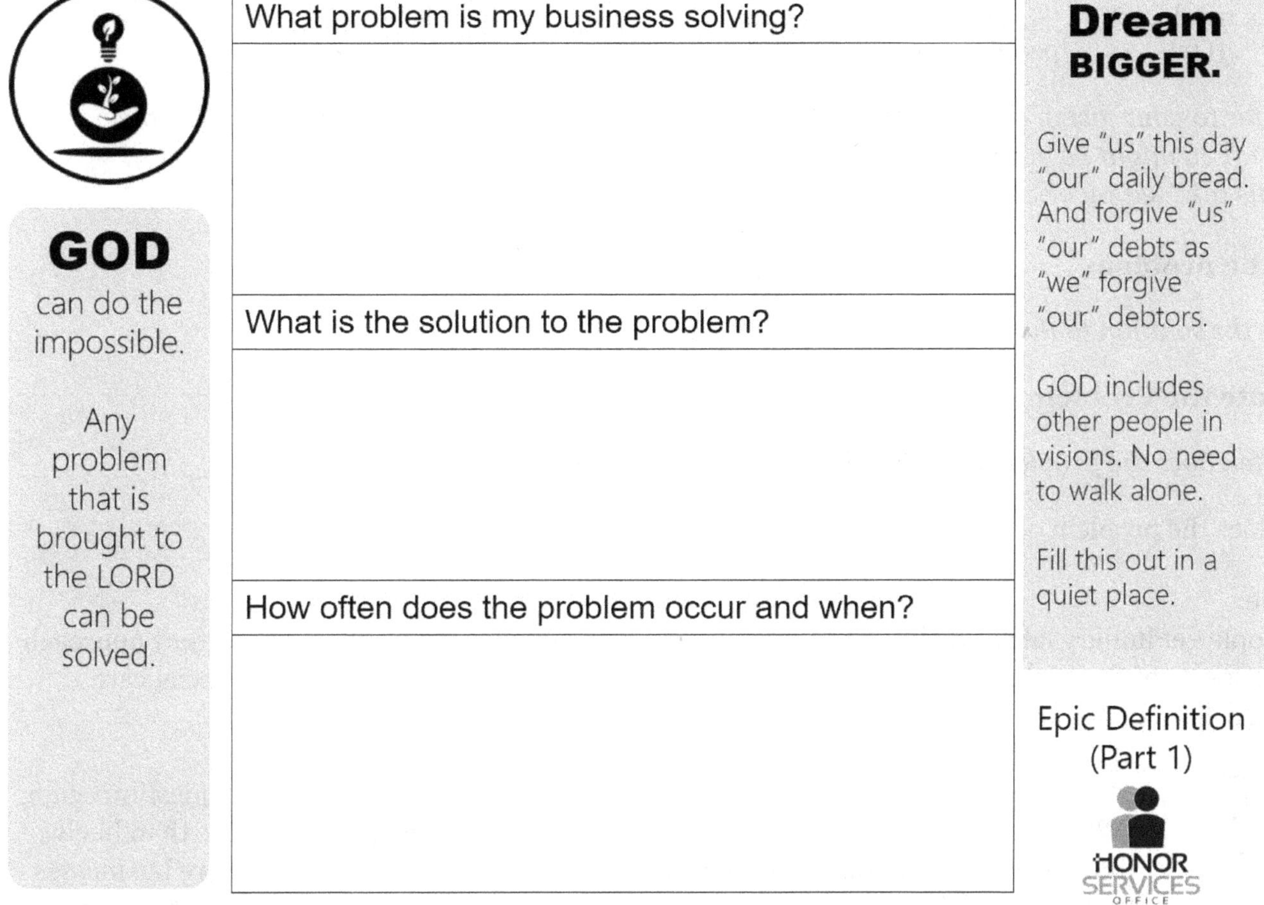

Matthew 6:11-13:
Give us this day our daily bread.

And forgive us our debts, as we forgive our debtors.

And lead us not into temptation, but deliver us from evil: For thine is the kingdom, and the power, and the glory, for ever. Amen. (KJV)

What do you notice about the statement in the upper box on the right side of the image. The words us and our in the LORD's prayer stand out. Sometimes we have a mindset of mine, rather than our—belonging to GOD and to us—when it comes to our work. Businesses that are thought of alone—just as coming up with the idea without seeking GOD and the feedback of potential customers—will remain alone—a solo venture that might not go as far as it could go. By asking GOD and your customers, "What problem should I work on?" your success rate increases exponentially.

Answer this important question:

What problem is my business trying to solve?

For existing businesses, you may be adding new items you are selling, new services, or revamping products and services that are not selling.

A problem is not always a problem. Some people simply want a new flavor of food, something repaired, or a better tool. Write your problem statement.

Here are a few thought starters. ______ people would like to ______ but there is gap in ________ and there is a need for ________. (Or) ________ people want _____ but there is not _____ and there is a need for _____. (Or) ______ people need _____ but there is a barrier of ______.

Refer to your list of gifts and talents. Circle the talents you will use to solve or resolve the problem. You might be missing some of the skills needed to solve the problem. But that's okay. Problems take teamwork to solve.

Solve the problem.

What is the solution to the problem?

Calculate the Problem.

How often does the problem occur?

When does the problem occur?

Example:

People get hungry late at night and desire a snack. (Or) People need training before they approach certain aspects of their job. (Or) Child athletes wear uniforms over and over and need special care cleaning before games and repair once a month.

> The first idea is usually not the one that will lead to success.

When it comes to your business or business idea, ask yourself the question again, "What do I own and what does GOD own?" If you own any percent, more than likely that percentage will ultimately fail in GOD's eyes. Unfortunately, there are businesses that appear to be successful, that are not GOD centered. These businesses bring in a lot of money, so the world claims their success, even if the business hurts people in the process.

GOD has a different currency, namely people. Our entire existence is for GOD. HE created humans and said, "It was very good" (Genesis 1:31 . Satan, wanting to be GOD, tempted the first humans in an attempt to get them to follow him. He also knew there was a scroll that existed, sealing his condemning fate. If he could just make all humans sinful, the scroll would never be opened. But GOD had a different plan. HIS SON JESUS volunteered to become human, live a sinless life, be blamed for the sins of mankind, die, and be risen from the dead, accepting all power.

So why should GOD go through all that and not be mentioned every day by HIS creation? Well, GOD does want to be mentioned every day, in every way. Unfortunately, many businesses of the world never acknowledge GOD but put profits over the people HE is trying to save.

Target Audience Introduction

> If you do not like yourself, you may not like the people around you.

Will you be able to identify which is a true audience? If you do not like yourself, you may not like the people around you either. You may want to leave your neighborhood because you do not like them. Put yourself in their shoes for a moment as I discuss the target audience.

Scenario 1

Let's pretend we are a shop that sells and cleans uniforms for women. Are women age 30 and over a good target audience? Why or why not?

(Answer) Micro businesses do not have the resources to reach an audience of this size. The audiences needs to be narrowed. This audience is too broad and unreachable for even the largest of companies. There are millions of people in this demographic with a variety of tastes, needs, and problems. Not everyone in this demographic will need your product or service.

Scenario 2

Let's pretend we are in the employment and resume writing business. Is unemployed people who are looking for a job is a good target audience or not?

(Answer) While the audience is narrowed and there is a need identified, the population may be too worried about finances to purchase anything. Some unemployed people may be too worried about their income loss and may not be able to hear the solution you present. This audience also is still too broad. How would you narrow the audience?

Scenario 3

Let's pretend we are in the pet sitting, walking, or grooming business. Is homes with pets in the area of X Street and Y street, a good target audience or not?

(Answer) While true, more research needs to be done specifically in that area. The more specific you can be with the target audience, the easier it will be to develop ideas to fix problems. In this example, these homes might be in muddy areas. The pet walker could provide booties to keep pets from tracking mud into the homes; the sitter may bring her own portable indoor running area to avoid taking pets out into the elements, and the groomer may increase his schedule to keep pets well groomed. See how these are specific to the area?

Target Audience Summary

A successful target audience is one that you have spoken to, or they told you they have a specific need, or your company can actually fulfill their orders based on a specification. In other words, look around you to see what problems GOD will have you solve.

Exercise 2—Identify GOD's Target Audience

Objective: Seek the true target audience that comes from asking GOD to fill your heart with an unexpected audience.

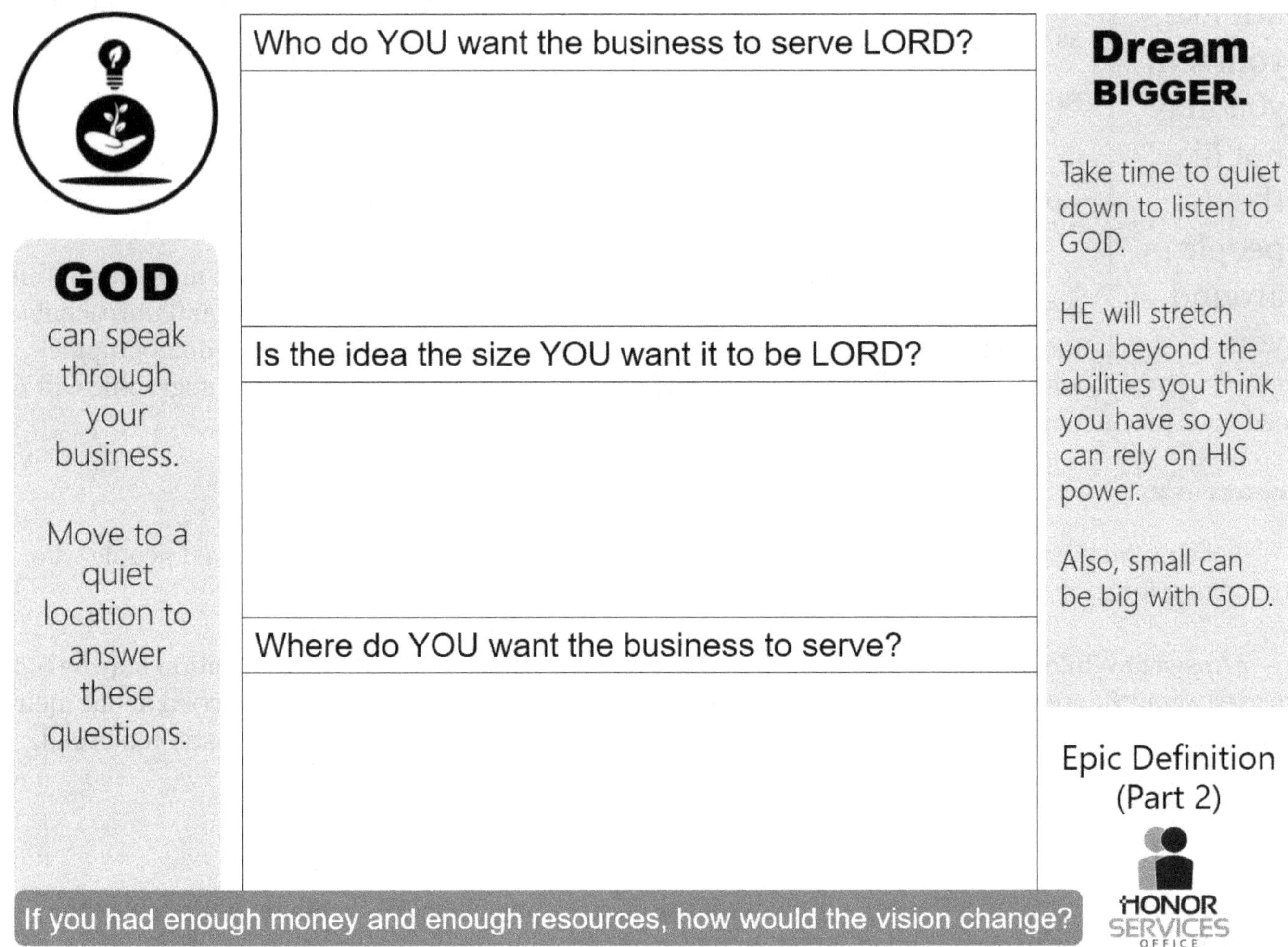

If you had enough money, would you still be doing your business idea? How would the vision of your business change? Would you serve people? GOD can speak through your business. This can start by you asking GOD, "Who do YOU want me to serve, LORD? You do this by quieting down versus getting noisy.

GOD's audience is sometimes an unlikely one who can most benefit from your gifts and talents. This does not mean you have to lose income all the time.

Describe the audience GOD guides you to serve.

Write a prayer about the people GOD told you to serve. Ask HIM to reveal who you need to serve if HE has not already done so.

Audience Size

Size matters to GOD. Is the idea the size GOD wants it to be? How do you know?

Some people want to be great among humans. Other people do not want anyone to know their name. Be willing to let GOD stretch or shrink your vision to HIS size.

Write the true size GOD wants your business to be. You should also write your anticipated number of employees (including yourself; the number of people you will serve; any fear of meeting new people; and any barrier to meeting 22 new people a month (or one person per business day each month).

Ask About the Audience and Idea Size.

Prayerfully ask, "Lord, is the idea the size You want it to be?"

Write a prayer about the people GOD told you to serve. Ask Him to reveal who you need to serve if He has not already done so.

Ask About the Location of the Business.

Lord, where do You want the business to serve?

What are the characteristics of this area or people?

A great question to ask GOD is, "Where do YOU want the business to serve?". Ask GOD about your current neighborhood, part of a town or part of a city. GOD may want you to serve special-interest groups.

Selecting a product or service without GOD can be detrimental to the business because the choice may be from of a path GOD wants to remove you from. If, for example, the business owner is a greedy person, then the target audience he chooses may not be the one GOD's message will be heard. The GOD-centered business owner listens to GOD for the audience, location and size of the business. GOD is the center of the choice, versus answering the question, "How much can I make from these people?"

When the GOD-centered business owner surrenders the audience choice to GOD, she becomes more open to hearing the needs of the audience. The product or service is then adjusted to fill the audience's need versus trying to search for an audience as an afterthought. GOD's message can be heard from those willing to be sent. Whoever is ashamed of me and my words, the Son of Man will be ashamed of them when he comes in his glory and in the glory of the Father and of the holy angels. – Luke 9:26 (NIV)

GOD's vision for your business includes a plan to grow you as well. Let's look at your leadership style.

GOD-First Leadership Style

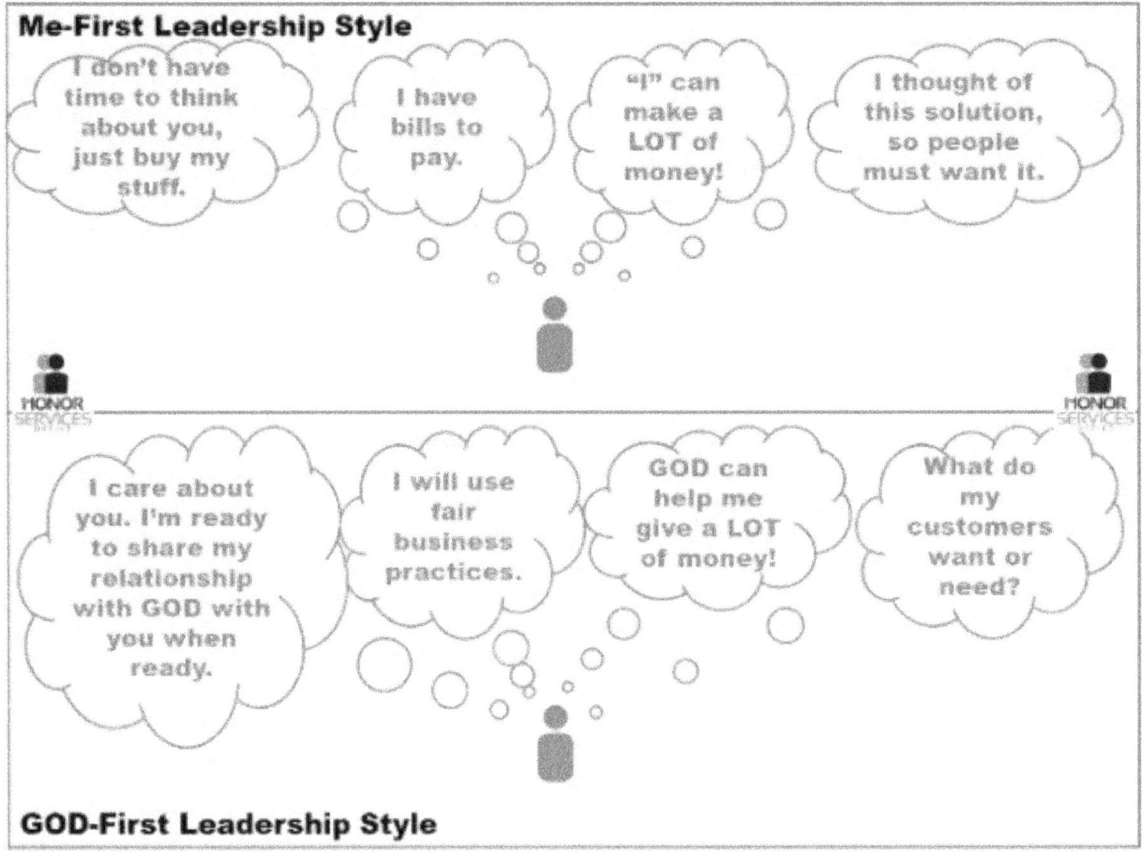

What does it mean to be a leader? Who do you care about? Would it be alright if you got money from your customer without delivering the product or service? Does leading mean bossing people around or being alone? Why or why not?

Leaders Care , Are Fair; They Give and Live

When you chose to go into business, you chose to be a leader. When GOD chose you, HE meant for you to lead people by your gifts and talents. Leadership is something more than bossing people around or not having to answer to anyone. Leaders do things first and people look to the leader as the primary example.

The first leadership style to adopt is the GOD-first leadership style. Have a purpose in your life, be intentional with everything you do, and remember, you are being watched as the example by everyone.

Caring is an often overlooked feature of business. Being "fair" is the first approach to business that will keep you balanced. For example, fair prices assumes you will make a profit but not cheat the customers.

*Write how you will **care** for your customer, how you will be **fair** in your pricing and practices, and write a prayer to get a generous heart (**Give**) and how you will seek the needs of your customers (**Live**).*

Putting GOD first takes effort. It is counterintuitive to put GOD first versus profits or self. The world will give free profit calculators and business plan templates focused only on maximizing money. Again, profit is nice, but GOD centered business owners look for profit and people they can serve for HIM.

When GOD said, "But seek first the kingdom of GOD and His righteousness, and all these things shall be added to you" (Matthew 6:33), HE was not looking at making yet another person so wealthy, that he or she could not see HIM or might think he or she is GOD. HE does, however, have a heart for the poor. JESUS said, "For you have the poor with you always, but Me you do not have always" (Matthew 26:11). HE wants people to reach the poor not only with money, but with love so they can believe in JESUS as their Savior.

> Revised ideas have a greater chance for success. Know and test with the target audience.

1. **Reach out to people with a purpose.** Putting GOD first means you are looking for opportunities to share HIS love with as many people as possible. Your business can be the source of this love.
2. **Be intentional.** Thinking about how GOD operates takes intentionality. This may lead to fair business practices, above-the-level services, and perhaps business offerings that align more to GOD's heart.
3. **You are being watched.** The GOD centered business owner will be scrutinized according to his or her actions. A double-minded person trying to serve GOD and money will fail. "*Their loyalty is divided between God and the world, and they are unstable in everything they do*" (James 1:8 NLT). By accepting the fact of being watched, one can more easily point people to GOD rather than oneself.

Acting counterintuitive in business is not easy when much of the information one can find is derived from concepts such as "sex sells" or "the person with the most money wins." GOD says, "*Come to Me, all you who labor and are heavy laden, and I will give you rest. Take My yoke upon you and learn from Me, for I am gentle and lowly in heart, and you will find rest for your souls*" (Matthew 11:28-29).

Exercise 3—Summarize the Vision GOD Gave You

Objective: 1. After listening to GOD, summarize what they heard HIM.
2. Listening to GOD takes time and quiet.

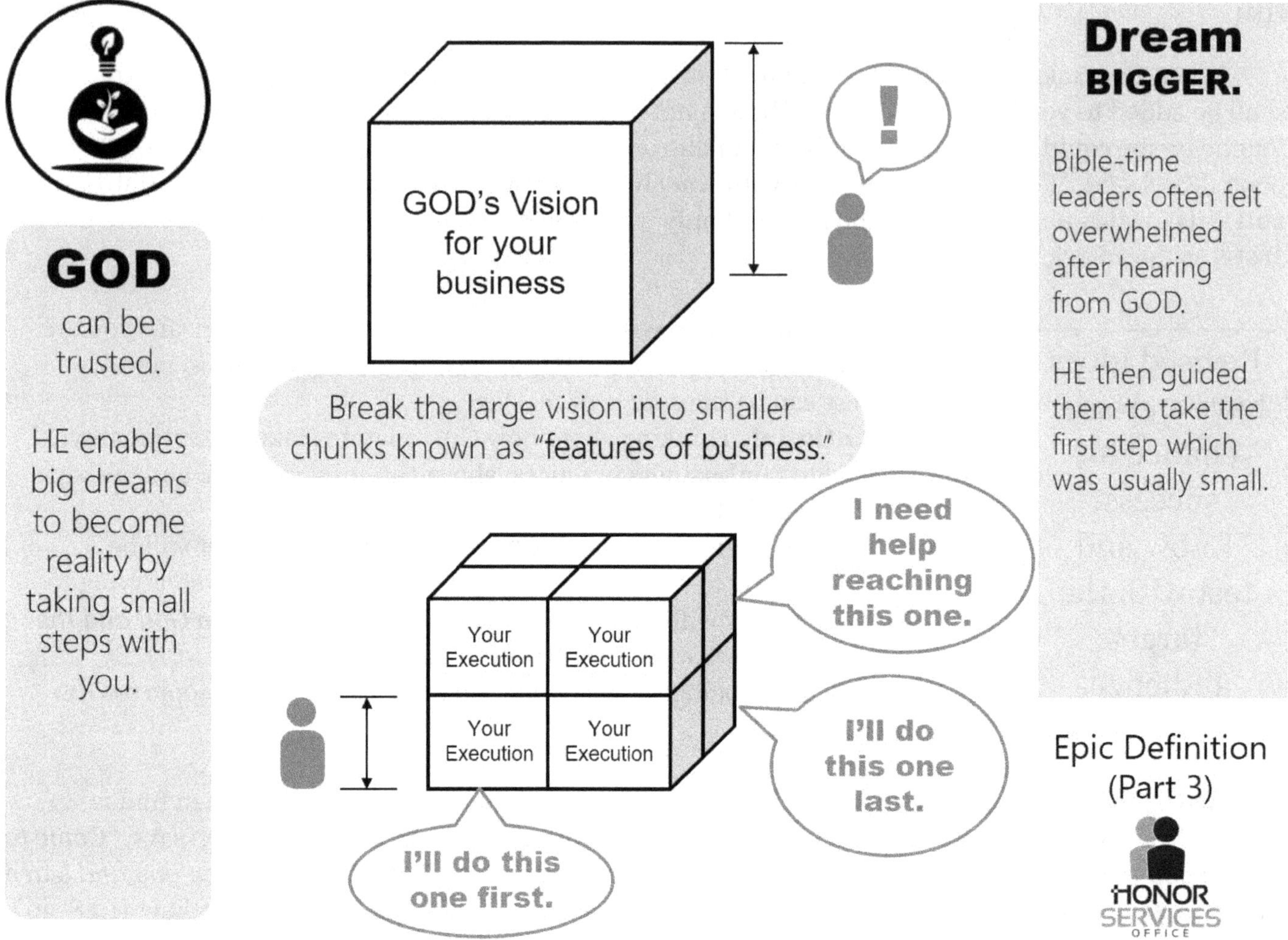

After quieting down and listening to GOD, as we discussed in the previous exercises, you should be able to summarize the vision HE has given you.

Example:

A statement felt in your heart from GOD may be: "Reach surfers for ME."
What this may translate to is: "Sal's Surf Supplies Shoppe"

In this example the owner has skills and talents relating to surfing. The urge to reach surfers for GOD drives the owner to open a shop to reach surfers for HIM.

Here is my example:

Sitting back and complaining about how someone was leading wrong was easy. I could see the flaw in the leader a mile away. Meanwhile, I kept doing "my" job as told by the leader. It was easy. But one day something strange happened. I was told I would be the leader of the group. I felt excited, then overwhelmed. I mean, what if I messed up? Entrepreneurs ask the same question.

Is GOD's Vision for Your Business Wrong?

GOD may have larger plans for your business than you expect. The first reaction is to question if you heard what HE said correctly. With no money, employees or knowledge of how to run a business, GOD may call you into business from that cushy job where it is safe and dependable. Just look at the Hebrews in Egypt. GOD saw how harshly they were treated and wanted them delivered from the cruel slavery they faced.

"Go lead millions of people out of bondage" were the words spoken to Moses by GOD. After living a life of solitude in the desert for killing a man, Moses was told by GOD that he would lead the slaves out of Egypt (Genesis 3). Moses quickly felt overwhelmed and made up excuses. The best one was "I cannot speak well." (Genesis 4:10) Was GOD's vision wrong for wanting HIS people freed from Egypt? No. Was GOD wrong for choosing Moses? No. Is HE wrong for choosing you? No.

Other Overwhelmed Leaders

Moses wasn't the only person who felt overwhelmed. Naomi lost everything and had to lead people in the middle of her pain. She was so overwhelmed that she tried to send everyone away from her so she could just die alone (Ruth 1). Solomon was possibly a teenager when appointed King. He was so overwhelmed that he asked GOD for wisdom (1 Kings 3).

Cure for Being Overwhelmed

After quieting down to hear GOD, He may tell you to do something large or small, depending on your relationship with HIM. If HE tells you to do something small, it is usually to see if you can handle something larger. The more faithful you handle the small, the more GOD can trust you with the large. But one day, GOD may call you to lead the large. What will you do then?

After getting over the initial shock of what GOD wants you to do, take a breath and start asking questions. GOD does not mind answering questions. Ask "Who do YOU want me to serve?" and "Where do YOU want me to serve? And "How can I do this with the resources I have?" HE is willing to answer these questions.

Act with faith and immediacy. Pray about the vision for the business HE has given you and start breaking that vision apart into smaller pieces. Each smaller piece is called a "Feature" of your business. Instead of trying to think of all the features, just think of a few and begin working on them. Ask questions of the customers GOD wants you to serve. They will define how your product or service should look and act like.

Stay Organized

Whether working on something small or large, write down what you will work on to ensure you will not miss anything. Mistakes are made because ideas are not thought out or flawed. When something is not working well with the business, the owner quickly questions GOD. "Are YOU sure I was supposed to be doing this?" GOD wants your confidence that HE is there with you. Slow down and ask HIM for guidance. Your trust in the vision for the business helps you to take things one step at a time.

Look at the talents GOD has given you, the experiences you learned by living life, and the need from the audience GOD wants you to serve. The vision will come from all of these factors.

Begin to break the larger vision you came up with in Exercise 1 into smaller pieces you or others can easily understand and execute.

Think in iterations or revisions. As you think about the steps of your vision, you do not have to get everything right the first time. Later, you will need to get input from strangers and others who may purchase from you.

Elevator Message Exercise

Objective: That participants will create a short summary of the vision.

The summary of the vision is what is known as an elevator message. This will be the beginnings of how to tell people what your business does and is.

People will ask, "What does your business do or sell?" This is an opportunity to quickly explain the product or service without coming across as salesy.

Summarize everything in your mind that defines what the business does and is. This is the beginning of your elevator message. Instead of starting from a blank page, use the following format as a thought starter. You do not have to follow this exactly.

________ is a product or service that provides ________. It addresses ________ need and will do ________. ________ number of people will be served in ________ area. I (We) will be able to pray for ________ daily.

Epic Wish List Exercise

GOD provides insight at random times. It is best to write these ideas down on a wish list. This is a list of features your business provides or will provide in the future. Do not worry about filling your list with ideas right away. This will be used to keep a running list of things you want your business to do or improve on. Later I will discuss discerning GOD's voice from your own.

Exercise 4—Take Your First Pass At Breaking Down the Vision

Objective: Develop a list of smaller parts of the vision to begin building them with customer input.

Breaking apart the vision helps the GOD-centered business owner stay organized while deciding how to explain the product or service on your website and other places.

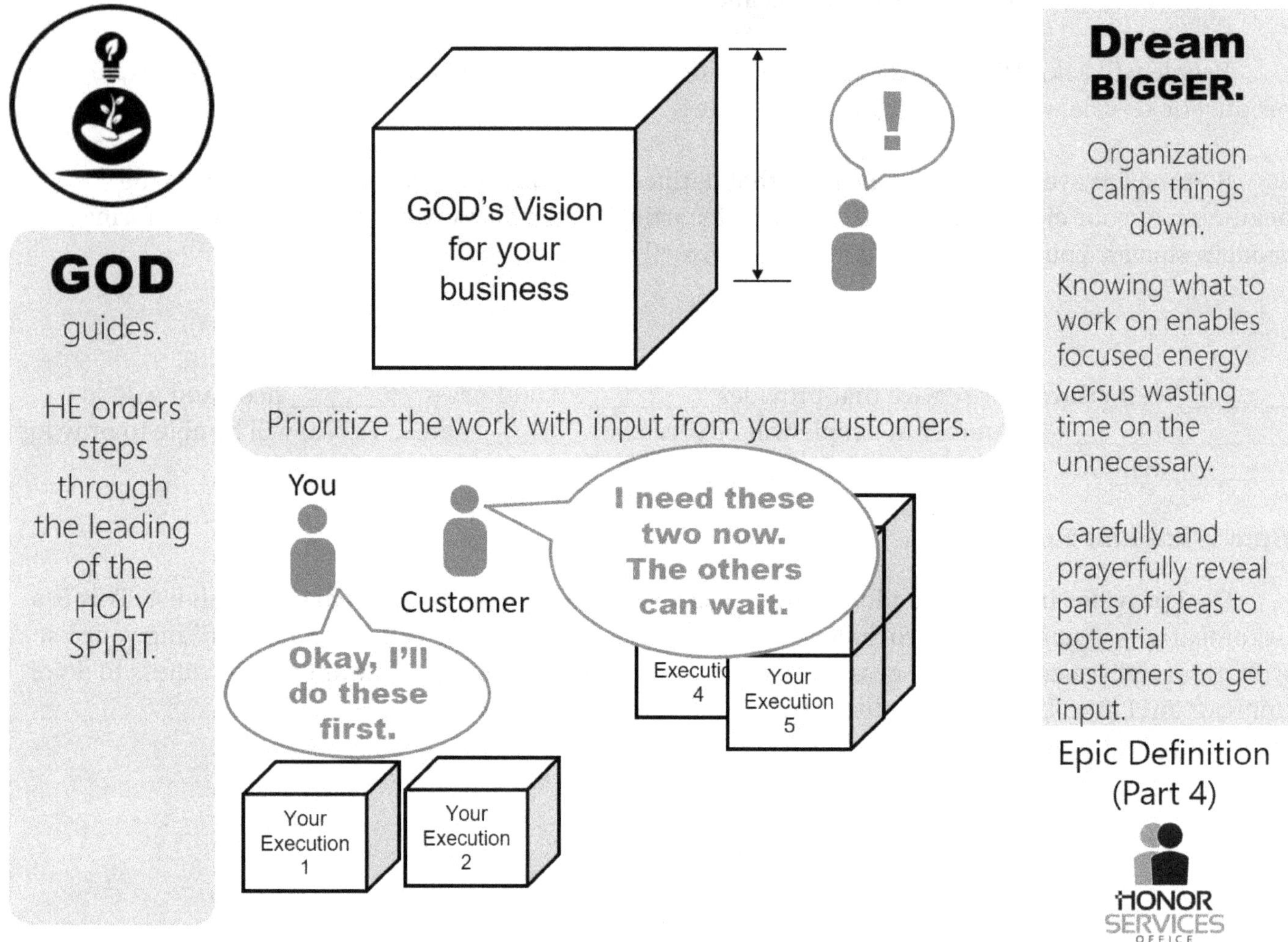

GOD looks forward to guiding you. How do you know this? HE said *"For I know the plans I have for you," declares the Lord, "plans to prosper you and not to harm you, plans to give you hope and a future."* Jeremiah 29:11 (NIV)

What are some of the ways you discern GOD's guidance?

Responses might include the Bible, the wise counsel of others, answers to prayer, etc.

How have you sensed GOD's leading in regard to the vision for your business? Let's talk about ways to break the vision for a business into smaller piece.

Let's suppose, through prayer, a business owner discerned that GOD was saying, "Sell surfboards to reach surfers for the Kingdom of GOD." As it stands, that might sound overwhelming. But this is where the vision is broken into components. Some include:

1. Sell
2. Rent
3. Buy Used
4. Recycle

You might wonder, *Where did these components come from?*

Psalm 119 requested of GOD: "*Order my steps in Your word* (Psalm 119 BSB).

Why? Because "*GOD is not a GOD of disorder but of peace*" (1 Corinthians 14:33). When GOD provides a vision, HE often challenges the person to do something he or she may not normally do. Yet the steps HE provides follow a natural progression. Selling new surfboards could lead to renting surfboards that are not selling fast, which could then lower the price to be sold as used.

List the smaller components of your business. Avoid "marketing" language at this time.

Each stage of the framework/methodology will have a list we will refer to as a *wish list*. At the vision stage, this wish list is for bigger and broader ideas as compared to the latter stages where detail is required.

What should be worked on first? Talk to the audience GOD wants you to serve. Try to identify the smallest need that can be fulfilled in the shortest amount of time. This is called the "Weighted Shortest Job First" or WSJF. The WSJF can also be used to prioritize the work not seen by your customers. By completing smaller tasks that have value first, it will be easier to break apart the more complex tasks because the smaller tasks enable the GOD-centered business owner to get into a rhythm of consistent delivery.

Prioritize the Vision

Objective: To prioritize tasks and define the MVP of your business or service.

Have you ever had one of those weeks when everything was due at once? Perhaps you had several deadlines, urgent meetings, and family issues. Staying focused requires the work to be prioritized from highest priority to the lowest. You can start to prioritize by breaking larger tasks into smaller tasks.

Do the easiest and most valuable item first. This is known as the Minimal Viable Product (MVP).

Write what should be done first, next, and so on until they get to the last. Try to keep it high level and avoid "how" language. Focus on "what" needs to be done.

For existing business owners reprioritize the features of your business based on what is working and what is not working. Ask GOD to help let go of what is not working or ask how to modify the feature to gain more quality or appeal.

New Business Exercise

As you consider how to order the steps of the vision GOD has given you, write what should be done first, next, and so on until you get to the last task. Try to keep it high level and avoid "how" language. Focus on "what" needs to be done.

Existing Business Exercise

For existing business owners, reprioritize the features of your business based on what is working and what is not working. Ask GOD to help let go of what is not working or ask how to modify the feature to gain more quality or appeal.

Business prioritization takes leadership. Let's look at another leadership trait, namely being a faithful leader. Now let's talk about the components of the Faithful Leadership style.

Faithful Leadership Style

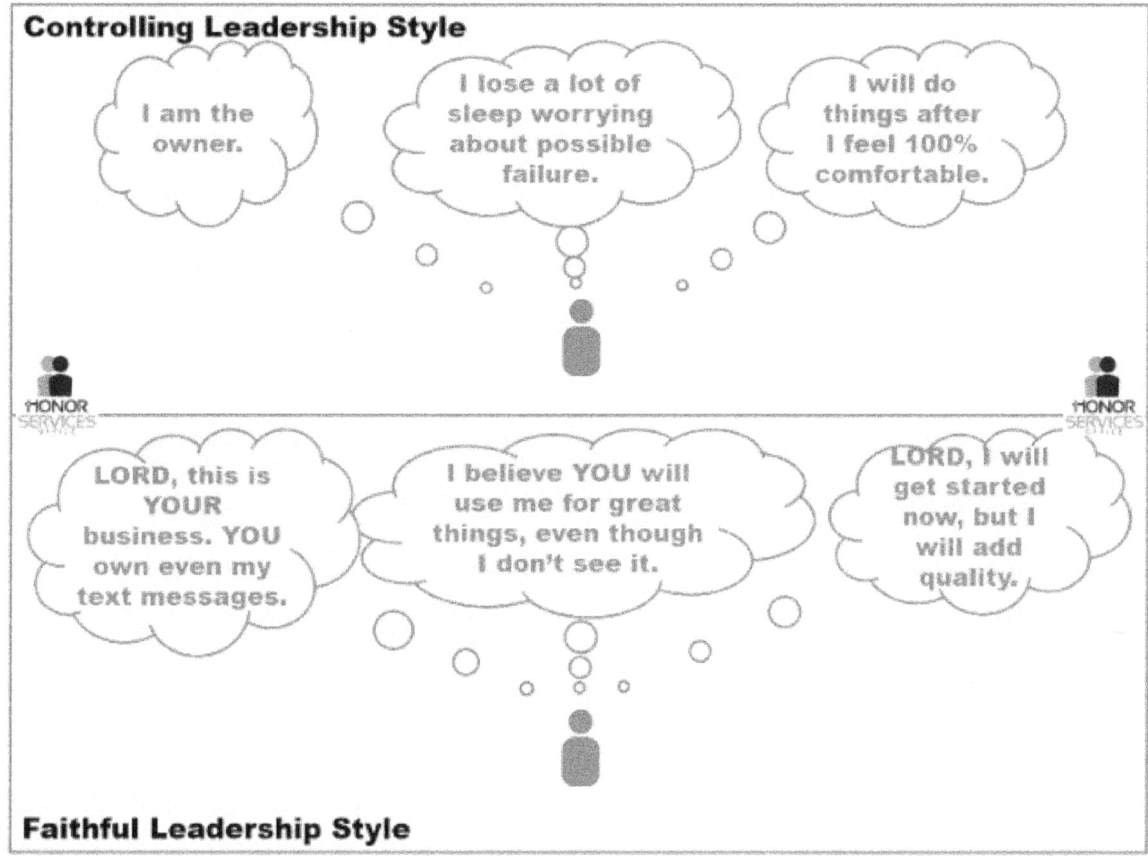

What does it mean to have faith? Do you have faith in yourself only? What do you put your faith in? Does having faith mean you have to control everything? Why or why not?

Leaders Give Problems to GOD – Believe in HIS Power – Act with Immediacy

Have you ever worked for a good boss? On the contrary, have you ever worked for a bad boss? What were the things that made them a good or bad boss?

It takes faith to run a successful business.

Hebrews 11:1: "*Now faith is the substance of things hoped for, the evidence of things not seen.*"

Faith, however, does not mean control. In fact it means quite the opposite. All areas of your business should be given to GOD. This means checking your heart and your business concept to see if they align with GOD by reading the Bible, praying, and letting GOD reduce your worries. Obedience with GOD is required, so that is why regularly reading GOD's Word is important.

What part do you think faith plays in running a business? Why?
What does your business reveal about your faith? Why?
List your concerns, thoughts text messages, and websites you will ***give*** *GOD.*
Write a belief statement, using this sentence starter: LORD, I ***believe*** *YOU will use me for...*
Write your promise to act with ***immediacy****, but still have patience to do it with quality.*

Faith fights your attempt to control. Jumping into the deep end of a swimming pool can be scary, especially if the person jumping does not know how to swim. Even if surrounded by people who can help him swim, there may be a natural hesitancy that causes a cautious approach.

Successful businesses have faithful leaders.

Business is no different. Sometimes, the guards get put up and the life jackets get strapped on before the nervous business owner jumps in the water. Unfortunately for the cautious business swimmers, a life jacket prevents them from learning how to swim.

The life jacket in this case is *control*. Micro-business owners want to do everything themselves, blaming their lack of money as the reason for this controlling behavior. Even if they got someone to help, it usually would be a person they could control, like a family member or a friend.

When seeking financial help, control comes into play. The person loaning the money wants a percentage of "control" in the company. If the money lender sees you are not meeting expectations, that person will use her control to get you out or take over the business assets or idea.

Here is GOD's perspective:

1. **GOD wants 100% control.** Obedience to GOD is paramount in the GOD centered business. Fearing GOD is more important than fearing a shrinking bank account. GOD may ask you to do something like giving the first portion of your revenue to a person who has a financial need. Though most experts may advise you to reinvest in the business, GOD may guide you to grow and bless HIS kingdom, which in turn brings blessings to you.
2. **GOD wants you to have faith in HIS vision for your life.** If GOD has said that He wants you in business and you accepted, HE wants you to believe HE will take care of you. HE cannot wait to supply all of your needs. It takes tremendous faith to be in business in the first place. GOD wants to grow that faith as you face a larger vision, one you've never dreamt of.
3. **GOD wants immediacy.** Childlike faith does not require analysis. The child immediately believes in the bearer of the information. Same with GOD. When HE says you will be successful based on HIS power, the immediate action should be belief.

Some business owners jump into water without knowing how to swim, but having no one there to help, they drown. These over-confident business swimmers never looked for help, thinking they could do everything themselves because they took the dangerous leap.

Jumping into business does not preclude you from doing the work necessary to stay in business. If your business is regulated, then you must abide by those regulations and get everything in place.

Jumping in means you cannot turn back. The faithful GOD-Centered business owner sees more at stake than her business. She discerns that reaching people for the kingdom is also important. Whatever barrier is placed in front of this person, faith will overcome the obstacle. The faithful person leads by asking GOD what HE wants versus telling GOD what she wants.

Exercise 5—List the Promises GOD Made You

Objective: To practice remembering the promises of GOD for use in difficult days. Write scripture or what the HOLY SPIRIT has told you.

We think of faithfulness as being committed. How do you show that you're committed to someone or something? Someone might mention giving an engagement ring as a sign of commitment. Others might mention signing a contract. GOD showed His faithfulness by the promises found throughout the Bible.

GOD keeps HIS promises.

Example: *I'll never leave you nor forsake you.**

*I will be with you always.***

*I will lead you.****

Promises GOD has for me.

Dream BIGGER.

Take time to write down the promises GOD has for you.

When you get quiet, GOD will make unbreakable promises to you.

Revisit these often.

Epic Definition (Part 5)

Read the Scriptures in the above illustration. Circle the promise that resonates the most with you. Why did you choose that promise? What other promises can you think of that GOD has for you? List those here.

How do you think the promises listed above will aid you in your business?

Hebrews 13:5. *Keep your lives free from the love of money and be content with what you have, because God has said, "Never will I leave you; never will I forsake you."* (NIV)

** Matthew 28:20 *"and teach them to obey everything I have commanded you. And I will be with you always, to the end of the age."* (GNT)

*** Isaiah 42:16 *I will lead the blind by ways they have not known, along unfamiliar paths I will guide them; I will turn the darkness into light before them and make the rough places smooth. These are the things I will do; I will not forsake them.* (NIV)

Sometimes things do not go as planned or happen as fast as we'd like. This may causes us to question GOD's promises. GOD means what HE says when HE promises something. HE has already done what HE said when HE says "I will." Whatever HE promises to the GOD-centered business owner has already happened to HIM. HE is not waiting on the conditions to be perfect. HIS "I will" is simply used to inform us of the things that have already occurred. Listen to GOD for the promises HE has for you

Ever had one of those days when it seemed like everything that could go wrong did go wrong?

Entrepreneurship is not as easy as some stories embellish. For some, it will be easier to get the business up and running than others. You read a story about how he or she started a business in their garage and five minutes later their success was multinational, meanwhile something else falls apart in your business. What happens when things go wrong with your business? Should you quit and give up? No. The solution is to remember the promises GOD told you.

GOD's promises provide confidence. Revisit the promises GOD gives your regularly.

What other promises does GOD have for **you**?
What promises does GOD have for your **business**?

Knowing GOD has promises will help with the Trusting Leadership style. Let's look at this style.

Be Content with GOD not the Situation

No one likes uncomfortable situations. Many bible authors were given words by GOD to enable us to hear the promises HE made to us. Paul writes in Hebrews 13:5. *"Keep your lives free from the love of money and be content with what you have, because God has said, 'Never will I leave you; never will I forsake you.'"* (NIV)

Lack of money sometimes brings on major worries. The love of money means the greedy will never have enough and will worry no matter how much money they have. GOD wants us to be content through all stages in life. While waiting on the business to make the first bit of revenue, be content with GOD, knowing HE is in this with you and you are not alone.

Be Obedient to GOD's Commands to Keep a Clear Conscience

Matthew 28:20 "*and teach them to obey everything I have commanded you. And I will be with you always, to the end of the age.*" (GNT)

Following GOD requires surrender to HIS ways. HE will sometimes allow you to try your own way and when things fail, HE is there to pick you up. But HE would rather that you show HIM the same faithfulness HE showed you. HE promises to be with you. Keeping a clear conscience helps when life's storms come. You can be assured you have been forgiven for all sins. This provides confidence that the storm is not punishment, rather a trial to grow you and make you stronger.

Be Guided

Isaiah 42:16 *I will lead the blind by ways they have not known, along unfamiliar paths I will guide them; I will turn the darkness into light before them and make the rough places smooth. These are the things I will do; I will not forsake them.* (NIV)

Confused and don't know where to turn? GOD will guide you out of difficult situations. HIS specialty is seeing all blind spots and delivering HIS sheep to green pastures. GOD is willing to guide you, remove barriers and make the difficult easy.

Following GOD enables hope that others do not have. You can show others that, while life can get difficult, you have GOD's promises to rely on.

Did GOD promise you HE will provide? Yes. What other promises did GOD tell you for your business?

Now let's talk about the components of the Trusting Leadership style.

Trusting Leadership Style

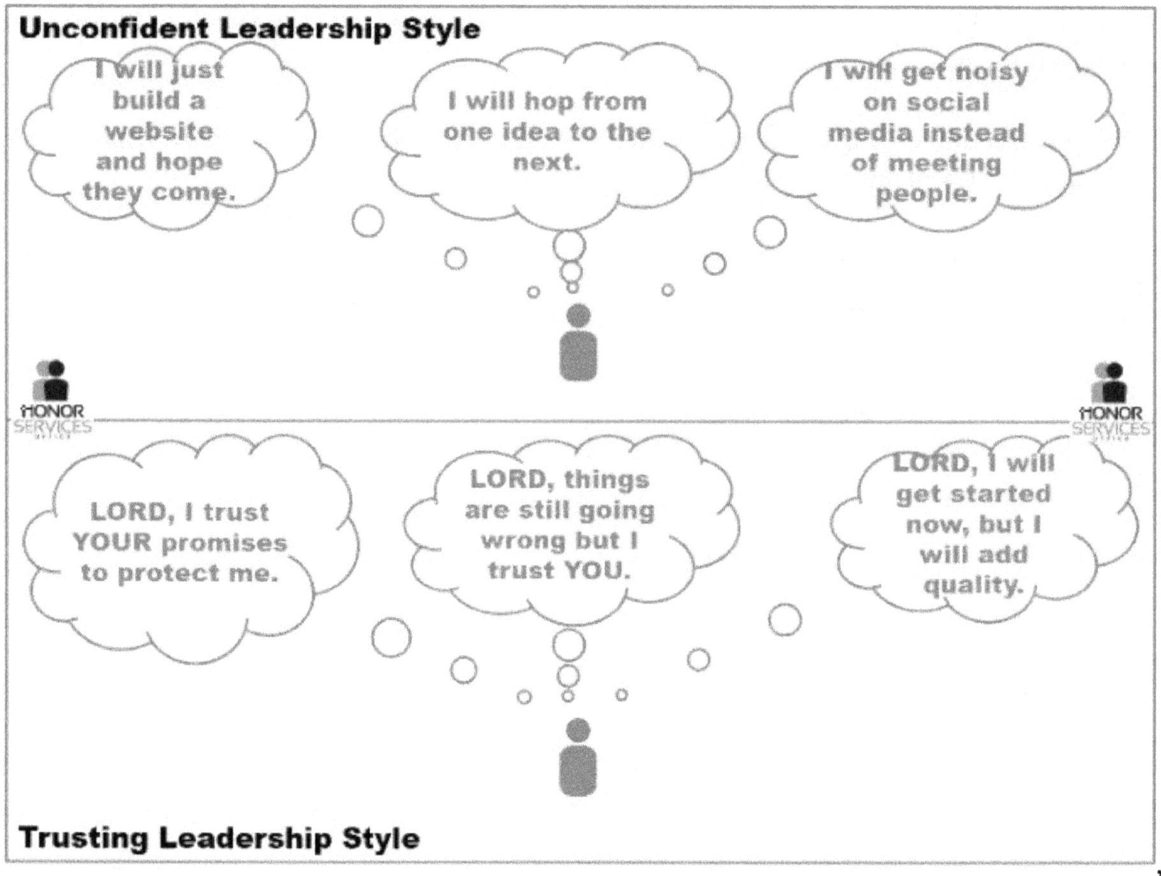

What does it mean to have trust? Who do you trust? What do you trust? Does trusting mean you never ask questions? Why or why not?

Leaders Pledge, Plea, and Pray

How would you feel getting on a plane with a pilot who is sweating nervously? How about going to a doctor who wasn't sure of herself? How would you feel?

> Trust in GOD means you will not give up.

Unconfident people spend enormous time trying to feel like they are doing something to make progress. When times get difficult, these unconfident people give up easily. You are a leader sent by GOD! You will be victorious when you put your trust in HIM.

Trust means you will not give up because you trust that God is for you and not against you.

Sample pledge

I pledge not to give up when it is hard. I pledge to trust GOD especially when things get hard. I also **pledge** to... (finish the sentence).

Revisit this once a month by adding a reminder on your calendar.
Write down a **plea** for areas of need. Though this may have been done earlier, it is another place to pray as your **plea**.

Pray, Sample prayer: "LORD I trust YOU to guide me, grow me and govern me as YOU please. I trust YOU to handle all my worries. Amen.

Trust is a requirement of following GOD. Fear breeds a lack of trust. It seems like the bigger the vision, the more people fear failing. Consequently, many micro-business owners play it safe, chasing less risky, low-rewarding routes. They listen to risk-adverse people, never meet new customers, and hide at home waiting on referrals.

Trust in GOD builds your confidence in HIM.

1. **GOD wants total trust in HIS abilities.** "*Trust in the LORD with all your heart, and lean not on your own understanding; in all your ways acknowledge Him, and He shall direct your paths*" (Proverbs 3:5-6). If a person is filled with fear, that person may believe in fearful directions labeled as "safe." But what if GOD does not want you to play it safe? GOD would prefer your relying on HIS abilities instead of your own. This may throw "safe" out the window.

2. **GOD wants obedience.** Not all areas of trust are fun. You may show a tiny bit of trust for a short time and things may still go wrong. Will you still obey GOD? The GOD-centered business owner expects things to go wrong but continues to obey GOD, knowing HE is trustworthy to clear up mistakes.

3. **GOD wants you whole.** Knowing that GOD wants you whole strengthens faith. Even when difficulties arise, trust shows up and guides you through the situation.

Addressing fear takes trust in GOD. When life has been tough and problems have beaten you up, it may be difficult for you to trust GOD. HE knows this and is gentle in HIS guidance. HE wants total trust from you, allowing HIM to guide your business, finances, family, friends, and your health. Trust builds obedience to HIM. Unshakeable trust enables GOD-sized things to happen through you.

Exercise 6—Listen to People

Objective: To make plans to listen to people to get vital feedback.

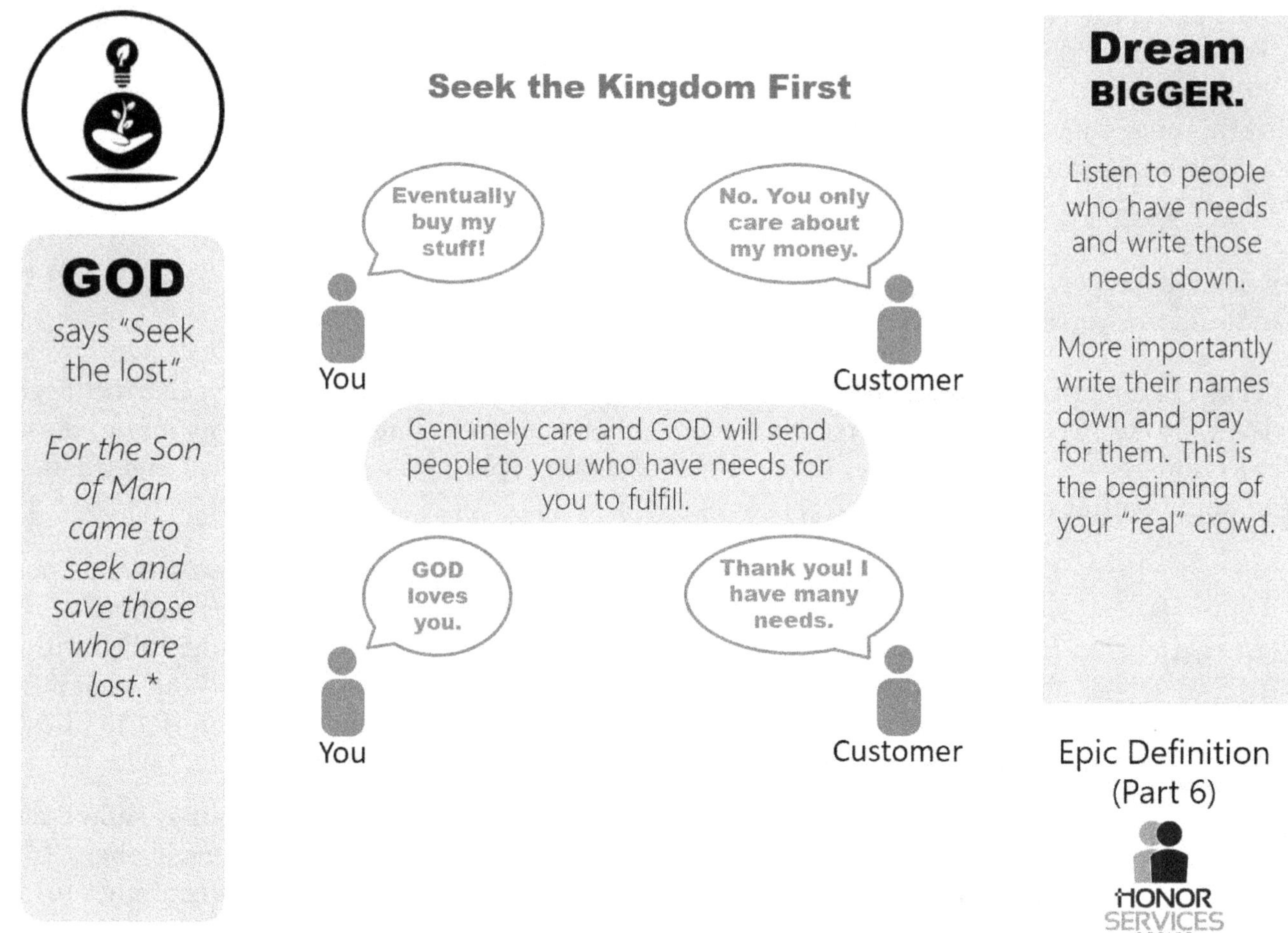

When was the last time you felt heard? By whom? How did the person communicate that he or she heard you? How does someone listen well? What are some of the characteristics of a listener?

Business should not be done in the dark or alone. Seek the needs of your customer by listening to them. Write down their needs. Remember, GOD's currency is people, so listen to their personal needs as well so you can pray for them.

GOD wants you to seek the lost.

Luke 19:10 – *For the Son of Man came to seek and save those who are lost.* (NLT)

Write the names of people who have told you about <u>a specific problem or need</u>.

Eventually the names you write will go into a Contact Relationship Management (CRM) system, where you will document their needs. You will contact this group or people to refine your problem statement, audience, and location.

What would make the product or service excellent?

Write the name of people who will review your product or service here.

Your proposed solution to the problem or need	Reviewer name

By seeking GOD's kingdom first, the GOD-centered business owner keeps his or her priorities straight. Kingdom growth before business growth is always the priority. Business growth will follow. *But seek first his kingdom and his righteousness, and all these things will be given to you as well. Matthew 6:33 (NIV)*

Everyone needs GOD. Find out the other needs that your business can supply and provide the kingdom and the solution to their problem. Now let's talk about the components of the Humble Leadership style.

Let's learn a leadership style that helps approach people, namely the Humble Leadership Style.

Humble Leadership Style

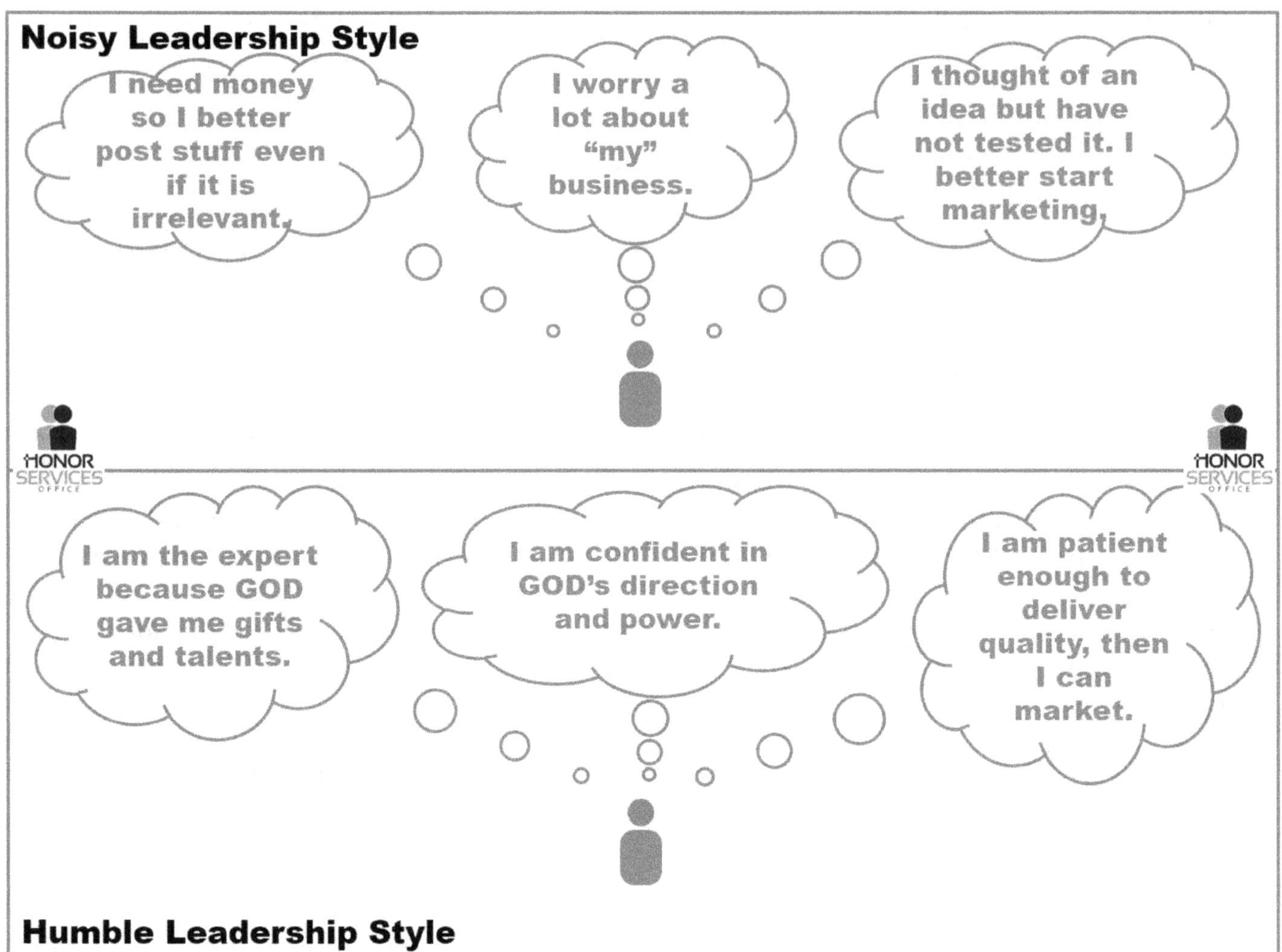

Humility/ humbleness means strength. Being in business is a humbling experience, especially if you are not financed. Each customer becomes precious and requires the best of care and attention. The GOD-centered business owner seeks opportunities to serve people with her hospitality, friendliness, competence, and refreshing attitude. The HOLY SPIRIT shines through you.

if my people, who are called by my name, will humble themselves.

1. **GOD wants humbleness.** *"if my people, who are called by my name, will humble themselves and pray and seek my face and turn from their wicked ways, then I will hear from heaven, and I will forgive their sin and will heal their land.* " (2 Chronicles 7:14). GOD knows how difficult life can be. Arrogance has no place in HIS kingdom. HE wants the best for those who believe in HIS SON, but the approach needs humbleness.

2. **GOD wants to be first.** "And seeing the multitudes, He went up on a mountain, and when He was seated His disciples came to Him. Then He opened His mouth and taught them, saying:

'Blessed are the poor in spirit,
For theirs is the kingdom of heaven.'" (Matthew 5:3)

The very first Beatitude JESUS presents is a poor or humble spirit. To the humble, GOD will gladly give HIS kingdom.

3. **GOD gave up everything.** "*Who, being in very nature God, did not consider equality with God something to be used to his own advantage;*" Philippians 2:6 . (NIV) JESUS, being GOD, never used HIS power as an advantage over HIS creation. Instead, HE served them. HIS humbleness shows true power.

What does it mean to be confident? Does confidence mean being noisy? Does confidence mean hiding faults? Have you ever met a person who can relate to many people? What about him or her stands out?

Leaders Are Confident, Capable, and Customized

What is your weakness? You don't have to tell us, but what thing do you fall to that is between only you and GOD? Are you trying to mask your weakness by being strong in front of people?

Confidence comes from trusting in GOD's power.

Confidence comes from trusting in GOD's power, not your own. Remember the thankfulness exercise? GOD provided you with many gifts and talents that you are thankful for. GOD provided your capabilities too. How about that idea? GOD enables you to make it special. Only you can make your product or service unique and customized to the people GOD wants you to reach.

"I am confident because" finish the sentence
"I am capable because" finish the sentence
"I am customized because I provide" finish the sentence

Knowing you get your confidence and capabilities from GOD enables you to steer clear of bragging or boasting about yourself and giving credit to GOD. Let's take the Humble Leadership style into refining the vision to achieve excellence.

Exercise 7—Refine the Vision for Excellence

Objective: To think about revising to achieve excellence rather than thinking the first draft will be excellent.

How do you know when something is excellent as opposed to something that's just good?
Do you think excellence is achieved on the first try? Why or why not?
Also, perfection is never reached, rather the business continuously improves.

Practice refining validation. This comes over time. The first vision God gives you may take several revisions that require input from your customers in order to get it right. Build your product or service with input from your potential customers and strive for excellence.

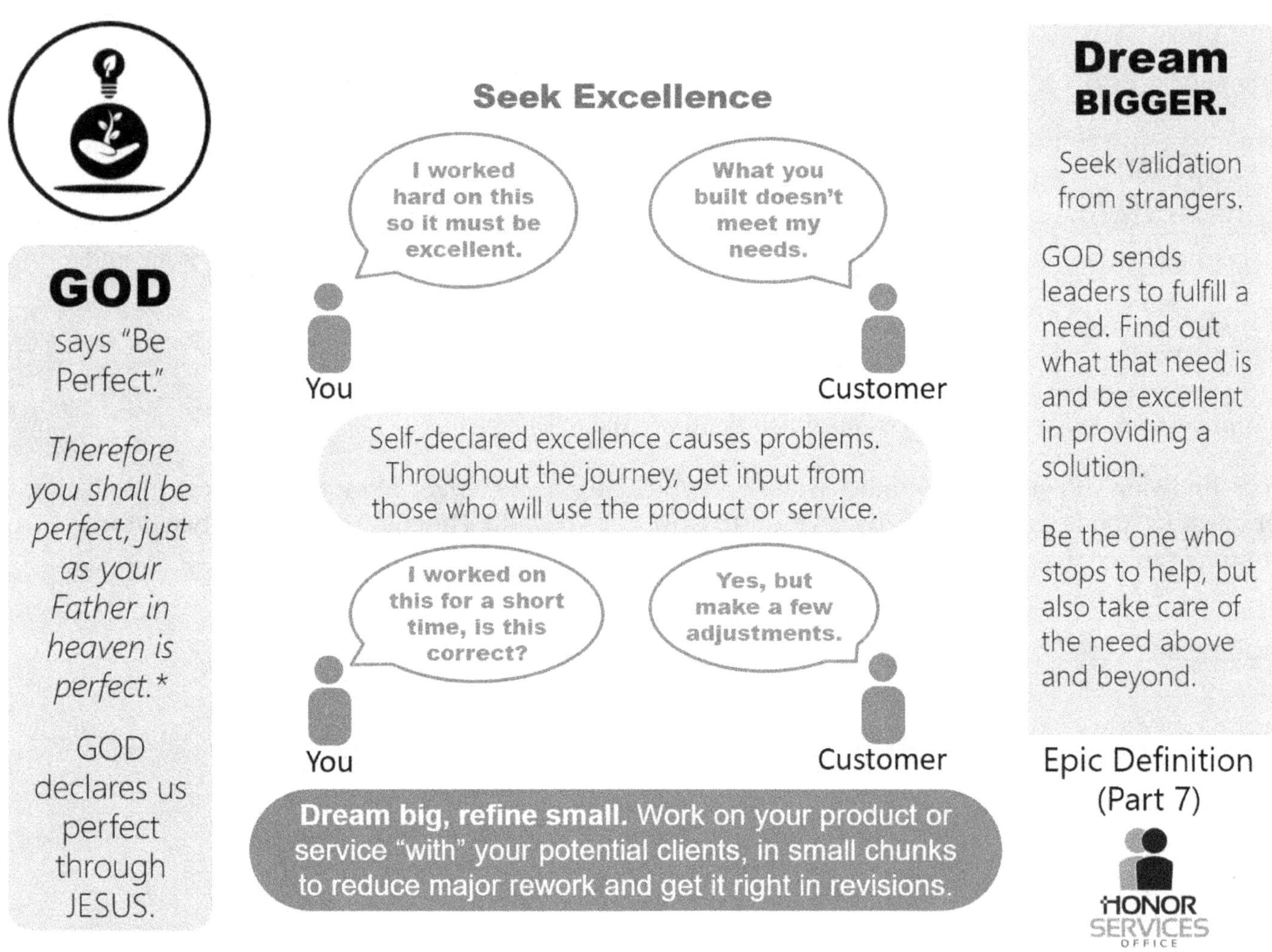

Perfection is the condition, state, or quality of being free or as free as possible from all flaws or defects. But how can this come from imperfect humans? GOD made a way for imperfect humans to be declared perfect. Through belief in JESUS as our Savior, we are made perfect. Only JESUS makes us perfect.

Matthew 5:48 *Therefore you shall be perfect, just as your Father in heaven is perfect.* (NKJV)

Take excellence seriously. The first idea will be revised and revised until it meets the need of the customer.

1. **Showing love is the goal.** Do you love the person you are selling to or love getting rich? The person matters more than your bank account. This strange approach is validated by GOD. The more love you show people, the more responsibility GOD will give to you. HE will then sustain you to love a larger crowd.
2. **Pride of ownership gets thrown away.** Your first idea may not be the true idea—the idea GOD has for your business. Abraham was told to sacrifice his son Isaac (Genesis 22). Abraham followed GOD's instructions and was obedient, even though losing his son would have hurt him dearly. GOD stopped Abraham before he killed his son and then provided him with the true sacrifice. Pride of ownership causes a person to hold onto "his" idea too long, missing out on how GOD wants to refine it.
3. **The spotlight becomes a compass.** For those who love to be seen and heard, your time in the spotlight can become a pointer to GOD. When you speak to new potential customers, the SPIRIT of GOD will shine through you, thus taking the spotlight while you take a lesser role. For those who are too shy to be in the spotlight, GOD wants you to step in so you can become a pointer to HIM, overcoming the urge to shy away from meeting and speaking to new people. It is about GOD, not you. Your product or service can open doors to form relationships, thus enabling you to speak about CHRIST in words and deeds.

True Solution Requires True Identity

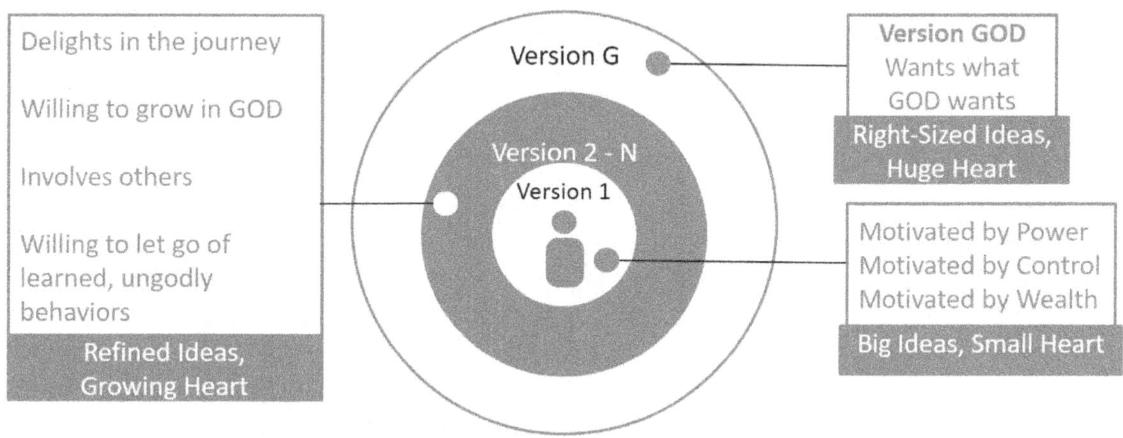

What you start with is usually not where you will finish. GOD made you special. Just because your were trained in something, doesn't mean it is your talent from GOD.

GOD wants a growing person with a heart filled with HIS love. By listening to the true needs of your customer, GOD helps you provide the solution based on the gifts and talents HE gave you from birth. Revisions can help the overconfident, who jump in without plans, slow down to revise. Revisions also can help those who are not confident and who over-plan to start with the MVP.

Write your pledge for excellence. This will be a promise you can display to your customers. In the next chapter, you will learn how to remove the trash, which is any obstacle to a true breakthrough in your business or relationships.

Exercise 8—Get Feedback From Specific People About Specific Parts

Objective: To make plans to solicit feedback <u>*once more*</u> *in order to seek excellence. Soliciting feedback should happen regularly.*

List potential customers/clients who will validate your idea. Remember, playing it safe is not the goal. Get validation even from harsh critics and refine your product with GOD'S assistance.

GOD

loves HIS people.

*You shall be My people, And I will be your God.**

The following **potential** customers review my initial work.

Dream BIGGER.

Take time to write down the people who will provide feedback.

This is the start of your "real" crowd. Try to enlist strangers. Family and friends mean well, but may not give necessary, objective feedback.

Epic Definition (Part 8)

GOD loves HIS creation. We have all been put here for a reason, namely GOD's purpose. Meeting HIS people to solve problems is part of the GOD-centered business owner's day. Listening to feedback is also part of a great product or service. What strangers will you encounter to provide feedback to you?

Your customers are never an inconvenience. Give them your best. Serve them well. Look for the best solutions and trust GOD to deliver.

Have you ever met a person who made you and everyone around you smile when they walked in the room? How about a person who helped you simply because you were you? GOD loves HIS people, especially you! You were made for HIM and HE made you to work with other people.

Jeremiah 30:22 - *'You shall be My people, And I will be your God.'* " (NKJV) As you can see, GOD wants to be GOD to HIS people. HE wants you to be there for HIS people.

List people and the specific feedback you are looking for. This will refine the vision and help you get a better grip on the problem. Use the STEP process to think of who you will get feedback from.

STEP Process for Feedback

S is for **Strangers** who tend to give the most honest feedback, because they have no emotional ties to you or your business.
T is for **Thought leaders** in your industry who can broaden your perspective.
E is for **Emotional** review which comes from family and friends. Their feedback enables them to be involved.
P is for **Professional** validation such as content editors, compliance groups, and regulatory agencies.

Refer to the "Remove the Trash" chapter if you are reluctant to have people review your work. This chapter deals with removing barriers to achieving true success. I will discuss this in depth later.

We did this exercise of identifying people for feedback before when we identified reviewers of our work. This time we are using the STEP method. Remember, the GOD-Centered Business is a framework from which you will, listen to GOD, listen to people and build your business ideas into features of your business you will sell and operate. If you run out of room, use a spreadsheet on your computer to log feedback. Keep in mind that regulatory agencies may require a specific method of providing feedback.

Feel free to invite these people to attend this community.

Name	Feedback Needed	Feedback Given

Now let's set some goals for your business.

Exercise 9—Set GREAT Goals

Objective: That the participants will practice setting goals.

A GOD-centered business needs great goals. By that HE means: **GOD**-sized, **R**elevant, **E**ngaging, **A**ttainable and **T**imely (GREAT) goals. These can only come from GOD.

What do people usually need to practice?

Someone might mention a musical instrument, someone else might mention something in relation to a sport, like practicing a basketball jump shot or bowling. Business goal setting requires practice as well.

Setting goals is important to remain hopeful and focused on GOD's vision. Every day you should know what you plan to do. Set a goal to get something accomplished. The goal should be GREAT

List GREAT goals. Here are some pointers to help:

1. **God Sized.** The right size could be tiny or huge when it comes to God. *He said, "Whoever receives one little child like this in My name receives Me"* (Matthew 18:5). He brings respect to the small and the large. God's vision for your business will succeed. He will not put more on you than you can handle, but He will stretch you more than you think.
2. **Relevant.** Listening to your customers' needs and using your God-given expertise to develop a solution that meets their needs. Great does not always mean big, rather, it can mean one who delivers and meets a need with a solid solution.
3. **Engaging.** Leveraging the list of people God wants you to serve will provide valuable feedback as to how they want to use your product or service. Capture how they wish to engage with your business.
4. **Attainable.** Reaching God's large vision can seem daunting at times. Take the vision God gave you and break it into smaller pieces so you can develop plans that are reachable in the near term—not next year, rather in the next **two weeks**.
5. **Timely.** Do not hurry through anything, but act with immediacy. The difference is, hurrying causes poor quality whereas acting with immediacy puts priority on the things God wants you to deliver.

GREAT Goal Exercise

Great—Write the original goal versus God's goal for your business.
Relevant—How is your business going to meet the needs of your customers? Write specific numbers of how often you plan to meet their needs **over the next ten weeks**.
Engaging—How useful is the product or service? Why is it useful? (This will be used later in the marketing.)
Attainable—Were you able to break God's vision into smaller pieces? If not then, ask God for clarity. If yes, then write feedback from potential customers about the products services you plan to offer.
Timely—What can you build or refine **over the next ten weeks?**

GREAT goals are broader than day-to-day goals. Every day you should know what you are going to do. We will discuss how to manage your day in the next chapter.

Why ten weeks? What is this two week constraint mentioned above? Agile AFB is structured to plan in ten week increments. No more. The world changes too rapidly to plan any further out. Two weeks is the most you should be focusing your efforts. Adjustments can be made every two weeks to stay on top of things.

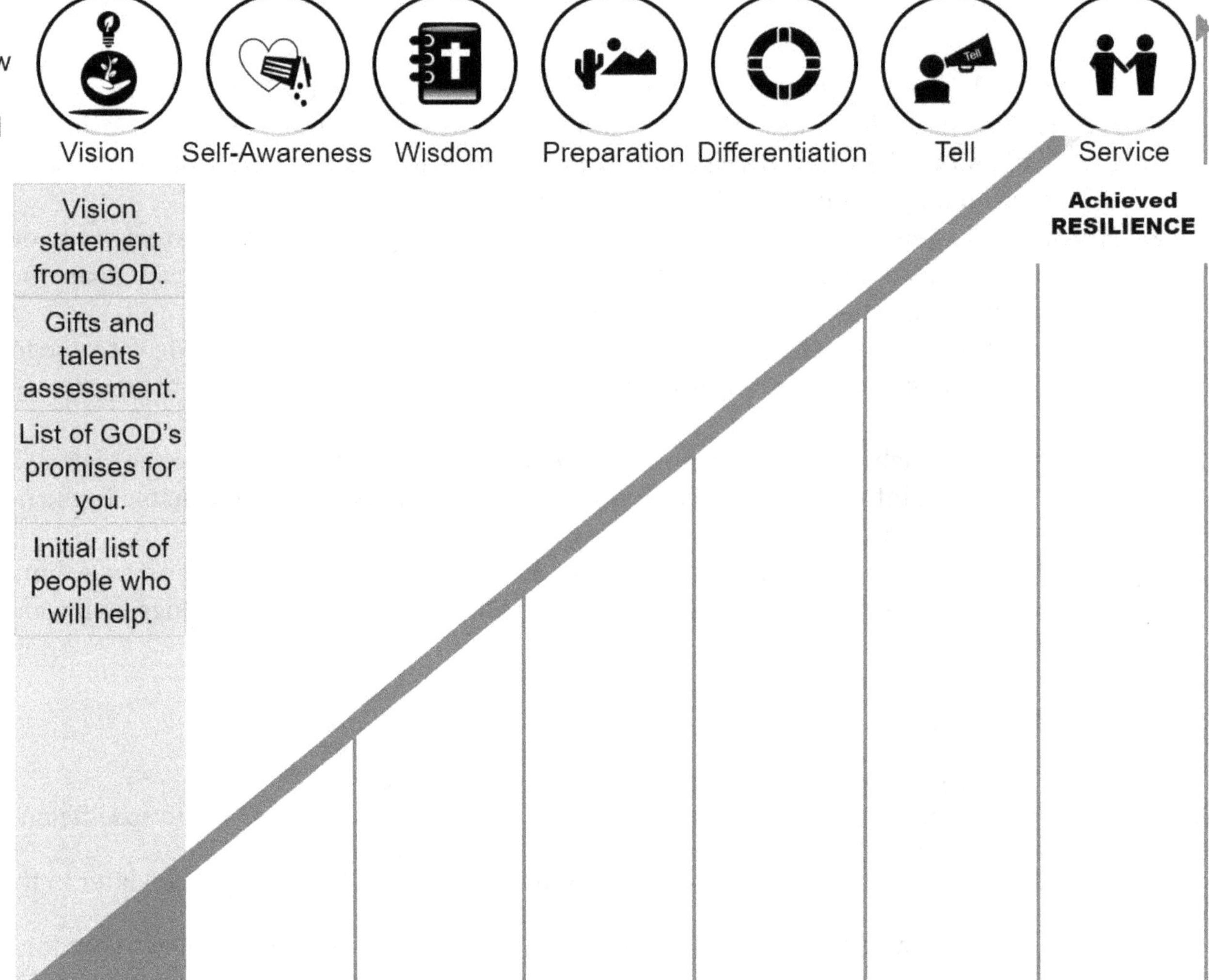

A resilience chart will be at the end of each chapter. This as a list of components to make your business more resilient and able to withstand life's challenges. By now you should have a vision from GOD broken down into smaller pieces. You should also have a list of people who will review your work.

Dream BIGGER.

Believe. **I**gnite **GOD**'s **G**race **E**verywhere **R**elationally!

For homework, go old school for one week: Turn off TV, radio, social media, and news. Carry a pad and pen. Ask GOD to speak to your heart.

If this is a weekly class, ask for any prayer requests and dismiss in prayer.

Remember to start your personal journal found at the end of this book.

NEXT STEPS

Review the vision GOD gave you in a quiet moment before Him. Plan for many revisions to the original vision through people GOD has sent to you. Strive for excellence.

WARNINGS

Letting go of self takes practice. Be patient with yourself and others and get rid of false deadlines. You are starting the journey to becoming a better leader. This does not happen overnight.

PRAYER

- Ask the LORD to guide you during this quiet time.
- Ask that you be decreased and GOD be increased.
- Pray to be sent to the group to which HE wants you to go.
- Admit any fear or doubt.

Chapter 2 – Remove the Trash: Self-Awareness

"What is blocking true success?"

"Could you be in your own way?"

"Are you salvageable?"

Remove the Trash preparation (Week 2)

Greet participants and remind them of the goal to unplug from TV and social media. Were with us last week, how did it feel being unplugged?

Prepare to drop the defenses we all have. This chapter will address your leadership style, enabling you to look introspectively regularly. You are GOD's leader.

Introduce the Remove the Trash Chapter

This chapter is to be used make adjustments to your current leadership style.

We are in part 2 of the framework. This methodology teaches you what to do to prepare your business for resilience. I will cover how to work with others. I will also cover time and schedule management.

Lastly, I will cover forgiveness. There are 12 leadership adjustment exercises, 1 foundation quiz and 1 time and schedule management quiz.

Be prepared to grow.

Remove the Trash Objective

You will learn; how to make adjustments to your leadership style to truly gain success, to manage time and schedule and to manage relationships.

Remove the Trash Prayer

Pray:
That the LORD will provide a clean heart.
That your motives will be aligned with GOD's desire.
For purpose.
For HIM to open your eyes to HIS leading.

The Remove the Trash chapter is to be used monthly to refine and grow your leadership style.

Leaders Reflect

GOD gave each person gifts and talents. Serving customers with these gifts enables a thriving, GOD-centered business. But what happens if the business is not thriving or the idea is not gaining traction? This makes some people doubt you even heard from GOD regarding your business. How can this doubt be removed? I keep asking you "Do you like you?" Are you ashamed? Are you filled with something that may cause you to overlook your gifts and talents? This fear, doubt and questioning could be trash in your heart that requires hearing GOD.

Believe

Hearing from GOD starts by knowing GOD. You can know GOD and experience the power of HIS daily provision by first accepting what HE's already done on your behalf. HE sent JESUS to die for the death all of us deserved "*For God so loved the world that He gave His only begotten Son, that whoever believes in Him should not perish but have everlasting life*" (John 3:16). "*But God demonstrates His own love toward us, in that while we were still sinners, Christ died for us*" (Romans 5:8). If you have not done so already, why not accept CHRIST as your Savior today. You are salvageable. HE does love you.

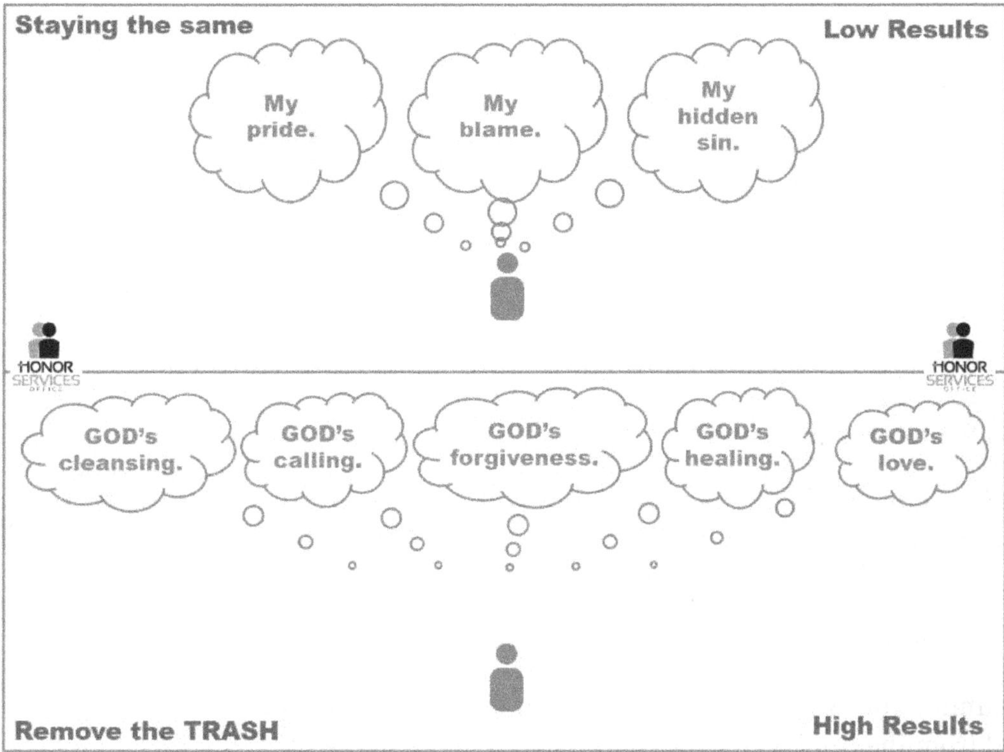

Have you ever seen a toddler grab something they should not have, yet they say "mine" when a parent tries to take it away from her? Leadership is more than getting your own way.

Accept the responsibility of becoming the best leader you can.

The GOD-centered business owner looks introspectively more than at the faults of others.

Leadership Character Development

Objective: *Share the plan of salvation. Be led by the HOLY SPIRIT to believe in JESUS.*

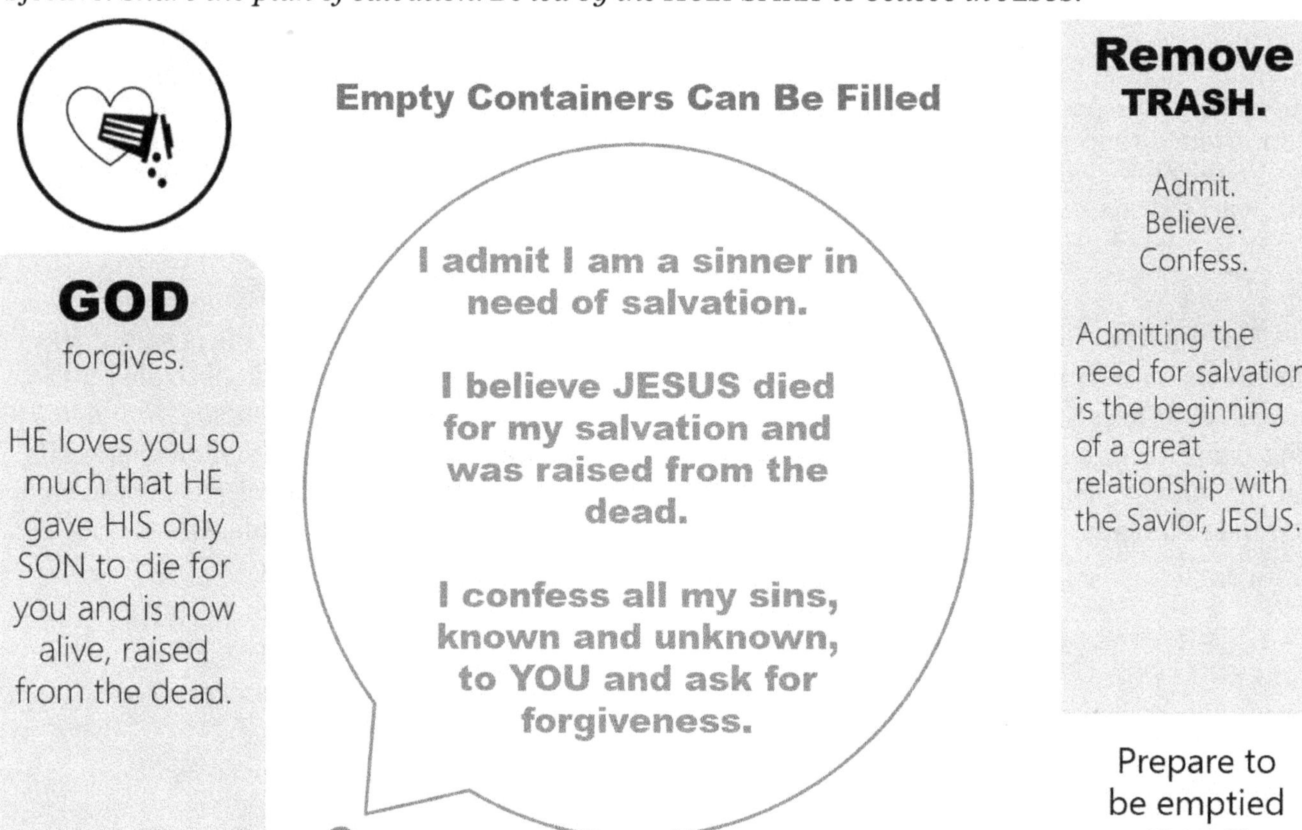

Preparing to Remove the Trash

– *For God so loved the world that He gave His only begotten Son, that whoever believes in Him should not perish but have everlasting life For God sent not his Son into the world to condemn the world; but that the world through him might be saved.* John 3:16 – 17

Whether you already believe or this is the first time, please join in praying this prayer:

LORD , I admit I am a sinner and I need YOU to forgive me. I believe JESUS died for my salvation and was raised from the dead. I confess all my sins to YOU and ask for YOUR forgiveness.

Congratulations! By believing and praying that prayer, you now have eternal life. This is the great news GOD wants everyone you know or meet to have. GOD has a special plan for you.

Introspection is important. "*Search me, O God, and know my heart; try me, and know my anxieties; and see if there is any wicked way in me, and lead me in the way everlasting*" (Psalm 139:23-24) was David's cry. This was an act of introspection or self-examination. The GOD-centered business owner does not strive for the perfection that only JESUS could provide, but rather seeks continuous improvement as a GOD -declared perfect person.

1. **Use healthy admission generously.** Healthy admission enables the GOD-centered business owner to admit his or her need for GOD'S correction and the growth that follows. It is healthy to come to grips with the fact that all humans are flawed and your flaws can sometimes get in the way of seeing GOD work in your business. "*If we confess our sins, He is faithful and just to forgive us our sins and to cleanse us from all unrighteousness*" (1 John 1:9). Unhealthy admission (or over-confessing) comes from not believing GOD has or can forgive all sins. Use healthy admission in introspection.
2. **Wonderfully made.** When GOD made you, HE said "This is very good." HE did not make a mistake when making you. Self-doubt can be overcome through understanding the purpose GOD has for you. As a business owner, GOD wants you to use the gifts and talents HE gave you to bless many.
3. **Forgiven.** Made a mistake? You are forgiven. Made the same mistake? You are forgiven for that too! But how about employees or rude customers who said they would purchase but did not? GOD wants you to express healthy grace that is combined with mercy. Power is implied with mercy and is given where not deserved. Grace and mercy are signs of strength.

Self-examination enables a bold, yet humble business owner. It also gives time to look at areas to improve, little by little.

Exercise 1 – Identify the Hidden Reason for Going into Business

Objective: *Recognize any hidden motives for being in business, and because of that, decision making can be hindered.*

List the "real" reason you went into business. Be honest. Some may say because they have a great idea, others may say they just felt like trying something new. But there may be reasons that are hidden that can cause harm if not dealt with properly.

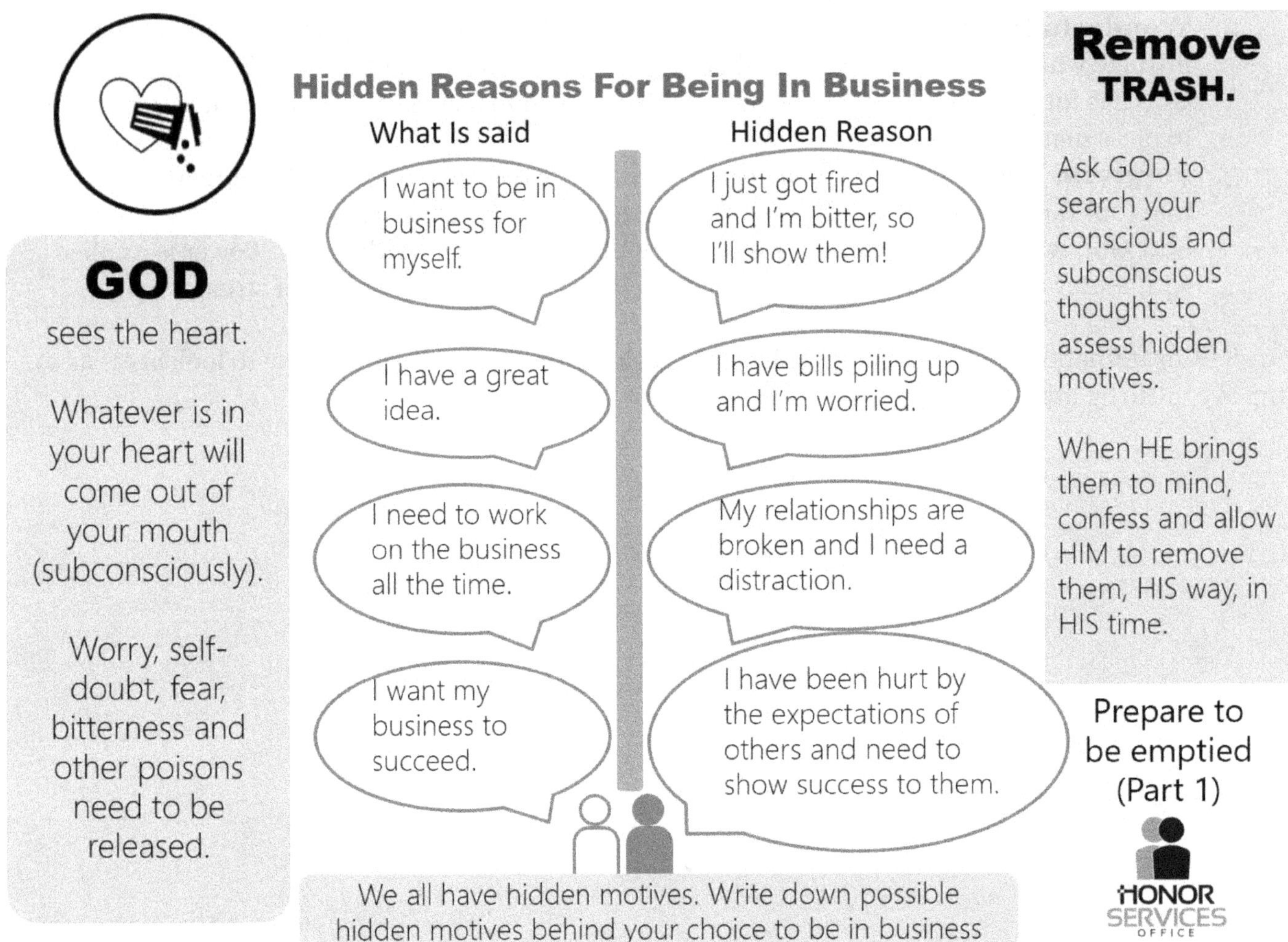

Have you ever been told to apologize? Did you grumpily say "I'm sorry and did not mean it?" (Add – "I have" if true.)

GOD looks at the heart.

Ask GOD to reveal what is hidden in your heart. The GOD-Centered Business Owner needs to be truthful to themselves and especially to GOD. Why did you **really** go into business? *Write down reasons you told people as to why you went into business. review the picture above.*

Use the examples on the image to write down possible hidden motives for going into business. Pray that GOD remove any hidden motives as these can block true success.

Exercise 2 – Identify the root to remove

Objective: *Grow by self-reflection rather than self-degradation.*

Modify an Unstable Leadership Style

Have you ever worked under a supervisor whose leadership style left you feeling unheard, ignored, or demeaned in some way? We easily see the faults in others, but not always in ourselves.

I may not be perfect, but I am better than I was.

The GOD-centered business owner understands he still has to move forward though flaws remain. "*For all have sinned and fall short of the glory of God*" (Romans 3:23).While perfection is not achievable by self, growth is expected from God. But sometimes we're blind to our own faults. Like Paul, I pray that "*the eyes of your understanding being enlightened; that you may know what is the hope of His calling, what are the riches of the glory of His inheritance in the saints* " (Ephesians 1:18)" GOD is willing to open your eyes.

Blind spots are not always your fault. Circumstance after circumstance can trip anyone up and cause a fall. These can be reversed by looking at the symptoms and being willing to allow GOD to heal. GOD is willing to help open your eyes to blind spots.

There are two sets of blindness the GOD-centered business owner faces.

1. **Business blind spots.** This involves a lack of knowledge in foundational business practices that enables sustainable growth. This will be discussed in more detail in the "Seek Wisdom" section.
2. **Spiritual blindness.** This can be an area of struggle that can only be removed by surrender to the leading of the HOLY SPIRIT.

Continuous improvement is provided in abundance to the GOD-centered business owner. "I may not be perfect, but I am better than I was" is the attitude to carry. Ask GOD to open your eyes to spiritual blindness you may be facing and address these daily while pursuing correction to business blind spots.

Hidden, harmful reasons why some go into business:

You are forgiven. Go and tell others they can be as well.

1. **Vengeance.** Starting a business to get back at those who harmed you can ultimately leads to a dead end. Focus on a place of strength, namely forgiveness, for a good foundation for your business.
2. **Worry.** Financial worries drive many to start a business. Businesses take much longer than expected to get up and running. Focus on a different source of income while the business is built properly.
3. **Ruined relationships.** Bringing people together is not easy when starting a business. Focus on strong relationships before you start a business.
4. **High expectations.** Lower everyone's expectations of when you will be profitable and ready to provide quality to your customers, including your own to a manageable state.

By facing the real reason why you went into business, success will come easier. Pleasing GOD is the number-one goal for the GOD-centered business owner. GOD gives patience, wisdom, knowledge, and understanding.

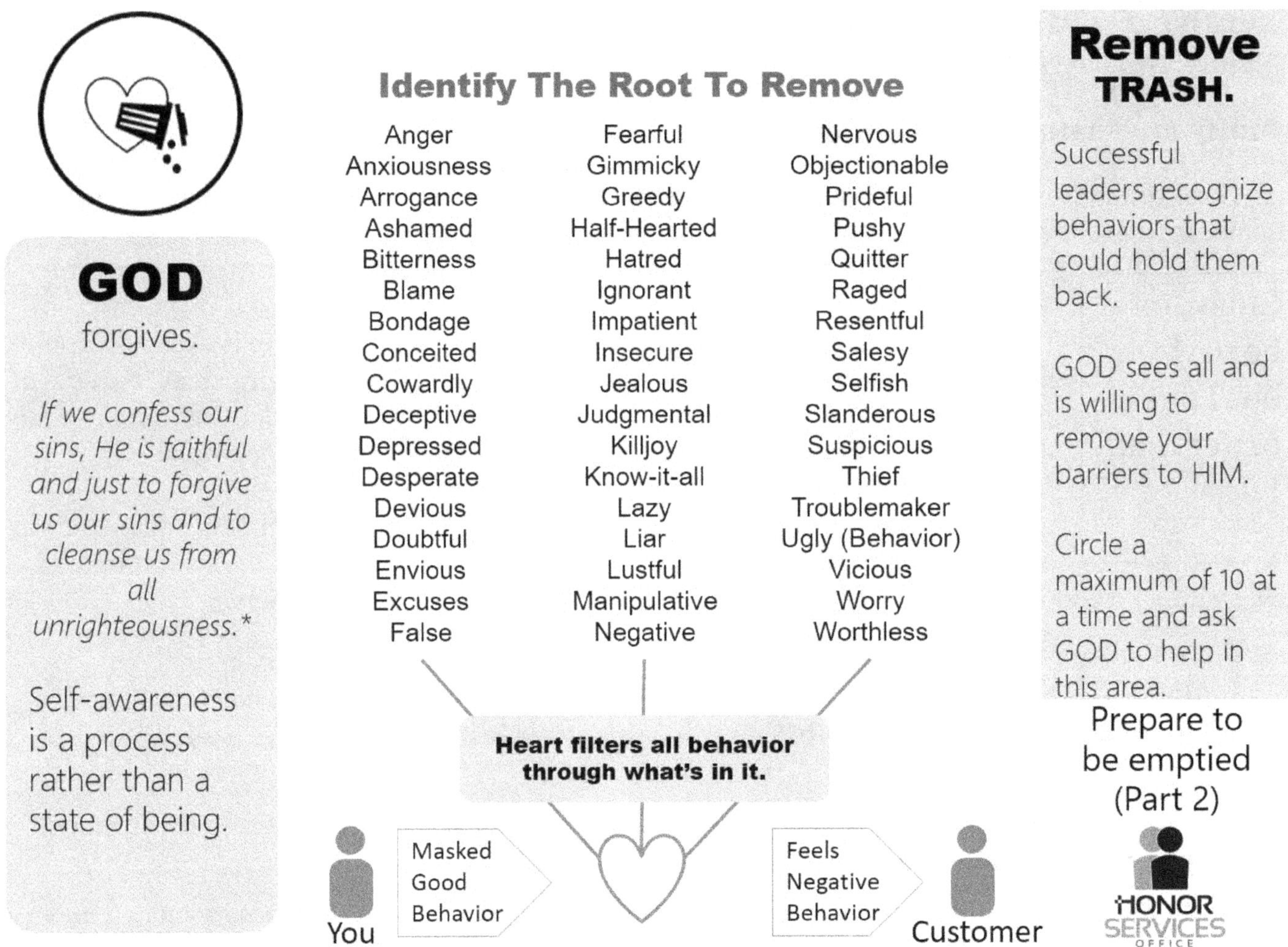

Have you ever done something wrong and wanted to hide what you did from everyone? Have you ever lied to yourself so long that you started believing in the lie?

GOD forgives.

1 John 1:9 – *If we confess our sins, He is faithful and just to forgive us our sins and to cleanse us from all unrighteousness.*

Have you failed at something? Are you afraid to fail so you fake it until you make it?" Admitting failure is the foundation of a great leader.

Successful leaders seek to improve. The heart will tell on you. If lying, lust or laziness is in your heart, then practicing a polished pitch will only magnify the negative behavior that's deep inside.

Matthew 15:18 – *But the things that come out of a person's mouth come from the heart, and these defile them.*

What should we do about our heart? Identify up to a maximum of 10 behaviors you wish to remove. Continue the exercise as long as you need to. The strength of the framework is building habits that will over time become second nature.

Blind spots can block you from the intended result. We call these blind spots "blockers." Here is a list of blockers one could address with GOD.

Blocker	Effect	Approach
Anger	Feeling annoyed or displeased can lead to hostility.	Ask GOD for a peaceful spirit, releasing the situation to HIS solution or vengeance.
Anxiousness	Increases worry, doubt, fear and decreases the desire to approach new people.	Ask GOD to reveal the true source of the anxiety.
Arrogance	Having or revealing an exaggerated sense of one's own importance or abilities can turn off customers.	Ask GOD for a heart of praise and appreciation for others.
Ashamed	Embarrassed or guilty because of one's actions, leads to lack of confidence to say the message.	Ask GOD to enable confidence to speak boldly.
Bitterness	Keeps looking at past hurts or an imaginary utopian state	Ask GOD for help to spit out the poisonous thoughts or words and identify the root of the bitterness. Once the bitterness is removed, ask GOD to fill the void with compassion.
Blame	Assigning responsibility for a perceived fault or wrong can push away customers.	Ask GOD for gentleness and outstanding customer service that includes listening, problem-solving questions, and root-cause analysis.
Bondage	Trapped in something harmful or negative	Ask GOD to tear down the stronghold to release you from whatever is holding you. If self-inflicted, ask for accountability.
Conceited	Focusing only on self excessively can cause one to overlook people in need.	Ask GOD to identify the root of self-centeredness and how to turn the attention to HIM.
Cowardly	Lacking courage keeps one from reaching out to others or speaking boldly about GOD.	Ask GOD for courage to be HIS bold servant. Focus on being prepared and ask GOD for confidence in what you know.
Deceptive	Misleading people or giving false appearance leads to mistrust and resentment.	Ask GOD for courage to face or tell the truth. Start small and add more and more truth in your life.
Depressed	Feelings of severe despondency and dejection can lead to a lack of motivation to grow the business or meet new people.	Ask GOD to send people in your life who can help guide you through times of depression. Also ask to identify the root, knowing HE loves you as you are.
Desperate	A hopeless sense that a situation is beyond your ability can scare away customers.	Ask GOD for patience, peacefulness, and quiet time with HIM to hear HIS guidance. He is the GOD of the impossible (Genesis 18:14; Luke 1:37).
Devious	The use of underhanded tactics to achieve goals can cause customers to complain to others about you.	Ask GOD to reveal the root of this behavior and to fill your heart with truth and courage to live that truth.
Doubtful	Uncertainty or lack of conviction leads to changing business direction often, never seeing full success.	Ask GOD for trust and patience to see things through to completion.

Blocker	Effect	Approach
Envious	Resentful longing of other people's possessions leads to lack of praise for GOD-given qualities for oneself or others.	Ask GOD for a heart of praise and for the humility to identify the source of wanting more than the needs GOD has already supplied.
Excuses	Attempting to lessen the blame can cause customers to not believe in you.	Ask GOD for trustworthiness, diligence, and responsibility for one's own actions.
False	Acting contrary to the truth could lead customers to doubt your product or service.	Ask GOD for HIS truth to speak through you, keeping what is best for those you are speaking to as your highest priority.
Fearful	To be afraid could lead to snap decisions, short unreachable deadlines, and low quality. Being fearful could also prevent the delivery of a solution.	Ask GOD to remove unhealthy fear, namely the spirit of fear, and replace it with faith in HIS power. Healthy fear is the fear of the LORD.
Gimmicky	Having a trick or device intended to attract attention, publicity, or business can lead to a feeling of disingenuity within your customers.	Ask GOD for genuine concern for your customers that shines more that trickery.
Greedy	With an intense selfish desire for a thing like wealth or power, the business will resort to gimmicks or an intense pushiness to buy from you.	Ask GOD for a truly generous heart and patience while being sustained during thin economic times.
Half-hearted	A lack of enthusiasm for what the business does can cause customers to lack confidence in your brand.	Ask GOD for excitement and confidence. Also ask GOD to identify the people who can help you to refine your product or service, thus creating excitement.
Hatred	Intense dislike or ill-will towards others leads to categorizing people and developing excuses for not loving them.	Ask GOD to remove this hatred, replacing it with love, compassion, and empathy.
Ignorant	Lacking knowledge could lead customers to a lack of belief in you and your brand.	Ask GOD for wisdom, knowledge, and understanding.
Impatient	Having or showing a tendency to be quickly irritated or provoked will cause customers to leave or react similarly.	Ask GOD for patience, joy, and thanksgiving.
Insecure	Lacking confidence or assurance shows uncertainty or anxiousness to the customers.	Ask GOD for faith in HIS power to sustain and protect you.
Jealous	Showing suspicion or envy can cause you to slander, oversell, or cling to the same customers in a needy way.	Ask GOD to open your eyes to HIS pure love for you and others.
Judgmental	Excessive critical thinking can promote a blaming spirit, or cause "over correction," leading to a controlling spirit.	Ask GOD for a grace-filled spirit for yourself and others.

Blocker	Effect	Approach
Killjoy	Deliberately spoiling enjoyment can lead to dissatisfaction in you, your product, or service.	Ask GOD to expose the root of this behavior and to help you be filled with hope.
Know-it-all	A person who behaves as if he knows everything will ultimately push customers away.	Ask GOD for humility. Also ask for courage to ask questions versus needing to provide answers.
Lazy	Unwillingness to work or use energy can lead to get-rich quick schemes, half-baked ideas, and unsuccessful efforts.	Ask GOD for strength and persistence.
Liar	A person who tells lies or untruths cannot be trusted by customers.	Ask GOD to identify the root of this behavior and for a truthful heart. Also ask for courage to live the truth.
Lustful	Strong sexual desire can be debilitating, derailing progress toward GOD's purpose.	Ask GOD for self-control and healthy relationships.
Manipulative	Influencing unscrupulously can create deeper deceptive behavior, leading to distrust within the customers.	Ask GOD for generosity, kindness, and excitement for other people.
Negative	Expressions of criticism or pessimism can cause a downward spiral, dragging those around you into lower, harmful moods.	Ask GOD for a spirit of joy and kindness.
Nervous	Easily agitated or alarmed actions can cause customers to lack confidence in you.	Ask GOD for confidence, competence, and composure.
Objectionable	Arousing opposition leads to a combative, defensive, disagreeable approach that turns people away.	Ask GOD for an agreeable spirit.
Prideful	Harmful deep pleasure in one's own achievements can lead to excessive self-confidence, bragging, and undesired self-promotion.	Ask GOD for humility, and confidence in HIM.
Pushy	Excessively or unpleasantly self-assertive or ambitiousness will turn off customers to the point of complaining.	Ask GOD for gentleness, kindness, patience, and a heart for listening to others.
Quitter	Giving up easily can lead to unmet desires.	Ask GOD for tenacity and healthy ambition.
Rage	Violent, uncontrollable anger is unacceptable to anyone.	Ask GOD to remove anger, malice, hatred, or bitterness that causes rage. Also ask for faithful self-control.
Resentful	Bitter indignation as a result of being treated unfairly can cause a poisonous heart, spilling out hateful words and results in wasted time replaying previous wrongs.	Ask GOD for innovation, looking forward to the future, and freedom from dwelling on the past.
Salesy	Always selling, never listening to needs turns off customers.	Ask GOD to open your heart to listen to needs, fulfilling them out of love. Also ask GOD to provide for your needs.

Blocker	Effect	Approach
Selfish	Concerned chiefly with one's own personal profit or pleasure shows selfishness, and customers will turn away.	Ask GOD for a selfless heart, one of generosity, compassion, and goodness.
Slanderous	False and malicious statements are heard by customers who, in turn, leave.	Ask GOD for gentle, kind words and a slow response to negative words hurled at you.
Suspicious	Having or showing distrust can breed the same behavior in customers toward you.	Ask GOD for HIS protection, faithfulness, trust, and hope.
Thief	A person who steals another person's property will be caught.	Ask GOD to open your eyes to the root of this behavior and for a better solution. Also ask for HIM to provide your needs.
Troublemaker	Habitually causing difficulty can lead to unnecessary fights and arguments.	Ask GOD for a collaborative and agreeable heart.
Ugly (Behavior)	Unpleasant or repulsive actions can turn off customers who will complain to many about you.	Ask GOD for a clean spirit that guides people to higher behaviors.
Vicious	Deliberately being cruel or violent can lead to harm of others.	Ask GOD for a gentle spirit that cares for people and shows love for enemies.
Worried	A state of being troubled about actual or potential problems can be seen by your customers.	Ask GOD to own every problem, and to help you understand that HIS grace is sufficient and HIS power unmatched.
Worthless	Having no real value or use leads to selling something people do not want or need.	Ask GOD to reveal the root of this behavior. Also ask to recognize the value HE places in you so you can show it to others.

While many other words can be added to this list, these are only examples of some blockers to ask GOD to guide out of your life, enabling a stronger you, suitable to operate the GOD-sized business He has planned for you.

Find a maximum of ten blockers to work on at a given time. The process can be exhausting but worth it. Be honest! Now let's look at what stable leadership looks like.

Identify **up to 10** behaviors to remove from the heart. Write them on a list and revisit them monthly.

List One	List Two	List Three
1.	1.	1.
2.	2.	2.
3.	3.	3.
4.	4.	4.
5.	5.	5.
6.	6.	6.
7.	7.	7.
8.	8.	8.

9.	9.	9.
10.	10.	10.

Blockers to Success

The list you write is more than a list of to-do's,. This list may block success. Over the next week fill in and revisit the list daily, asking GOD to give you action steps to address the blockers. Be patient with yourself as it may have taken you years to learn these behaviors. For example, impatient people will not learn patience in one day.

You do not have to share your list with the group, but it may be necessary for some of you to do so.

If some of these issues are deep rooted, then the group of GOD-centered business owners is here to help you. We will pray for deliverance. This is not a confidential group. Someone in the group may struggle with lying and gossiping, so anything said in this group is now public to them and everyone else they speak to.

Public knowledge of sin provides freedom to the person who confesses. This takes courage. The more courageous you and I can be, the less the sin will hold onto us. This can be the start of the road to recovery.

Please do not judge someone for their confession or provide immediate suggestions. Some behaviors may need a special or professional guide, gifted in leading people out of certain behaviors and back to GOD's instructions as listed in the Bible.

JESUS warns us about stopping too short of true deliverance.

Matthew 12:43-45

Matthew 12: *"When an impure spirit comes out of a person, it goes through arid places seeking rest and does not find it. Then it says, 'I will return to the house I left.' When it arrives, it finds the house unoccupied, swept clean and put in order. Then it goes and takes with it seven other spirits more wicked than itself, and they go in and live there. And the final condition of that person is worse than the first. That is how it will be with this wicked generation."* (NIV)

People return to doing the same sins over and over. In the passage of Scripture, JESUS implies a twostep process for getting "clean and put in order." It takes an emptying of the "trash." But there is a problem. An empty vessel needs to be filled. That is why it is imperative that the guide, special or professional, is willing to take the full next step of providing what can fill the person up.

Revisit this exercise and start a new list monthly, knowing they will never be perfect. Also know it is alright to have something on your list that appears over and over several times. This shows you are human.

GOD is willing to help.

Stable Leadership Foundation

After being emptied of negative behaviors and approaches, the GOD-centered business owner needs to get filled up with positivity that only comes from HIM. Many seek happiness and, therefore, want customers to be happy. The problem with this approach is motivation. Like a thermometer that changes based on external forces, the person who seeks happiness based on other folk's actions will be doomed to have unstable relationships.

GOD is willing to help because HE loves you.

The GOD-centered business owner seeks joy rather than happiness. Joy supersedes bad moods, anger, and dissatisfaction. Once filled with the joy of GOD, you become an unparalleled leader. Joy is only one part. GOD wants us to operate with the fruit of the SPIRIT to be successful (see Galatians 5:22-23).

Leaders cannot see into the future; only GOD can do this. But leaders are not surprised by issues because they are ready for life's turmoil and situations.

Unstable Leadership	**Stable Leadership**
Reactive/Not Ready (Fearful)	Proactive/Ready (Faithful)
Surprised by issues (Unhappy)	Expects issues and plans (Joy)
Untested (Rough)	Tests to improve (Gentleness/Goodness)
Cannot wait (Impatient/Wild)	Waits for right time (Patient/Self-control)
Expects others to help (Needy)	Leads/Helps (Peace/Kindness)
Works alone often (Control)	Works with others (Love)

Exercise 3 – Stabilize your leadership style by filling the heart

Objective: *Use the fruit of the Spirit to purposefully replace negative behaviors.*

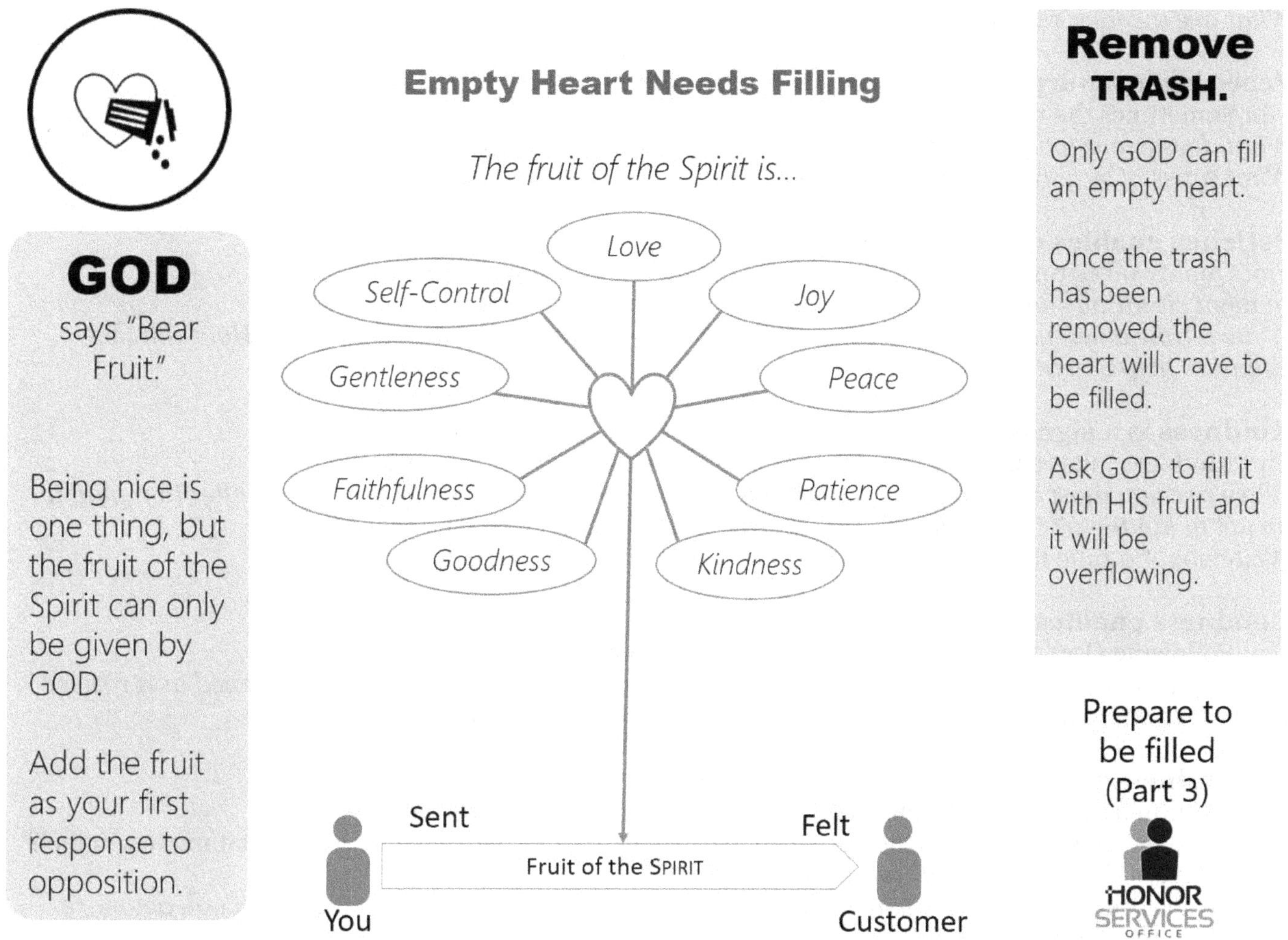

Have you ever run out of gas when driving a car? Was it on the side of the road? You needed fuel didn't you?

Only GOD can fill an empty heart.

– *"But the fruit of the Spirit is love, joy, peace, longsuffering, kindness, goodness, faithfulness, gentleness, self-control. Against such there is no law."* (Galatians 5:22-23)

Removing the trash from the heart is not enough. The heart needs to be filled with something. If left alone, then self or the world or evil will fill the heart. You, the instructor, and the GOD-centered Business owner have the responsibility to seek GOD, asking HIM to fill your heart.

The fruit of the Spirit is the foundation for the remainder of the GOD-Centered Framework. You will see this appear in numerous exercises.

Resilient leaders have joy.
Tip: Choosing joy over happiness leads to stable decision making.
How would you define joy? How would you define happiness? Describe a time when you chose joy over happiness. What was the result?
What are the factors that tend to rob you of your joy?

Peace is used purposefully by resilient leaders.
Tip: Sometimes the most peaceful times are in the middle of a storm.
What does peace look like in your life? How do you know when you have peace?
What types of situations rob you of peace?

Patience enables quality.
Tip: Quality takes time. Customers appreciate quality and complain less.
In what situations do you find yourself getting impatient?
Write a time when you were intentional about being patient. What was the result? How can that situation help you be more patient going forward?

Kindness is a sign of strength.
Tip: Kindness takes considerable self-control, thus producing a stronger leader.
When are you most challenged about exhibiting kindness? What part, if any, does obligation play in an act of kindness? Does guilt stimulate or deter a genuine act of kindness? Explain.
Write about a time when someone was kind to you. How can you do the same?

Goodness enables you to finish first.
Tip: Following GOD's rules stirs up many rewards that come from HIM.
Describe a time when you willingly chose to be wrong or behave badly. What happened as a result?
What does being good look like to you?

Faithfulness means dependable.
Tip: Faithful leaders not only show courage through faith, but are there for people.
List a time when someone depended on you and you let him or her down. How did that make you feel?
What did you learn about faithfulness as a result?
Write an example of someone who was there for you or you for him or her. How can you act more faithful in the coming week?

Gentleness calms situations.
Tip: Gentle approaches reduce potential arguments and tames combative talks.
Name someone in your life who is gentle. What do you admire about him or her?
Sometimes people erroneously equate gentleness with weakness. Why do you think this assumption is made?
List an example of someone, like a dentist, who could have been rough, but was gentle with you. How did that make you feel? How does gentleness calm volatile situations?

Self-control enables leaders to reach large goals.
Tip: Try self-control to regain control over the "out of control."
What area of your life, if any, currently feels out of control?
How can self-control help you? If you need accountability, who can help you?

Love erases bad recordings or negative thoughts that play over and over in your mind.
Tip: Love as an action lowers stress and increases rest.
When have you felt most challenged to show love when you least felt like doing so?
Write down a time when you sensed the love GOD *has shown you. How did that help?*

Over the next week, ask GOD *to add an element of the fruit of the Spirit that speaks to you most*

Purpose is needed to sustain the fruit of the SPIRIT. Adding purpose to your life to share this fruit enables the heart to be filled to overflowing. The GOD-centered business owner recognizes that profit is important, but ultimately bringing people to GOD is the higher purpose.

Let love, joy, peace, patience, kindness, goodness, faithfulness, gentleness, and self-control fuel your actions. When difficulties arise, the fruit of the SPIRIT is there to stabilize, giving wisdom to navigate life's trials.

A Serious Need for Change

Success is a very distorted word. To some it could mean how much money they have, to others it is the number of followers or social media likes they receive. But what is *success* to GOD when it comes to business? The GOD-centered business owner shines GOD's light before those to whom he is sent. "*A new commandment I give to you, that you love one another; as I have loved you, that you also love one another*" (John 13:34).

Love customers as you love yourself.

Do you love your customers? GOD wants you to love them. HE wants to radiate through you as you pray for and serve people. A question may arise: "Should I give away my products and services?" The answer is "Sometimes." Be led by the HOLY SPIRIT in your generosity. If you struggle with greed, then you may need to give away more.

Loyalty is built by loving your customers. When starting out, try to know your customers by name. If you grow, have your employees do the same. This personal touch becomes a differentiator.

Exercise 4 – Assess the heart of your business

Objective: *Implement the fruit of the Spirit in business activities.*

The heart of your business is seen whether you like it or not. Words of worry or hurry or greed flow even when you try to hide the fact that you feel that way. List the current heart of your business and write how the fruit of the SPIRIT can help. Be honest.

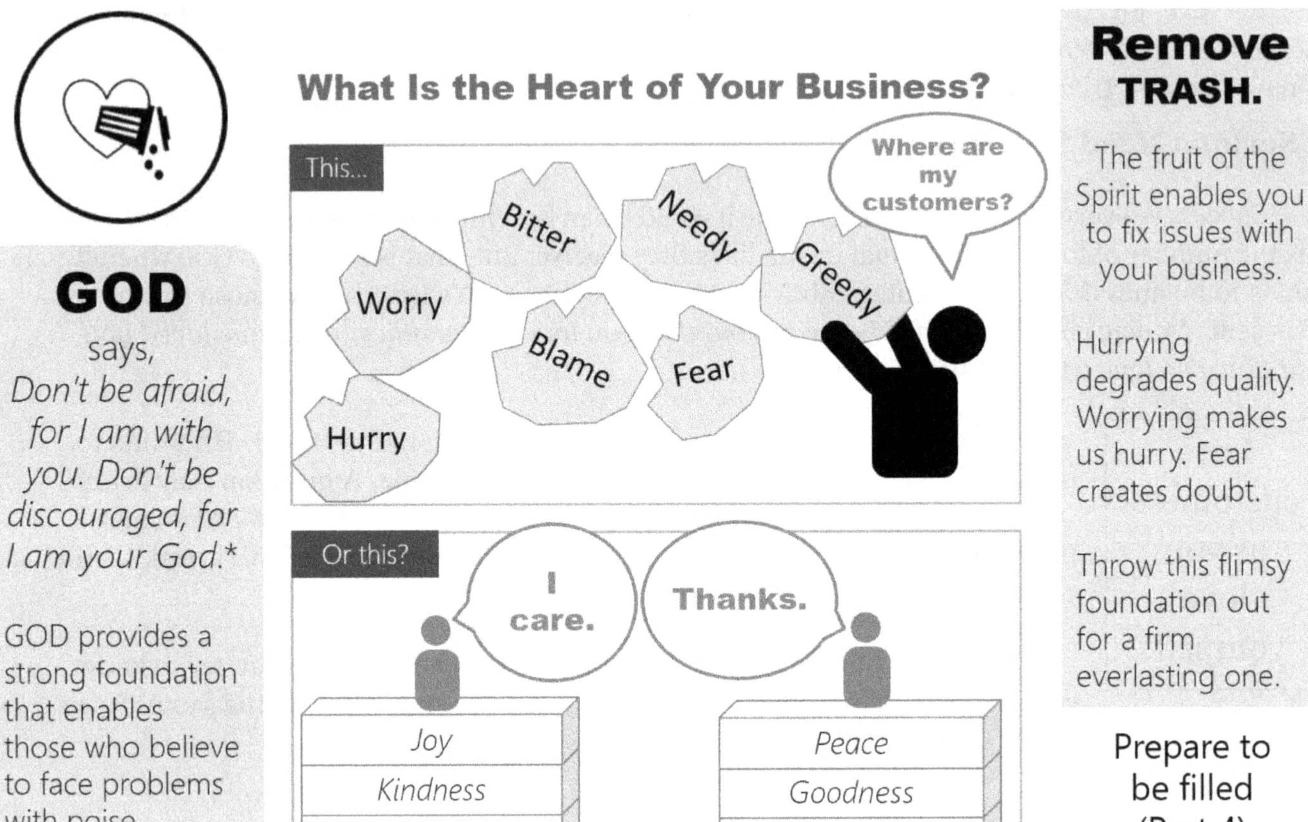

Have you ever seen an impatient driver? Maybe I should ask, "Are you an impatient driver?" – Smile. How do impatient people make you feel? How do you feel when you a deadline approaching when you have a lot of work to do?

GOD wants you courageous and patient.

Isaiah 41:10 *Don't be afraid, for I am with you. Don't be discouraged, for I am your God. I will strengthen you and help you. I will hold you up with my victorious right hand.* (NLT)

Have you ever ran into a pushy business? How about a business that seems desperate or made you feel guilty for not buying their product or service?

These feelings cannot be hidden. The heart of the business needs to be assessed. Whether you work alone, or collaborate with others, it is best to work with the right heart. Let me give you a term that we will use for the rest of the class. Desperate Expecting Acquisitive Dollars (DEAD). If you are D-E-A-D you will always sound dead. The opposite is to be Appreciative, Loving, Inviting, Victorious, and Everlasting. (ALIVE.). We are A-L-I-V-E ALIVE!

Are you and your employees calm or worried?
Is the atmosphere you set patient or hurried?
What do you do when you feel nervous?
How can you use the fruit of the Spirit to combat any negative feelings?
Who will you give generously to this week?

Changing the heart of the business takes practice. Here are some tips:

1. **Serve the poor.** Practice a generous heart by serving the poor. Truly loving people who have less enables the heart to grow.
2. **Serve widows.** Loneliness is a silent killer. Practice being there for those in need. This will provide solutions you never considered.
3. **Serve neighbors.** Own your block, apartment complex, or other area you live in. Be responsible for the whole area, praying for each person you encounter. Pick up that piece of paper without complaining that the neighbors threw it down. All of this increases your territory.

Exercise 5 – Foundation Quiz

Objective: *Recognize and value every area of operating a business.*

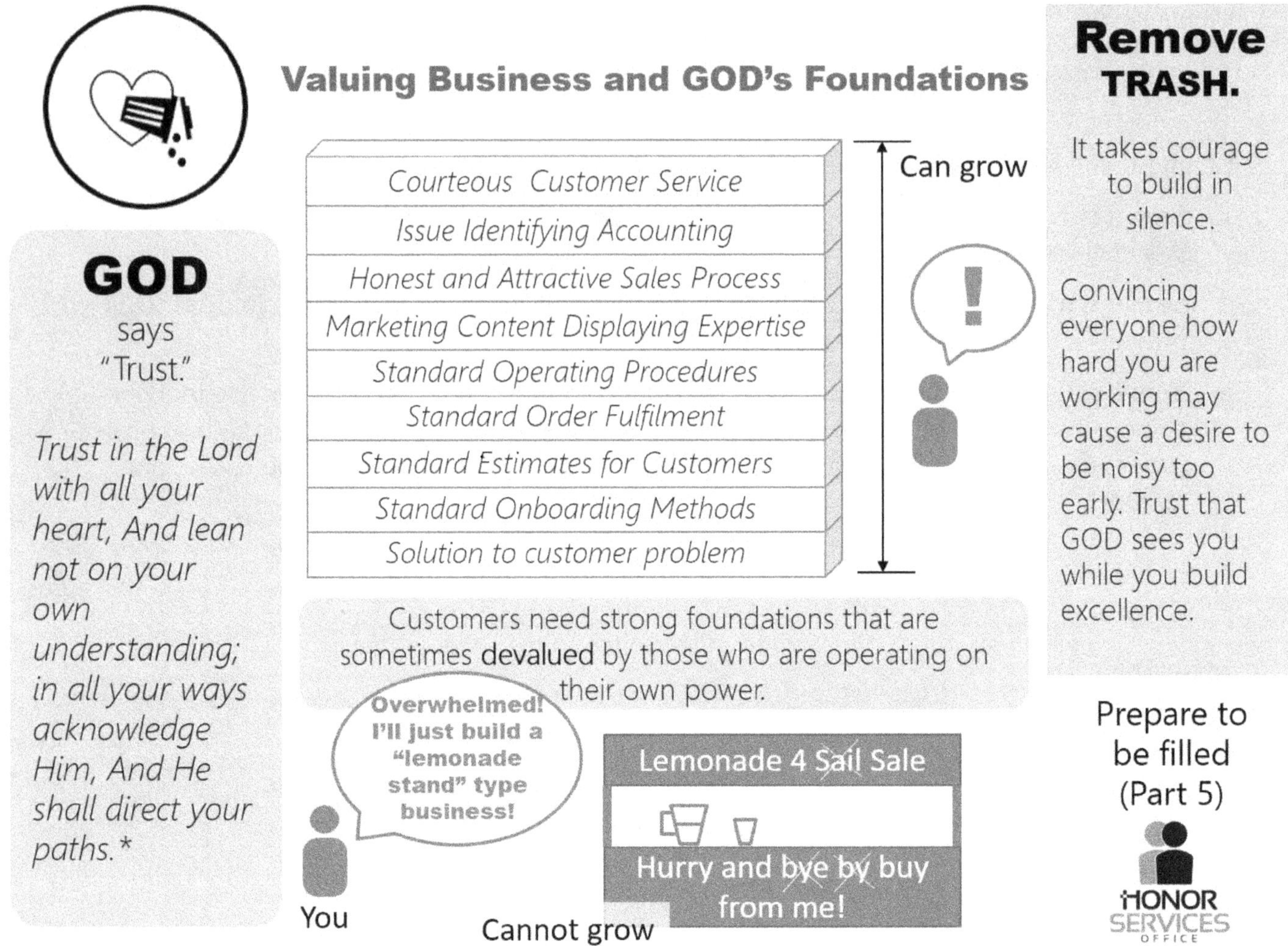

Have you ever ignored the instructions for putting something together? Perhaps it was a bike or a piece of furniture. What happened when you found some pieces left over after you thought it was built? Did you return to the instructions? Did you have to take apart what you put together?

Building takes time. For the impatient or worried, the time that it takes to build a resilient business is perceived as being "too long." Unfortunately, that person decides to build a business built on weak principles and will set themselves up for failure. As Jesus said in a parable,

> *Therefore whoever hears these sayings of Mine, and does them, I will liken him to a wise man who built his house on the rock: and the rain descended, the floods came, and the winds blew and beat on that house; and it did not fall, for it was founded on the rock .*
>
> *But everyone who hears these sayings of Mine, and does not do them, will be like a foolish man who built his house on the sand: and the rain descended, the floods came, and the winds blew and beat on that house; and it fell. And great was its fall.* (Matthew 7:24-27)

Without addressing foundational components, the business cannot grow profitably. Consider the idea, service, or business venture as being in "test" mode until the full foundation is ready. Here are some foundational components:

1. **Solution fully designed to customer liking.** After receiving the vision from GOD, you will work with your client to determine her needs and design the solution to her liking.
2. **Standard onboarding method.** Customer intake for some could be as simple as them buying from you. For others, it could mean upfront agreements, preparation, and in some cases, legal signatures.
3. **Standard estimates.** Having an estimating methodology that is sound grows the customer's trust.
4. **Standard order fulfilment.** A consistent method of receiving your product or service is highly appreciated by customers. They will refer your company based on your consistency.
5. **Standard operating procedures.** This is how you and your employees perform the expertise within your business. Even if you work alone, you should have a document detailing your standard operating procedures. Having an accessible standard operating procedure guide enables consistency without your needing to remember everything. Also, some entities may want to see if you are following standards before they award you a contract.
6. **Marketing content.** This content is often overlooked, but just as important as the product or service. Having supporting content enables your company to be accepted as the expert. The more content supporting your business, the more customers will trust your organization.
7. **Honest sales process.** Having a sales process that helps people make decisions rather than pushing them into buying is paramount.
8. **Issue identifying accounting.** Can you readily tell how much you spent? If not, then this foundation is missing. Accounting is not just record keeping, it is the practice of controlling expenses, understanding profit, and managing cashflow.
9. **Customer service.** Another highly overlooked foundation is customer service. This is the follow up after the sale has been made. Stand by your product or service and your customers will be loyal.

The GOD-centered business owner is patient enough to build a business that is strong enough to grow and flourish.

Foundation Quiz Assessing Micro–Business Resilience

1. Do you have a solution to customer's problems?

   ☐ Yes (Add 10 points)

   ☐ No (Subtract 5 points)

   ☐ I have to think about this (Subtract 2 points)

2. Do you have written standard onboarding methods to bring new customers on board?

   ☐ Yes (Add 10 points)

   ☐ No (Subtract 5 points)

   ☐ I don't know what this is (Subtract 2 points)

3. Do you have a written standard estimation methodology to give an estimate to your customers?

   ☐ Yes (Add 10 points)

   ☐ No (Subtract 5 points)

   ☐ I don't know what this is (Subtract 2 points)

4. Do you have a written standard order fulfilment methodology?

   ☐ Yes (Add 10 points)

   ☐ No (Subtract 5 points)

   ☐ I don't know what this is (Subtract 2 points)

5. Do you have a written standard operating procedures?

   ☐ Yes (Add 10 points)

   ☐ No (Subtract 5 points)

   ☐ I don't know what this is (Subtract 2 points)

6. Do you have marketing content that shows you as the expert?

   ☐ Yes (Add 10 points)

   ☐ No (Subtract 5 points)

   ☐ I don't know what this is (Subtract 2 points)

7. Is the marketing content accessible online?

- ☐ Yes (Add 2 points for every online page) – When tallying the responses shock the class with a value of "100" as the minimum points they should have here. Content is half of your business and requires more effort than people are willing to put in.
- ☐ No (Subtract 5 points)
- ☐ I don't know what this is (Subtract 2 points)

Subtract 1 point for every existing page that has not been reviewed by your customers and feedback acquired to revision wording.

8. Do you have an honest sales process that clearly explains how to purchase from you, offers deals, enables a win for everyone and captures new customers?

- ☐ Yes (Add 10 points)
- ☐ No (Subtract 5 points)
- ☐ I don't know what this is (Subtract 2 points)

9. Do you have an accounting system outside of your bank account that keeps track of categorized expenses and income?

- ☐ Yes (Add 10 points)
- ☐ No (Subtract 5 points)
- ☐ I don't know what this is (Subtract 2 points)

10. Do you have a way for customers to report issues and a written method to resolve them consistently?

- ☐ Yes (Add 10 points)
- ☐ No (Subtract 5 points)
- ☐ I don't know what this is (Subtract 2 points)

Add up your score. Be encouraged. Every business has to start somewhere.

Unfortunately some businesses do not put priority on some vital business practices, rather they focus on branding, or deciding if they should be an LLC versus incorporated or spending precious time posting on social media posting. Circle the items you want to work on. While there is a time for these actions, focusing on the elements listed in the quiz will make your business resilient, able to withstand hard times.

Get these foundational items together first before making huge investments in other aspects of your business. Add the elements that you did not score high on to your wish list.

Did you get 100? What did you notice about the point system? There is a penalty for not having the item on each quiz question. It is less of a penalty if you don't know about something and more of a penalty if you know about it, yet have not started working on this item.

This exercise is designed to instill the value of business systems that are foundational. It is not to give you more work to do. Work a little at a time until you have these systems in place.

Optional Deeper Discussion

This section is optional. It lists types of questions or statements that could be asked or said by the class. You could also ask the questions on this page if you want to add more interaction.

Solutions

Should you have a solution versus a good idea? Solutions tend to have more "pull", in other words, the customer desires to purchase the product or service. Solutions require refinement. Some people may not think through the idea to make it fully useful to their customer. Unrefined ideas fail most of the time.

Written Standards

Why are written standards important? Written standards enable consistency. Like following a recipe, the cook always knows how much of the ingredient to use. Even if you work alone, it is best to document standards. Whether it is an operations procedure or an intake method or something else, this document will help you. Some of you who go after government contracts may be asked to produce a **capabilities statement**, listing your capability to produce the product or service. The standard documents will help you win contracts that require it.

Also, it is important to do things consistently. If you have documented standards, then you don't have to waste valuable time making up new processes each time the work is done. If you ever need someone to temporarily fill in for you, then the standard will help the person get up to speed quickly. If you have employees, then standard documentation is mandatory.

Standard Onboarding Methodology

What is a standard onboarding methodology? This is the method you build for a customer to use your product or service for the first time. Some people use automated systems to capture name address, email and phone number. Vital information is collected or disseminated during the onboarding process. Policies, procedures, agreements can all be part of the onboarding process.

Marketing Content

What is marketing content? Marketing content is 50 % of your product or service. It describes the product or service using facts, test results, studies, the materials you used to obtain your credentials and many other sources that enlighten the customer on your industry or business.

This is a highly neglected area because some people feel they cannot write well or that creating content is too time consuming. I strongly suggest you overcome this obstacle as this could hinder success. If you feel you cannot write, then use pictures and few words. Video content, showing your audience examples. Do demonstrations. What example of content can you think of?

Sales Process

What is a sales process? A sales process shows customers how, when and why to purchase your product or service. The sales steps should be standard and easy to use so customers can easily purchase from you. Your customers will refer your company if the sales process is easy and the solution meets or exceeds their expectation.

Accounting System

Why should I use an accounting system? Bank accounts are difficult to use when trying to understand if or where you overspent. Use an accounting system like Honor Services Office to keep track of income, expenses and profit.

Customer Service

Where can your customers go to ask questions get issues resolved or provide feedback on your product or service? Add customer service processes that enables questions to be answered, resolves issues and records customer feedback.

Exercise 6 – Improve Internal Problems

Objective: *Implement continuous improvement versus fixing everything right away. Also to persevere, which ultimately leads to true hope.*

It's one thing to understand the foundation you need, it is another to put that foundation into practice. The GOD-centered business owner prayerfully seeks GOD's help to assess areas that need improvement.

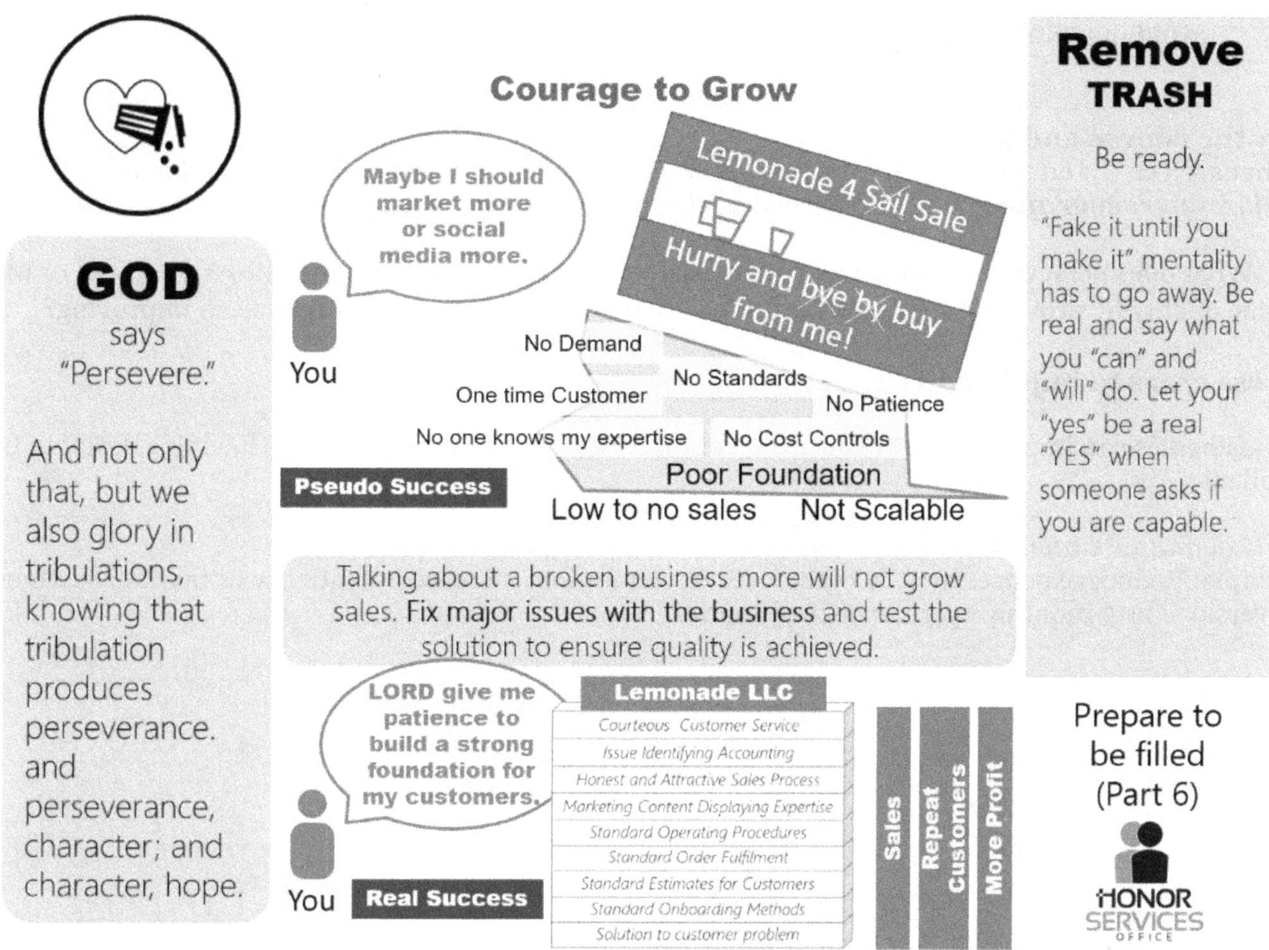

Have you ever lost your keys in your house or apartment? What if you had to go to work and couldn't find those keys? Did you just give up and say you are never going to drive again?

Here are some common methodologies some business owners adapt to their detriment, as well as some tools to help you work toward change.

1. **The need to quickly make money myth.** This methodology is meant to develop a minimal viable product within a short span of time. Some think they have to have the entire business ready in order to launch. By breaking the vision into smaller pieces, you can deliver value to your customers while working on building other components of the business.

2. **Pseudo-success versus real success.** Sometimes the worst thing that could happen to business owners is to be paid for their product or service. They view payment as "success" and seek more of it without putting a foundation in place to assure they will keep receiving the income. The GOD-centered business owner is not fooled by short-term success. Realizing that he is still in the "test" phase of operation can add the self-control needed to refrain from

screaming "success" too early. Real success is making profits in a scalable way for those who plan on a large business or automated for those who will remain a sole-proprietor operation.

3. **Real courage.** Good cooks know that excitement is in preparing the meal, not eating it. They carefully select the proper ingredients and taste everything in the preparation process, rather than cooking everything and then tasting after everything is cooked. It takes courage to wait until the business idea is fully tested and approved by your customer. Ask GOD to help you avoid implementing half-baked ideas.

Stay the course and persevere.
Romans 5:3-4 - *And not only that, but we also glory in tribulations, knowing that tribulation produces **perseverance**; and perseverance, character; and character, hope.*

What does perseverance look like in your business? Does it mean hanging onto a dead idea or to pursue quality by providing solutions to your customers? How will your business keep improving?

Assess areas to improve in

All businesses can improve but it takes perseverance. Being GOD-centered means having a desire to be excellent.

Write definitive statements with quantitative results as a goal to improve.
Example: Reduce expenses by 10% in the next three months. Increase potential customer to customer conversions by 5 monthly over the next 4 months.

Exercise 7 – A serious need for change

Objective: *Recognize the need for change in many aspects of your life.*

Return to what you wrote for Exercise 1 (Identify Motive) of this chapter. What have you identified as needing to change? After reviewing "A Serious Need for Change," update Exercise 1.

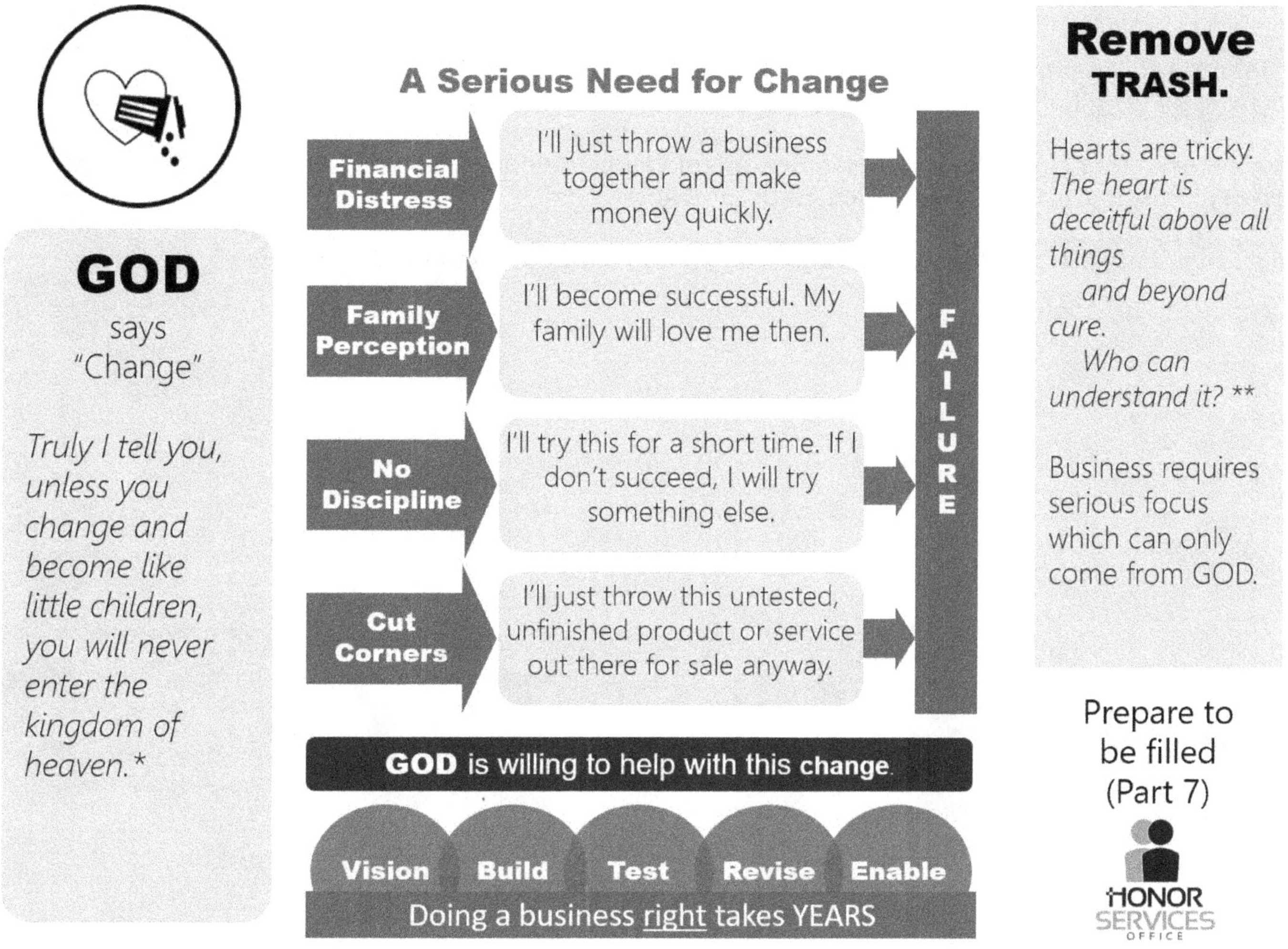

Have you ever been so distracted that you put your phone or something else valuable someplace strange? Did you do this more than once? Did you ever eat or drank too much of something and got sick? Did you feel the need to change? Did you find out a place where you will always put your phone? Did you set limits on how much you will eat or drink?

If so, you made a change. GOD wants a change of heart.

Matthew 18:3 – *And he said: "Truly I tell you, unless you change and become like little children, you will never enter the kingdom of heaven.* (NIV)

**Jeremiah 17:9 – *The heart is deceitful above all things*
and beyond cure.
Who can understand it? (NIV)

Change is sometimes difficult; yet it is a recurring theme throughout life. You are a leader, so it is your responsibility to adapt needed change to sustain the heart of your business. Recognize the need for change management in your business. Identify issues and gradually come up with solutions to address them. Changing the heart requires GOD. HE promised to cleanse us of all unrighteousness if we just ask HIM.

1 John 1:9 *If we confess our sins, he is faithful and just and will forgive us our sins and purify us from all unrighteousness.*

Review exercise 1 (Identify the Hidden Reason for Going into Business) and refine it based on ideas listed in this image and in the Hidden Motives chapter.

Write a plan to address the hidden motives or simply areas you want to improve in.

Exercise 8 – Plan to address internal issues

Objective: *Develop action steps to continuously improve.*

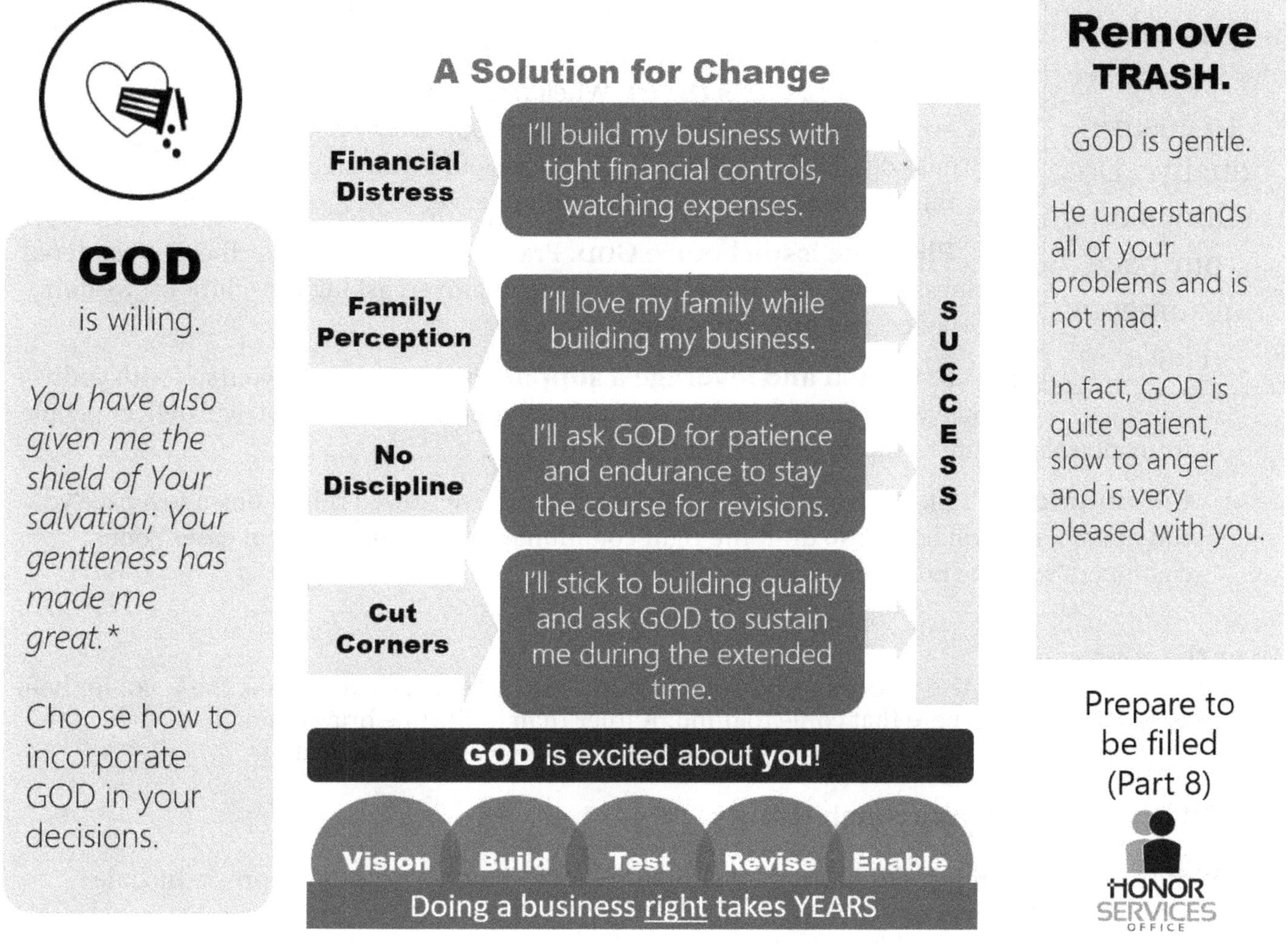

Have you broken something that was special to someone else? Did the person get mad at you? Were you ever afraid to tell a person you messed up? Do you ever get afraid of telling GOD you messed up?

GOD is willing to help you and is gentle. HE wants to make you and your business great so HE can bring many people to HIM through you.

Psalm 18:35 – *You have also given me the shield of Your salvation;*
Your right hand has held me up,
Your gentleness has made me great.

Over the next week, develop a plan to address internal issues you may have with your business. Write actual plans that include G.R.E.A.T. goals.

Write a plan to address the hidden motives or simply areas they want to improve in.

> Act with immediacy versus hurry to ensure quality. Do things on your pace not someone else's.

Every business runs into internal issues. While it is important to resolve issues customers have, it is equally important to resolve internal issues and leadership styles.

1. **Slow the process (STP).** When things are going fast and out of control, slow everything down to your pace. If someone is trying to hurry you because you may miss out on an opportunity, then miss out if you are not ready. Leaders who slow things down to their pace show confidence.
2. **Place the issue before GOD.** Prayer is a foundation for the GOD-centered business owner. Take everything to GOD in prayer, asking for solutions, wisdom, knowledge, and understanding.
3. **Establish and leverage a support base.** Surround yourself with godly people who will pray and have your best interest in mind. GOD will deliver people from all walks of life to supply your needs.
4. **Communicate.** Talk to people about issues. Since you have slowed things down to a pace you can handle, you will be able to draft the right communication to put people at ease. Your customers will love honest communication.

Over the next week:
Write how you will **slow the process** when quick decisions are being asked for. Ask the LORD for help and helpers. Write names here that come to mind. Rather than hiding, be brave enough to **communicate issues**. What is the main message that needs to be communicated?

Adjust how you will approach things

Write a plan to address internal issues or simply areas in which you want to improve. Include how will you **slow the process** to fit your speed.

Write prayer needs here that will address internal issues. Ask the LORD for help and helpers. List names here that come to mind.

Rather than hiding, be brave enough to communicate issues. What is the main message that needs to be communicated?

For existing businesses, write down what is working well and what is not working so well. Develop a plan to improve the features of your business where things are not working so well.

Add the improvement items to your wish list located in Exercise 3 of the Dream Bigger chapter.

Exercise 9 – Implement Time Management

Objective: *Use a schedule to realistically estimate and accomplish tasks.*

Scheduled people have more time. The better you get at scheduling, the more efficient your time will be. Eventually you will get to the point where you can estimate how long things will take to create and execute in your business.

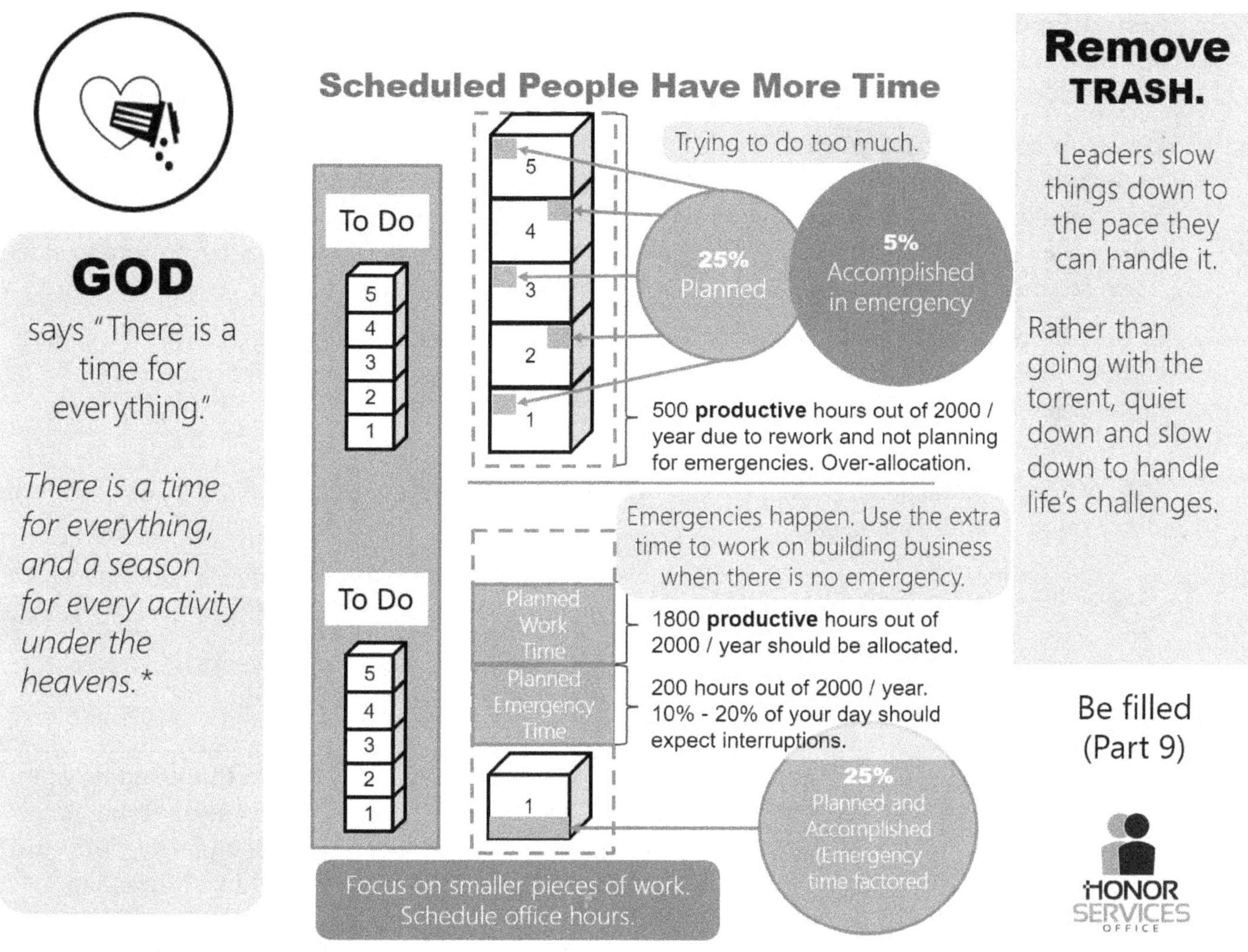

Have you ever tried to pick up too many things and wound up dropping everything? Did something break when you dropped it? Were you trying to save time?

There is a time for everything. Leaders leave gaps on their schedule so they can be prepared.

Ecclesiastes 3:1 – *There is a time for everything, and a season for every activity under the heavens* (NIV)

Prayerfully write a plan you can achieve. Each day ask three questions. "What did I do yesterday?" "What am I going to do today?" "What barriers am I facing that I need to give to GOD?"

1. **Give yourself enough time.** Many business owners underestimate how much time it really takes to build and introduce a new product or service. Break larger tasks into smaller ones and estimate the time needed to implement each task.
2. **Schedule emergency time.** Instead of overscheduling, try scheduling yourself to get through 25% of what you thought you would do that day. If you complete this without an emergency, then start on the next 25%, knowing there will be interruptions.
3. **Develop contingency plans.** GOD is in control of each day. Ask GOD to protect your time but be open to HIS interruptions. HE may send you to someone in need, so why not plan for it. Set aside time in your day to help someone. When things go wrong, plan for what you will do to get things back on track. Contingency plans are different for every situation and require you to slow down so you can quiet down to listen to GOD's solution in prayer.
4. **Schedule administrative time.** Set aside one day each week for administration, cold calls, communication, and financial reporting. Add a high priority on slowing down to become organized.

Many people make the mistake of overscheduling or underestimating how long it really takes to develop a quality product or service.

Example:

There are 2000 work hours available in a year, 40 hours per week for 50 weeks and 2 weeks' vacation. Ten percent of that time is 200 hours that should remain unscheduled.

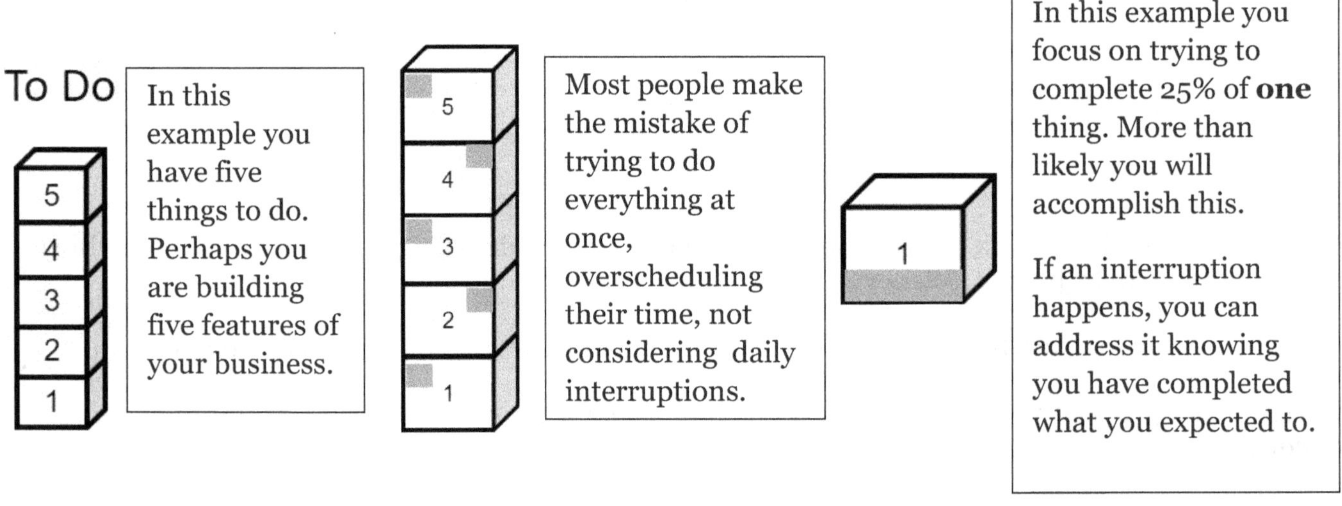

Schedule and Spend Exercise

Let's play Schedule and Spend.

Identify the correct amount of time and how much it will cost. Will you be able to create a good estimate?

Let's pretend we are a going to make a cake. Have you ever made one of these?

How long will it take to **make** a Box Cake?

Box cake is a box of dry cake mix that can be purchased at a grocery store. What do you assume goes into the time?"

Did you guess 3 – 4 hours?

Preparation time could include shopping for the items. The assumption in that case is 30 minutes travel to the grocery store, 30 minutes shopping and 30 minutes to return. Another 30 minutes to unload groceries, wash hands and get ingredients opened and ready.

Bake, cool and frost time = 1.5 - 2 hours

How much do you think it will cost to make the box cake?" Will it cost as much as $10?"

Cost assumptions: The person baking the cake does not have any ingredients. The person owns a mixer, pots, pans and utensils.

The prices in this example may not be accurate, but used to explain a concept.

Let's pretend we are a cake making business. How much do you think it will cost to make the first cake?

Will it cost over $7,000?"

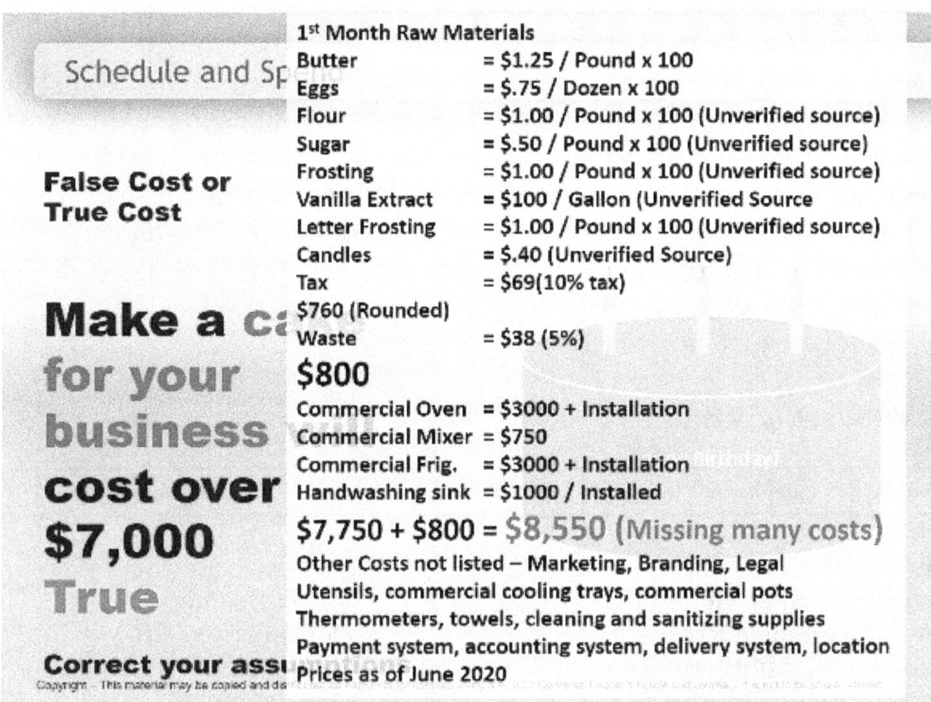

The assumptions are; this is a start up with no equipment or raw materials. The assumptions also include using commercial equipment because home equipment will wear out regularly causing an interruption of income. Commercial equipment may also meet regulated requirements in certain instances.

Another assumption is; instead of using ready mixed box cake, raw ingredients would be purchased. One last assumption is cross contamination avoidance processes add more costs. People have to buy more utensils to keep raw ingredients from touching baked or prepared items.

The prices are for new equipment based on prices in 2020. Also, many costs are not listed and these are investment costs. The **first** cake could cost the price of the equipment, build out of the shop, raw material purchase and installation of equipment. Every cake sold after that would eventually make profit once the costs have been recouped.

People usually underestimate how long things will take and how much they will cost.
When you underestimate, you wind up rushing to meet the deadline and many times make costly mistakes.

The GOD-centered business owner can use the P.R.A.Y. approach to managing time.

P is for **Proact** versus react – Host the meeting instead of being invited meetings.
R is for **Respond** versus react – Be ready with refined, structured features instead of trying to build features on the fly as a reaction to a request from a customer.
A is for **Act** versus react – Be self-motivated versus having to be told.
Y is for **Yield** versus react – Know when to "not" do something that will be a time waster.

Know what you will be doing each day. Each day ask three questions. "What did I do yesterday?" "What am I going to do today?" "What barriers am I facing that I need to give to GOD?"

Scheduled people have more time to do things because the schedule lists what you are doing and gives an amount of time to do them, whereas the unscheduled person may not allocate time to do tasks or forget to do important tasks. Scheduling also prevents them from chasing time-wasters. Look at the examples below and alter the Business, Personal and Spiritual Growth Weekly Ritual suggestions to fit your schedule.

Business Growth Weekly Ritual

Magic Monday	Telephone Tuesday	Win Wednesday	Talk Thursday	Follow-up Friday
Search, search, search. Spend about 4 to 5 hours looking for new people and leads on the Web or physically. Goal is 22 people / month.	Time to call people. Get on the phone and set up 15 minute coffee dates. Prepare yourself; ask for their needs.	Have at least one coffee networking meeting. Meeting new people is the most important time of the week.	Have another coffee networking meeting. Are you getting it? This is the most important time of the week.	Follow up on any leads. Call the people you were referred to. Send thank-you notes as a reminder.

Take time to put business growth activity on your calendar to ensure you make time to grow the business.

Personal Growth Weekly Ritual

Mentor Monday	Teaching Tuesday	Wise Wednesday	Thrifty Thursday	Fun Friday
Spend about an hour **mentoring** someone.	Spend about an hour **teaching** someone.	Spend some time **learning** something.	Spend some time **saving** money.	Spend some time having **fun!**
Builds advisory soft skill	Builds step-by-step soft skill	Builds listening / comprehension soft skill	Builds fiscal skill; gives you a place to schedule your financial worries. Use this as your administrative day to do some accounting reconciliation.	Builds the skill of letting go

Take time to put personal growth activity on your calendar to ensure you make time to sharpen your skills.

Spiritual Growth Weekly Ritual

Meditation Monday	Translate Tuesday	Worship Wednesday	Thoughtful Thursday	Fearless Friday
Spend time meditating on GOD's Word. I like to do my quiet time in the morning. How about you? Check out our daily devotional on Honordevotional. blogspot.com if you don't have a routine picked out for yourself.	Spend time telling someone about CHRIST. It doesn't have to be face to face. Write a blog post, a social media post, or an article. It's time to wring out the sponge and give back.	Spend time worshiping and praising GOD. Put on some praise music and have a good time talking about blessings.	Spend time thinking about how wonderful GOD made you. Your skills and talents came from HIM. Find HIS promises for you in the Bible.	Spend time in prayer giving GOD your fears, doubts, and worries. Read about fearless people who met great obstacles in the Bible and how GOD helped them.

Last but not least, take time to put spiritual growth activity on your calendar to ensure you are listening to GOD for direction daily.

Exercise 10 – Implement a Schedule

Objective: *Develop immovable hours and a cadence everyone can understand.*

GOD

says "I AM with you."

*This is My command— be strong and courageous! Do not be afraid or discouraged. For the Lord your God is with you wherever you go.**

My **dedicated** quiet time is
My **dedicated** family time is
My **dedicated** me time is
My **dedicated** Business Hours are:
My **dedicated** administrative day is

Remove TRASH.

Be there for people and they will be there for you.

Take time for structure. Set up boundaries with these hours.

Try to make them immovable, like a job, only you are the boss.

Be filled (Part 10)

HONOR SERVICES OFFICE

Have you been in a store and couldn't find what you were looking for? Did you ask someone to help you find what you were looking for? *State a time you felt relieved when someone gave you directions to a place or thing.*

Take time for quiet each day. Every day will have its challenges, which is why the GOD-centered business owner quiets down at the beginning of the day to listen to the LORD. Give HIM HIS time, then sort out the rest of the day.

1. **GOD's time.** Quiet time is meant to be a special time between you and the LORD. Spend it learning about HIM, praising HIM ,and worshiping HIS power.
2. **Stand firm.** Expect trouble to happen every day. This is not a pessimistic view, but rather, a move to be prepared. Trials from GOD strengthen you and make you unshakable.
3. **Prepare.** Some days will be harder than others, especially if feeling like a failure or if sin is involved, or if a trial that is out of your control happens. Confess, ask, request and put it behind you. "*Put on the full armor of God, so that you can take your stand against the devil's schemes*" (Ephesians 6:11 NIV).
4. **Practice being a new creation.** As with all things that are new, it takes practice to solidify true behavioral change. Ask GOD for the practical steps HE would have you take as you grow.

> "Therefore, if anyone is in Christ, he is a new creation; old things have passed away; behold, all things have become new" (2 Corinthians 5:17)

Be there for people as GOD is there for you.

Joshua 1:9–*This is my command—be strong and courageous! Do not be afraid or discouraged. For the Lord your God is with you wherever you go.* (NLT)

Put boundaries for "quiet time", "family time", "me time", "business hours" and "administrative time." Communicate these hours to people as **dedicated time**. Remind people of these times until they are accepted by your family, friends and customers.

Quiet, Family, and Personal Time

*My **dedicated** quiet time is (finish the sentence)*
*My **dedicated** family time is (finish the sentence)*
*My **dedicated** me time is (finish the sentence)*

Business Hours

*My **dedicated** Business Hours are (finish the sentence)*

Schedule time to post your business hours on your website, Google, social media and CRM tools like Honor Services Office.

Administrative Day

*My **dedicated** administrative day is (finish the sentence)*

Setting aside time to take care of administrative tasks. By incorporating this in your week or every other week, you can remain organized to review expenses, return proposals, or tackle the other administrative tasks that rise, seemingly daily. Set up time on your calendar on your smartphone.

Make the times you listed in this section immovable.

Special Prayer Before Forgiveness

Pray for:
Hearts to be opened to hear the HOLY SPIRIT.
Hurt hearts to be healed.
Reconciliation of relationships.

Now we are about to move into a very necessary time all GOD-centered business owners will need to face, namely forgiveness.

Exercise 11 – Forgiveness

Objective: *Avoid being affected by external issues people may place on you and to be infectious with GOD's love.*

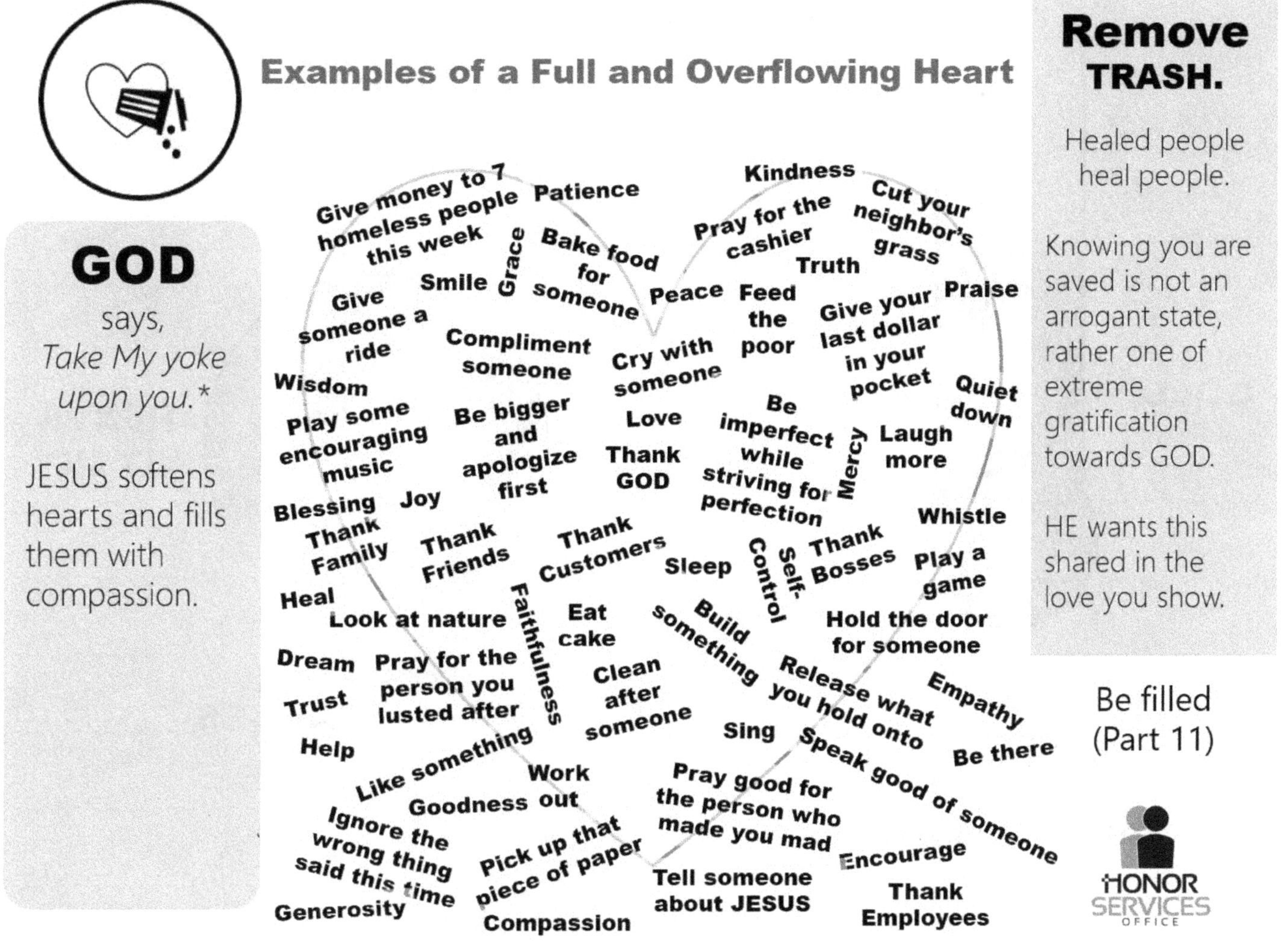

Have you ever heard the term "Hurt people, hurt people?" What do you hear twice in this statement?

Let's try a new statement. **Healed people heal people.**

Matthew 11:29 – *Take My yoke upon you and learn from Me, for I am gentle and lowly in heart, and you will find rest for your souls.*

GOD wants to heal hearts. HE is willing to yoke HIMSELF to anyone who wants HIS love.

Love them

Take time to review some items listed in the picture above so you can place as much in your heart as possible. This takes practice.

Thermostat versus a Thermometer

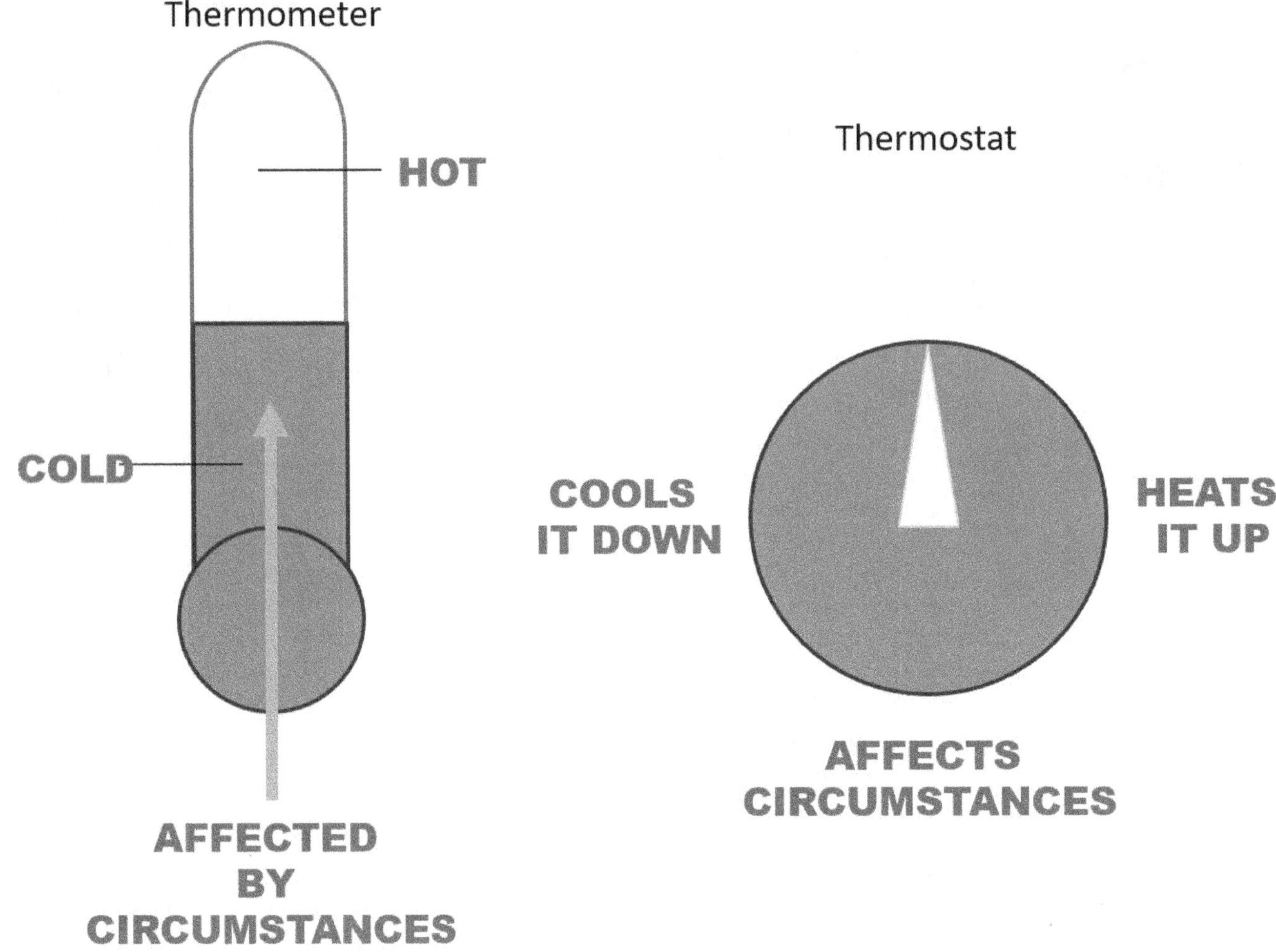

What is the difference between a thermometer and a thermostat?

An overflowing hearts enables the GOD-centered business owner to become a thermostat versus a thermometer. Thermostats control the temperature of the surroundings, versus a thermometer that reacts to the temperature. Become a thermostat, setting the temperature of the situation versus reacting to it.

Exercise 12—Forgive Them

Objective: *Gain freedom by learning how to forgive.*

Pain from being hurt by someone shows up in unexpected places—like your business. People say "forgive and forget." But this practice makes matters worse because the painful memory is replayed over and over, rather than forgotten. Real forgiveness takes strength from GOD.

GOD

says "Forgive."

JESUS told Peter to forgive a person "up to seventy times seven." *

Turn Hurt into Love

I have been hurt by:
In this way:
I accept the power of love by forgiving myself and them for:

Remove TRASH.

Forgiveness enables strength.

When you forgive those who hurt you or hate you, the power of love is placed in your heart.

Use this power of love to heal many people.

Be filled (Part 12)

HONOR SERVICES OFFICE

Has anyone ever hurt you? Did they offend you or say something the wrong way? Did someone deeply hurt you? Was it a family member? When you think of the hurt, does it drain you? Does it cause your mind to think of the hurt over and over?

Forgive to regain lost power. When someone hurts you, the hurt steals your power.

Matthew 18:21-22 *Then Peter came to Him and said, "Lord, how often shall my brother sin against me, and I forgive him? Up to seven times?"*

Jesus said to him, "I do not say to you, up to seven times, but up to seventy times seven.

Forgive Them

Take a moment to think about who hurt you, what they did and why it still hurts. This may or may not include the people you thought you had reconciled with and moved on. Think of the person or people you still need to forgive. Maybe the person you need to forgive is yourself.

Write who hurt you. ***On a separate sheet of paper****, write out what the person did and how it made you feel.*

This may not be easy right now, especially if the wound is still fresh. Start a prayer that begins with "I accept the power of love by forgiving myself and them for hurting me." Add additional words.

Let Go of the Person

Now that you have written down how the person hurt you... *tear up the page and throw it away*. Say "I release you by forgiving you" as you tear the paper up.

Repeat this exercise as many tines as you need to until you can release this person, in other words, until the hurt they put on you hurts less and less.

Please note that true forgiveness means you do not have to see evidence of them changing.

Only when the pain has subsided enough for you to keep your emotions level, approach the person with forgiveness. Let the person know you forgive them. Do this with caution and discernment, as they may not know they hurt you.

Feel better? It may not last, so let's discuss what may keep you up at night.

1. **Change the recording.** When the pain replays in your mind, ask GOD to forgive the person who hurt you. This will not come easy; however, stand firm and continue. The deeper the wound, the more time it may take, but relief comes when you know that person no longer has power over you. "*Then Peter came to Him and said, " 'Lord, how often shall my brother sin against me, and I forgive him? Up to seven times?' Jesus said to him, " 'I do not say to you, up to seven times, but up to seventy times seven"*" (Matthew 18:21-22)
2. **Forgive to regain power.** Forgiveness restores power that was stolen from you. Trading bitterness, hatred, and anger for love, joy, peace, patience, kindness, goodness, gentleness faithfulness, and self-control, restores power that was lost, namely the ability to reach GOD's people.
3. **Forgive yourself.** Blame is a dangerous weapon that works against us when we blame ourselves. Knowing GOD has forgiven you gives you permission to forgive yourself, even when it is hard. "For God did not send His Son into the world to condemn the world, but that the world through Him might be saved"" (John 3:17)

Let Go of Pain

How to regain lost sleep and peace

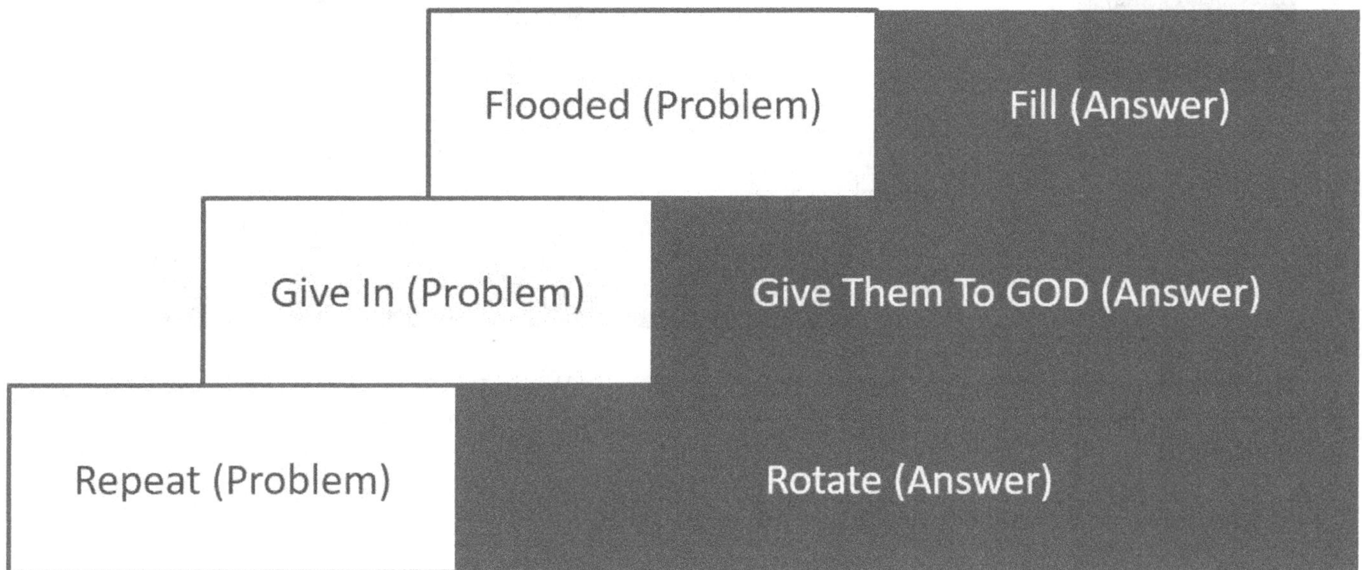

When someone has hurt you, three things can happen.
1. You repeat the hurt over and over trying to resolve the issue as best you can.
2. You give into a wrong solution which is usually a fight or hatred or fall prey to an addiction like alcohol, drugs or porn.
3. You carry the hurt to other situations and become hypersensitive to the hurt others are doing, therefore becoming flooded.

Have you ever lost sleep over the hurt someone imposed on you?

As a GOD-centered business owner, you cannot afford to lose sleep. So how can we deal with the pain? R-G-F.

Rotate – Give – Fill Methodology to Regain Sleep

How to regain lost sleep and peace – Rotate Your Thinking to GOD

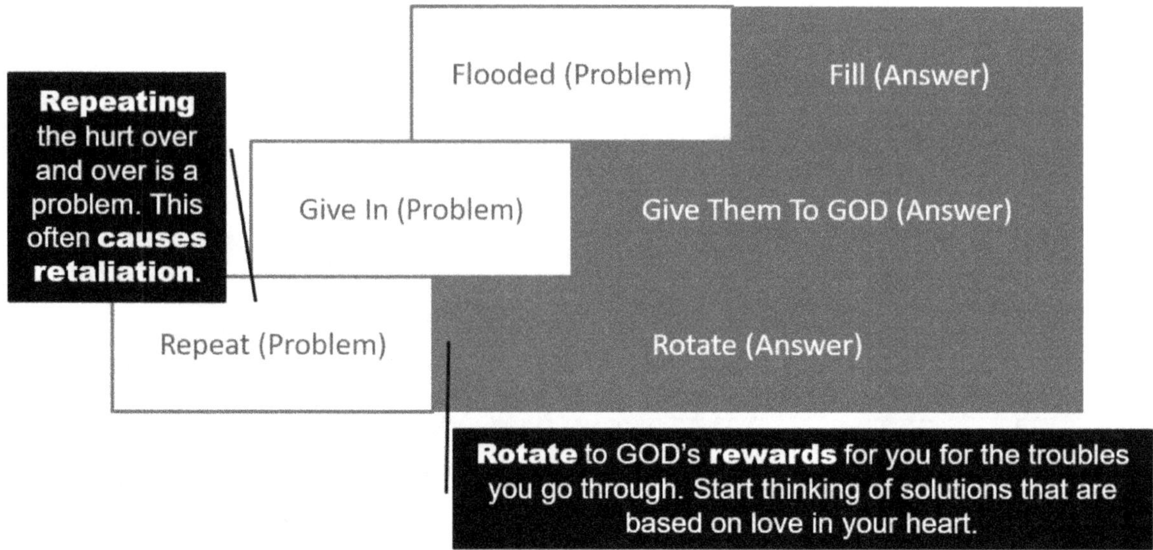

The first method of letting go of the pain is to R-Rotate. When you keep replaying a problem over and over in your head, you can get stuck and even worse, it can cause you to experience fear, anxiety and depression.

<u>Rotate</u> your thinking to what GOD wants you to think about.

Philippians 4:8 *Finally, brothers and sisters, whatever is true, whatever is noble, whatever is right, whatever is pure, whatever is lovely, whatever is admirable--if anything is excellent or praiseworthy--think about such things.*(NIV).

When do you have the best ideas? Is it when you love to do something or when you hate doing something? Instead of retaliation, can you rotate to love as your weapon and approach? Instead of writing that nasty note, practice asking GOD to bless the person with HIS love and forgiveness. Fill your heart with love and watch the power flood back into you. This will take practice.

– Romans 12:14-16 *Ask God to bless those who persecute you—yes, ask him to bless, not to curse. Be happy with those who are happy, weep with those who weep. Have the same concern for everyone. Do not be proud, but accept humble duties. Do not think of yourselves as wise.*

Blessing people releases bitterness from your heart. Rotating to a loving plan enables you to be above the situation.

How to regain lost sleep and peace – Give Them to GOD

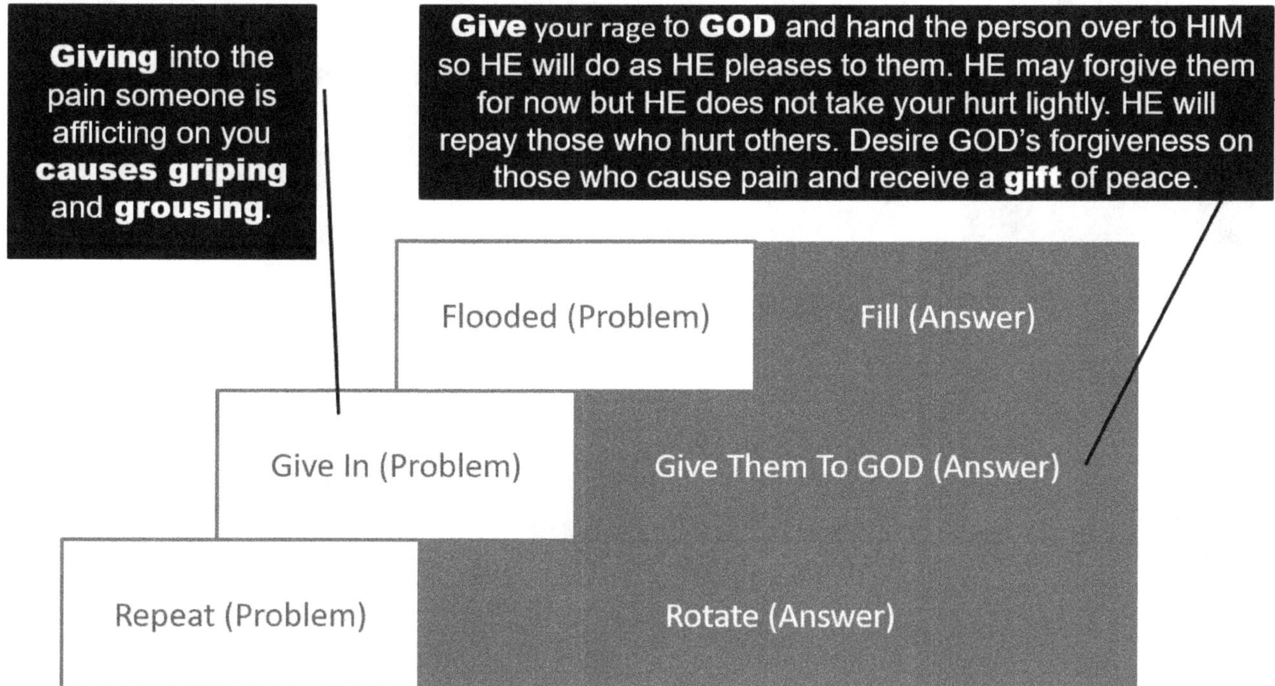

The next method to regain sleep and peace is to **G-Give** the person over to GOD. This means releasing the thought of getting revenge. Get off the dangerous path or trying to win the argument or trying to hurt them back.

Romans 12:18 – 19 *Do everything possible on your part to live in peace with everybody. Never take revenge, my friends, but instead let God's anger do it. For the scripture says, "I will take revenge, I will pay back, says the Lord."* (GNT)

Do you have anyone you can ask GOD to forgive?

Grow in grace by **G-<u>Giving</u>** them to GOD. Ask the LORD to have mercy on the person and then ask for GOD to have mercy on you. This takes practice.

Story of a man who loved GOD more than retaliation
There was a man who GOD loved very much. He chose to use love as a weapon instead of using retaliation. When his employer tried to kill him, he did not retaliate. Instead, he showed love. Everyone knew this person would someday become the boss. They even told him, "You will rule someday."

That person is David, a man after GOD's own heart.

When king Saul tried to kill David, recorded in 1 Samuel 19, David did not retaliate because he knew he would someday be the king and chose to use love versus hate. He was above the situation. You can be above the situation.

You can read about David in the book of 1 Samuel.

How to regain lost sleep and peace – Fill Your Heart with Love

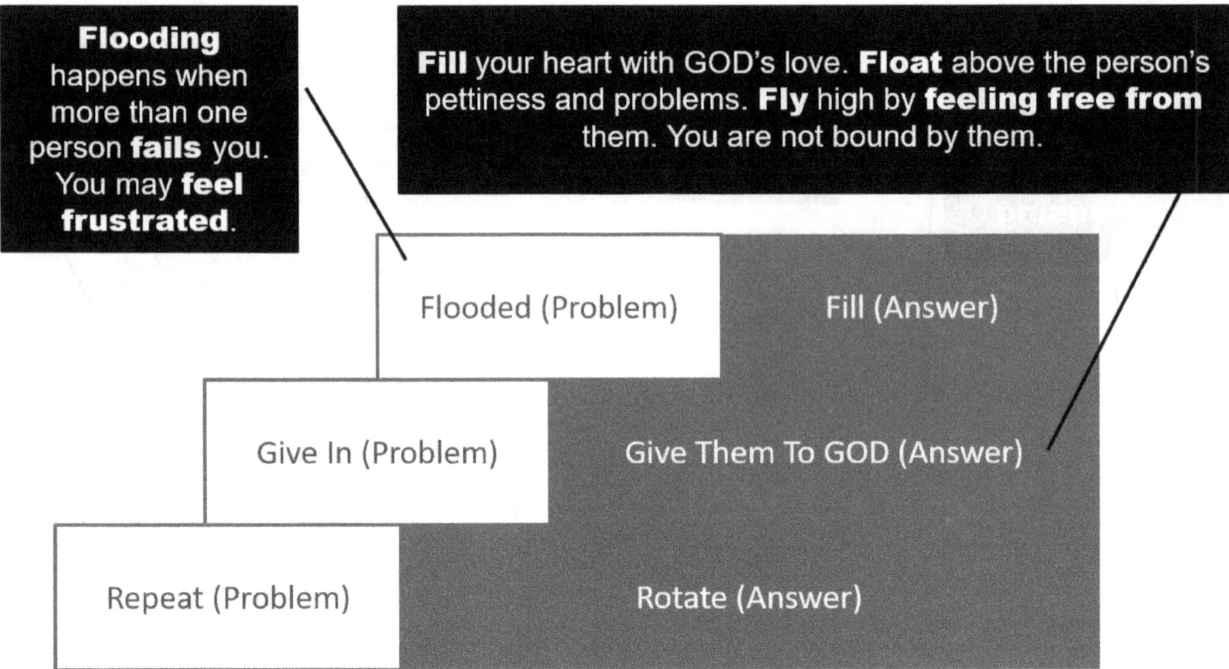

The last method to regaining peace and sleep is to **F-Fill** your heart with love. The person causing pain may be trying to rob you of peace. This can provoke you into anger and rage. Reduce the rage and fill your heart with love for them.

Love provides freedom they may be trying to steal from you.

Luke 6:27-36. *"But to you who are listening I Love your enemies, do good to those who hate you, bless those who curse you, pray for those who mistreat you. If someone slaps you on one cheek, turn to them the other also. If someone takes your coat, do not withhold your shirt from them. Give to everyone who asks you, and if anyone takes what belongs to you, do not demand it back. Do to others as you would have them do to you.*

"If you love those who love you, what credit is that to you? Even sinners love those who love them. And if you do good to those who are good to you, what credit is that to you? Even sinners do that. And if you lend to those from whom you expect repayment, what credit is that to you? Even sinners lend to sinners, expecting to be repaid in full. But love your enemies, do good to them, and lend to them without expecting to get anything back. Then your reward will be great, and you will be children of the Most High, because he is kind to the ungrateful and wicked. Be merciful, just as your Father is merciful.

GOD is not saying become a wimp, rather be strong enough to choose love over petty retaliation. **You are a leader** who is above the situation. **You are bigger than this**. Your leadership in the area of forgiveness is necessary. The more people you can release, the more successful you can be. Using RGF, "Rotate", "Give" and "Fill", enables you to focus on love for the person, giving vengeance to GOD and filling your heart with love and genuine concern for people. You will have peace.

Exercise 13—Seek Forgiveness

Objective: *Seek forgiveness to grow as a leader.*

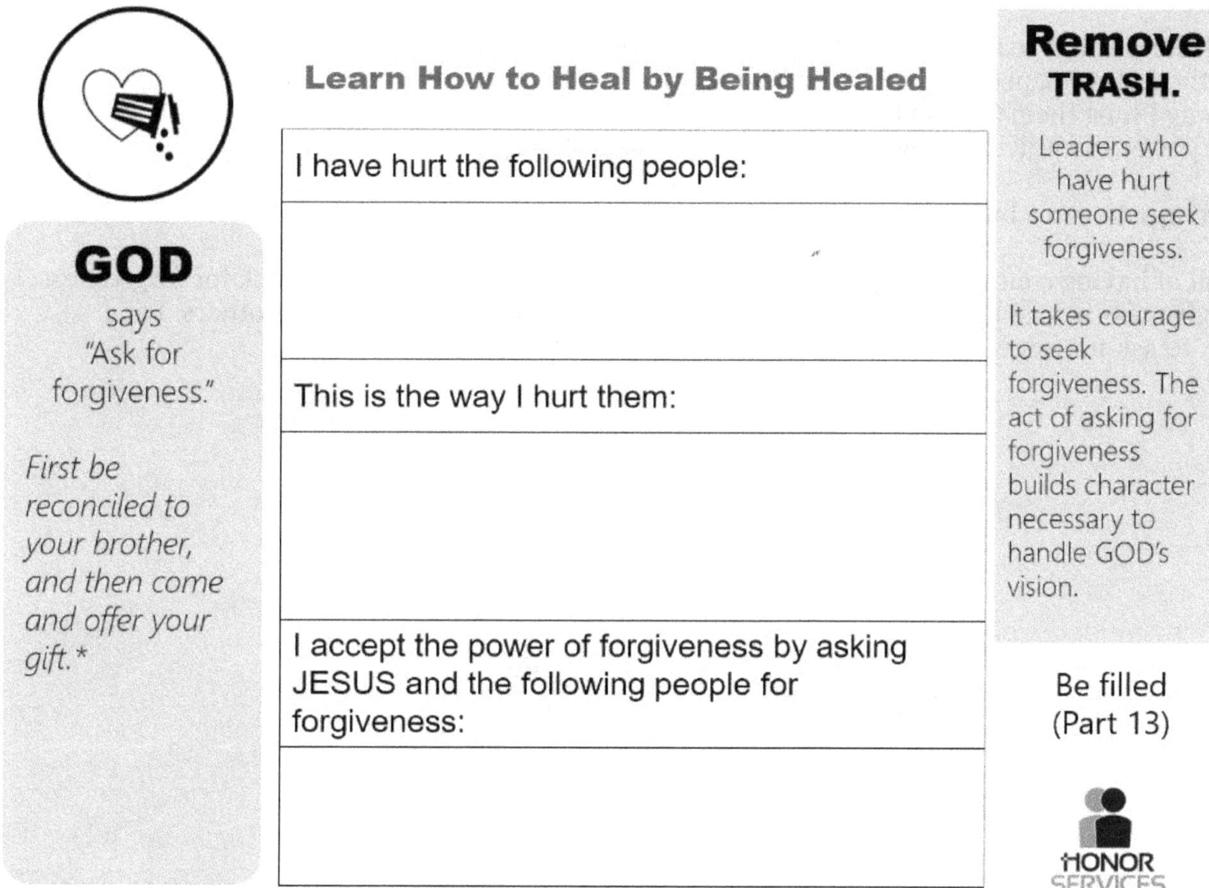

Person 1 – Have you ever experienced a salesperson at a store who received your complaint well? Think of a time when the salesperson listened attentively and then apologized for the issue. How did she make you feel?

Person 2 – Have you ever experienced a salesperson who blamed you for the problem she caused? How did you feel about their attitude?

Between the two people, which one showed more leadership to you?

Ask for forgiveness as an act of leadership.

Matthew 5:24 – *leave your gift there before the altar, and go your way. First be reconciled to your brother, and then come and offer your gift.*

Leaders know that forgiveness is more important than being right. By seeking to be right, blame inserts itself into the heart and blinds the leader causing a failure. By seeking forgiveness, the blindness is lifted and the heart becomes cleanses and healed.

Ask for Forgiveness

Courage to ask for forgiveness is needed right now from you.

Ask GOD for the courage to admit when they have wronged someone.
I have hurt the following people (Finish the sentence)
This is the way I hurt them (Finish the sentence)
I accept the power of forgiveness by asking JESUS and the following people for forgiveness:

It takes **courage** to run a business.

The skill of having courage is acquired when you forgive people and when you ask for forgiveness. Seeking forgiveness from a leadership role may be new to some and very familiar to others. Let's explore how to ask for forgiveness.

Let go of the Pride

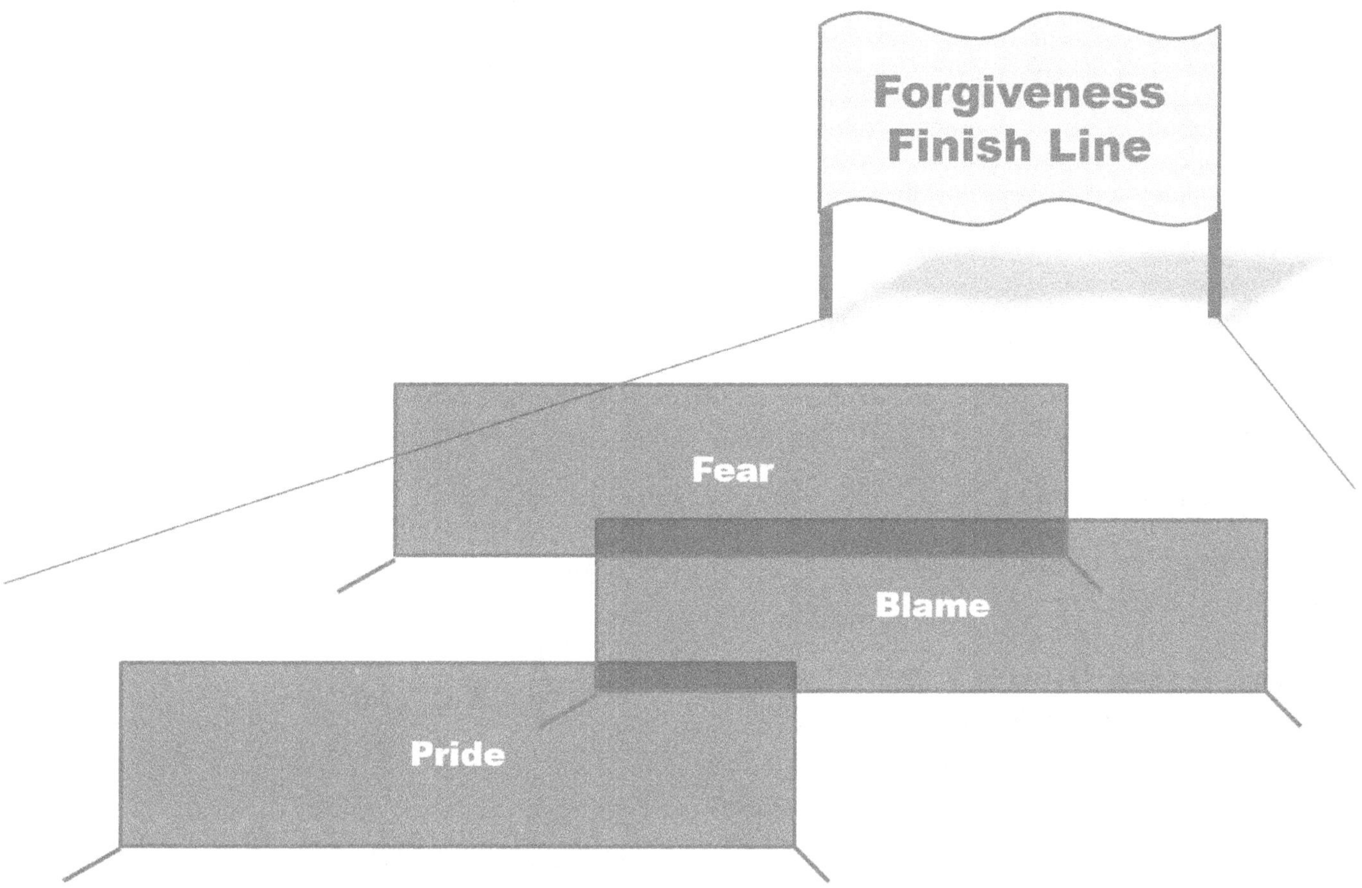

Asking for forgiveness can be just as hard, if not harder, than forgiving others. Here, you are relinquishing power and becoming vulnerable. There are many blockers to asking for forgiveness, but these three truly hurt your leadership.

Pride blocks you from thinking you need to ask for forgiveness.

Look at Satan's pride by reading out loud Isaiah 14: 13-15 *You said in your heart,*
"I will ascend to the heavens;
I will raise my throne
above the stars of God;
I will sit enthroned on the mount of assembly,
on the utmost heights of Mount Zaphon.
I will ascend above the tops of the clouds;
I will make myself like the Most High."
But you are brought down to the realm of the dead,
to the depths of the pit. (NIV)

Blame blocks you from necessary admission of guilt. Romans 2:1 You, therefore, have no excuse, you who pass judgment on someone else, for at whatever point you judge another, you are condemning yourself, because you who pass judgment do the same things.

Fear blocks you from growing as a leader. Matthew 16:24 --27 : *Then Jesus said to his disciples, "Whoever wants to be my disciple must deny themselves and take up their cross and follow me. For whoever wants to save their life will lose it, but whoever loses their life for me will find it. What good will it be for someone to gain the whole world, yet forfeit their soul? Or what can anyone* *give in exchange for their soul? For the Son of Man is going to come in his Father's glory with his angels, and then he will reward each person according to what they have done.*

Pride was Satan's main problem. Do you know that if Satan asked for forgiveness, he may not have gotten thrown out of heaven? Instead, he stuck with the thought that he could be higher than GOD. He thought he could control his own life rather than surrender it.

Blame was the problem Paul wrote about in Romans 2:1. Whenever the leader blames other people, it never looks good. Blame is detestable to GOD. He wants people who are strong enough to admit wrong.

Fear causes people to self-protect. He spends most of the day worrying about bills, making more money and what it would be like to have more and more. He never once asks GOD, "What do you want to do with my life?" GOD wants him to let go of HIS life so it can be saved. The more fearful control the person has, the less GOD can work through him.

Do you have pride or blame or fear? If so, what can you do about it?

Answer to Pride is Appreciation

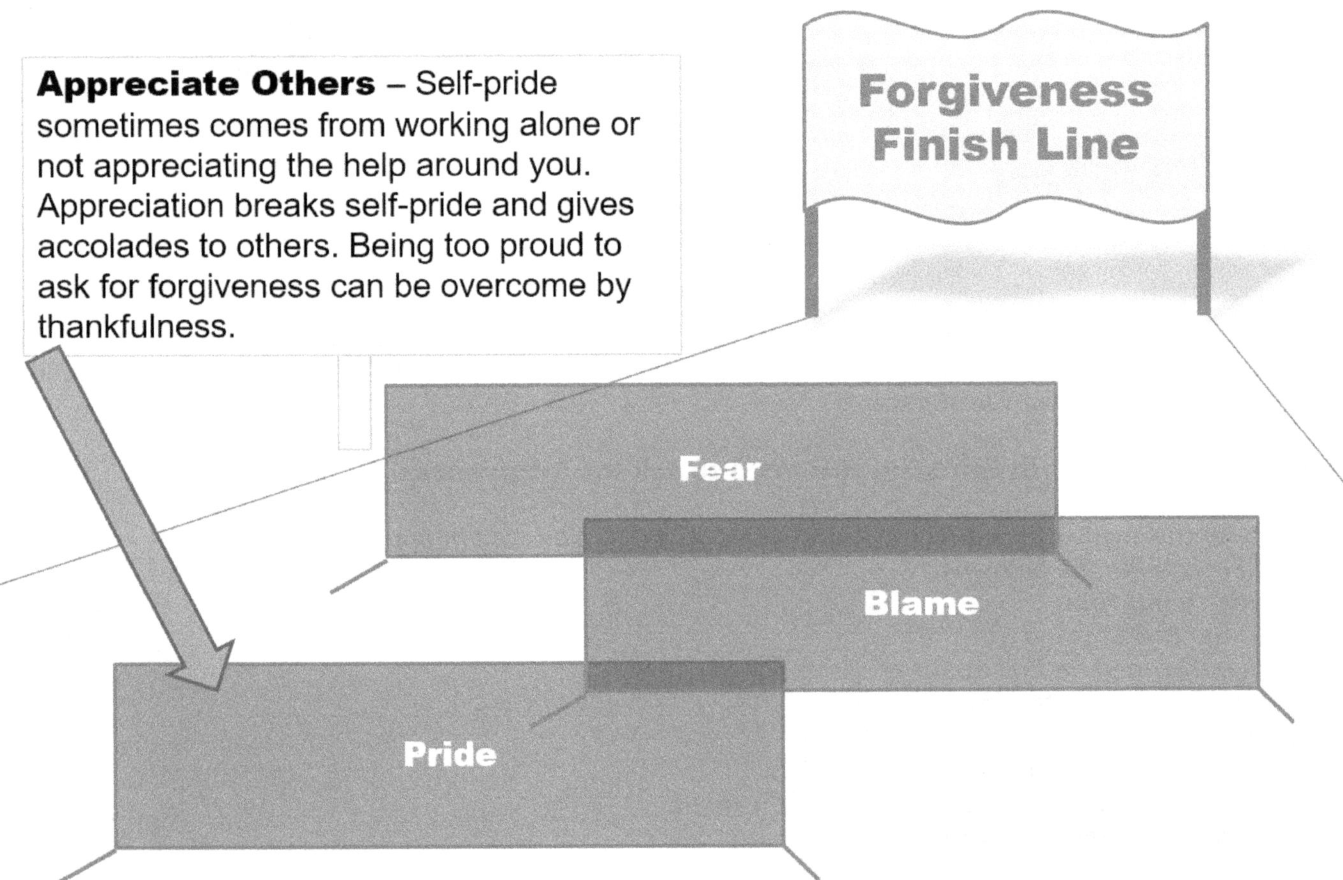

Appreciation erases harmful pride. If you are too proud to approach the person you harmed to ask for forgiveness, then it will affect other relationships. It is a heart thing that cannot be masked.

Fill your heart with appreciation for him or her. See them as GOD sees and values people. They deserve a sincere apology.

Answer to Blame is Accepting Responsibility

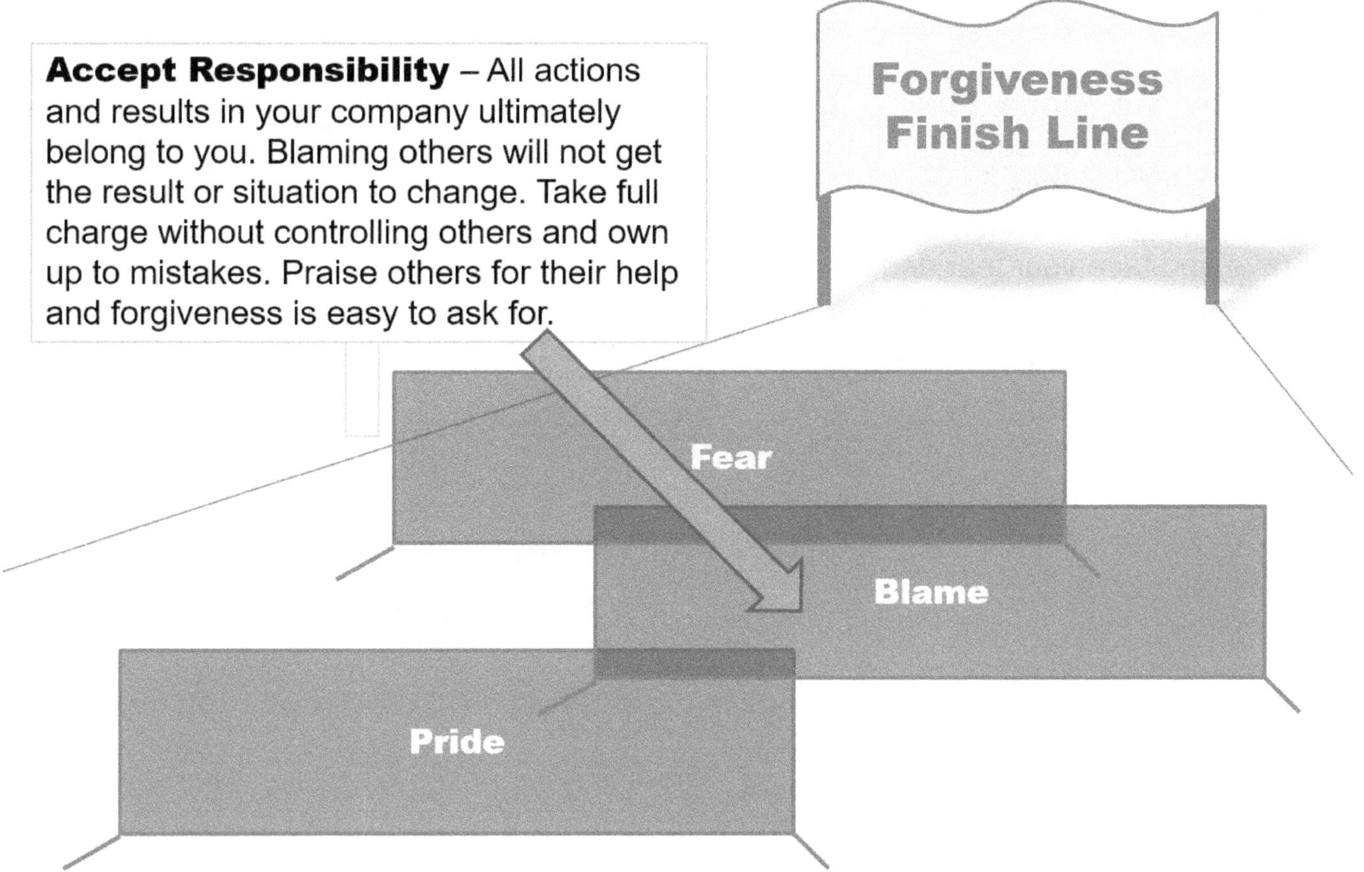

Have you ever asked a kid, who clearly broke your stuff, "what happened?" How do kids respond if they are guilty and don't want you to show their guilt?

Accepting responsibility is a must for the GOD -Centered Business owner. Leaders who own the mistakes of their employees and sometimes their customers, shine brighter than people who blame.

Answer to Fear is Abbreviate Alone Time

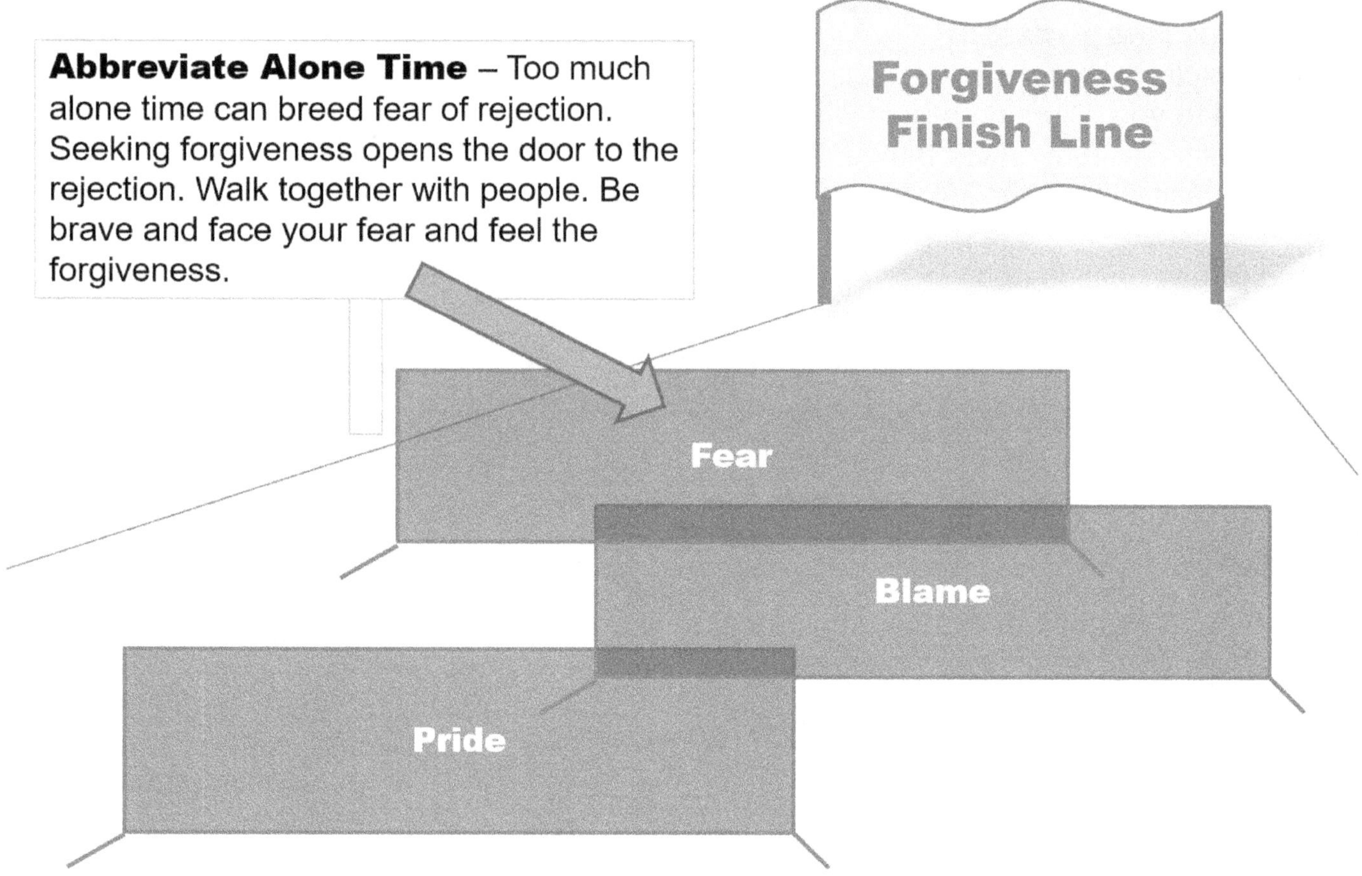

Have you ever said "Well I don't need them anyway?" How many times can you say this until you are alone?

Abbreviate alone time to rid yourself of fear. This is your group who will be there for you to help face fears and to talk about problems. Some of you may enjoy being alone, but if you have fear, it is best to be with a group to help you.

This fear that some people face may cause them to be too scared to ask for forgiveness. "What if the truth comes out you might ask?' Good, then now you are free.

GOD wants you to be free, so ask HIM for the courage to admit wrong.

When JESUS forgives, it is permanent. HE saw every sin you and I did, yet HE died for us and took the blame anyway. When HE rose from the dead, HE received all authority to forgive, pardon and make people right with HIM.

Over the next week, write down the people who have hurt you. On the separate sheet of paper write how the person hurt you and tear it up, saying "I release you." Rotate your thinking to love. Give the person to GOD. Fill your heart with love as a weapon. Appreciate people. Accept responsibility. Abbreviate walking alone.

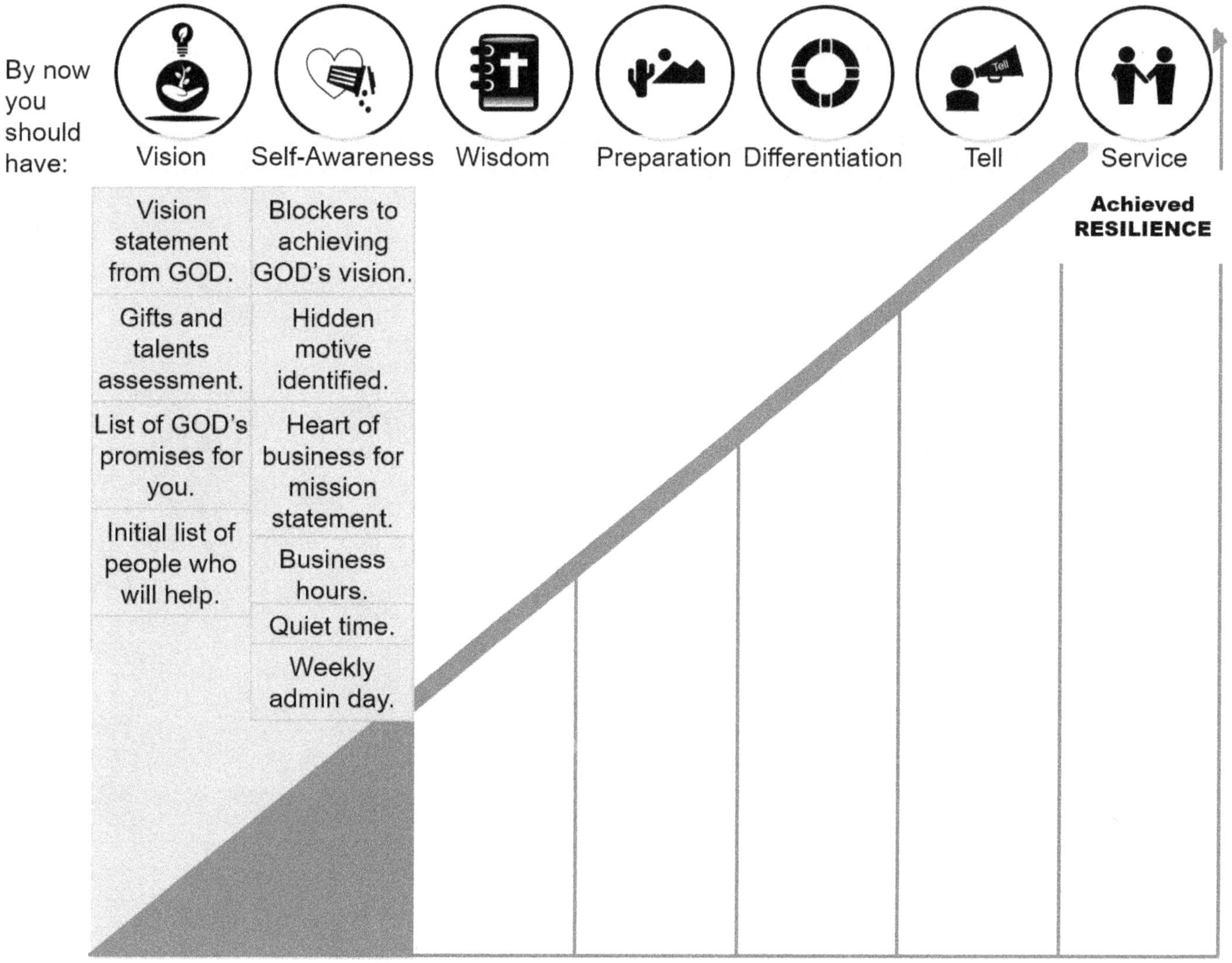

By now you should have:

Vision	Self-Awareness	Wisdom	Preparation	Differentiation	Tell	Service
Vision statement from GOD.	Blockers to achieving GOD's vision.					
Gifts and talents assessment.	Hidden motive identified.					
List of GOD's promises for you.	Heart of business for mission statement.					
Initial list of people who will help.	Business hours.					
	Quiet time.					
	Weekly admin day.					

Achieved RESILIENCE

Use T.R.A.S.H. to remove the TRASH.

Tame **R**age **A**nd **S**elfish **H**abits.

For your homework, count your negative thoughts for the next week. Each time you want to experience anger, frustration, doubt, blame, fear, anxiousness, worry, hatred or any other negative feeling, rotate your thinking to the fruit of the Spirit.

Ask for any prayer requests and dismiss in prayer. Remember to use your personal growth journal at the end of this book

WARNING

- Change takes time. The longer a habit has been in place, the longer it may take to change the habit. Ask GOD for the courage to persist.
- Leaders are responsible for their actions. This may require uncomfortable admissions at times.
- Avoid skipping the process toward change if you are an existing business owner.

NEXT STEPS

- Set aside time to prepare yourself before you begin creating your product or service.
- Implement business hours.
- Implement an administrative day.
- Implement a set quiet time.
- Review examples of a full heart.

PRAYER

- Pray that the LORD will provide a clean heart.
- Pray that your motives will be aligned with GOD's desire.
- Pray for purpose.
- Pray for HIM to open your eyes to HIS leading.

Chapter 3 – Seek Wisdom: Get Resources / Skills

"Are you as smart as GOD?"

"When should you ask for help?"

Seek Wisdom preparation (Week 3)

Greet participants and remind them of the goal to use the fruit of the Spirit as a guide to controlling their thoughts. Did you see a difference in your week by using the fruit of the Spirit?

If you were with us last week (or whatever your time frame), how did it feel to reduce negative thoughts?

Did you implement the fruit of the Spirit? How about the other assignments? Did you complete your lists of behaviors you want to reduce? Share your thoughts with your community.

Now let's talk about seeking wisdom for your business. None of us is as good as all of us. Seek GOD's knowledge first, then assess what you can do and what you will need help with. Be honest with your expectations. It takes thousands of hours for a person to become an expert. But GOD can make a person wise enough to handle business at levels they would never imagine.

Introduce the Seek Wisdom Chapter

This chapter is to assess current skills and identify gaps to fill them. We are in part 3 of the framework. This methodology teaches you what to do to prepare your business for resilience. We will cover true wisdom. We will also cover appreciating how GOD made you, and managing your business mood.
There are 6 Wisdom Exercises.

Be prepared to seek new skills."

Seek Wisdom Objective

You will learn; how to make adjustments to your leadership style to truly gain success, to appreciate how GOD made you, to manage your business mood, to manage time and schedule and to manage relationship.

Seek Wisdom Prayer

Pray:
To follow HIS power.
For wisdom to be the leader GOD wants you to be.
For an understanding of the skills you may be missing.
For the right resources to be brought into your life at the right time.

The "Seek Wisdom" portion of the class is to enable you to not only hear GOD daily, but to seek expertise that will grow your business.

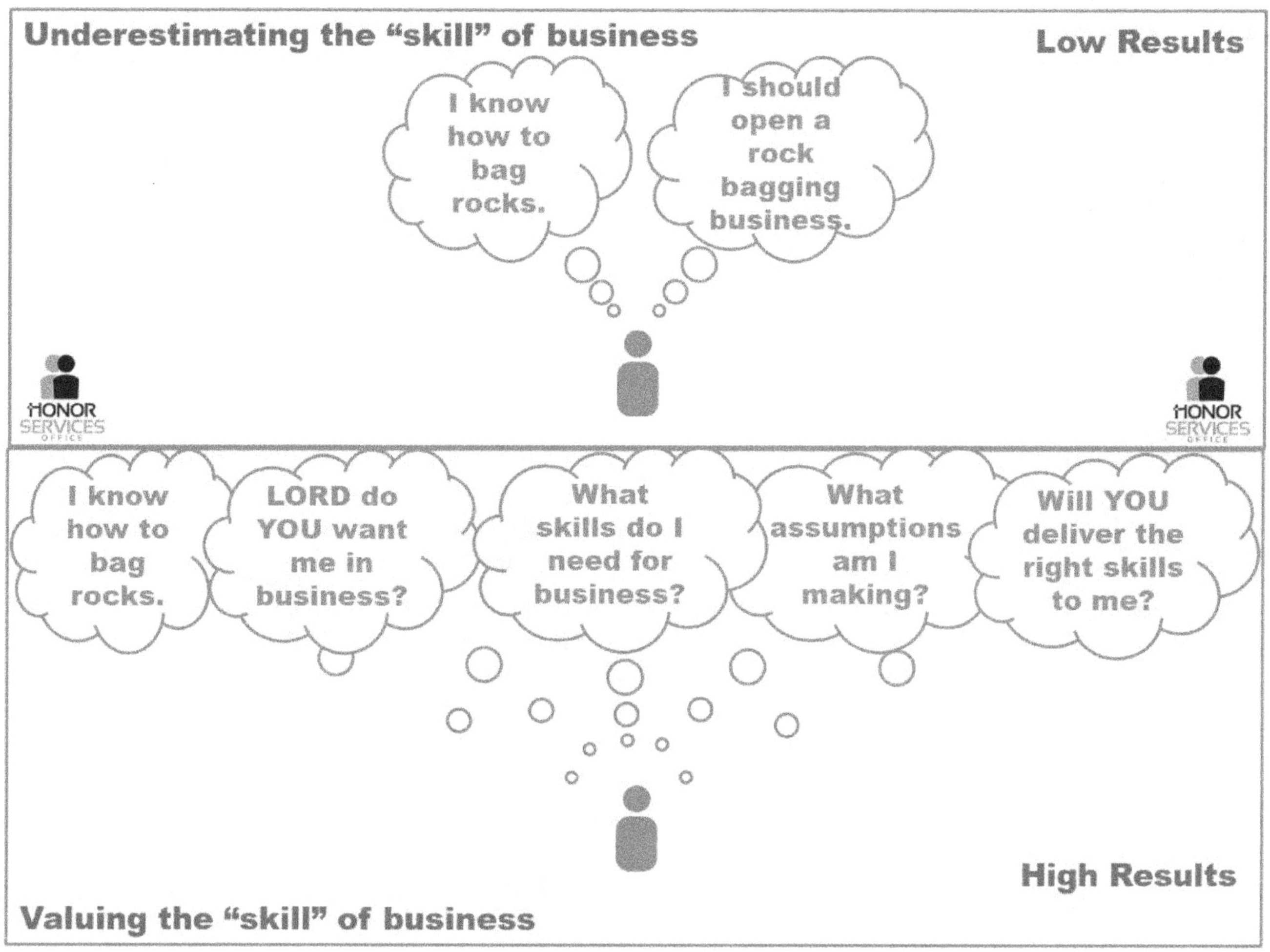

Do you remember learning how to ride a bike or drive a car? Did it look easy? How many people got it right the first time?

The skill of operating a business is just as important as the skills needed to do what the business does.

The GOD-Centered Business owner looks for missing skills and asks GOD to provide for their needs.

Let's begin by seeking GOD's Word First.

Seek GOD's Kingdom First

Objective: *Seek time with GOD by reading the Bible daily.*

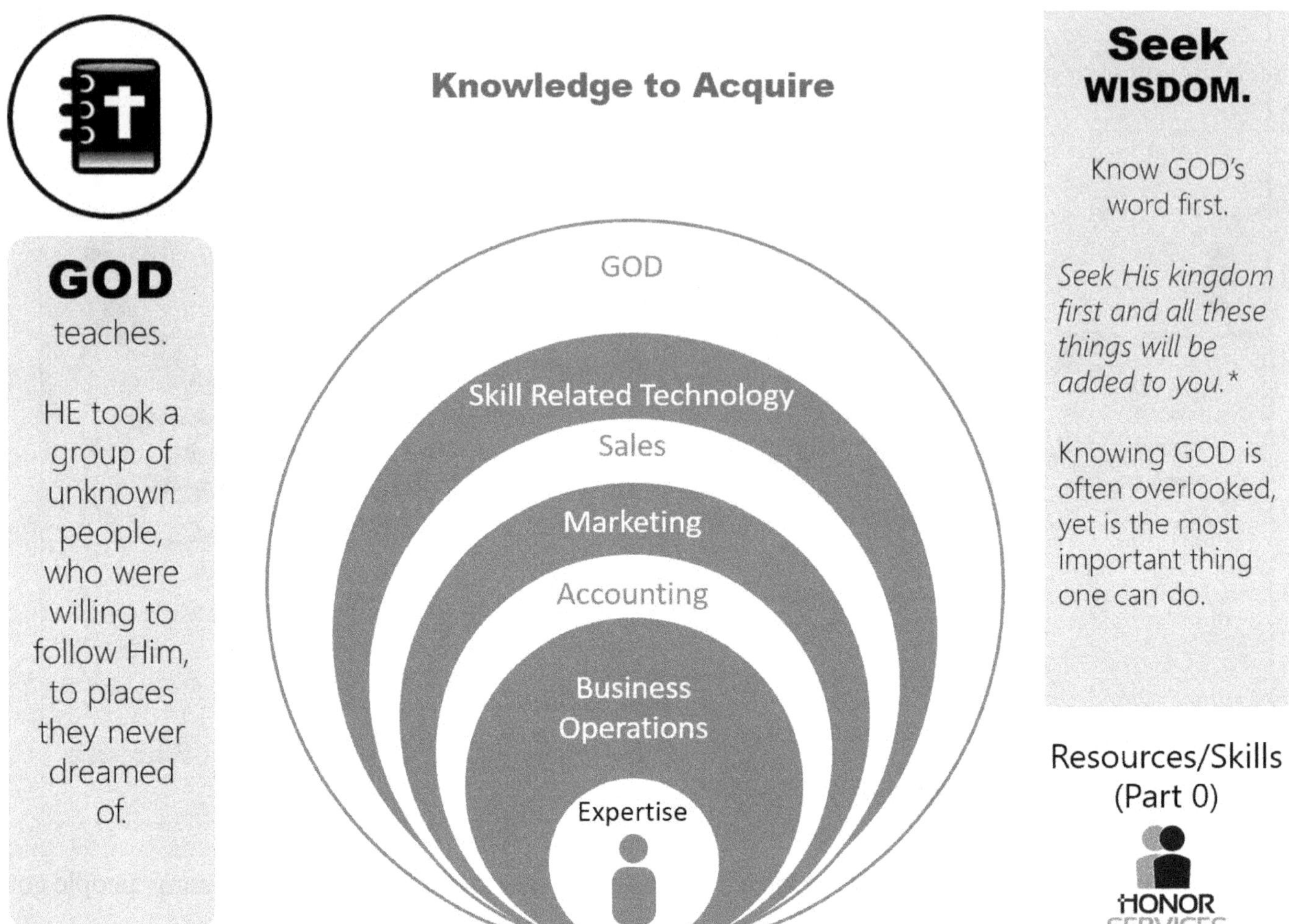

Have you ever liked someone enough to find out more about him or her? Did you ask questions to them or talk to their friends? GOD wants to be known. By seeking GOD, HE will teach you and add the right things you need.

Matthew 6:33 *But seek first the kingdom of God and His righteousness, and all these things shall be added to you.*

Let's look at two sections of the bible. One scripture written in the new testament and one written in the old testament, thousands of years before the new testament was written.

Read John 1:1-3.
In the beginning was the Word, and the Word was with God, and the Word was God. He was in the beginning with God. All things were made through Him, and without Him nothing was made that was made.

Now read Genesis 1:1 and compare it to John 1:1-3.
In the beginning God created the heavens and the earth.
What similarities do you notice? Write your observations.

Read John 1:1-5, 9-14 and **circle** the references to JESUS.

The Eternal Word
1 In the beginning was the Word, and the Word was with God, and the Word was God. 2 He was with
God in the beginning. 3 Through him all things were made; without him nothing was made that has
been made. 4 In him was life, and that life was the light of all mankind. 5 The light shines in the
darkness, and the darkness has not overcome it.

9 The true light that gives light to everyone was coming into the world. 10 He was in the world, and
though the world was made through him, the world did not recognize him. 11 He came to that which
was his own, but his own did not receive him. 12 Yet to all who did receive him, to those who
believed in his name, he gave the right to become children of God— 13 children born not of natural
descent, nor of human decision or a husband's will, but born of God.
14 The Word became flesh and made his dwelling among us. We have seen his glory, the glory of the
one and only Son, who came from the Father, full of grace and truth.

What do you observe about the role of the Word? Write your observations ,

Did anything stand out personally to you? If so, then write this down. What words seem to jump off the page at you? Remember them.

Let GOD measure your success. Allow HIM to guide you while obeying HIS direction.

Exercise 1 – Seek by being you

Objective: *Value GOD's design for you and know HE did not make a mistake when HE created you.*

GOD believes in you, why don't you?

Staying who you are is very important. If you are a shy person, forcing yourself to be gregarious is not recommended. Your personality and behaviors are what make you special and unique. There are people who need your style and GOD is willing to send them to you or you to them.

"Be yourself" is an action accepted by leaders. It means be confident to approach people just as you are. This does not mean you should not modify behaviors that may be harmful to others. It simply means be comfortable with your personality and appearance. GOD loves you and considers you wonderful!

GOD made you.

When HE thought of you, HE knew every sin and great things you would do. Then HE made you anyway.

Be Yourself

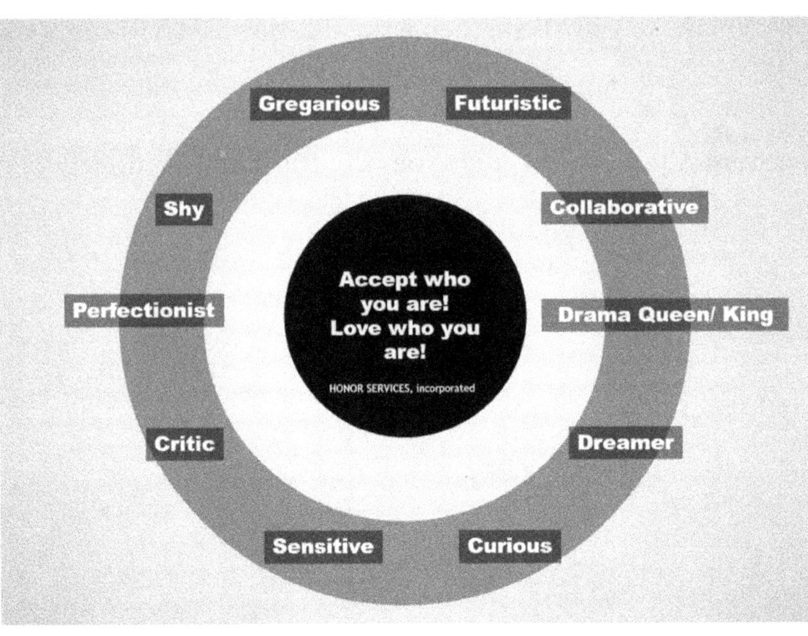

Seek WISDOM.

Accept who you are and love how GOD made you.

Some people may have an opinion about you that is opposite of what GOD thinks about you.

Know that HE loves you dearly.

Resources/Skills (Part 1)

Does GOD love you?. Do you love yourself?

Love and accept who you are. review the image and identify a few behavioral traits that describe who you are.

GOD was pleased when HE made you. Some people may have a different opinion about you, but GOD thinks you are wonderful! The first step to loving you is to accept your behaviors. Look at the image and identify one or more behaviors that describe how you behave sometimes."

Write your observations.

GOD's currency is people. HE will never have a shortage of people who need to hear about HIS love, grace, and mercy. The dilemma arises in the greedy person who wants to exploit GOD's kingdom for her own wealth or power. This person wrestles with questions like, "Should I sell in church?" or "Should I throw some Scripture on my product so I can sell more?"

"God is Spirit, and those who worship Him must worship in spirit and truth" (John 4:24). HE guides, HE supplies, and HE grows people and businesses. But what does seeking GOD's kingdom mean to the GOD-centered business owner? Let's revisit our foundation.

On your own, look at John 1:1-3 and compare it to Genesis 1:1. Then return to the Gospel of John and finish the first chapter. This is a start of getting to know who *JESUS* really is.

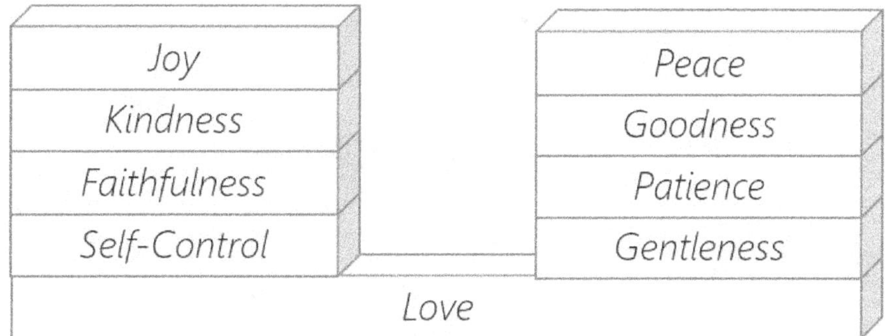

1. **Carry the fruit of the SPIRIT into business dealings.** Knowing people will try to take advantage of you is still a requirement, however by carrying the fruit of the SPIRIT into every aspect of your business, you will see notable changes in the business mood.
2. **Pray for everyone you meet.** Seeing everyone as someone who needs GOD reduces arguments and increases the desire to enable people to have the best. You never know what people are going through, even those who put on an "I'm healthy" mask.
3. **Love them.** Love everyone you meet. Even a smile can show love to someone. GOD said, "But I say to you, love your enemies, bless those who curse you, do good to those who hate you, and pray for those who spitefully use you and persecute you" (Matthew 5:44). Imagine what HE wants us to do for those who do not hate us.

You are Unique

Meeting new people can be exciting or scary, depending on your personality. GOD made you and said, "Very good." HE does not want you to be like other people because HE made you unique to reach a certain group of people only you can reach.

Exercise 2 – Adjust Yourself

Objective: *Value the variety of styles you will encounter while working with other people by knowing GOD made other people the way they are.*

Working with others takes effort. Whether customers or employees, each person is different. See if you need to make some minor adjustments to reach people while staying in your comfort zone.

In the chart below and in the following pages, identify your behaviors and the suggestions for interacting with other people

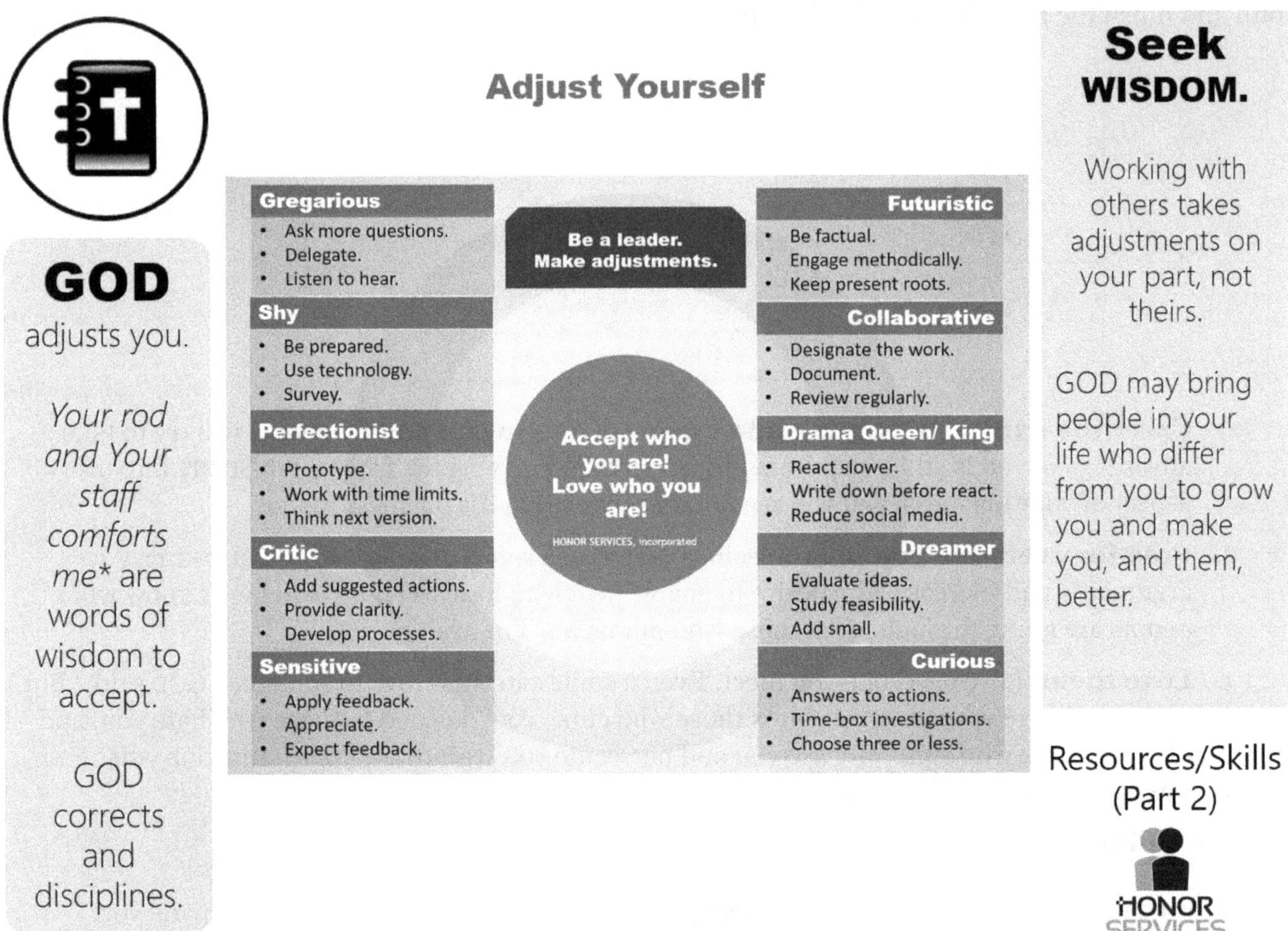

Have you ever met someone who just rubbed you the wrong way? I mean, they just got on your nerves. Is it hard to listen to that person? What if that person was saying something valuable to you that you needed to hear? Would you close your ears to what they had to say?

GOD adjusts us.

Psalm 23:4 – *Yea, though I walk through the valley of the shadow of death, I will fear no evil; For You are with me; Your rod and Your staff, they comfort me.*

GOD gently corrects us with HIS rod of truth. This brings comfort.

When engaging with potential customers/clients, know yourself and make adjustments on how you approach people. Look at the list below and identify an approach to how you will meet people.

Behavior	Strengths	Opportunities	Suggested Approach(es)
Futuristic (aka the Innovator)	Visionary, innovative, imaginative, inventive	May move to the next thing too quickly, sometimes speaks without facts, may be discontented	Be factual. Engage with a methodology rather than winging it. Spend a balanced time in the present and in the future.
Collaborative	Brings people together; energized by groups; serves people	May miss details by talking and not documenting or by being involved in all conversations; puts people over process once too often	Delegate the work. Keep conversations short but meaningful. Document needs. Review processes with those you are working with.
Dreamer	Imaginative; likes big ideas; visionary; solutions driven	Sometimes thinks all ideas are good ideas; may skip testing or may take on too much and not deliver	Evaluate ideas and test before implementing. Study feasibility. Break ideas up into smaller implementable pieces.
Drama Queen/King	Excited; passionate; enjoys the spotlight (center of attention)	May react without asking for clarification, speaks before thinking; often posts irrelevant information on social media	React slower. Write responses after a 24-hour cool down period. Reduce social media posts to relevant information only.
Curious	Inquisitive; research driven; factual	Prone to over-analyze; looks for problems where there may not be any; presents too many options to customers	Timebox investigations. Provide answers only to problems given to you. Choose two or three solutions to present.
Sensitive	Empathetic; understanding, reads nonverbals	Adverse to feedback; withholds improvements; may boil over and lash out	Seek feedback on regular intervals versus whenever you feel like it. Expect and accept feedback as a gift. Add appreciation.
Critical	Solves problems; looks for root cause; provides improvements.	May provide too many improvements than others can handle; can come off as abrasive; never seems satisfied	Bring others in on solutions and accept their ideas. Delegate improvements and inspections. Accept the pace of others with patience.
Perfectionist	Likes high quality; high performance; high standards	May take longer than needed or expected; frustrated easily by mistakes; comes across as hard to please	Develop prototypes to get feedback, rather than waiting on finished product. Work timebound. Think of putting improvements in the next version.

Behavior	Strengths	Opportunities	Suggested Approach(es)
Shy	Great listener; observant, thinker/ intellect	May feel uncomfortable speaking to strangers who can grow the business; may overthink what others are thinking based on insecurities; may look for self-fulfilling failure	Be prepared and use technology to focus the audience's attention away from you. Focus more on the valuable message needing to be heard by the receiver, thus relieving him or her of a problem.
Gregarious	Meets new people easily; public speaker; has a host of prepared messages and wisdom to impart	May speak before listening; takes over the conversation; may not seek input	Ask more questions. Listen to hear. Delegate to others. Seek advice before giving it.

Insecurities and self-doubt could prevent you from giving a valuable message to the person who needs to hear it. On the other hand, speaking at people rather than hearing their needs creates a situation where the speaker could miss out on what is needed to be said.

Again, GOD made you wonderfully and is pleased with you. Use the gifts and talents He gave you to grow His kingdom through your business. He is excited and has a plan for you!

Working with strangers takes humility that only comes from GOD correcting us, sometimes gently, sometimes harder than we'd like. Self-Control is the only control worth seeking. This is a part of the fruit of the Spirit. Write adjustments you will make to work with people who look and act differently than you do. Now let's adjust the mood.

Exercise 3 – Seek a Better Mood

Objective: *Use emotional intelligence, the ability to identify and manage one's own emotions, as well as the emotions of others, to recognize the mood and make adjustments.*

Your mood affects your business. Each day, the GOD-centered business owner will need to choose how to approach the day.

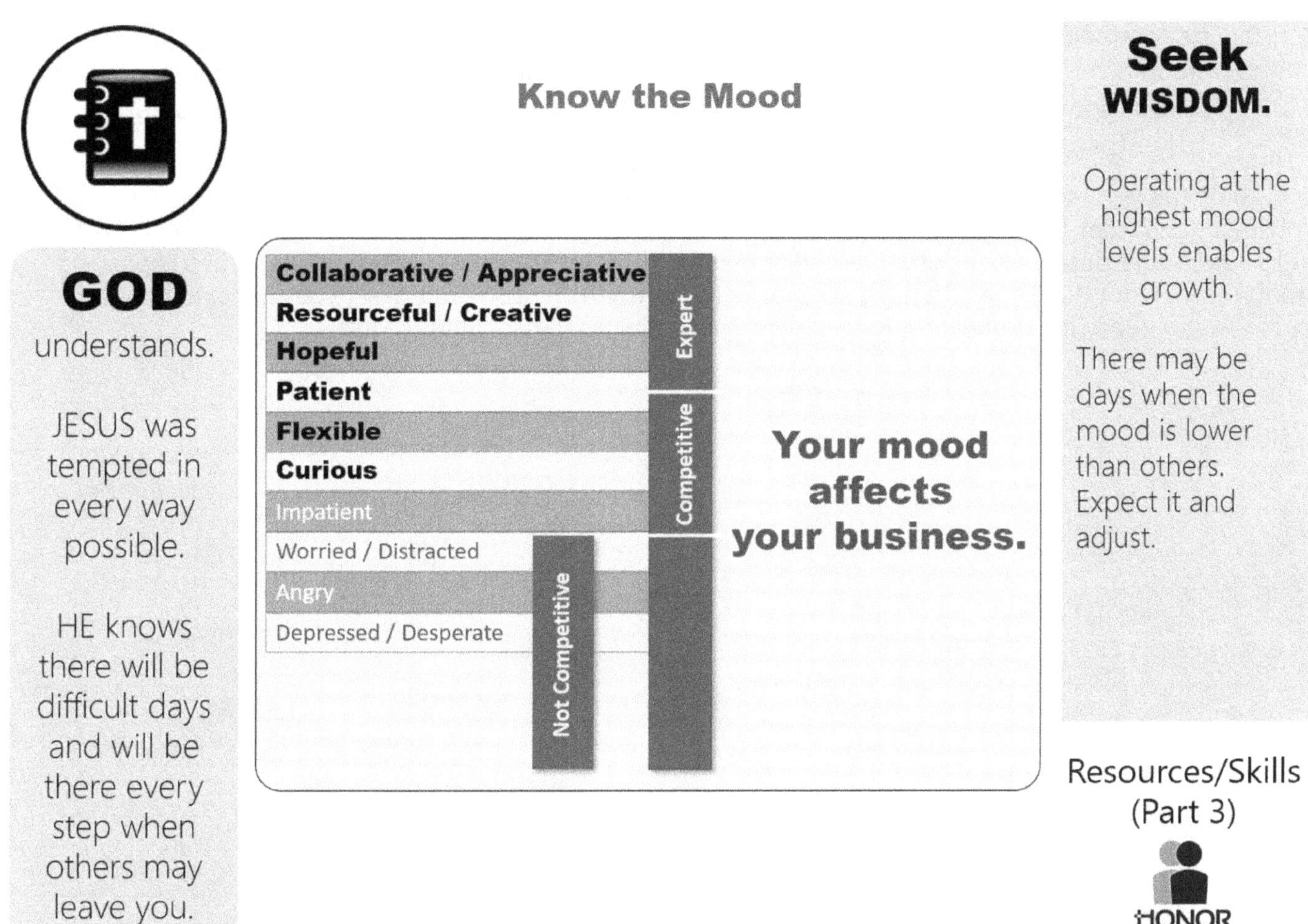

Have you ever met someone who just lights up the room? I mean their very presence makes everyone smile even though they haven't said a word? On the flip-side, have you ever met someone who seems to work bad or negative news into every conversation? Can you recognize when someone is sad?"

Their mood shows up on their face, yours does too. Do you ever assess your mood? What is the mood of your business? The mood of the business will affect the performance of the business. JESUS understand having a bad day.

Expect to operate in the lower moods every now and then, but do not stay there. What do you notice about the image? The higher moods showcase your expertise.

Write down the mood of your business.

1. **Assess your mood.** Before self-examination or quiet time with the LORD, purposefully and honestly check what mood you are in. You cannot always operate at the highest levels of the mood elevator; however, operating at the lowest levels too long can cause exhaustion.
2. **Identify the root.** What is the cause of the lower or higher mood? Higher mood levels enable praise while lower mood levels trigger prayer. Be specific.
3. **Expend healthy energy.** Have grace for yourself, knowing it is all right to be in a lower mood level. The desire is to operate at a higher level. Depending on other humans or a change in situation can cause disappointment. GOD wants you to be insulated with permanent joy, rather than temporary happiness.

By being honest about moods and identifying what put you in this mood, you can give GOD praise or surrender the issue to Him. Giving GOD praise may come harder for those who need to feel wanted and desire attention. Surrender may be difficult for those who have been in a lower mood for an extended time and have no energy to do anything. In either case, you may need help from those skilled in guiding people to operate in higher levels in a godly way.

Exercise 4 – Plan the Mood

Objective: *Plan to use emotional intelligence to plan the mood. See the objective in the previous for the definition of emotional intelligence.*

Adjust the Mood

Seek WISDOM.

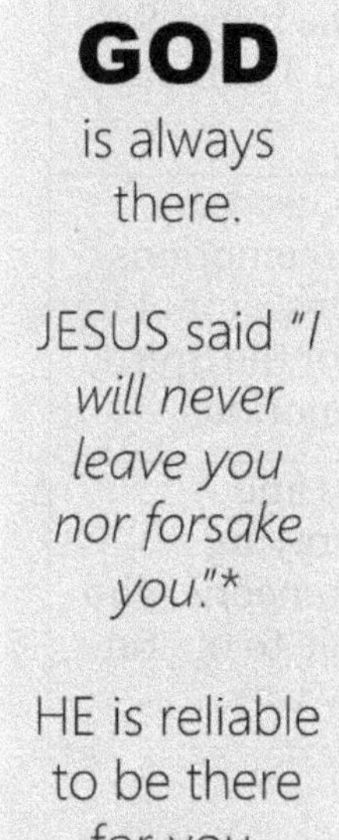

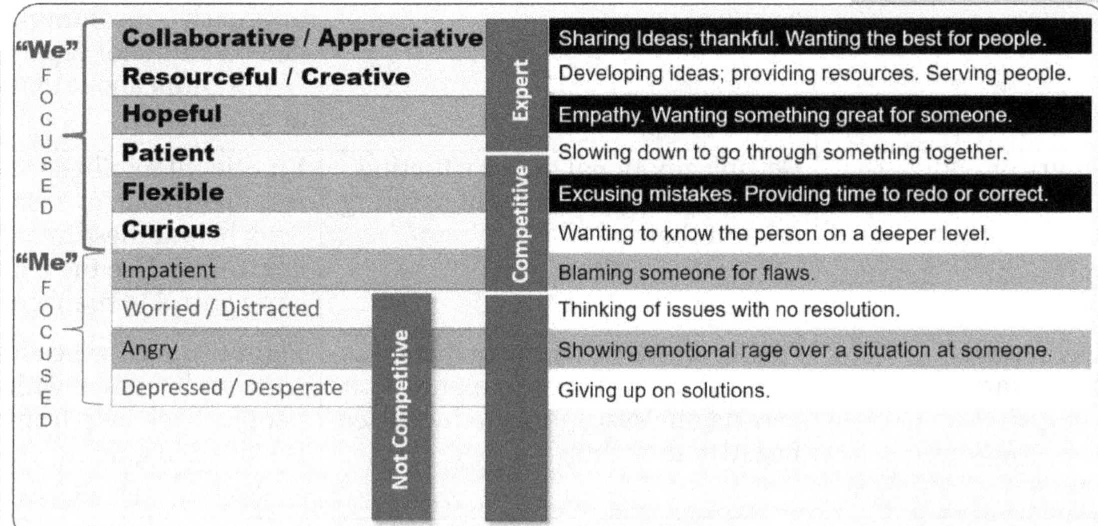

Resources/Skills (Part 4)

Have you ever been let down when you expected someone to come through for you?

GOD's promises are never broken. HE will always be there for you.

Hebrews 13:5 – *Make sure that your character is free from the love of money, being content with what you have; for He Himself has said, "I WILL NEVER DESERT YOU, NOR WILL I EVER FORSAKE YOU,* (NASB) (or) *Let your conduct be without covetousness; be content with such things as you have. For He Himself has said, "I will never leave you nor forsake you.* (NKJV)

GOD never leaves you. This comforting and reassuring message can help you.
Operating at higher mood level is usually "we focused."

Higher Mood	Description
Collaborative/Appreciative	Sharing ideas; thankful; wanting the best for people
Resourceful/Creative	Developing ideas; providing resources; serving people
Hopeful	Empathy; wanting something great for someone
Patient	Slowing down to go through something together with others; taking time to include quality; increase proactive responses
Flexible	Excusing mistakes; providing time to redo or correct
Curious	Wanting to know the person on a deeper level

Operating at lower mood levels can be "me focused."

Lower Mood	Description	Suggestion
Impatient	Blaming others for their flaws does not fix the situation. This can cause the recipient to lose courage.	Seek patience little by little with this person and others. Also, be patient with yourself.
Worried or Distracted	Thinking of issues with no resolution over and over can cause a state of worry.	Schedule a day and time to consider the issue and possible ways to approach a resolution. This way you can rest and not replay the issue. Say, "I will think about that on Thursday at 2:00 PM. "
Angry or Sad	Getting emotional over a situation increases the possibility of harming self or others.	Emotional intelligence is used to rationally control harmful emotions. Seek help if these emotions cannot be controlled. Use the fruit of the Spirit, self-control to manage emotions.
Depressed / Desperate	Giving up on all solutions increases the desire to work or be alone, thus leaving one susceptible to increased negative thoughts.	Fight the urge to be alone and surround yourself with praying people. Seek help from someone who is skilled in guiding people to operate in higher levels in a godly way.

When operating in lower moods, it is imperative to meet with people who can open your eyes to the root cause of the negativity so you can get to a place where you can hear GOD again. For some, it may take a professional who is skilled in bringing people to higher mood levels. For others,, a wise, prayerful person who listens well might be the answer. This is a great time for prayer and surrender to GOD.

When operating in higher mood levels, it is imperative to meet the people to whom GOD wants you to speak, bringing them along, growing them, and serving them. Higher or positive moods bring positive results. This is a great time of praise.

Remember, if you are D-E-A-D (desperate expecting acquisitive dollars) you will always sound dead. We are ALIVE! Appreciative, Loving, Inviting, Victorious, and Everlasting."

Go into your day with a planned mood. Expect difficulties and plan how you will handle them beforehand.

Working in the higher mood levels takes practice. Some days it will be harder than others to work in the higher moods, but return to the image monthly to assess how you are performing in this vital area.

Write activities you will perform to work in the higher mood levels more often.

Who do you like hanging out with in your industry? Are there certain customers you know who will give you some great feedback as well as new ideas? Are there people you are thankful for?"

Fill in the responses to the following questions to set the mood for your business.

Who do I collaborate with?

Who do I appreciate and value?

Who do I go to for ideas and who can I provide ideas to?

What issues should I be more flexible on?

Who do I want to get to know more so eventually I can share my experiences with GOD with them?

Exercise 5 – Learn or Outsource

Objective: *Identify skills to "learn" or "outsource to someone else." You should also* ***value operating the business*** *versus only focusing on providing the product or service. Both must be done.*

We all have a skillset. But most of us would admit that we're not a jack-of-all-trades. Sometimes we need the skill of others to help us in our business. And sometimes, we need to take the time to learn how to develop the skills we need. Identify the skills you are missing and fully understand why you need them.

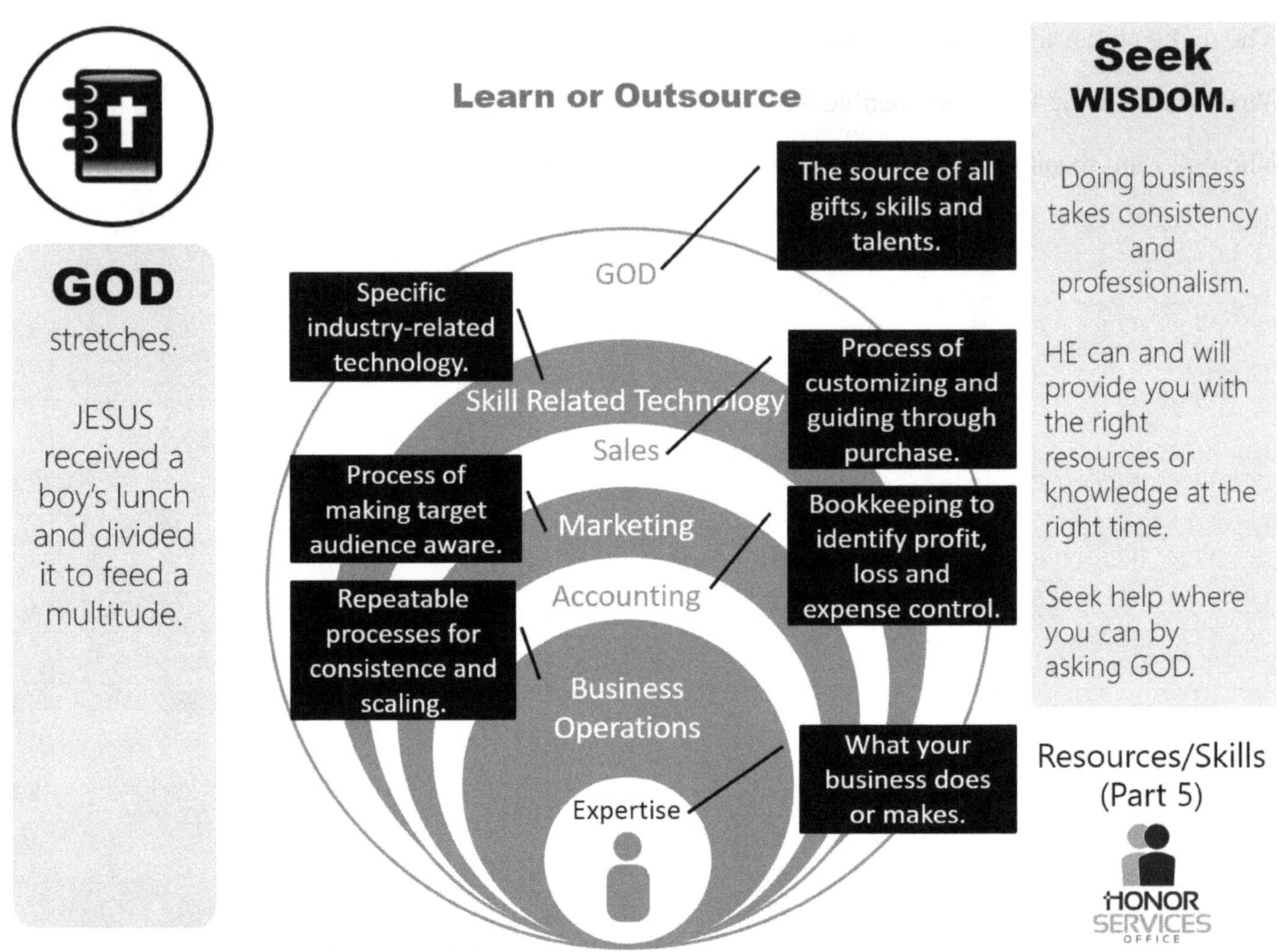

Have you ever made dough or seen it being made?

The baker kneads and then stretches the dough until it is just right. The purpose of stretching the dough is not to tear it apart rather to stretch it to fulfill the purpose for the dish being prepared.

GOD stretches.

Matthew 14:18-21 – 18 *"Bring them here to me," he said. 19 And he directed the people to sit down on the grass. Taking the five loaves and the two fish and looking up to heaven, he gave thanks and broke the loaves. Then he gave them to the disciples, and the disciples gave them to the people. 20 They all ate and were satisfied, and the disciples picked up twelve basketfuls of broken pieces that were left over. 21 The number of those who ate was about five thousand men, besides women and children.*

GOD stretched the resources and multiplied them. HE can do the same for you.

Professionalism increases credibility in your business. But professional services can be expensive. If you do not have the money, then take a moment to quiet down and schedule time to speak to GOD for direction on how to develop you through training or His provision of volunteers to help your business.

1. **Profit brings resources.** Set aside 10% of what you just made on a sale to reinvest in your business. For those who have a lot of bills, try this if you can. Use this set-aside money as funds to eventually get training to develop the missing skill.
2. **Seek one example.** If you have a little money to sow, have a professional show you how to do something—a personalized training. While that person performs the service for you, take notes so you can do the rest yourself. Be honest with that person to set the right expectation.
3. **Barter skills.** Instead of a direct payment, offer a service to someone in lieu of payment. For example, if your business is website development, offer to design the website for someone whose skill is needed for your business.

Skilled help needs prayer too. Always remember, you are dealing with a person GOD loves and prayer always helps. Instead of throwing the work at the professional help, remain involved and engaged. Remove any desire to blame the help and be responsible for the outcome of the skill you outsourced.

GOD stretches in amazing ways.

The purpose of learning a new skill means you will become proficient to, not only do the skill but to perform at a level to achieve high results. Outsourcing means you know about and value the skill, but you are not proficient in performing the skill and need an expert.

A word of caution. Outsourcing does not mean, throw it over the fence and let someone else do it. In other words, you must fully be aware of every aspect of the outsourced skill, so you know how to guide the expert in your customized need.

Many business owners do not know or appreciate other aspects of operating their business and fall into the trap of doing the business, thinking they are operating the business. Now let's walk through each definition. I will not try to convince you to incorporate these skills into your business, rather I am here to make you aware.

You may possesses the skill of doing the business, but let's discuss the skill of operating the business.

Business Operations

The necessary skill to develop written Standard Operating Procedures (SOPs) for yourself and others to follow to perform at a consistent level of excellence. Once you write an SOP, it can live as long as the procedure does not change. Usually changes are made when the procedures written out. Verifying the written steps work as expected.

Let me give you a quick example... A professional bowler may have learned a skill of knocking down bowling pins, therefore she wins tournaments. The skill of operating the professional bowling business may consist of creating and following checklists to ensure bowling supplies, such as powder, shoes, bowling balls for various lane conditions, bandages for wounds, and various cleaning supplies and towels, are available. Transportation for the bowling balls would then be considered and procedures for special handling written.

In this example why would transportation procedures be written down?

One assumption, she may be holding a traveling bowling clinic that she puts on prior to a tournament, which requires demonstration equipment, sign-up and waiver forms.

Write out your standards to be prepared, consistent and efficient.

Now that we know how to consistently operate the business, let's look at the skill of accounting.

Accounting

The necessary skill of keeping track of income, expenses and profit. This is your job, not an accountant. Why? You are the one who gives the accountant the correct information for them to do your taxes and other vital services. But you must be the one who understands all expenses and all income. You must also understand how to control expenses to maximize profit.

Let me go back to the professional bowler example. Let's say she knows how to knock down pins better than most people, so she wins a tournament. How much were her entry fees to the tournament she just won? How much did it cost to transport all of the equipment from one town to the next? How much did it cost to travel, eat and stay overnight? Now, compare that to the winnings to see how much she really earned.

In this example how can the bowler modify her spending if she is not sure if the expense has truly gained her profit? What can she adjust to maximize her winnings?

Now that we have a consistent way to operate the business, and a way to make adjustments to maximize our profits, let's make people aware of our product or service.

Marketing

The necessary skill of making people aware of your product and service to gain their trust in purchasing from your business. Trust is earned, and not easy to acquire. Getting certified helps, but does not prove you know how to operate the business. It only says you know how to do the skill.

Let me go back to the professional bowler business. One feature of the professional bowler's business may be teaching others how to bowl. Her lessons need to be made known to the public. Her back story of how he became a professional bowler, the awards he achieved, and a list of tournaments she won, shows her expertise as a professional bowler. This puts the customer at ease that she can in fact teach bowling.

What content would make you interested in this professional bowler? How could she incorporate a message that displays her faith?

Now that we have a consistent way to operate the business, and a way to make adjustments to maximize our profits, and a way to make people aware of our expertise, let's help the customer make a purchase through our sales process.

Sales

The necessary skill of leveraging a standard process for understanding the customer's needs, developing a deal that provides a "win-win" environment, guiding the person through the order and payment process and following up with promised goods and services and customer service after the purchase.

Let's revisit our professional bowler business. The pro may do a free assessment to identify if a person is a beginner versus someone who has been bowling for a while and needs minor adjustments to their skills. She would develop a customized deal to work with the individual that ranges from 1 to 8 weeks at a price per week. She would then leverage the written standard sign up process she created and guide the new customer through her standard payment process, using her standard pricing.

What can she do to make the customer feel comfortable before the sale happens? Can she provide a video assessment of the problem? What kind of deal can she offer?

Now that we have a consistent way to operate the business, and a way to make adjustments to maximize our profits, and a way to make people aware of our expertise, and a way to help the customer make a purchase through our sales process, let's stay proficient with our industry specific technology.

Understanding Skill Related Technology

The necessary skill of knowing your industry. Most people feel very comfortable learning this because they like "doing" the business. Learn the skill while keeping GOD's word in all aspects of your belief.

Let's go back to the professional bowler example. Knowing about the right type of bowling ball to address problems like oily or dry lanes is important. The pro also needs to know how to repair balls and shoes during a tournament within the rules of the professional bowlers association (PBA). The weight of the ball, and the type of shoe are also important parts to the technology of bowling. The GOD-centered professional bowler has the integrity to follow the rules of the PBA, using her skill to reach others for HIM.

Which association was responsible for the rules and standards to abide by in this example?

Does your business need to adhere to standards or rules that protect the customer?

Check your industry to see if it has rules to follow, certifications needed, or standards to be met.

Now that we have a consistent way to operate the business, and a way to make adjustments to maximize our profits, and a way to make people aware of our expertise, and a way to help the customer make a purchase through our sales process, and we have stayed proficient with our industry specific technology, let's look to the one who gave us the skill in the first place.

Knowing GOD is the necessary skill of knowing where your skills, opportunities and triumphs come from. HE may expand the business to bring on other professional bowlers and since there are written standards, there is no confusion to what they should be doing. One last item. HE taught you all of this to serve HIS kingdom. Somehow, HE wants the professional to reach people for HIM. This needs to be the most import addition to the business.

Now it's your turn. Which skills will you learn or outsource? Can GOD grow the business large enough to need these roles? Yes.

Review the image at the beginning of exercise 5 to identify areas they need to outsource or learn. Write the skills you will learn or outsource. The goal is to operate the business, not just perform the expertise.

If you see a vital skill you do not possess, do you automatically say 'I don't understand the missing skill, so I don't need the skill?

What factors can you think of that cause a business to fail?

Some people may answer lack of money. This is far from the truth. A successful business starts with the vision from GOD who will guide them to people with a need. Fulfilling the needs of people with simple solutions and strong business practices enables GOD-centered success.

How long do you think it will take to start or grow a business? Remember in "Remove the Trash" what a hurried business will do?

Many entrepreneurs don't have time to develop good business practices, but have plenty of time to go out of business.

If you are missing a vital skill, will you ignore it or add this to your wish list to build a feature of your business?

How will the gap in a specific skill affect your timeline?
Write out a prayer for patience, wisdom and resources. Pray for bravery to ask for help.

Let me give you some encouragement. "GOD will provide." HE is the one who has you in business for HIS purpose. HE will equip you with the right skills or people. Also, pray for the helpers GOD sends to you. They are people too.

If you don't finish this exercise today, then complete this over the next week.

Exercise 6 – Identify Symptoms of Missing Skills

Objective: *Recognize gaps in your business processes to develop a plan to address those gaps.*

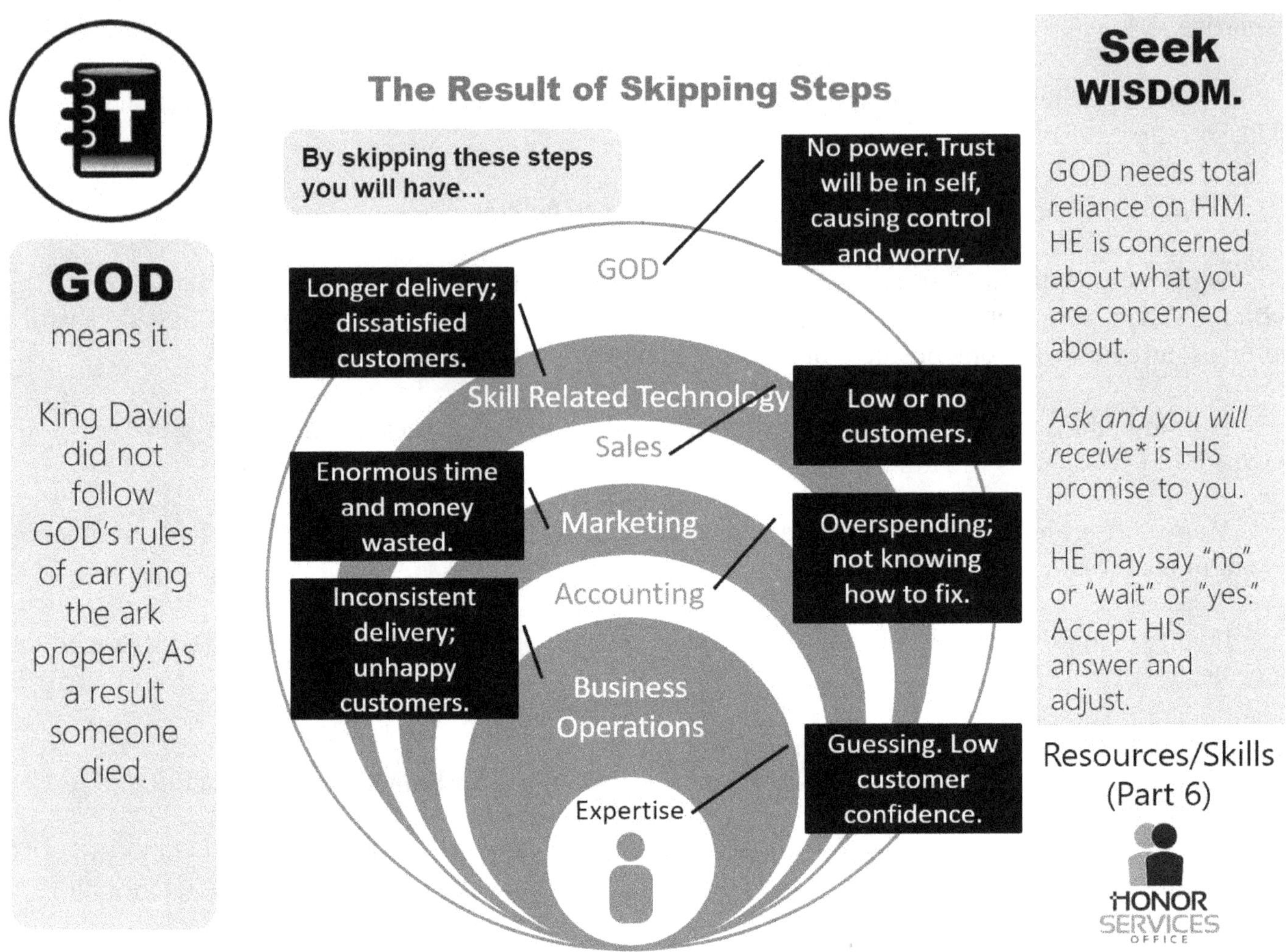

Have you experienced getting the right thing at the right time? Was it a ride from a neighbor when you were walking in the rain? Did you get help picking up something heavy you could not lift? What help, other than money, have you received at the right time that you did not expect?

GOD wants to help. Ask HIM for the missing skills instead of ignoring them.

Matthew 7:7 – *Ask, and it will be given to you; seek, and you will find; knock, and it will be opened to you.*

Approaching missing skills as an opportunity rather than a barrier enables the GOD-centered business owner to meet many people of all walks of life. Not everyone has your best interest so be wise while seeking help. "Behold, I send you out as sheep in the midst of wolves. Therefore be wise as serpents and harmless as doves" (Matthew 10:16). Getting help is important, but getting the right help is imperative. For example, Jesus' disciples asked GOD to help them choose another disciple when one was lost (see Acts 1:15-26).

1. **Pray and ask GOD.** Seek GOD's answer to your skill gap. Be open to whomever HE sends or sends you to as a probable resource.

2. **Get references.** When outsourcing, ask for three references and follow up on the references. Check on the person's work so you can be sure he will provide the quality you are looking for.
3. **Pay your bills.** Immediately pay your workers and other resource people the agreed-upon price. You are worth your wages and so are they. Thank GOD for having the cash to be able to pay bills.

Let's ask for vital skills. Here are some symptoms you may experience that can be addressed by GOD sending you the right resource at the right time.

Guessing Expertise.

If you are not the expert in the business you are running, the result will be a low confidence in your business. Customers are very savvy. They research and compare. Take time to know your industry. Ask GOD for patience to learn the skills needed to be viewed as the expert.

Has anyone experienced a business that did not know what they were supposed to know?

Let's discuss a symptom of not having standard operations.

Inconsistent Delivery.

If you do things different every time without following a standard, your customers will be reluctant to refer you. Customers like to refer businesses to other people if they can know what to expect. If one customer is happy with the results and the other unhappy, then address the inconsistency by finding out what went wrong. Ask GOD to open your eyes to what is inconsistent in your business.

Have you eaten at a restaurant and enjoyed the food so you returned to that restaurant a second time? What happens if you do not enjoy the food the second time? Will you return?

Do you have a phone that can take pictures? Can some of you use pictures to show the steps you need to provide the necessary consistency? What other examples can you follow to ensure consistency?

A relationship with your customers helps. Some business owners want to skip the relationship part to make a lot of money. Be brave enough to ask the customer if you delivered consistently. Be transparent when there is a problem.

Let's discuss a symptom of not having accounting that tracks expenses.

Do you have a credit card? When you first got the credit card, did you pay off the balance? Did you ever go through the credit card statement, looking for unnecessary expenses?

Without accounting practices that regularly looks at expenses, you can overspend without knowing how to fix it. Account for how much you paid out in expenses and compare that to how much income you made. Subtract your expenses from your income to determine if you are profitable. Ask GOD for cost effective, profitable ways to doing your business while producing quality.

What happens to businesses when they get desperate for money?

Let's discuss a symptom of not having an expert message when marketing.

Can you recognize a gimmick? Did you ever see a product or service that seemed too good to be true? What happens when many people find out this product or service is a gimmick rather than a real solution?

Marketing with gimmicks, catch phrases or the wrong information to wrong audience can lead to a negative reputation. Without saying the right words to the right audience, you will waste a lot of time and money. Ask GOD for a message that shows you as the expert and HIM as the provider of that expertise.

What happens to your business when people expose your lies or exaggerations?

Let's discuss a symptom of having an aggressive or absent Sales Process.

Have you ever been pressured to do something you did not want to do and later regretted you did it? Have you ever been pressured to buy something you were not really interested in, yet the sales person was really convincing and aggressive?

Aggressive selling is usually done poorly and with the wrong motive. The pressured customer may purchase, but will resent the process and may complain about the experience. Guilting or coercing people into purchasing will eventually cause customers to leave.

Secondly, if you do not have a sales process, then customers may become confused to how you can work specifically with them. Some business owners make the "build it and they will come" mistake. Customers need education. They need steps, solutions, explanations and confidence you can deliver quality. Ask GOD to guide you to the right audience for HIS purpose first, then HE will provide the increase and a process for handling HIS people.

Have you ever been part of a group that cares for you? If not, now you do with us. How does it feel to belong?

Make your customers feel welcome, loved and engaged.

Let's discuss a symptom of using outdated business practices.

Using archaic, outdated methods

May result in slower or harmful delivery of a solution to your customers. Check to see if your industry requires more up to date methods. Be careful not to get on the "bleeding edge", in other words, using methods that are tested but have not proven that the solution is one that will remain. Use tested -- information, processes, technology, software and hardware. Ask GOD for the timing and means to change.

Can you imagine life before the smartphone? How about life before the automobile?

Be comfortable with change. You do not have to jump into change right away. Change at the pace GOD wants you to. Sometimes HE may want you to change your business practices when you are not ready and sometimes HE may want you to use discernment to lag on the change.

Let's discuss a symptom of making decisions without consulting GOD.

Doing things without consulting GOD

Can result in attempts to control circumstances out of your control. When something goes wrong, worry emerges. Ask GOD for direction, contentment, patience and purpose.

What does success look like?

What does success look like to GOD through your business?

When GOD puts you in business, it is not to fail but to successfully bring people to HIM.

Place your trust in the LORD.

I use caution when saying this... not every skill is needed for every business to be successful. While that may sound relieving to some, use caution when deciding what you will do without..

Write the skills you will do without and the reason.

If you don't finish the exercises today, then complete this over the next week.

GOD-Centered Business: A Foundational Framework to Grow with Resilience

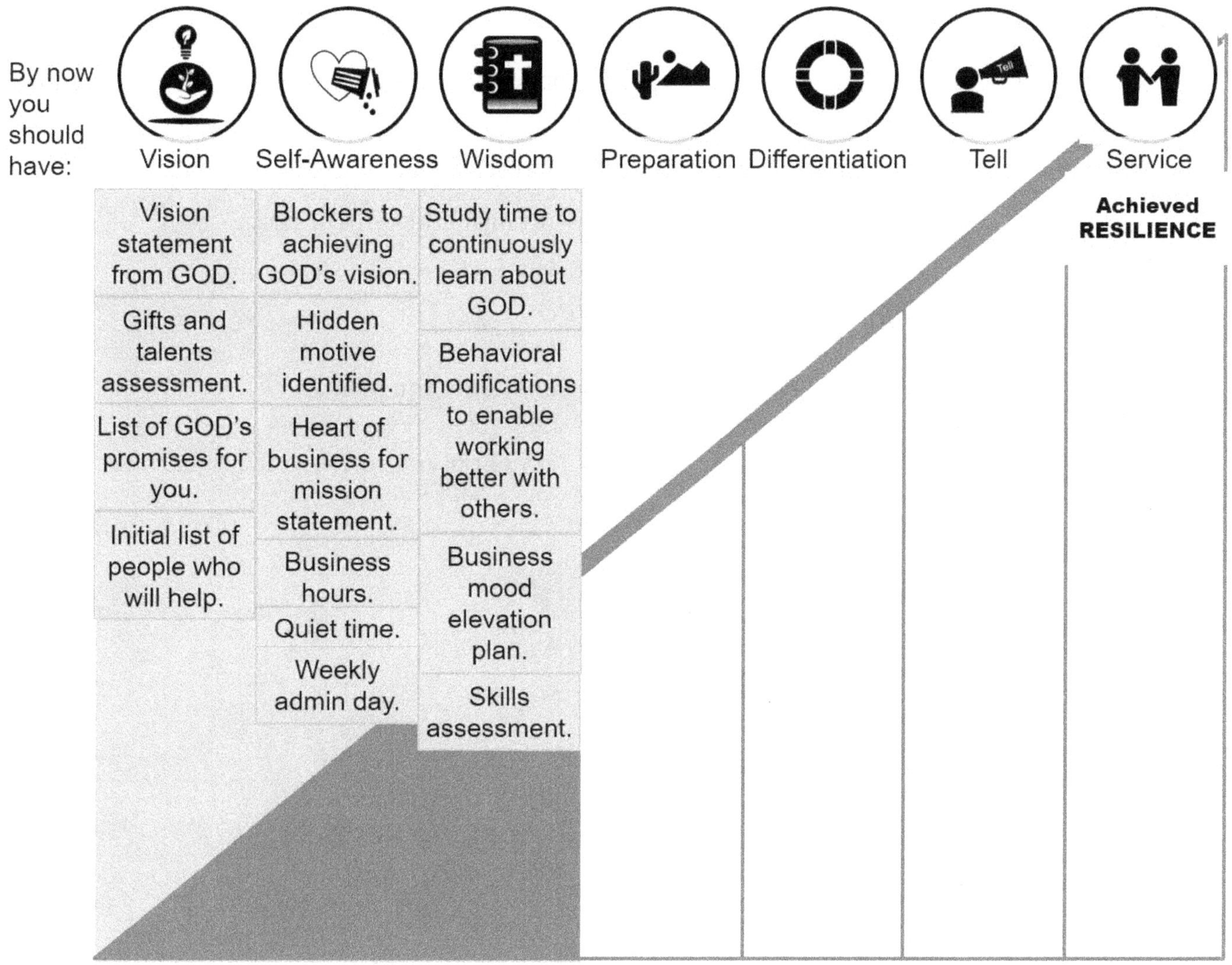

By now you should have:

Vision	Self-Awareness	Wisdom	Preparation	Differentiation	Tell	Service
Vision statement from GOD.	Blockers to achieving GOD's vision.	Study time to continuously learn about GOD.				Achieved RESILIENCE
Gifts and talents assessment.	Hidden motive identified.	Behavioral modifications to enable working better with others.				
List of GOD's promises for you.	Heart of business for mission statement.	Business mood elevation plan.				
Initial list of people who will help.	Business hours.	Skills assessment.				
	Quiet time.					
	Weekly admin day.					

SEEK.

Study **E**xcellent **E**nriching **K**nowledge.

For your homework, spend a day or a week, if you can, having someone else do some or "all" of your work (even if it is housework). (You cannot complain or correct).

Ask for any prayer requests and dismiss in prayer. Remember to use your personal journals found at the end of this book.

WARNING

- Avoid giving up too soon just because a skill is missing.
- Seek feedback from strangers if self-taught on a skill.
- Slow down! Hurrying will cause a drop in mood which will affect your results.

NEXT STEPS

- Establish a regular quiet time where you seek GOD for His perspective on your life and business; where you spend time in prayer and praise.

- List the minor adjustments needed to help you become a stronger leader.
- List mood behaviors to facilitate working better with others.
- Document available and missing skills and a prayer for the gaps.

PRAYER

- Pray for wisdom to be the leader GOD wants you to be.
- Pray for an understanding of the skills you may be missing.
- Pray for the right resources to be brought into your life at the right time

Chapter 4 – Go to the Desert: Planning/Preparation

"Is it too noisy to hear GOD?"

"What are the priorities?"

"What should be tested before going to market?"

Go to the Desert preparation (Week 4)

Greet participants and remind them of the goal to use have someone do some or all of their work.

Did you identify areas you will gain skills on or outsource? : If you were with us last week (or whatever your time frame), did any of you try the exercise where you allowed someone to do your work without correcting them or complaining? Was it hard to let go of telling them what to do and how to do it? What did you learn? How did it feel to watch someone do your work?

The need for quiet

Move to a quiet location away from responsibilities, when you are not in a class setting. This chapter will need as much quiet time as you can possibly get. Turn off all electronic devices and go to a place where you can think over the next week. Some may choose a place by the water, others a quiet room.

Introduce the Go to the Desert Chapter

Going to the desert is a place of preparation and planning. Valuing God's preparation is what's important. In this chapter of the class, we will walk through a case study as an example for you to do with your own business.

There are 11 exercises and 1 case study.
Ready? Be prepared to get prepared.

Go to the Desert Objective

We are in part 4 of the framework. This methodology teaches you what to do to prepare your business for resilience. You will learn; how to define features of your business from the vision God gave you. These features will eventually end up on your website and other advertisement channels. You will also use them to standardize how you operate the business.

Explain Group Reviews of Participant's Business

From here on out we will work as a group on one or more aspects of your business.

Go to the Desert Prayer

Pray:
For participants to have patience in preparation.
That GOD will give the participants purpose.
For guidance in leading HIS people.
For participant's revisions to go well.

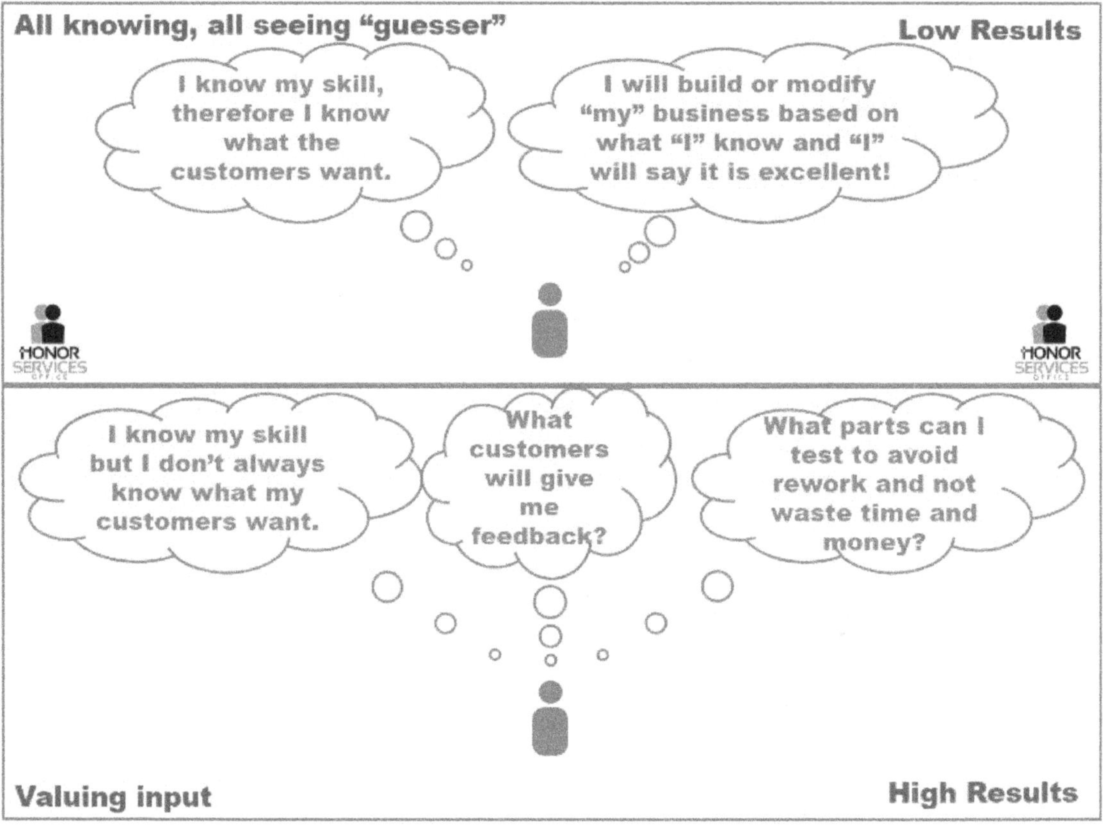

Have you ever bought the wrong thing from the store and had to return it? Did you avoid going back to the store because it is easier to just keep the item?

It probably depends on how much you spent on the item, right? What if the product or service you bought was not what you had in mind or did not meet your expectations? Would you ask for your money back? Let's try to prevent this from happening in your business.

Value input from customers and employees. The GOD-centered business owner looks for feedback to avoid costly mistakes, protecting precious time.

Let's prepare ourselves with a plan.

Go to the Desert to Plan and Prepare

Objective: *To value quiet time with the LORD.*

Moses spent time in the desert before GOD gave him the huge responsibility of leading (see Exodus 3). Moses learned to hear from GOD in the middle of a quiet place where there was nothing to desire. Many entrepreneurs despise quieting down to plan, no matter how long or short the planning session may be.

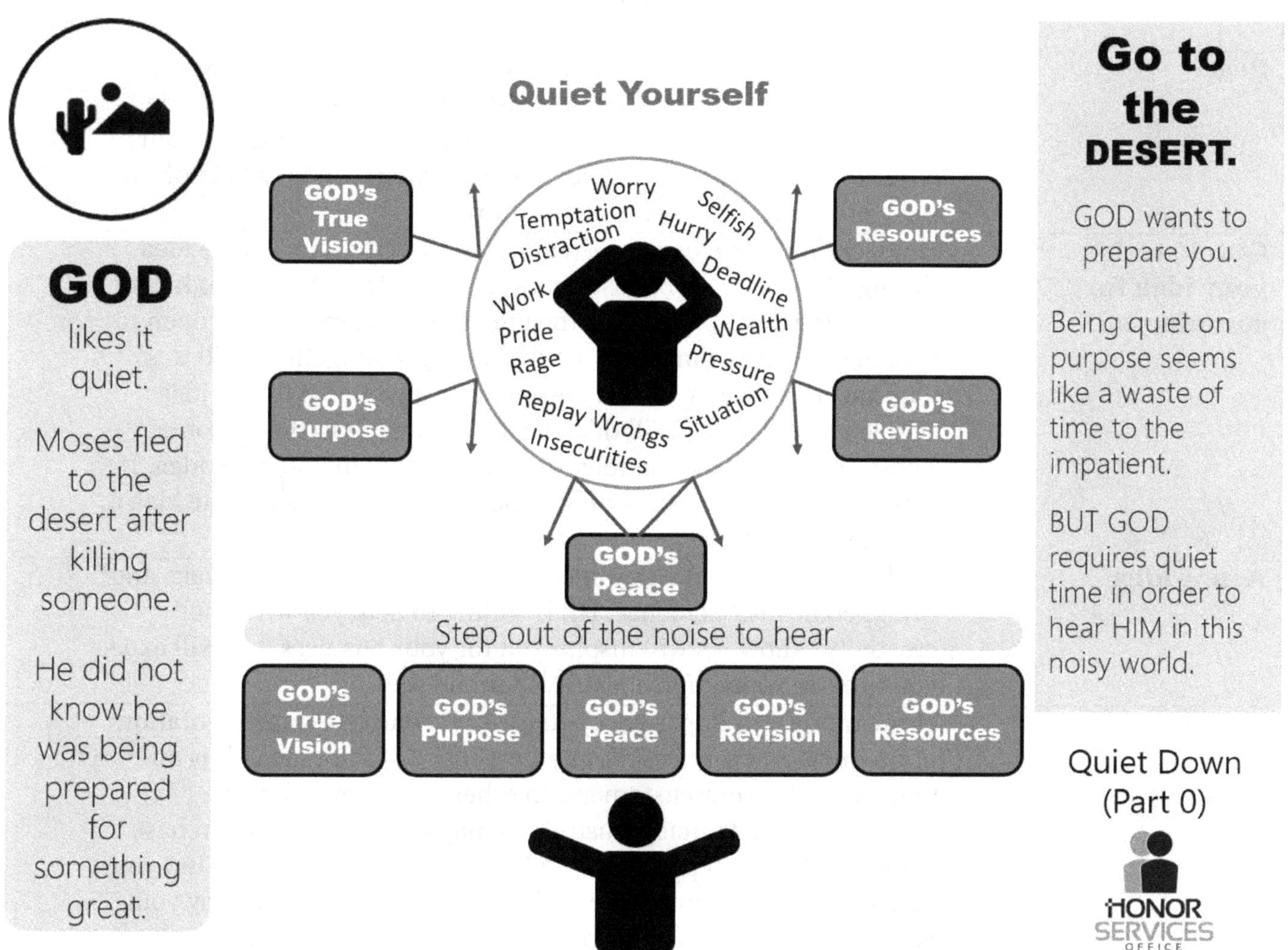

Have you ever been in a place that was too noisy to think? Was noisy place also fast paced? Did you feel unprepared for the fast pace, noisy place?

Quiet Down on Purpose

Go to a place regularly where you can and spend time with GOD in the quiet. Try to remember that your life is GOD's and not your own. Operate your quiet time like a tithe. For every ten days you work, spend one with GOD. This would equate to one month and one week spent specifically with GOD.

Is this even possible? Yes, but if you cannot take large chunks of time with GOD, take smaller ones. Try a few half-hour chunks a day, and maybe an hour more here and there.

Seven Things to Ask GOD

Ask for . . .

Direction. "What do YOU want me to do?	Be honest. You can say "I would like to do..." during this conversation with the LORD, but give HIM the right to say "No" or "Wait" or "Yes."
Clarity	HE is the only one who can handle complex concepts. HE enjoys clearing up confusion. Yet it takes quiet to hear HIM.
Peace	Schedule time to think about issues rather than letting the worry over them paralyze you every day. GOD is willing to show you the source of the worries and also to take control of the situation. This requires your willingness to surrender, letting GOD take hold of the issue or person you are trying to control.
GOD to test your idea for soundness.	Hold loosely every idea you dream of until GOD validates the idea through the feedback of customers HE sends to test your product or service. Being willing to have the idea tested means you are open to revising the idea to improve it or dropping it altogether. Will this idea harm anyone? Will this idea exclude anyone? Will this idea enable an addiction? Will this idea fail to benefit to the customer? These are only a few examples of allowing GOD to break the idea. If you answered "yes" to any of the questions, then consider the idea a fail and move on.
A new idea	Feel blocked without a new idea? GOD is the creator. HE speaks and things come into existence. HE is willing to help you with your creativity. Know HE will inspire you for your business, but will expect you to carry yourself in a loving, thankful way.
Patience	Desperation and impatience can cause incomplete implementation of products and services. Your emergency does not mean it is an emergency for your customers. In other words, even if you desperately need money, customers may not be ready to purchase from you. GOD will provide. HE always has and always will. But your idea needs to be strong, thorough, and worthy of purchase by your customers. Desire the best for them. It may take a little more patience to do what is right versus cutting corners.
The right audience	Some will serve many and some will serve few based on the gifts GOD has given. Asking GOD for the right audience means that when HE brings people to you, accept their honest feedback to improve your product or service. GOD will also provide you with methods of reaching the number of people meant for you to reach.

Planning time with GOD should be prioritized first. Desperate, greedy feelings make people throw planning time out the window. Think of it this way: If a driver spent all her time driving and no time filling the car up with fuel, she would eventually run out of gas.

1. **Invisible things are important.** GOD wants you to see HIM in everything, small and large. By quieting down in a place with no television, internet, or other distractions, GOD can open your eyes to the invisible things HE is working on that are necessary for your journey.
2. **Stewardship starts small.** GOD calls you to treat a small group of people like you would if you had infinite resources for them. In other words, you should always give them your best. Rather than complaining and begging GOD for more people to "buy your stuff," thank GOD for those who will.
3. **Practice makes perfect.** During this planning time with GOD, practice with your product or service, getting it ready for the masses. Would you like to get in an airplane that has not been tested? Before starting the business, build a prototype of your product or service and try it out on a small group of people. Take their feedback seriously and make adjustments. This will take the patience for which you asked GOD.

Building a Plan to Execute Now

When people hear the word *plan*, some get scared, because they don't know where to start. They also think planning will delay the act of making money. Using Agile Adopted for Business (AFB), the GOD-centered business owner can plan short-work efforts that deliver a minimal viable product (MVP).

What is Agile AFB? It is a **community** method of getting things done. That's it. This is the division of tasks into phases of work and frequent reassessment and adaptation of plans.

Write your discussion with GOD.

Hearing GOD

How do you know you are hearing from God and not yourself? For me... (Use your own testimony).

For some of you, this may be your first time trying to hear God. Here is how I know God is speaking to me. Usually He speaks to me through reading His word. I read the entire Bible, a few verses each day, until I complete the whole thing. It takes about 7 years. This provides me with correction and direction.

It is uncanny how the situation of the day matches my daily reading. God also confirms what I heard from Him through people I interact with. They may mention the very scripture I was reading. Sometimes the situation I just read about is identical to the situation of the day. This happens often.

Another way I hear God is when He tells me to do something I really don't want to do, but I know it will benefit or grow His kingdom. I may want to treat myself to a tasty meal, BUT God may say, "give the money to that person over there." I may pout and ask "Do I have to?" I feel great when I obey.

He may also "Apologize" especially when I know I'm right when arguing or fighting someone. He then may tell me not to fight in the first place.

He tells me to "let go" when I want to control and "trust" when I want to know everything. These are all examples of me listening to God. It has never steered me wrong. God told me to stay away from porn. When I looked at porn, I liked it, a lot. From pre-teen to adult, I looked at it every now and then. BUT God simply said "I need you to do a greater work and lust is in the way." "Sigh" I let go, even though I didn't want to. I mean, this sin was easy to hide, BUT God wanted me to worship in spirit and truth.

After listening and obeying for years, I became accustomed to hearing from Him. I grew to discern when I hear my desires versus when the Holy Spirit is guiding me. My self-imposed timeframes soon disappeared. My false expectations of God melted away. That is when He spoke to me in a more powerful way. The participants of this class are here because I listened to God. I hope God is speaking to you through this class.

Cake and Pastry Business Case Study Overview

Let's walk through a case study. You will learn:

1. How to write a vision statement also known as an Epic
2. How to break the vision into smaller parts, also known as "what you sell"
3. How to translate "what you sell", also known as "Features of Business" from "User Stories" or customer's needs
4. How to get feedback on what you build, also known as your product or service
5. What parts of the business you should test

We will take time to walk through an example vision to prompt discussion for your company."

Before getting started with the case study, become familiar with the concepts of epics, features of business and user stories located in exercises 1 – 4 of this chapter.

Exercise 1 – Understand Agile AFB

Objective: *To begin using the terminology as described in the Agile AFB methodology to transform the business.*

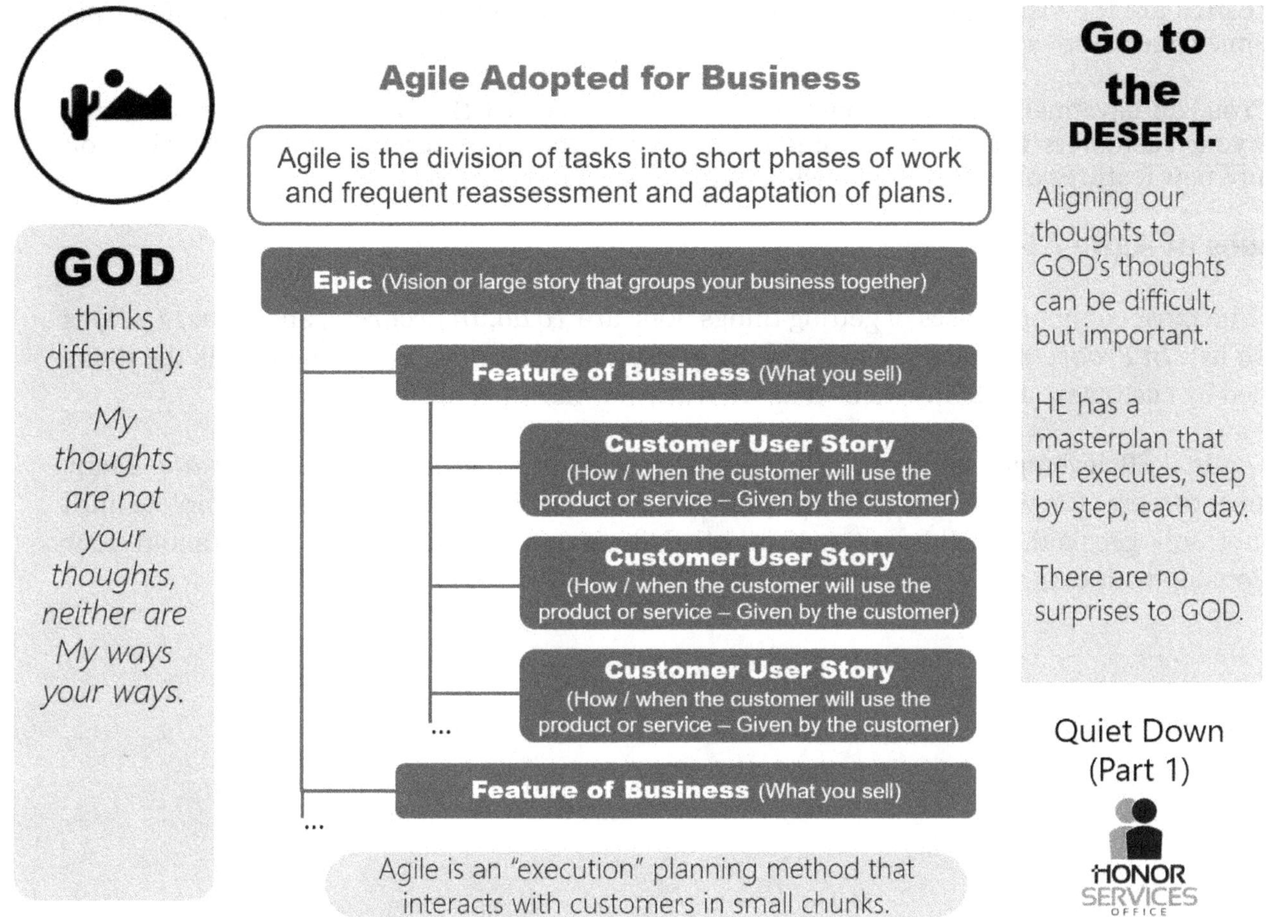

Name something pleasant you are doing today that you could not have imagined you would be doing. Is it driving? Is it drawing something? How about playing a game? What led you to what you are doing? Was it easy to learn? What problems did you overcome? Can GOD handle large problems? How about small ones? How about medium problems?

Can GOD give you something to do that is larger than the vision you had for yourself?

GOD wants you to align your thoughts to His when you make plans.

Isaiah 55:8 -9 *"For My thoughts are not your thoughts,*
Nor are your ways My ways," says the Lord.
"For as the heavens are higher than the earth,
So are My ways higher than your ways,
And My thoughts than your thoughts.

GOD has plans for you that you would never be able to conceive. Let's look at a methodology that includes listening to Him. Agile Adopted For Business (AFB) is an execution planning method that interacts with customers to fulfill their needs by building valuable business products and services in small chunks.

Review the image above to understand the structure of breaking the vision GOD gave you down into something you will sell to your customer. Note that you are seeking input from multiple customers to understand their needs and how they will use your product or service.

Agile is a proven technology industry methodology that has been adopted to enable micro-businesses reach success in a shorter period of time.

Epics are the vision from GOD. Multiple Features of Business make up an **Epic**. Multiple Customer User Stories make up a Feature of Business.

You can have many epics (visions) and many **Features of Business** which include many ways your customers would like to interact with your product or service. Agile AFB helps you capture new features of your business when rapid change in your industry occurs.

Phases of Agile AFB

The most common phases of getting things done are *To do*, *In progress,* and *Done*. *To Do* is a wish list. *In Progress* means the items being worked on right now, and *Done* means the items verified by customers as quality items that are ready for many people to purchase.

Agile AFB leverages additional short-phased principles: *Growth* and *Perpetuate*. Many business owners stop when they build the product or service. But Agile AFB is not complete until you not only get paid, but the customer is satisfied enough to listen to you speak about your relationship with GOD.

Exercise 2 – Understand the Parts of Agile AFB

Objective: *To create the Minimal Viable Product (MVP) as it relates to building operational processes of the business.*

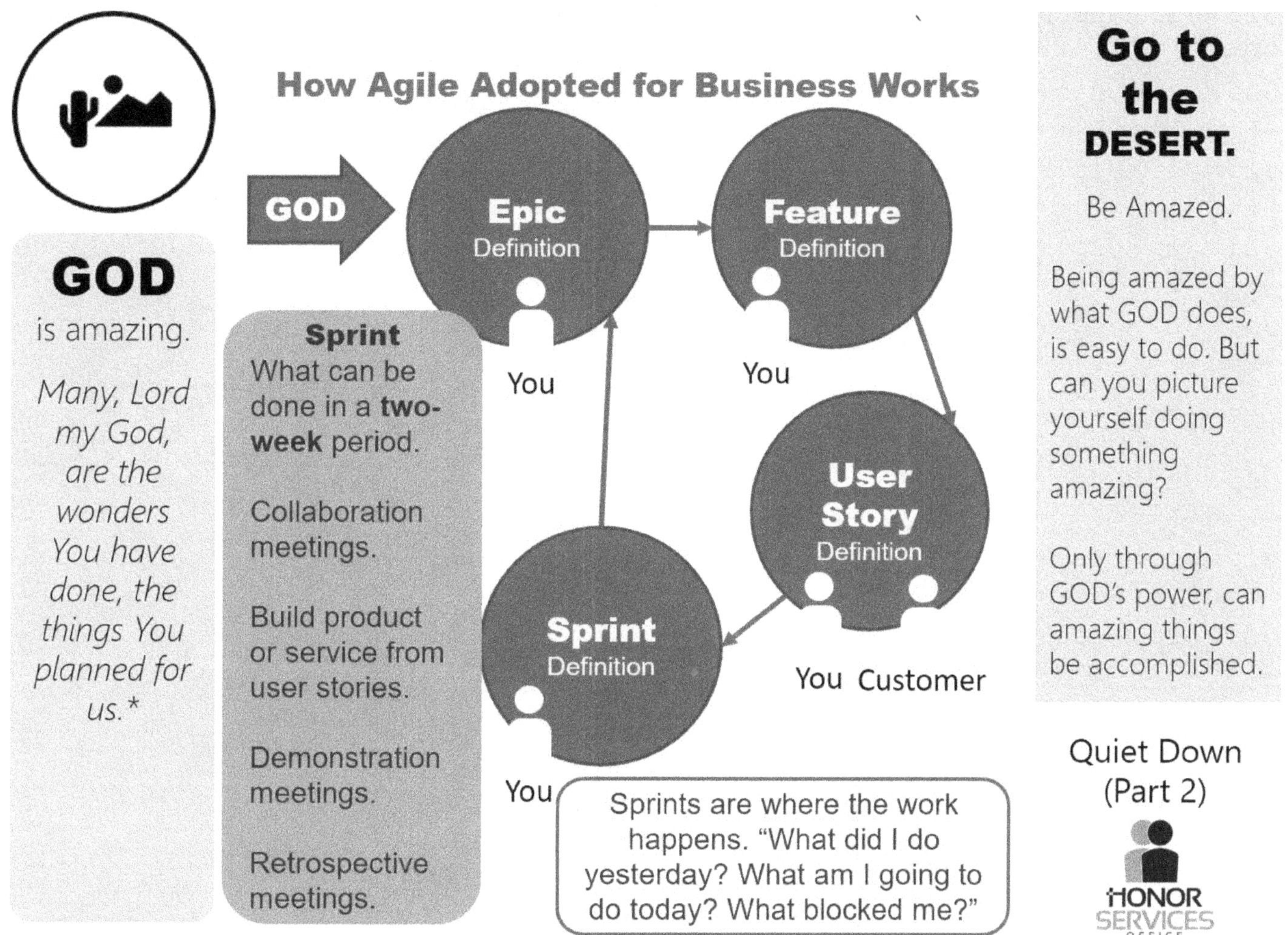

Let's pretend it's raining outside. How would you prepare to go out in the rain? What are your assumptions?

Did you say you need 11 umbrellas, one for yourself and 10 for your neighbors? Is GOD amazing every day to you? Do you give Him credit for more than controlling weather and nature? Be amazed by GOD and His plans for you and your business. Open your eyes to opportunities He puts in front of you, especially when situations seem difficult.

Psalm 40:5 – *Many, LORD my God, are the wonders you have done, the things you planned for us. None can compare with you; were I to speak and tell of your deeds, they would be too many to declare.* (NIV)

Being amazed with GOD is the beginning of HIM being able to do amazing things through you and your business.

Review the image on this page to understand the iterative nature of Agile AFB. Instead of building everything all at once, you will build small, valuable pieces enabling quick use, instead of waiting for all the work to be done.

Have a mindset that uses a "wish list" to document ideas that come from GOD, so they can prioritize the work to be done now or in the future. Work on small parts until you have something "viable" to sell. This will be known as the Minimal Viable Product (MVP).

Having verified products and services is not enough. Growing and perpetuating the vision GOD has given for your business is the goal. This is done by taking HIS large vision and breaking it into smaller parts.

Exercise 3 – Choose to Work Smaller

Objective: *To value planning.*

GOD

says "Peace be still."

When GOD wants to show HIS might, HE tells us to "sit" or "stand still."

Myth	Result
Too busy to plan	Will cost four times as much and take twice as long
If I stop working to plan I will not make money.	Will have serious long gaps with no income
I'll just wing it.	Will have many flaws and failures resulting in refunds or dissatisfied customers

Go to the DESERT.

Ideas need up to seven revisions to get it ready for customer consumption.

The disciples spent years working with JESUS. HE prepared them for something much greater than expected.

Quiet Down (Part 3)

Have you ever made a mistake because you were moving too fast? Did you lose something? Did something break? Were you stressed out?

GOD wants you to have peace and confidence in HIM and HIS timing. A confident person does not have to rush when others are rushing. Remember, **people who do not have time to plan to succeed have plenty of time to fail.** Working smaller will help you get started writing the Epic, aka vision.

Review the myths on this illustration. No one will remember if your business started two months later, but they will remember if the product or service is shoddy or poorly made. Planning saves time and money. Use the analogy of jumping in the car with no direction and just driving until the person runs out of gas. It is better to not only know the destination but also know the route and stops along the way.

Finally, guessing cost more money because of flaws and misses. People who fail to break their vision into smaller, executable chunks are doomed to failure. They will bite off more than they can handle and not deliver the quality their customers expect.

Work in small chunks and deliver the minimal viable product (MVP). Customers will be happy to get quality products and services a few at a time rather than in a big blast.

Exercise 4 – Get the Vision

Objective: To begin listening to GOD for all your plans.

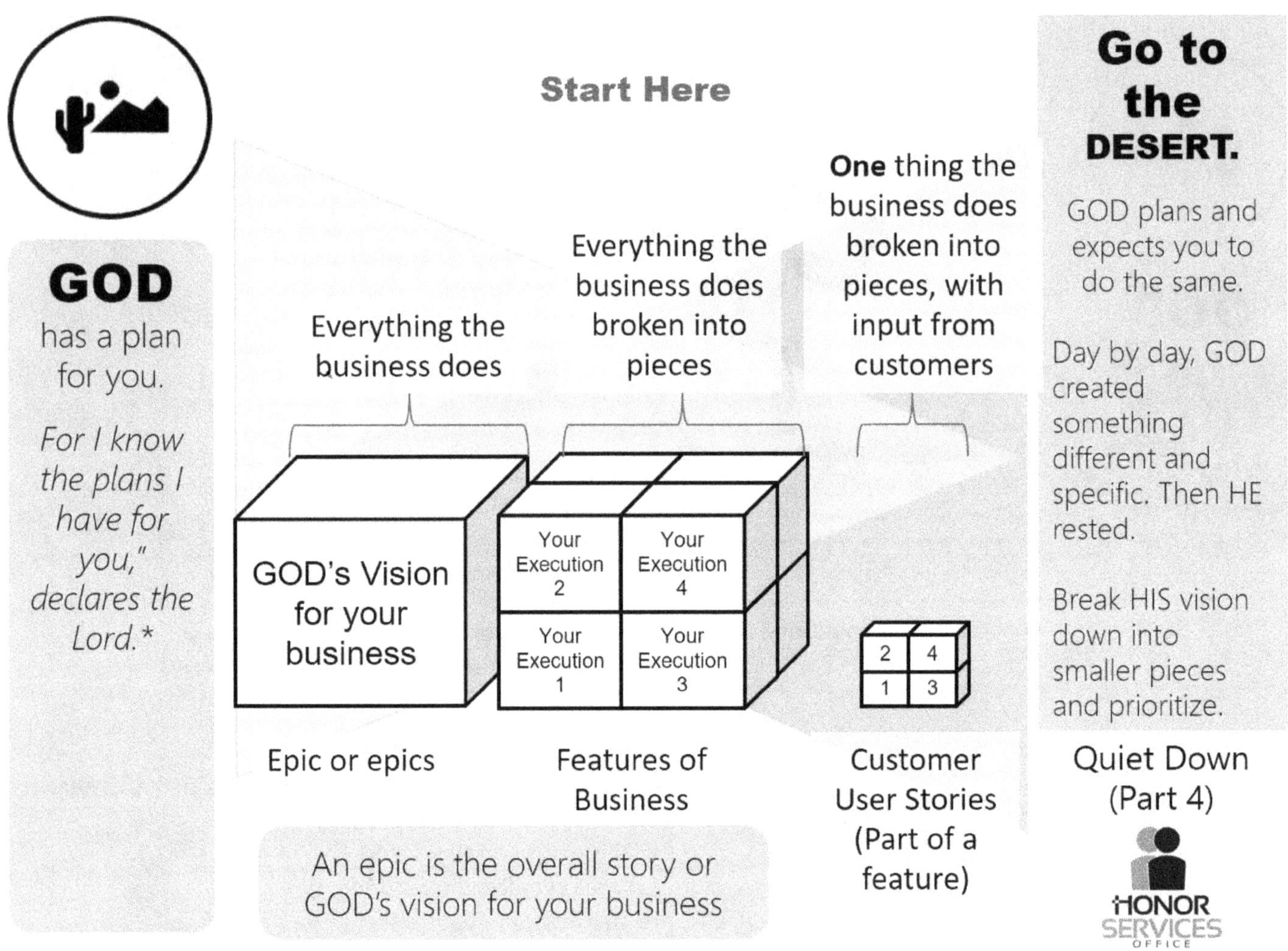

What is your purpose in life? Is it simply to have more stuff? Has life been so hard, you simply want it to be easier?

GOD has a plan for you and your business.

Jeremiah 29:11 - *For I know the plans I have for you," declares the LORD, "plans to prosper you and not to harm you, plans to give you hope and a future.* (NIV)

GOD's plan for you is amazing according to the scripture. Instead of being overwhelmed, listen to HIM and start doing what HE says.

Let's do a case study. You will need the vision from GOD you wrote in Exercise 1 of the Dream Bigger chapter. You will need your target audience you wrote down in Exercise 2 of the same chapter. All set? Let's begin the case study.

In the case study, we will walk from the inception of an idea all the way through building operational components and finally to marketing. I will guide you through examples. Take many notes and ask questions. There are 15 parts to the case study. There is a lot of material to cover. The first thirteen examples will take you from the vision GOD gives you all the way to defining the features of your business.

You will then understand how to do this yourself. We will then finish up with the user story case study which has two examples.

This case study is only an example. GOD may speak to you differently. Let's begin.

Cake and Pastry Business Case Study – From Epic to Feature

1. *The Process Starts with Giving Thanks*

In this example, the business owner starts by giving thanks to GOD by saying "Dear LORD, thank YOU for giving me the ability to bake and decorate pastries. Thank YOU for being able to drive, teach people and write. What do YOU want me to do with these talents?"

What are your observations? *When you write out thanks to GOD, circle the talents you can see use in business.*

Why does GOD want you in business? *HE wants ambassadors who want to make disciples of JESUS.*

2. *Pray for GOD's Response*

In this example, the business owner prays to GOD, asking "LORD, please show me what YOU want me to do with the talents YOU gave me."

The HOLY SPIRIT answers by giving an urge to reach people for HIM through a local bakery that sells cakes.

What are your observations? *Urges and desires need to be filtered through prayer and GOD's word.*

After communicating with GOD through quiet time, continue to clarify, asking "Is this what YOU want me to do? Ask for confirmation.

3. *Look For Empathy, Desire and Passion*

In this example, the business owner says "I feel excited and a bit confused. I know how to bake cakes, but I'm a little confused about reaching people for GOD through baking cakes. What am I supposed to do? I do feel the need to bring some delicious flavors to this neighborhood. I also feel the urge to teach people how to bake. Maybe this will help people feel good about what they can do."

What are your observations?" *Examine how you feel about your customer.* Do you have a desire to see something better for them?

4. *Ask GOD to Clarify*

In this example, the business owner says "LORD, please clarify what you mean 'reach people for YOU.' How am I supposed to do this through the bakery?"

What are your observations? *GOD does not mind clarifying.* Ask for clarification and allow HIM to sometimes say "no" or "wait." HE may want you to truly dedicate your heart to HIM first, before HE guides your business.

5. *Listen for GOD's Response to the Question*

In this example, GOD replies "Sell cakes for all occasions, emphasizing the ones that bring people to ME. Teach people about love in a couples baking class. Add hospitality to the business to show love for your neighbor."

What are your observations? *Quiet down to listen to GOD's response to the questions you asked.* Note that the HOLY SPIRIT asks people to do things that grow the kingdom. HE will use your business if you allow HIM to.

6. *Ask GOD about the Target Audience*

In this example, the business owner says "LORD, who do YOU want me to serve? I would like to serve the neighborhood I am familiar with."

What are your observations? *It is alright to give GOD idea you thought of, when asking HIM what HE wants you to do.* In this example, the person would like to start serving in their own neighborhood.

7. *Listen for GOD's Target Audience Answer*

In this example, GOD replies "Start with the neighborhood, but I will bring many to you so be ready to go to other locations in MY time."

What are your observations? *If your heart is truly open to what GOD has to say, HE may allow your wish to happen but HE may also stretch you to do something different.*

8. *Define Epic from GOD's Vision*

In this example, the business owner writes the vision based on ideas they got from GOD.

"Provide a slice of heaven and a word of encouragement. Our cake baking business will include 4 flavors to start. They will be decorated for any occasion using icing printers to print photos on sheet cakes. We will sell full cakes and slices out of a neighborhood location, providing a warm inviting atmosphere for people to sit and enjoy desert. We will also provide a pick up counter for phone in orders. With each slice, we will give a word of encouragement from GOD. Teach couples how to bake using our cake mix. We will also..."

Now that you have heard from GOD, start. What are your observations? *Write down HIS vision to gain clarity.*

9. *Name the Feature*

In this example, the business owner names the first feature of the business, "Cake by the slice "

"Cake by the slice" is the first feature. Note that the name is plain and not marketing related at this time. What are your observations? The business owner is focused on building out the operations rather than acquiring paying customers at this point. They will begin documenting SOPs.

10. *Develop the Feature 1 Long Description*

In this example, the business owner writes out the long description of Cake by the Slice.

We will bake 4 flavors of cake daily and slice them into 8 slices (Thick) or 16 slices (Thin). These will not be decorated, but iced. Sprinkles and other toppings can be purchased. The slices will be served on colorful paper or plastic plates for those who wish to dine in and special see through boxes for carry out.

Each carry out slice will be weighed and labeled to provide the customer with information such as possible allergens, gluten free or other specialty needs. The slices that are not sold will be given to the local homeless shelter daily. If all slices are sold, then we will bake a cake for the shelter.

Encouraging messages will include promises GOD made to protect and guide people. This will be either a message of the day or we will print a number of messages and randomly pick them to give with each slice.

Each slice will be baked using our super moist recipe. Gluten free options will be sold at a premium as the ingredients cost extra. Eventually we will expand the flavors to include fruit and nut flavors. We will do this once we have the operations worked out.

This describes the work that needs to be done to make this feature into something purchasable by the customer. What are your observations? Note that it only focuses on "Cake by the slice." What are the business operations components? Can you see standards starting to form? What part of the feature points to GOD? What cost controls do you observe?

11. Develop the Feature Short Description 160 Characters or Less

In this example, the business owner looks at the long description of the feature and translates it into something smaller. "Super moist heavenly cake slices come in 4 flavors: chocolate, yellow, white and marble. Each slice is served with a word of encouragement to brighten your day." This example is 159 characters with spaces.

The business owner describes the feature of business using meaningful words that will explain what is sold and why the customer should purchase it. What are your observations? The constraint by search engines is the description **must be 160 characters or less**.

12. Get Input from Customer (User Stories)

In this example, the business meets with many people and captures their perspective. Here are a few example responses that uses the agile structure for capturing the need from the customer's point of view.

As an expectant mother, I would like "his and her" bags for baby showers. The business owner writes when they will do this by noting (Do right away)

As a person who has gluten allergens, I would like to see the ingredients. The business owner writes when they will do this by noting (Do in 6 months of open). The business owner gives themselves time to develop and test the gluten free recipe idea.

As a smartphone user, I would like to pay with my phone. The business owner writes they will not do this by noting (Too expensive, may add later). The business owner may research payment systems and realize, while this is a cool idea, it may be cost prohibitive for now.

As an online user, I would like to place an order using my smartphone. The business owner writes when they will do this by noting (Do right away). The owner wants to make the business relevant by capturing orders through their website that is flexible enough to be used from a smartphone.

As a foodie, I would like to have a flavor of the day or week club. The business owner writes when they will do this by noting (Do in 6 months of open). Great ideas need time to develop and the business owner has enough to focus on right now.

As a party planner, I would like to have a full cake sliced and boxed. The business owner writes when they will do this by noting (Do right away) This aligns with the vision GOD provided.

As an eat in guest I would like to eat ice cream with my cake. The business owner writes when they will do this by noting (Far future) while this is a great idea, the startup costs for ice cream was not in the original vision. The business owner is mature enough not to react to every idea, but to put it on the wish list.

Do not guess. Ask. What are your observations? A formal or informal meeting could have been held to identify the customer's needs. This could have been done with trusted customers first followed by validation from strangers with "indirect" questions like "What do you like about your favorite bakery?" I will discuss User Stories in detail later.

13. Add Other Feature Titles

In this example, the business owner added more features to their wish list. Here are examples of what the business owner added.

Full Cake Sliced (From GOD's vision after you refine it)
Full Cake Sliced Thin (From GOD's vision after you refine it)
In Store Order Payment (From understanding that customers need to pay)
Online Order Payment (From understanding the next logical step from in-store payment)
An Encouraging Message with each slice (GOD's Purpose)

What other features would you like to see?

Always return back to the original vision and look at what GOD said and start dividing the vision using wisdom from your talents. What are your observations? Also look at the user stories to see what the customers want. Do not supersede the customers wishes with your knowledge, blowing off the customer's request. They may be requesting something that is valid.

Website Example

Now let's look at how everything translates into the website.

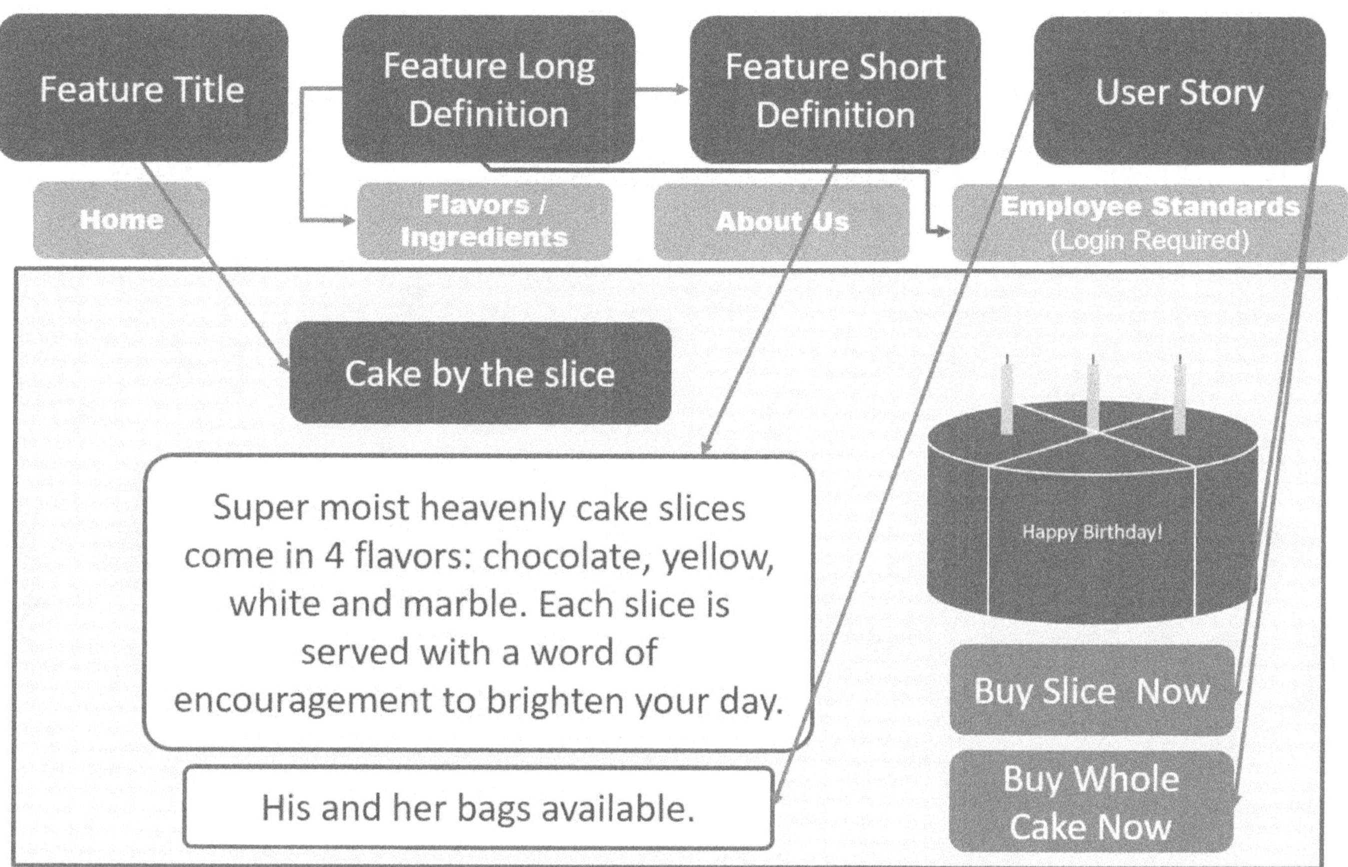

The title of the feature is displayed on their website in an area that is easily accessible by their customer.

The **feature long description** played a major role in how to consistently make the product or service over and over. In this example, the employees can see SOPs by logging in.

The **feature short description** is displayed near to the title and is limited to search engine optimization rules of 160 characters. Our example has 159.

The **user story** items came from direct feedback from your customers. Remember the "his and her" bag request and the whole cake request? They are implemented and displayed on the website.

The business owner knows how to store the "his and her" bags. He also knows how to slice the cake and box it. The website has been built in a way to accept payments.

Standard Operating Procedure Example

Standard Operating Procedures (SOP) were derived from the feature long description. This includes the steps used to execute or perform the feature. Think of following a recipe. It has the step-by-step instructions mixed in with the ingredients and finished product characteristics. SOPs should be developed and tested before the business is open to customers.

In our example the cake baking company would have the following standards:
Baking
Storage
Sales and Delivery
Cleaning
Payment

What others can you think of?

Exercise 5 – Prepare to Break the Vision into Smaller Pieces

Objective: *To begin to **list** the features of your business.*

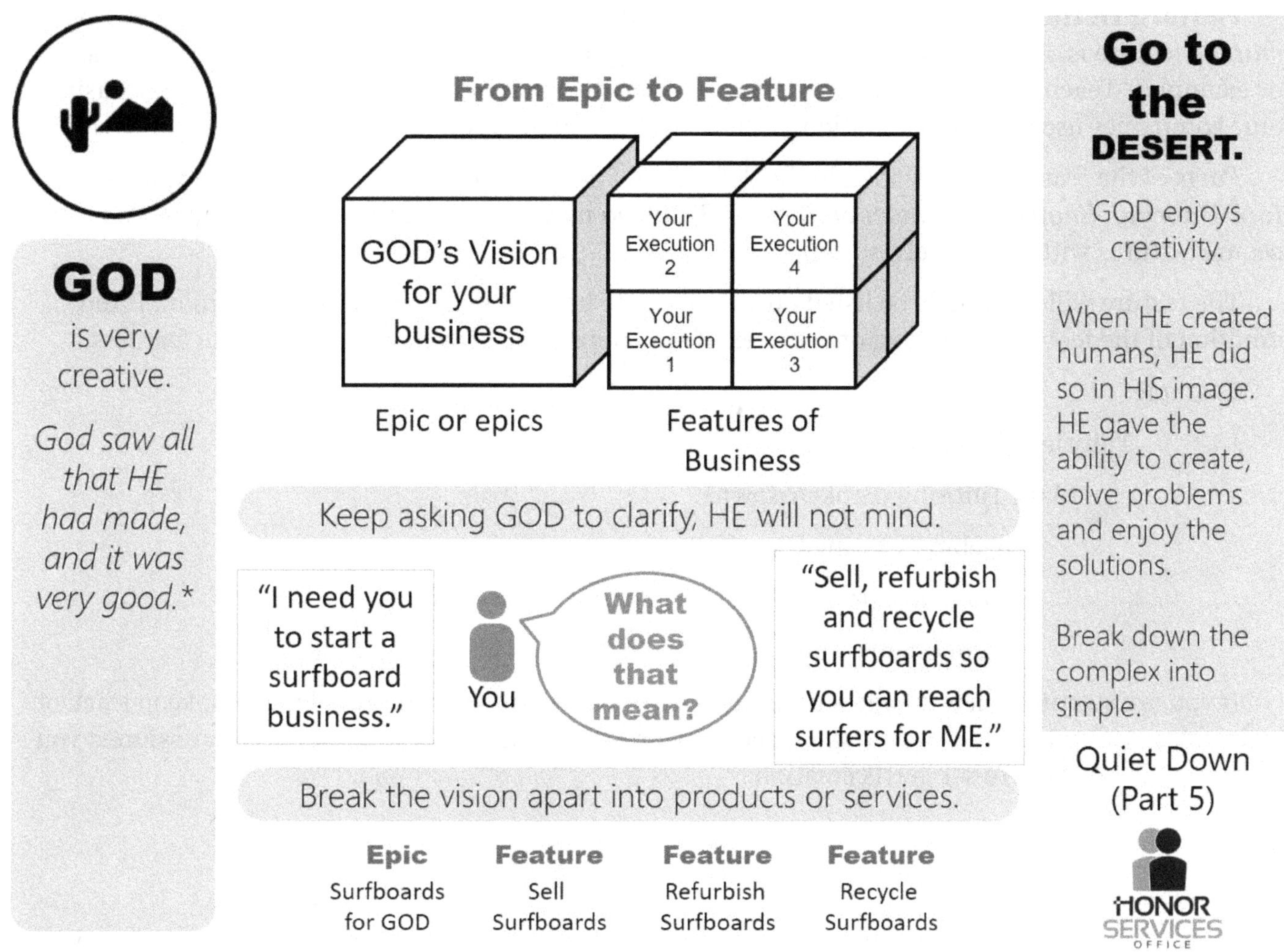

Flap your hands near your face. Feel it? As simple as this sounds, you just created wind. GOD created you to create.

GOD enables and enjoys creativity.

Genesis 1:31 – *Then God saw everything that He had made, and indeed it was very good. So the evening and the morning were the sixth day.*

When GOD created the heavens and the earth, He did it with deep imagination. He considered every little stone and every drop of water. He also did the same when He created you.

Now it's your turn to be creative in your business. Review this image and refer to the case study to see how the vision GOD provides, turns into feature of your business. You will also see that you can ask GOD for clarity.

GOD gives vision to those who are willing serve Him for His purpose.

What gift or talent are you thankful to GOD for? What solution to your customer's problem has God placed in your heart? Who will you talk to about the vision? Which customers will provide you feedback and input? How will you grow the kingdom with your business?

Feature of Business. This is the first step of breaking up the vision GOD gave you. This high-level grouping is one product or a single service. For example, a financial services business may have a feature of business named Tax Preparation.

Feature Definition (Long). List what this product or service is. The long definition describes *what* the feature is, not *how*, *when*. or even *why* it is used. Goals can be added to the long definition. For example: "Teach participants to grow their business through Agile AFB" is a feature of our business. Some companies use this long definition in their legal documentation or terms of service.

Parts of the feature are included in the definition. For example: *Tutoring* may be the feature but *Math Tutoring*, *English Tutoring*, and *Biology Tutoring* may be parts of tutoring. They may also become features within themselves.

The feature will eventually be listed on your website in search engine optimized fashion. If the definition of the feature is too long or complex, it may need to be broken up into multiple features.

Example:

- Tutoring (Larger vision)
  - Math Tutoring (Broken down)
    - Algebra Tutoring (Specific)
    - Geometry Tutoring
    - Trigonometry Tutoring

If you are starting a new business or adding more features to your existing business, keep track of these features as part of your wish list. Notice the words "for GOD" are not written as it is assumed you are doing this business to serve HIS creation.

Exercise 6 – Feature Title and Description

Objective: *To begin to **define** the features of your business.*

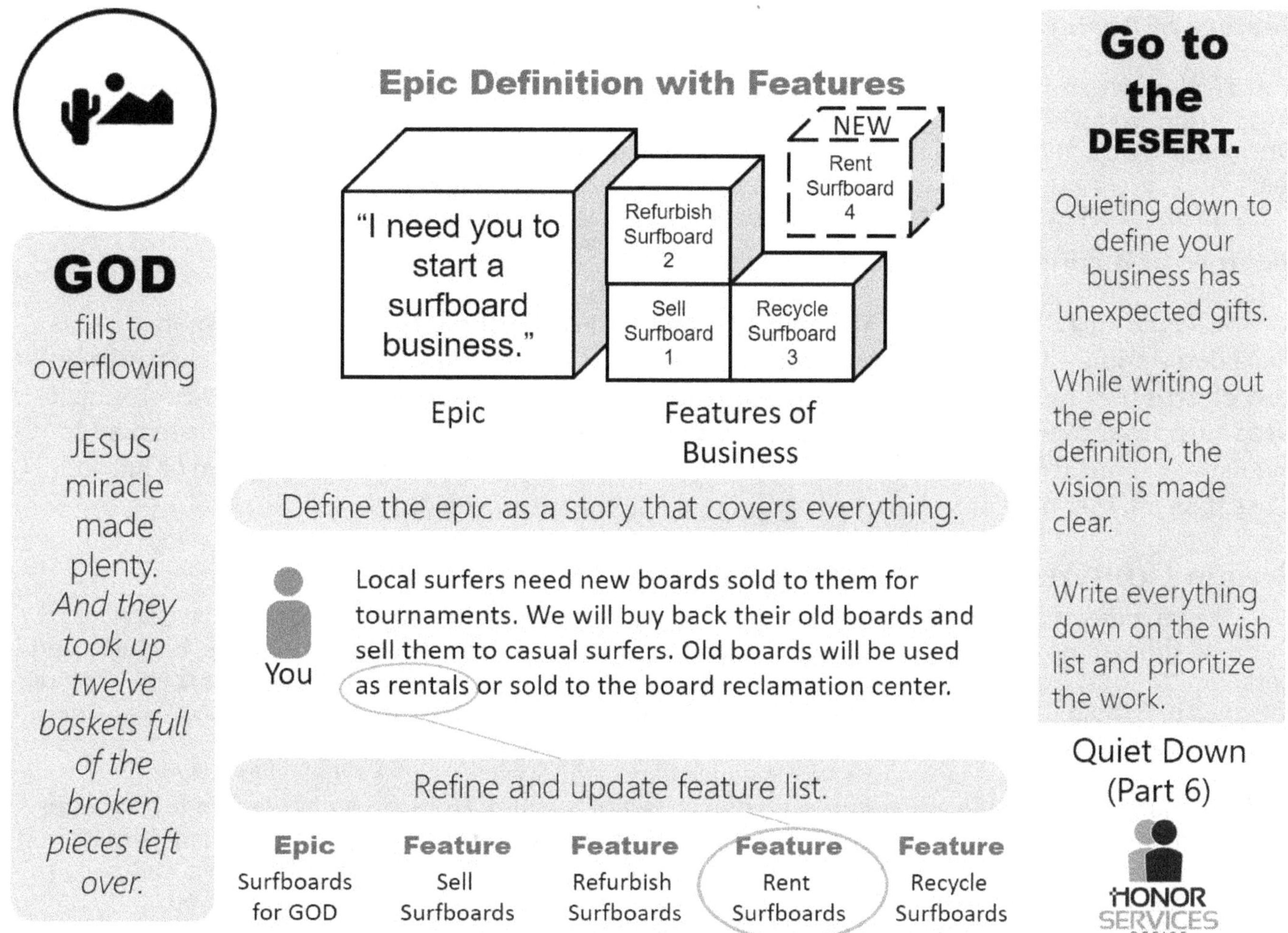

Have you ever moved? Did you put everything in one large box or did you divide all of your stuff into multiple boxes?

Even JESUS divided things up. HE fills in the gaps with overflowing blessings.

Matthew 14:20 - *And they all ate and were satisfied. And they took up twelve baskets full of the broken pieces left over.* (ESV)

When JESUS performed the miracle of feeding 5000 men, HE divided the bread so everyone had enough to eat. When they were all full, there were twelve backets left over.

What do you observe on this image? The example shown above illustrates a new feature added as a need that came from a customer.

Now it's time to start defining the features of your business. Write out your features of business.

Tip: Be more thorough than the examples given in the book and in the class. Remember, your customers need to understand what you sell and why they should buy it. Share your ideas with the group you belong to.

Feature Title

Try to keep the title to four words or less—ideally one or two words. The title should be self-explanatory, but will need a short definition to explain to the customers what they will really get.

Feature of Business Description (Long)

The long description is used to document everything the feature does and is. Inside the long description, you will keep a ideas, thoughts, and requests from your customers. All customer **User Stories** will be listed in the long description. Use this information as the beginning of your standards, marketing, accounting structure and sales definitions. While that sounds like a lot, make it small and work on one facet at a time. Refer to the Cake Business Case Study for thought starters.

Feature of Business Description (Short)

Scale the long description back to smaller pieces that can be understood by your customers. This short description will be seen on your website, blog, social media, and ads. This description **must be 160 characters or less**. This is the search engine optimization (SEO) standard for all search engines. Use words from your long description to fully describe this feature enough to make the customer inquisitive. If further definition is needed on your website, then add a *Learn More* button or link and place it on another page or web part where more detail can be provided.

Assign GOD-Centered Thought Groups

The purpose of a thought group is to figure out problems together. The purpose of the GOD-centered thought group is to pray for one another and help each other through problems, business and personal. Natural teams work best. If a few friends come in together, then it is alright for them to work together in a thought group. Suggest to the friends that it would be good to meet other people and get other perspectives.

You, the instructor, need to make sure everyone is part of a group. Here are a few ways to form groups.

1. Divide the class into equal groups of 4 or 5. This can be done many ways. If the class is in person have one person start with the number 1, the next 2, the next 3 and finally the next 4. Repeat this cycle until everyone has a number 1, 2, 3 or 4. Have all the 1's group, then the 2's, etc.
2. Group by birthday's closest to each other in a given week. All those born 1 – 7 work together. Those born 8-15, etc.
3. Group by industry or location.
4. Randomly put names in a bowl and pick a person for the groups you predesign.

Have the groups exchange contact information as they will be working together outside of class. The purpose of forming this group is for you to work through at least one feature of your business. I will explain what a feature is in the first four exercises of this chapter.

Be there for one another. Here are the rules:

1. Share your business idea, but do not share confidential information that is proprietary to your business.
2. Be conscious of everyone's time. Have a time to talk and a time to listen.
3. Try to refrain from controlling someone else's business, rather provide valuable feedback.
4. Help the business owner by focusing him or her on the target audience. You may not be the audience for the product or service, so your suggestions, while good, may be more confusing than helpful.

Have everyone in the group say "**I'm here. Persevere!**" Use this statement when one of your group members feels like giving up or are frustrated. Validate the features of your business with customers and the group you belong to. Ask if the feature solves the problem, as given by your target audience. Get feedback and modify your feature.

Exercise 7 – User Story Definition

Objective: *To collect and write the needs of your customers through user stories while tracking the creation of a feature.*

Cheating on the test by copying from someone else does not make you successful. **Learn and know your own business** by getting the needs directly from your customers. You will provide a better product or service than the one you want to copy.

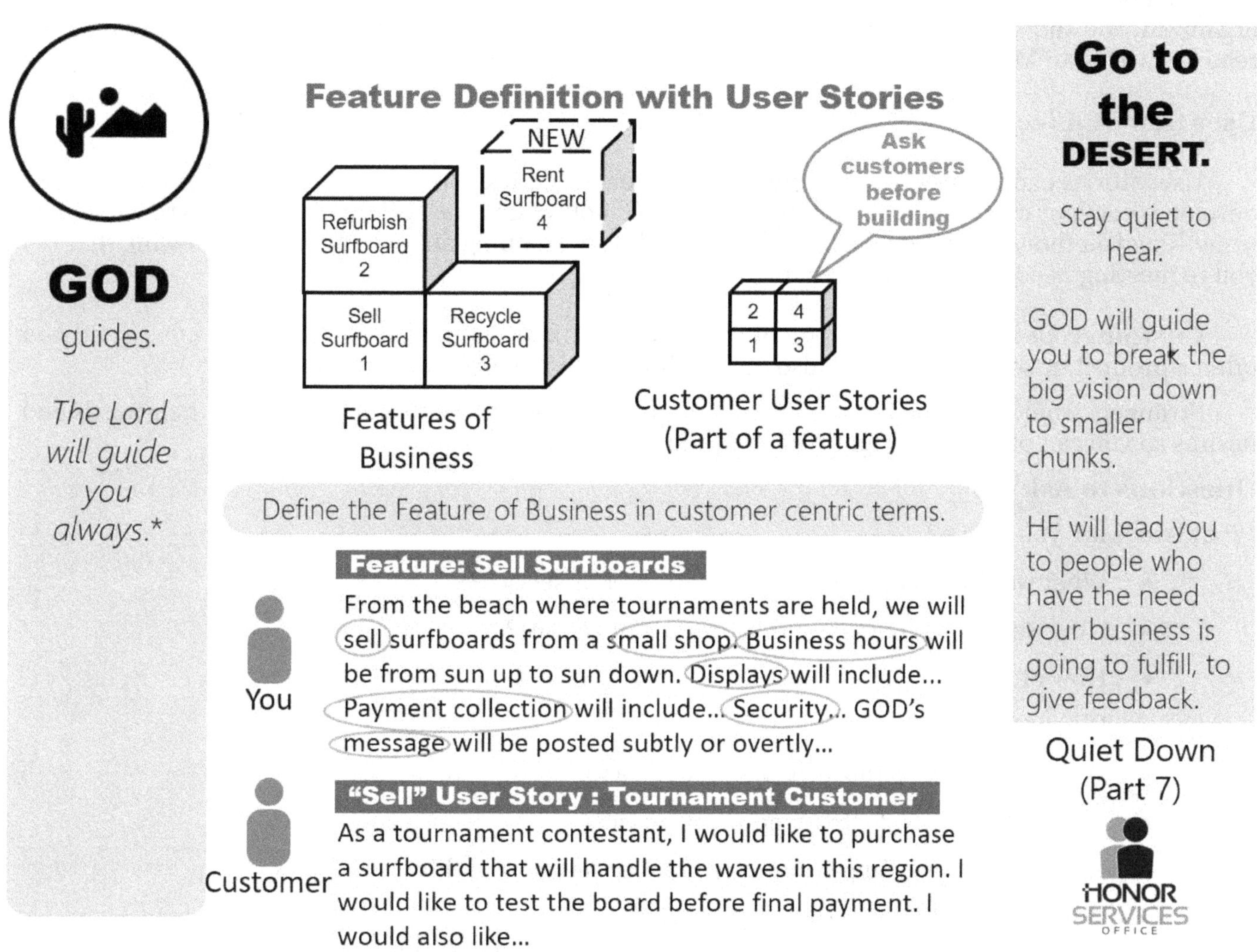

When you see a customer, do you see only an opportunity to get money? Do you use a person who has needs, wants and desires? Do you see a person who needs prayer and may not know who JESUS is?

GOD knows the heart. Seek excellence for your customer, HE will guide you.

Isaiah 58:11 – *The LORD will guide you always; he will satisfy your needs in a sun-scorched land and will strengthen your frame. You will be like a well-watered garden, like a spring whose waters never fail.* (NIV)

User stories express needs a customer has. Getting feedback saves time and money. When you develop what your customers are looking for, you will not waste time and money trying to rework something you thought would work, but did not. Be excited about meeting needs versus being the one who thought of the idea. Let's start working on how to build a feature of the business. We will begin breaking down the epic. Remember, the epic is the vision from GOD you got in the Dream Bigger chapter.

Example from Dream Bigger

There are four features of business to the Epic "Sell Surfboards for GOD."

1. Sell surfboards
2. Rent surfboards
3. Refurbish surfboards
4. Recycle surfboards

Each of these features need to be built so you can provide the service to the customer. To stay organized, you should build them, one at a time, until complete. Once complete, this feature may be ready to use as an MVP.

User Story Collection

User stories express needs a customer has. Getting feedback saves time and money. When you develop what your customers are looking for, you will not waste time and money trying to rework something you thought would work, but did not. While developing an idea is exciting, knowing that you're meeting needs is even more exciting.

Customer User Story. A statement from your customer listing *how, when, why, where* and *how often* a product or service is used. It also defines how it should look and behave.

Strangers would be ideal, but known customers are a good place to start. Ask them their needs and desires so you can provide the right type of product or service.

Questions to Ask

What issues are you facing?

- What would you like to see in this product or service?
- How would you like to use this product or service?
- How often?
- Where?
- What would make this product or service more convenient?
- Why did you choose this product or service?
- How much have you paid for a product or service like this?
- What feeling did this product or service invoke?
- What is the minimal lead time for delivering the product or service?

Next ask about exceptions.

- What actions or steps would you like to see if something went wrong?
- What does a good return policy look like?
- What examples of "bad" service have you experienced?
- What are your expectations if we run out of a product or service?

Customer Perspective. Now that we have the information, it is time to document it from the customer's perspective. This is important as the feedback will be used in collaboration and demonstration meetings. "As a customer, I would like to..." is the standard structure of the user story. You can get more specific. "As a tall customer, I would like to..."

Jewelry User Story Example: As an attendee of a formal event, I would like to wear a necklace that complements my after five, black garment.

From the customer's wish list, the God-centered business owner would create a title and definition that interests him or her. Example:

Feature Title: After Five Necklace

Feature Definition: Twenty-four karat pure, reclaimed gold necklace with a black hexagonal gem, complements formal attire while standing out.

Problem being addressed: The formal event and the need to complement an after five garment.

Differentiator: Reclaimed gold would appeal to those who are earth conscious.

Collaboration: The crowd this group serves desires reclaimed jewelry, not freshly mined gold from poorly run mines.

Credibility: Our shops purchase gold, recycling it into new jewelry. We are certified by . . .

Cleaning Service User Story Example: As a home seller, I would like my home cleaned and detailed to sell so I can maximize profits.

Feature Title: Home-Sales Cleaning and Detailing

Feature Definition: Clean and detail kitchen, bathrooms, bedrooms, and other living spaces, making them presentable for selling. Restoration services available.

Problem being addressed: Cleaning that is done beyond normal surface cleaning.

Differentiator: Detailing service versus normal home cleaning service; restoration service.

Collaboration: Realtor and home sellers requesting home cleaning services

Credibility: Listed on another page. "See our ten-year history."

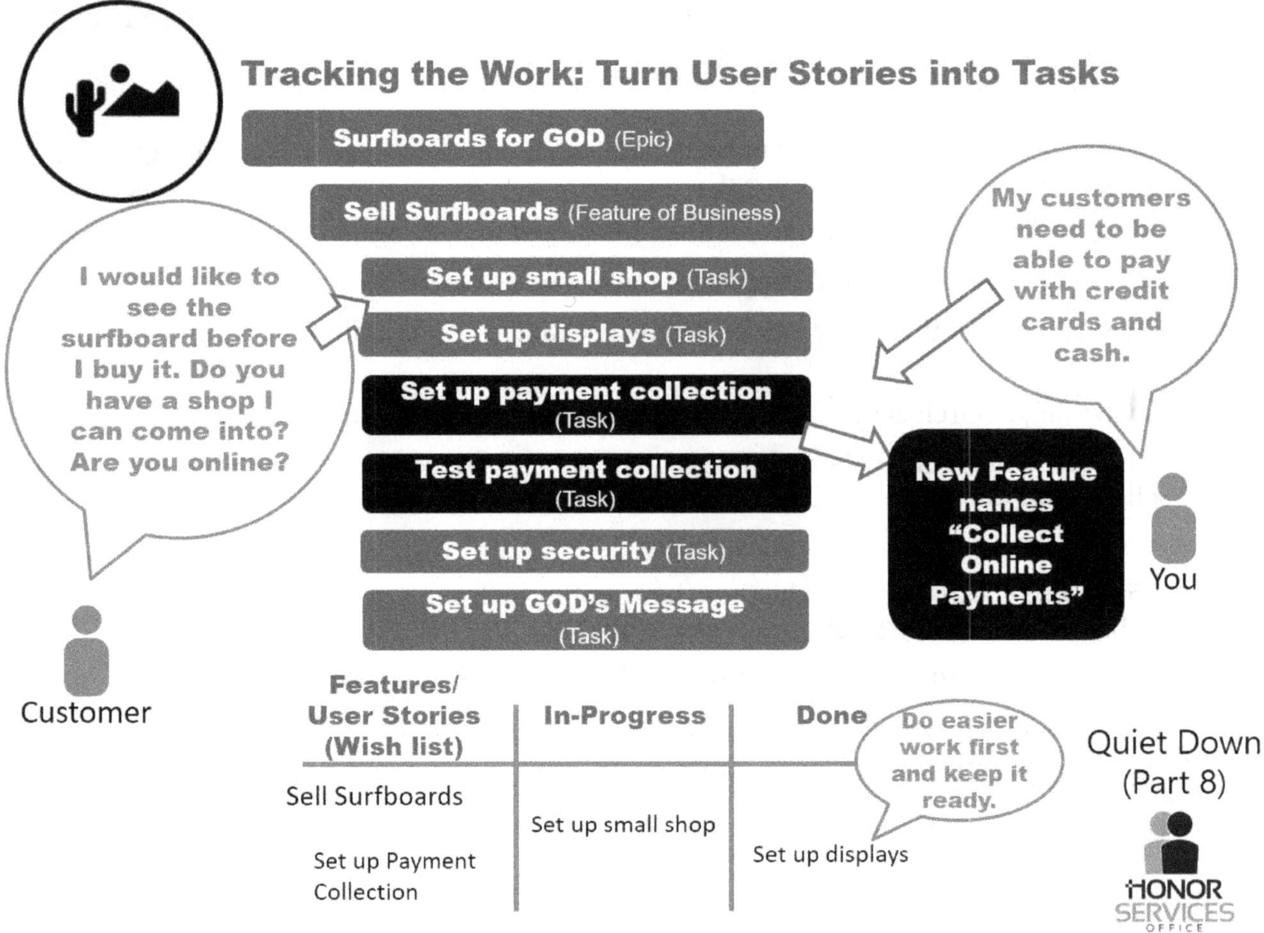

The starting point for building the feature is important. You must break apart the feature into "Customer User Stories" to begin your development. Ask yourself "What parts are customer facing, in other words what does the custom know about the product or service?

Does your company have secret recipes or patented materials?

Ask yourself "What features of the business will only the business know about? Getting back to the customer... How often will the customer use my product or service? Where will they use it? How will they use it?" These and many other questions need to be answered in your solution. The answers need to come from your customers.

Track the customer user stories you are working on. In this example, "Sell Surfboards is the feature the business owner is working on. A customer may have said, "I would like to purchase surfboards from a location where I can see them.

The business owner would then list that desire as a part of the feature by writing "As a purchaser, I would like to visit a small shop to see the surfboards." How do you, as the business owner meet that request? This question is answered by getting the details of how the customer wants to use your product or service, mixed with your expertise and solutions to their problems or requests. When you start working on the task, use a spreadsheet to keep track of what is "in-progress" and what is completely "done."

You, as the business owner also have the right to develop user stories. Your customer may want the surfboards for free, but they have to pay for them. In this example you have determined there is a need for a payment system. It must be easy to use, so the customers will still need to give you feedback on the solution.

In this example from the image above, there are only five users stories to be concerned with. You can have a lot more, but if you go over 10 or so, then consider breaking the feature apart.

1. Set up small shop
2. Set up displays
3. Set up payment collection
4. Set up security
5. Set up God's message to the customer

Note: "Test payment collection" is left off the list on purpose.

Notice, marketing or sales are not features listed here. They require their own features to fully build the right marketing and sales geared towards meeting your customer's needs.. Also notice "Set up" is in each customer user story in this example. Other action words like "build" or "develop" or "purchase" can be used for your list.

When you add action words to the customer user story title, it is now called a "Task." The task is what you will do to create the feature. Think of a set of tasks as a "To-Do" list to build the solution for your customer. In this example, the business owner can also have a task that is "Test payment collection" or "Test security."

This example now has six tasks.

Place all items in a spreadsheet, in a column labelled "Wish List."

Label the next column "In-progress" and the next column "Done."

When the you work on the task, moves it from the wish list column to the "In-progress" column. When you complete the task, moves it to the "Done" column. Repeat this until all "tasks" are complete. In this example there are now **six** tasks to complete.

1. Set up small shop
2. Set up displays
3. Set up payment collection
4. **Test payment collection (new)**
5. Set up security
6. Set up God's message to the customer

In our example, "Set up displays" was the easiest and most valuable task to that business owner, so it was placed in the "in-progress" column. More than one task can be placed in the "In-progress" column at a time. We will discuss this in sprint planning, later in the chapter.

What tasks would you add to this list?

How about adding "Demonstrate payment collection " as a task? Remember, these are tasks to keep you organized.

Does everything need to be demonstrated to the customer?

No, but the more feedback you can get, the easier it will be for your customers to use your product or service. Use discernment on what to get feedback on.

Let's continue the case study by writing user stories for the features.

Case Study – User Story

What are your observations about the title of the feature "Cake by the Slice?"

If you are thinking about marketing when developing a title for your features, then please refrain from it for a moment. Think about what needs to be done to make this feature sellable to your customer.

Too often business owners start with marketing terms for the feature versus creating what it will take to "operate" the product or service. We discussed this at length in the "Seek Wisdom" chapter. In this instance "Cake by the Slice" is not glamorous, however it says what the business is providing to the customer.

Customer Feedback

Now let's look at the feedback from customers.
First, let's look at how to write a user story. "As a ___ I would like to... Which customer user stories pertain only to "Cake by the slice?".

As an expectant mother, I would like his and her bags for baby showers. (Do right away)
As a person who has gluten allergens I would like to see the ingredients. (Do in 6 months of open)
As a smartphone user, I would like to pay with my phone. (Too expensive, may add later)
As an online user I would like to place an order using my smartphone. (Do right away)
As a foodie I would like to have a flavor of the day or week club. (Do in 6 months of open)
As a party giver I would like to have a full cake sliced and boxed. (Do right away)
As an eat in guest I would like to eat ice cream with my cake. (Far future)
[POSSIBLE NEW FEATURE] As a business-woman I would like a piece of cake to and a drink before I go to my meetings. I would also like to order slices for my team for delivery. (Do right away)

Notice some notes in parenthesis made by the business user of when he or she can work on this part of the business feature. This comes with experience and by making adjustments to the how you approach the business.

Prioritize the User Stories

Group the user stories based on what you will work on now versus the future.

As an expectant mother, I would like his and her bags for baby showers. (Do right away)
As a party planner I would like to have a full cake sliced and boxed. (Do right away)
As a business-woman I would like a piece of cake to and a drink before I go to my meetings. (Do right away)
Can you think of more user stories? How about thick versus thin sliced whole cakes? Should spacers be inserted to separate the slices in a whole sliced cake?

Why aren't the other user stories part of the "Cake by the slice" user story?"

Because they are part of another feature of the business. Divide the work to satisfy your customer while creating small, valuable pieces ready to be used right away." Adding a scoop of ice cream, for example, is not part of the "Cake by the slice" user story because it has a different handling, ingredients, storage and cleaning practices. This does not mean the features will not be combined for marketing and sales purposes.

My User Stories

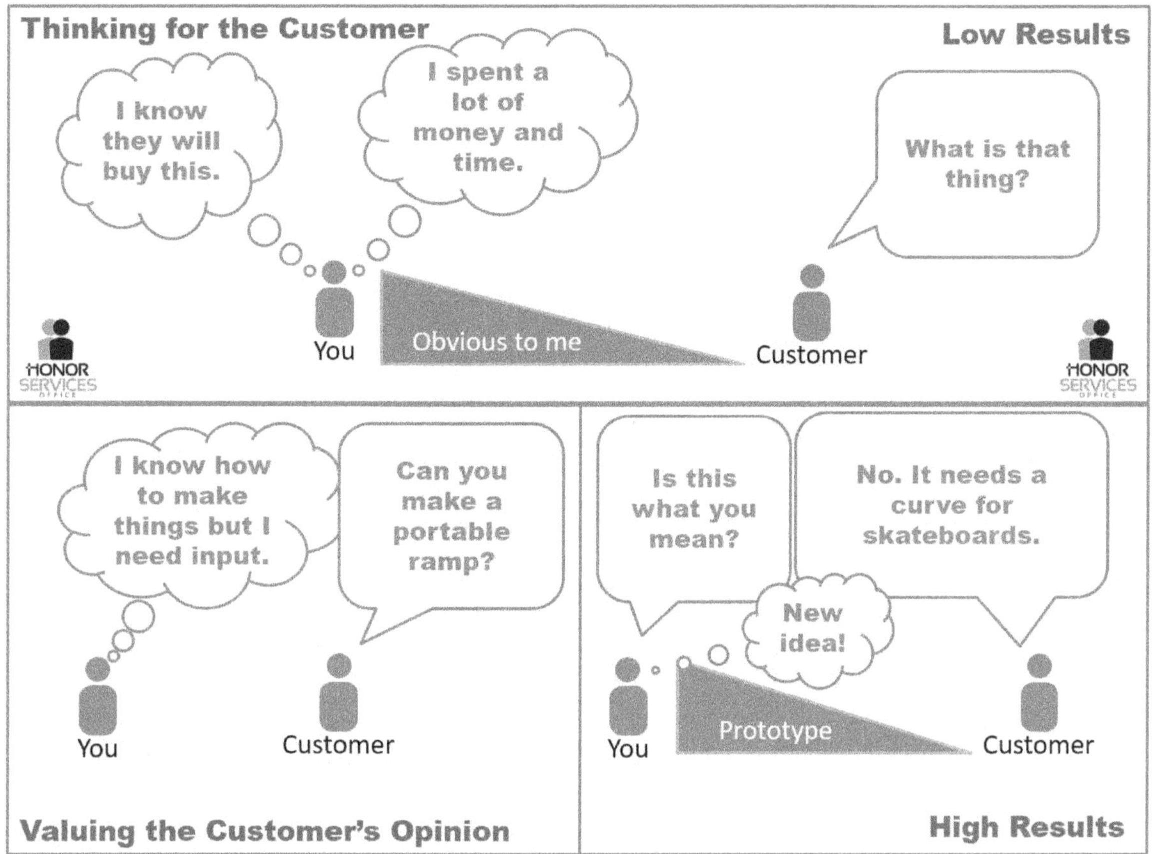

Has something been extremely obvious to the person who is doing the explanation, but you just were not getting what they were saying?

What is obvious to you may not be obvious to your customers. Be open to refining the product or service to fit the needs of their customer.

Clarifying and refining is not saying the business owner is not the expert, rather the business owner may be missing what the audience wants or needs. Then he or she will have a difficult time explaining the product or service him or her spent money and time on.

Now it's time to write user stories for the features of your business. Meet with your customers, aka users of your products or services. This will be used to build or refine the product or service. This section of the chapter should be done **<u>after</u>** you speak to your customers and people who may purchase from you. You can try to do this, hoping to think from their perspective, but the problem arises with how you want them to act versus how your customers really will use your product or service. Discuss your feature with your thought group outside of class.

Over the next week try to meet with customers and write your user stories. What do you notice about your user stories? Are there similarities? Are there any surprises? What is different than your original idea? As you get used to meeting with customers to get and meet their needs, you will get better at hearing what they really want. You will also begin hearing a pattern.

Exercise 8 – Refine the Product or Service

Objective: *To plan your design and build activities in two week chunks, getting input and feedback from your customers.*

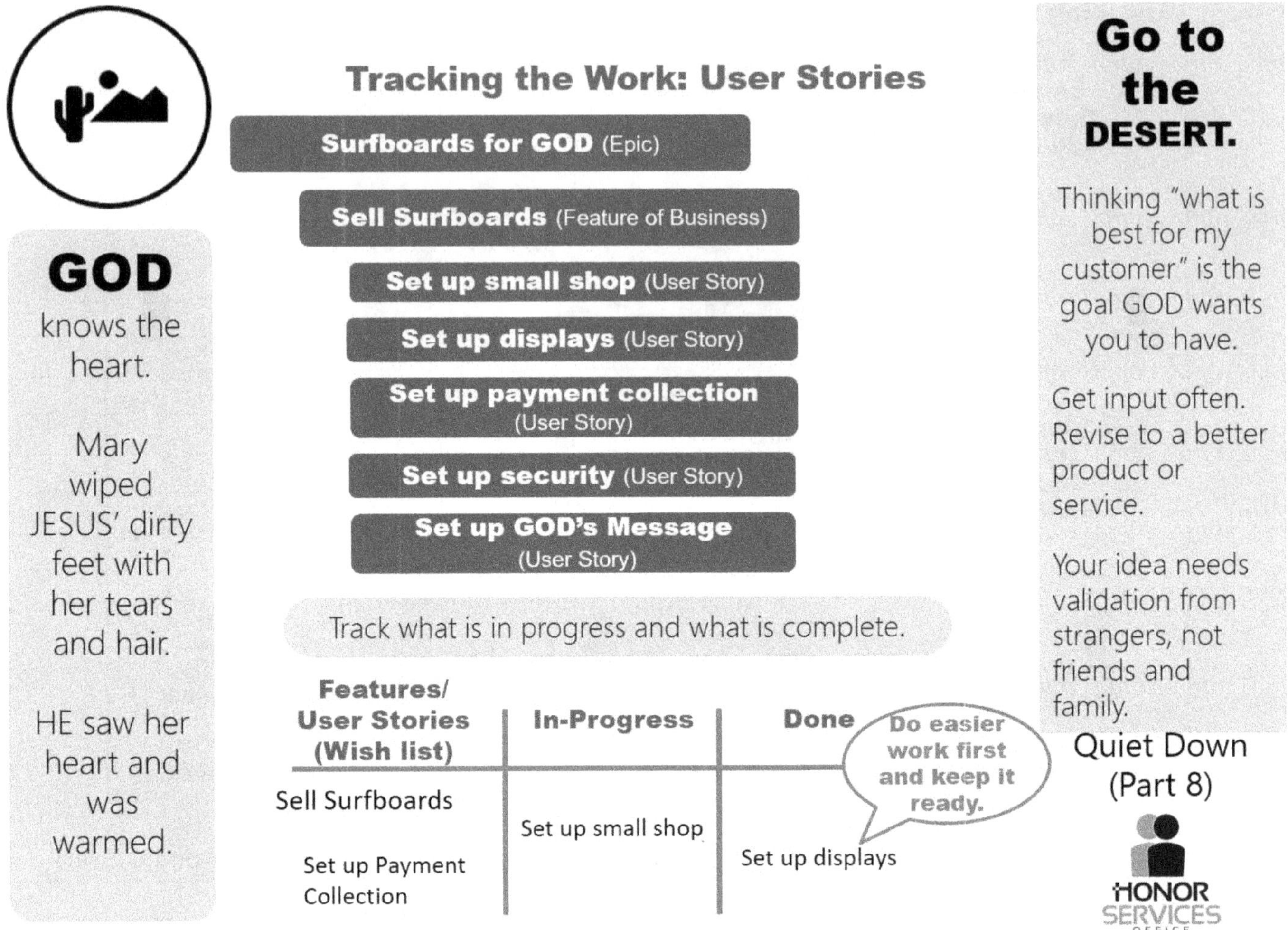

Would you like to be handed worn out clothes to wear? Would you give worn out clothes to the homeless?

Because GOD knows the heart, think about what is best for the customer.

The image refers to John 12:1-8 when Mary broke open expensive perfume and wiped HIS feet. JESUS saw her generous heart. HE will see yours.

Plan the Sprint (Two Weeks)

How much work can be done in two weeks? That is what you are tasked to plan out. How large of an effort is each user story to build? Do some things need to be broken into small pieces? If so, then give it a title so you can keep track of it. Update or add this to your wish list inside of the Feature Long Definition. Sprint planning should only take up to two hours. All feature definitions, user stories and prioritizations should be completed. Figure out how long it will take to build the user stories so you can place them in a sprint.

Prioritize the work

Look at the smallest most valuable user story you can work on first. This is technically known as the WSJF, aka the Weighted Shortest Job First, but simply put, do the easiest thing that brings the most value "to the customer" first.

Which would you do first?

1. **Design branded packaging.** (**Answer**: This is second in this example. Many other steps are needed before branding is developed, but this is an example only)
2. **Get a contract to sell your food item.** (**Answer**: This is done last in this example. You should be ready for the contract versus getting the contract and then getting ready)
3. **Develop the ingredients and allergens list.** (**Answer**: This is done first in this example because it provides the most value and is the easiest to do right away)

The customer needs to know it your product or service is safe, desirable and trustworthy. Developing this list would be fairly easy and could contribute to the documentation needed to get a contract. While many steps are needed before branding is developed, the allergen list will also contribute to the overall brand.

Once you complete the easiest work, then set the completed item to the side and work on the next user story. Do this until all "planned" work is complete. You will never be finished as your business will always be changing and improving.

Define the Sprint (Two Weeks)

Here is where the rubber meets the road. Look at your features and their associated user stories and divide the work into **two-week** chunks. What can you do in two weeks? Be honest. Include all of the activities you do in a two-week calendar. Now, purposefully take the user-story definitions and schedule the work.

Book Author's Customer User Story Example: *As a romance reader, I would like to read a story that mixes action and romance.* The sprint may have the defining of action and the definition of the romance structure due by a certain day in the two-week process.

Exercise 9 – Invite People to Meetings

Objective: *To plan meetings to get feedback and demonstrate **versions** of the product or service.*

Important Meetings

The best outcome for your business is to have your customers involved from beginning to end.

GOD wants gatherings.

Let us not neglect meeting together, as some have made a habit, but let us encourage one another.

Sprint Definition
Define what work will be done over "this" two week interval. Be realistic, listing possible distractions. Come up with a plan to mitigate roadblocks.

Collaboration Meeting
Work with the customer to understand how they will use the product or service. Time of day, how often, and where used should be considered.

Demonstration Meeting
Demonstrate what has been accomplished over the course of "this" sprint to get feedback. If the product or service needs adjusting, then schedule it for the next sprint or later.

Innovation Meeting
After 4 sprints have been completed, host an innovation meeting, looking for new ideas or needs from your customers. Look for problems to solve.

Go to the DESERT.

Healed people seek.

GOD wants you to be a leader who seeks the wise counsel of others so you can heal them and they can heal you.

Find your own crowd.

Quiet Down (Part 9)

In the past, how did it feel to hand your homework in to a teacher? Did you have a bad experience with a teacher who seemingly made you feel less than you are when they marked up your homework?

I apologize for those of you who have faced extremely critical people. This is not the same. GOD-centered business owners welcome feedback because it will be used to help , not hurt.

It is important to meet with your customer.

Hebrews 10:25 - *Let us not neglect meeting together, as some have made a habit, but let us encourage one another, and all the more as you see the Day approaching.* (BSB)

Meet with your customer to get input and bring a word of encouragement into your meetings. And meet with people to pray and encourage one another. The main purpose of meeting with your customer is to get input on your product or service. This means you have to build a rapport with your customers to identify willing participants who will provide honest feedback as well as contribute new problems for you to solve.

The main goal is to keep, you and your business, organized while building or updating features of your business. Three questions to ask yourself and your employees are:
What did you do yesterday?
What are you going to do today?
What barriers do you face?

You are not asking these questions to your customer, rather you are answering them for yourself and your employees. Let's get feedback on what you will build.

Turning the plan into a product or service is not easy work, but worth the effort. From your wish list of user stories schedule time to build the product or service with input from your customers.

> **Construction Company Owner's Customer Story Example:** *As a homeowner, I would like my basement remodeled to keep out water. I would also like to have a warm, well-lit basement. I like to walk barefooted and would like to have warm feet in the winter.*
> There are four stories that may go into multiple sprints because the time necessary might take may take up large chunks of the two-week period.
> *Waterproof basement:* Dig around the foundation filling in cracks from outside in and again from inside out. Seal exterior and interior walls. (FIVE DAYS + ONE DAY Inspection – SIX DAYS)
> *Frame/wall basement:* Purchase and deliver wood or aluminum to frame drywall and finish walls. (TWO DAYS + ONE DAY Inspection – THREE DAYS)
> *Install electric:* Install circuit breaker, electric lines, plugs, light fixtures, rewiring and replacing existing to customer specifications. (FOUR DAYS + ONE DAY Inspection – FIVE DAYS)
> *Install padding and carpet:* Install mold-proof padding and carpet in case of moisture. (ONE DAY)
>
> **Please Note:** There is too much work for the two weeks. Two sprints must be defined. All resources who will be working on this sprint cannot take on any more work. But what about sales, marketing, and the administrative day? If you factor these in as well, this would stretch the sprints into three. Days off, errands, holidays, emergency contingency time all get factored in.

When will you develop the user stories? When will you collect feedback from your customers during the development process? When will you demonstrate what you have built?

These meetings can be formal or informal. Formal meetings require an invitation, time, date, and agenda at a minimum. Informal discussions are harder to execute as they happen without a schedule. The value in informal meetings is collecting small amounts of feedback a little at a time directly from customers who may be using your product or service. Just note that people are tired of being surveyed, so face to face is highly desired. Try to schedule two weeks at a time.

Will you demonstrate? Will you provide a sample? Do you have documentation to review? Think ahead before having a meeting.

Sprint definition meeting

You and those who are helping will attend. The customer will not attend this meeting. Review the wish list and look at the features you have fully defined. Pull out the user stories you want to fulfill and plan accordingly. The meeting may last a couple of hours.

Sprint 1 (Two Weeks)

Monday	Tuesday	Wednesday	Thursday	Friday
1	2	3	4	5
6	7	8	9	10

At the end of the two weeks, see if you accomplished everything you set out to do. Set aside time to reflect on how you can improve your planning. Put this reflection time on your calendar.

Sprint 2 (Two Weeks)

If you did not finish everything you planned in Sprint 1, move it to Sprint 2. Incomplete work pushes out your timeline. Remember, the goal is not to cram work in, rather to build quality products and services that will be fully understood and accepted by your customer. Work on one thing at a time until that item is complete. Do this as much as you can.

Sprint 3 (Two Weeks)

If you did not finish everything you planned in Sprint 2, move it to Sprint 3. Incomplete work pushes out your timeline. If you moved too many work items around, then assess if you should be doing this right now or if you can increase the priority of getting your plans accomplished.

Sprint 4 (Two Weeks)

If the first three sprints went as expected, then reserve this sprint for developing marketing. Validate any marketing with your customers to make sure it resonates with them.

Will things move? Yes! At the end of each sprint, see why you completed the work and more importantly, why you did not. Don't just plow into another sprint thinking you have to work twice as hard. Re-plan your work, this time with more knowledge. Give yourself more time to actually complete the work.

After Sprint 4, the product or service features of business, that were worked on over the past 8 weeks, should be ready for customer use and purchase. Remember, only work on what can be completed and done well within this period of time.

Like any new process, the first time you do this, expect confusion and missteps. This is natural. You will get better and better at building and refining your business operational components and marketing messages.

Meeting Planning

Write a list of people you can invite to a meeting to discuss your product or service. Fill in the meeting planning list and invite them to your meeting.

Sprint	Collaboration Meetings	Demonstration Meetings	Innovation Meetings
Sprint 1	John and Jane Doe - Next week	John and Jane Doe – Two Weeks from today	John and Jane Doe – Next Month
Sprint 2			
Sprint 3			
Sprint 4			

Put your customer's problems, desires and feedback in a Contact Relationship Management (CRM) tool. This can be a spreadsheet or Honor services Office.

Exercise 10 – Meeting Agenda

Objective: *To prepare for meetings with your customers.*

Sprint Planning

Ask for accountability if extra discipline is needed.

monday	tuesday	wednesday	thursday	friday
Sprint planning for "this" 2 weeks (2 hours) Build	Build part of customer's need (User story)	**Collaboration meeting (15 Minute meeting) What you did yesterday. What you will do today. Road blocks** Build	Build part of customer's need (User story)	**Collaboration meeting (15 Minute meeting) What you did this week. What is remaining. Road blocks** Build
Build part of customer's need (User story)	**Collaboration meeting (15 Minute meeting) What you did yesterday. What you will do today. Road blocks** Build	Build part of customer's need (User story)	Build part of customer's need (User story)	**Demonstration meeting (30 Minute – 1 hour web or face to face meeting) Address their need. Demonstrate the solution.**

Become disciplined to stay the course on your plan. Collect, clarify, validate customer user stories and demonstrate you fulfilled the need.

GOD says "Be Ready."

*But sanctify the Lord God in your hearts, and always be ready to give a defense to everyone who asks you a reason for the hope that is in you.**

Go to the DESERT.

Step by step.

Knowing what you are going to do each day enables speed and increases quality.

Pray before, during and after each meeting, asking GOD to remove barriers and open hearts.

Quiet Down (Part 10)

Have you ever been caught off guard by someone giving you a criticism? How did you handle it?

Be ready to receive feedback and to present GOD at any time.

1 Peter 3:15 *But sanctify the Lord God in your hearts, and always be ready to give a defense to everyone who asks you a reason for the hope that is in you, with meekness and fear;*

Collaboration meeting

You, those who are helping, and the customer will attend. This is a very short meeting to discuss progress of developing the new product or service. Clarification of the user stories is allowed in this meeting. Ask or present what happened yesterday, what is going to be done today, and discuss the existing barriers.

Collaboration Meeting Agenda

Try to keep your meetings brief. Your customers time is very precious. Try to keep this meeting under thirty minutes. Collect user stories in your collaboration meetings. First, decide on the type of meeting you would like to host in order to collect your customers' feedback. Will you host a lunch? Dinner? A coffee session?

Demonstration meeting

You, those who are helping, and the customer will attend. At the end of the two weeks, demonstrate what has been created so far. Get input and test the product or service in front of your customer.

Demonstration Meeting Agenda

Getting feedback on what you are building is crucial. Since your product or service is not ready for use by your customer, it is important that they know they are part of a feedback group. Set their expectation that this is not a finished product.

If your product or service is confidential, then it is recommended that you have participants of the meeting sign a non-disclosure agreement until you get other protections in place like a trademark or patent or copyright. Unfortunately I do not have an example of a non-disclosure agreement. This is where someone else's expertise comes into play. Ask a lawyer or try to find an NDA that suits your business.

Demonstrate what you are working on to get feedback. Will you host a coffee meeting to collect their feedback? What is the agenda for this meeting?

Innovation Meeting

You, anyone who has been involved in the sprint and your customer will attend.

Innovation Meeting Agenda

After the sprints are complete and you have working products or services, plan to do go through another 10 weeks of development that include 2 weeks of planning and 4 two week sprints. Before starting the next cycle of developing more features for your business, consider hosting an innovation meeting to understand the needs of the customers. This is a period of time to look for innovations in your industry. It is also a time to collect new problems your customer may be facing.

What ideas has GOD given you? This meeting can be used to get feedback on your idea, before you do major investments in solutions.

Quiet down after this meeting to ask GOD, "Is this what YOU want me to work on?". HIS answer will go into your next vision. This is an ongoing process.

What new problems or ideas do people have? Will you host a workshop or a small meeting to collect their feedback? What is the agenda for this meeting?

1. **Pray before scheduling the meeting.** Ask GOD to reveal any flaws in your work so they can be corrected.
2. **Schedule the meeting.** Pick times that are convenient to your customers.
3. **Obtain feedback and acceptance.** For some businesses, a formal signature of acceptance may be required. In all cases, seek feedback. This will be used in marketing and sales.

Exercise 11 – Validation (Test) Planning

Objective: *To validate and refine every aspect of the business.*

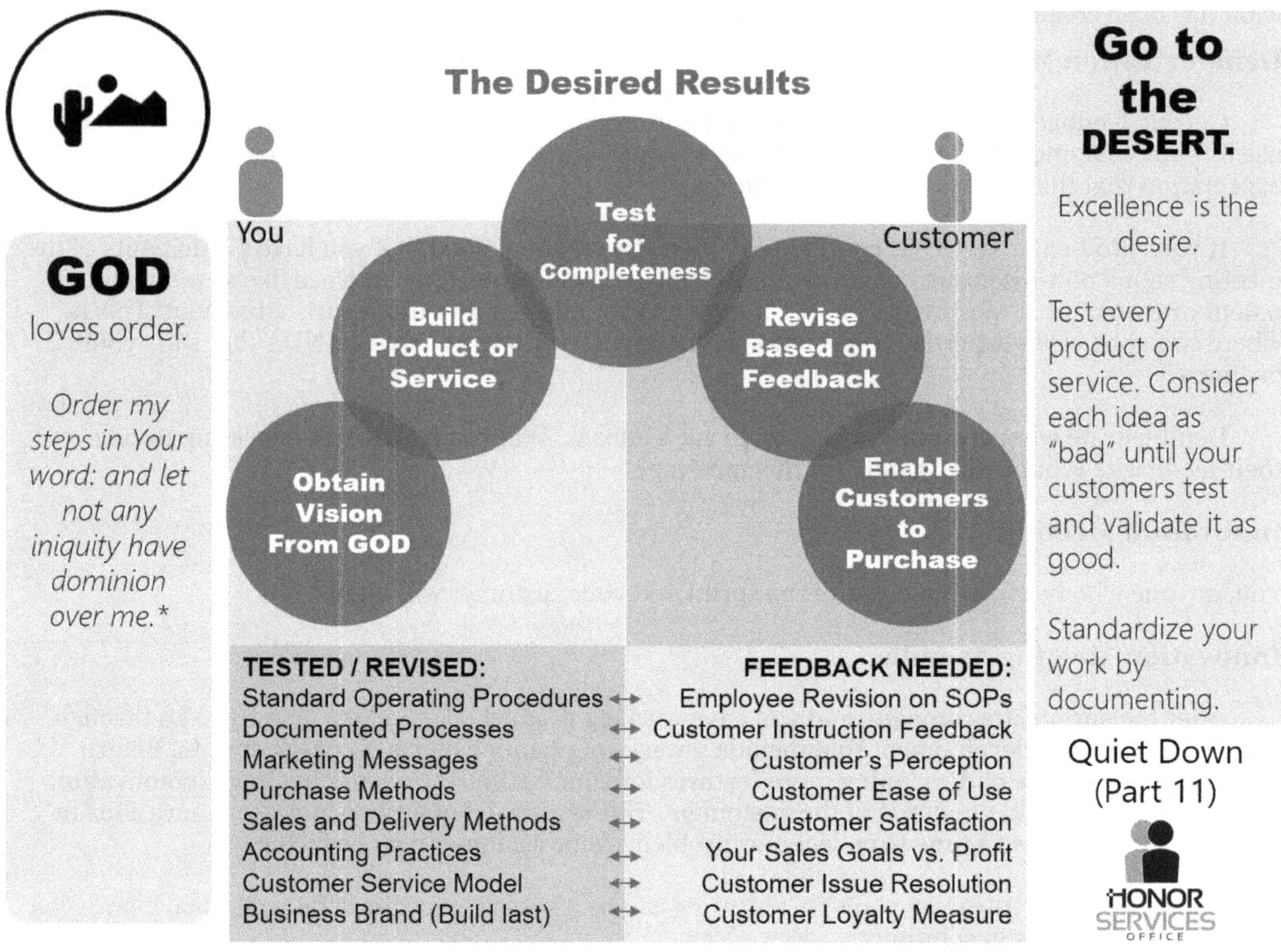

Have you ever been so distracted that you poured your beverage from the container onto the table because you forgot the cup? I have. What other distracted stories do you have?

GOD orders your steps when you feel distracted or overwhelmed.

Psalm 119:133 *Order my steps in Your word: and let not any iniquity have dominion over me* (AKJV)

When GOD gave you the vision, HE did not want you to be alone. HE is there every step of the way. GOD will give you the patience to validate your newly developed feature.

Validation varies from business to business.

The table only has space for three features just to get you started. *For each feature, write down how you will validate if it is repeatable (can be done consistently over and over), has quality, is easy to use, meets regulatory requirements, has value, looks pleasing and meets GOD's vision.*

After getting the vision from GOD and breaking it into smaller pieces, you will build the product or service to meet the needs of your customer. During the test with a few customers, listen intently. You are looking for the following:

If the product or service fails in any of the above categories, document the issue and add it to the next sprint. The validation should be done with your customers to get their feedback on your products and services you are building or modifying.

Validation	Feature Name	Feature Name	Feature Name
Is this process repeatable?			
What is the quality level?			
Is the product or service easy to use?			
Does it meet regulatory requirements (if any)?			
What is the intrinsic value? (The value does not have to be monetary.)			
Is the product aesthetically pleasing?			
Does this product or service align with GOD's vision?			

Exercise 12 – Validate (test) for Readiness

Objective: *To identify areas of your business to validate.*

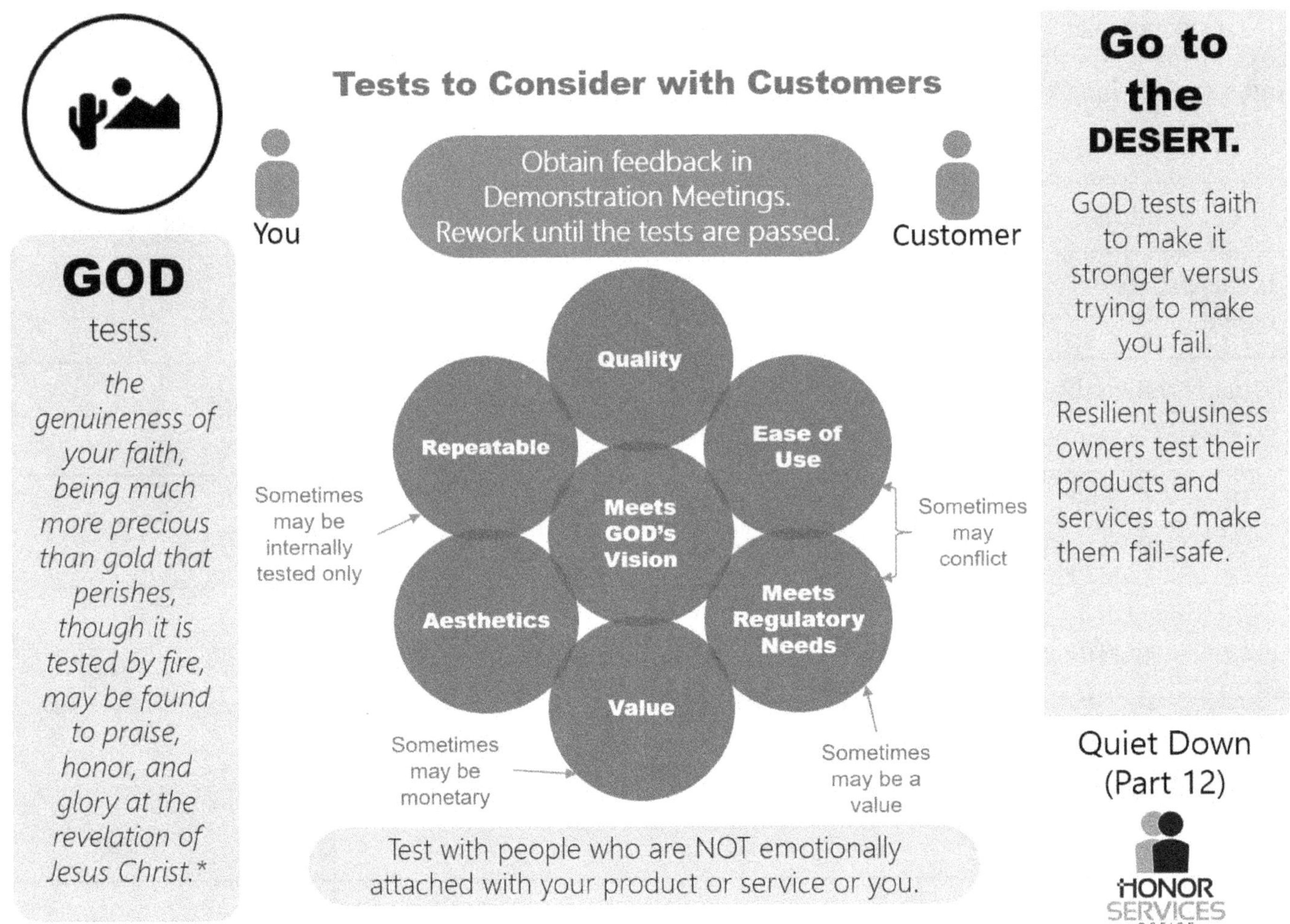

Have you ever tried exercising by lifting something heavy? Did you get stronger the more you exercised? Could you swim further or run longer?

When GOD tests you, it is not to fail you but to refine you.

1 Peter 1:7 - *that the genuineness of your faith, being much more precious than gold that perishes, though it is tested by fire, may be found to praise, honor, and glory at the revelation of Jesus Christ,*

The purpose of testing is to get stronger.

Readiness Checklist

No one is perfect, neither are your business processes. Customers need to test your documented process or instructions you may have. Your employees need to test the Standard Operating Procedures. Don't have employees?

Write your SOPs anyway. You will be surprised that you may be skipping steps even though you may have been doing the procedure for years. All the rest of the business items are to be tested by your customer.

What other tests can you think of to make sure you are ready to handle your customers? take a moment to fill in the table below.

Business Item to Validate	Who Will Validate	Acceptance Criteria
Documented Process		
Standard Operating Procedures		
Marketing Message(s)		
Purchasing Methodology		
Sales / Delivery Methodology		
Accounting Practices		
Customer Service Model		
Business Brand		

Sanity Check on Validation

Address the "No time" excuse.
Some may say, "I don't have time to do all this testing" or "I don't know people to help me validate." It is understandable to be overwhelmed by all it takes to be in business. If you do not have time, then you may want to revisit "Remove the Trash" chapter to gain confidence in GOD to help you with patience.

Address the "I do not know people" excuse.
If you do not know people, that is the main problem with starting a business or trying to grow one. Start the business after you have the relationships and have acquired their feedback.

Address the "I just want it to be done" feeling.
Rushing through the validation phase may make you miss out on valuable feedback that could have otherwise have enabled you to make necessary changes to your product or service that would have made customers more inclined to purchase from your company.

Address the "testing forever" feeling.
Validation should be concluded once the MVP is achieved. Keep checking with your customer to see if that is met. Keep improvements on a wish list for the next time you plan on doing work to change your product or service. This is why the build and feedback cycle is limited to ten weeks.

You may ask "But what if the business is not ready after I have built the first few features?" That is a fair question. Plan the next ten weeks to provide completeness to your business offerings, but also check to see if you have any blockers holding you back.

Remember, you are seeking the MVP that will be revised. In other words, if you have fear of failure, then remove this by adding confidence in GOD.

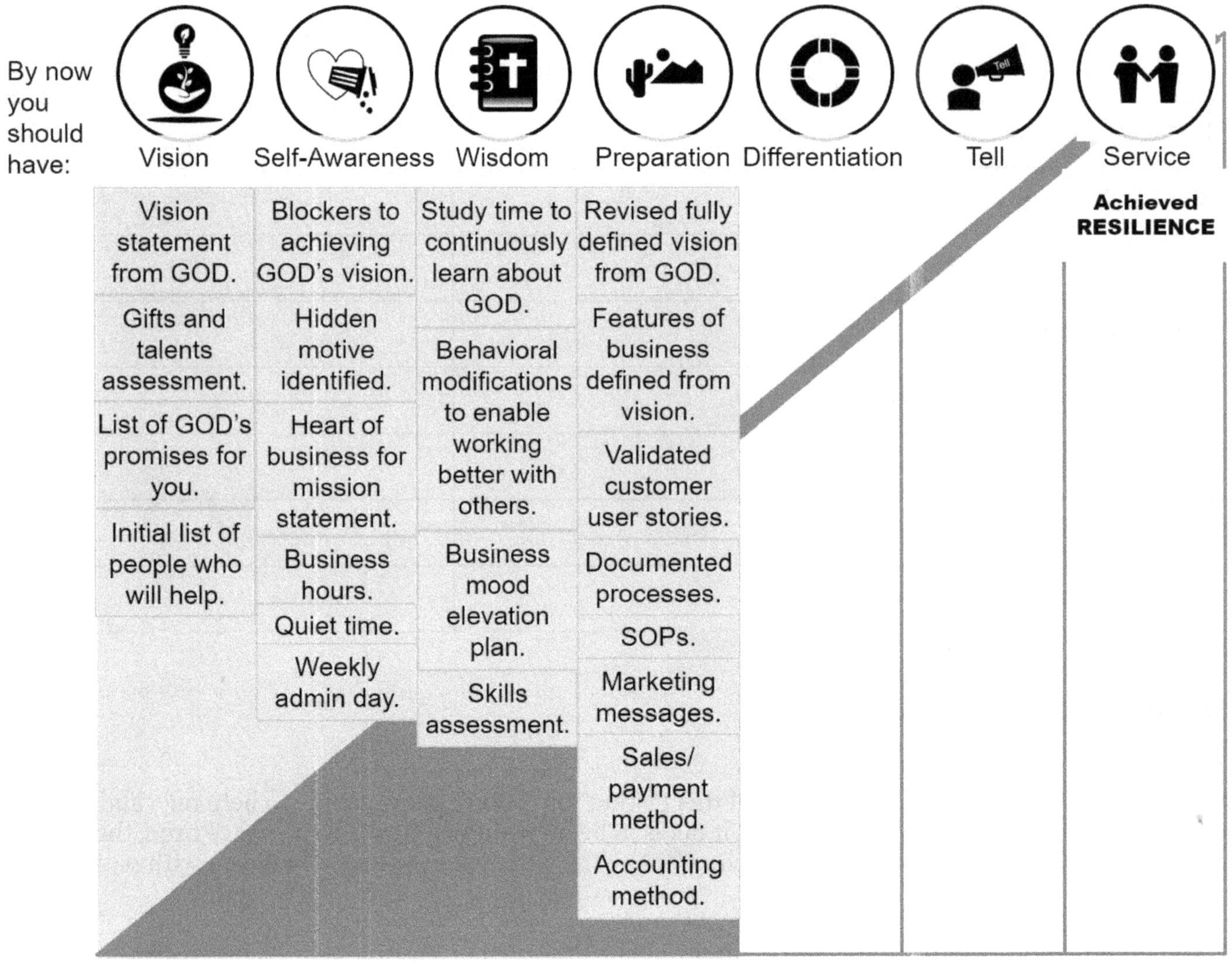

By now you should have:

Vision	Self-Awareness	Wisdom	Preparation	Differentiation	Tell	Service
Vision statement from GOD.	Blockers to achieving GOD's vision.	Study time to continuously learn about GOD.	Revised fully defined vision from GOD.			Achieved RESILIENCE
Gifts and talents assessment.	Hidden motive identified.	Behavioral modifications to enable working better with others.	Features of business defined from vision.			
List of GOD's promises for you.	Heart of business for mission statement.	Business mood elevation plan.	Validated customer user stories.			
Initial list of people who will help.	Business hours.	Skills assessment.	Documented processes.			
	Quiet time.		SOPs.			
	Weekly admin day.		Marketing messages.			
			Sales/ payment method.			
			Accounting method.			

DESERT.

Divide **E**verything. **S**eek **E**xcellence. **R**evise. **T**est.

For homework, sometime over the next week, plan time to understand and write out your customer's needs. Here is the hard part, get feedback on a feature of your business without defending it**.**

Ask for any prayer requests and dismiss in prayer. Remember to use your personal journals found on at the end of the book.

WARNING

- Avoid skipping planning.
- Avoid skipping documentation even in a sole-proprietor situation.
- Avoid being too clever in names and definitions.
- Check spelling and remain positive.

NEXT STEPS

- Document your features of business.
- Document feature definitions.
- Communicate with customers to get user stories.
- Develop test and validate completeness with customers.

PRAYER

- Pray for patience in preparation.
- Pray that GOD will give you purpose.
- Pray for guidance in leading HIS people.
- Pray for revisions to go well.

Chapter 5 – Emerge Different: Pricing/Marketing

"If GOD made you unique, why are you trying to be someone else?"

"What does a fair price look like?"

"Who should you partner with?"

"How do people know you are the expert?"

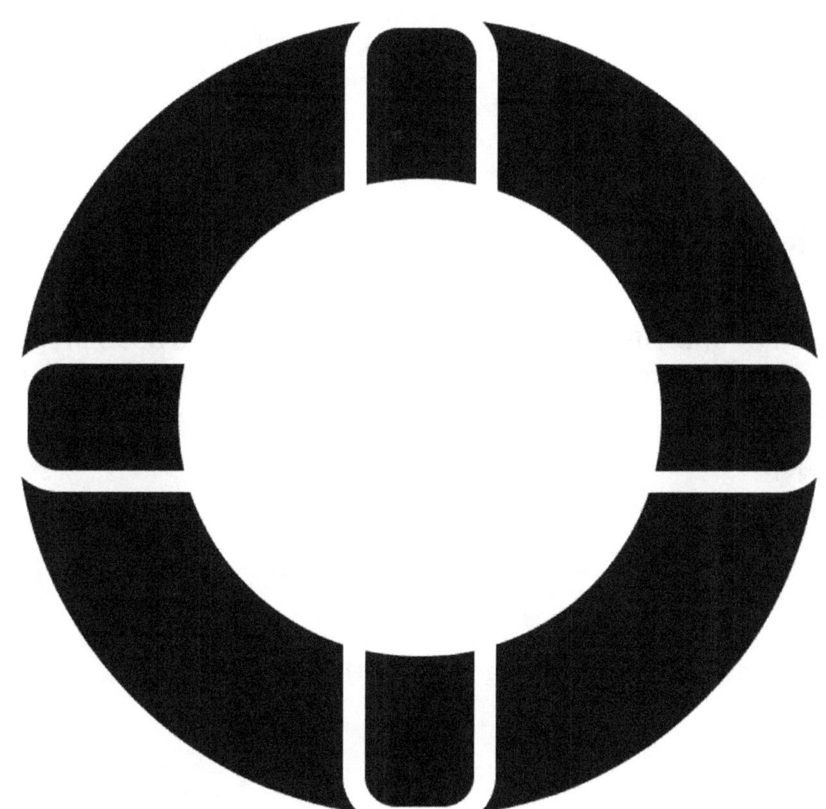

Emerge Different preparation (Week 5)

Greet participants and remind them of the goal to get feedback on at least one feature of their business from customers.

Did you meet with your thought group? If you were with us last week (or whatever your time frame), did any of you meet with your customers to get feedback on your idea or existing feature? Was it awkward getting feedback? Identify any barriers?

It takes time and practice to get feedback from your customers. The more you do this the better your business will be.

Tell the class to collect their test results, completed product or service, tested and refined marketing messages from Go to the Desert in preparation for Emerging Different.

Introduce the Emerge Different Chapter

Explain this chapter is used to develop their **expert** message which will be used in marketing.

There are 10 Marketing and Pricing Exercises.

Be prepared to get your expertise message together.

Emerge Different Objective

We are in part 5 of the framework. This methodology teaches you what to do to prepare your business for resilience. You will learn; about collaborative marketing, content marketing, pricing and scheduled time to take care of yourself.

Emerge Different Prayer

Pray:
That the class be used by GOD to encourage someone or to lead someone to the truth of salvation.
For truth in what they deliver.
To reach many for the kingdom of GOD.

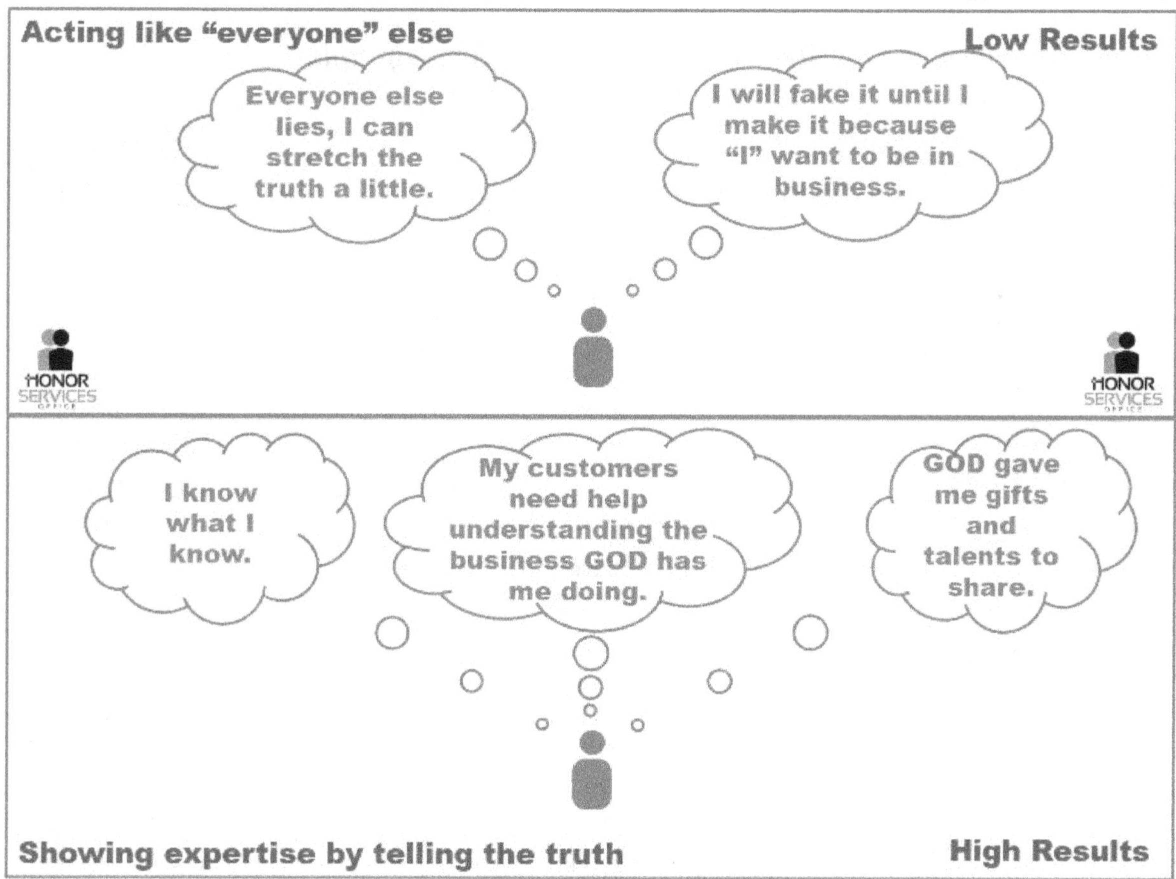

When you were a kid, did you ever break something and did not want the adult to find out? Did you pretend that everything was fine and you had nothing to do with the broken object? What other situation can you think of when you were faking it?

Customers look for experts who are truthful and skilled. The customer wants their expectations met or exceeded. The GOD-centered business owner tells the truth.

It may seem like you completed the task of creating marketing after your fourth sprint. You are almost there. Let's refine your marketing by adding your expert message. But first let's revisit your leadership style. How will you emerge different? In other words, how will you differentiate?

How to be a Servant Leader

Objective: *Revisit the fruit of the Spirit and apply it to your leadership style.*

Do you feel comfortable only around friends and family? Do you feel comfortable meeting strangers and starting conversations with them? What if the person were drowning and you had a life preserver in your hand? Would you withhold the fact that you have something important to give the person?

Be Different.

GOD wants you to go with HIS purpose.

Matthew 28:19 – *Go therefore and make disciples of all the nations, baptizing them in the name of the Father and of the Son and of the Holy Spirit*

Being a servant leader means, it is alright to run a business that makes money, but you are also an ambassador for CHRIST. This means you are always ready to be an example for HIM and to humbly speak about HIM.

Review the image to understand how to further adjust your leadership style.

Servant Leader Promise to Myself

Change takes commitment. Take a moment to write your commitment to becoming a Servant Leader by reviewing the definitions listed in the picture above. Set a date, 90 days from now, in your calendar to review your promise. Keep asking GOD for help in these areas. Write your promise in the response box provided.

I promise to (Finish the sentence)

When GOD placed you in business, it was for HIS purpose. All HE asks is that you surrender to HIM. This means HE has given you an extra desire that goes beyond profits. The GOD-centered business owner looks for opportunities to share his or her relationship with CHRIST with those to whom HE calls them. Being ready does not mean you have to change all your marketing material to mention GOD or slap verses on everything. It means being genuine, never hiding your relationship with GOD.

Serve people lavishly. Be excited for people, thanking them for listening to you as you make them aware of your product or service. Truly want the best for people, answering questions not only about your company and what it sells, but also why you believe in our LORD and Savior. HE will give you the right words at the right time to speak to the situation at hand.

The more you sow, the larger the harvest you will reap.

1. **Serve without demanding.** While marketing means making people aware, people are watchfully aware of how you treat others. Treat employees and all people you encounter as if they are the ones who need to be served, not you. Humble requests don't mean weakness; rather, restraint shows character.

2. **Be thankful.** Approaching everyone with a thankful attitude can transform a conversation. The GOD-centered business owner is grateful for being chosen by GOD to meet people and get revenue for doing so. A thankful attitude helps offset any rejection you receive. Thank GOD for HIS vision and all of the blessings HE has planned for you.

3. **Lead them.** GOD's currency is loving people. When they purchase from you, keep the relationship going in the hope of leading them to the true finish line, namely GOD's kingdom. This is the abundant life JESUS promised in John 10:10. The more you sow, the larger the harvest you will reap.

Now let's look at some marketing concepts.

Ideas are a gift from GOD. Once the GOD-centered business owner realizes the depth and breadth of HIS vision for your business, one must prepare to make people aware.

Do you have a detailed marketing plan? Many, but not all, business owners have a business plan, which includes a marketing plan section. This may contain valuable information about the market segment, competition, marketing channels, industry, and marketing strategies. Yet the plan often lacks detailed information business owners can use to get started marketing their business. The following information should be included in your marketing plan.

Collaboration marketing is an event held with other small businesses to make people aware of your product or service. This event is usually content driven, although gatherings to celebrate have been successful.

Content marketing establishes you as the expert.

It is a marketing technique of creating and distributing valuable, relevant and consistent content to attract and acquire a clearly defined audience—with the objective of driving profitable customer action. Content Marketing Institute (https://contentmarketinginstitute.com/what-is-content-marketing/)

Exercise 1 – Develop a Collaboration Marketing Plan

Objective: *Host a collaborative marketing event to grow business with a larger group.*

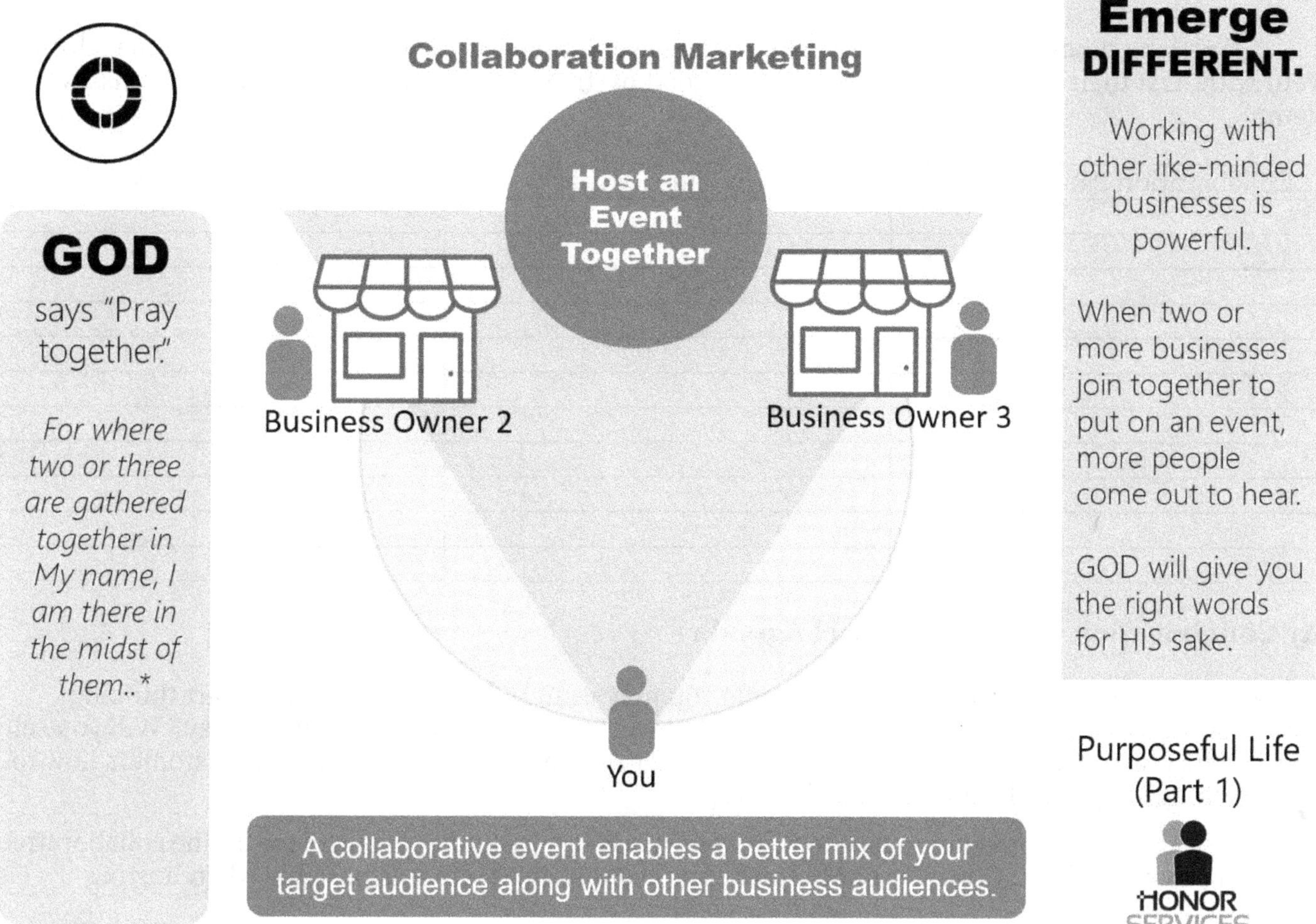

Have you ever been part of a successful team? Did you have to do everything or did you get help?

GOD wants you to help each other and pray together.

Matthew 18:20 - *For where two or three are gathered together in My name, I am there in the midst of them.*

> Collaborative Marketing increases your customers.

Your business does not have to be alone. Work with other businesses to help them succeed and seek other businesses to help you succeed. A marketing plan should be developed before doing any marketing or advertising. The two concepts we will cover are Collaborative and Content Marketing.

A **brand** is a type of product or service manufactured by a particular company under a particular name.

A **co-brand** is your brand coupled with their brand on advertising and other marketing material.

Collaborative Marketing is done by hosting events with other brands or by co-branding on advertising, with the intent of growing the client base, by exposing customers to one another's businesses." Also, not everyone is a good partner. Pray before partnering because you represent GOD.

Fill in the table below.

My Collaboration Partner List

If you plan on hosting a collaborative marketing event, then list the names of those you may host an event with. List their name, why they would be a good partner and possible event dates to discuss with them.

Collaboration Partner Name	Why This Partner	Possible Event Date

My Collaboration Event High Level Agenda

Now that you have a list of potential people you may want to host an event with, start thinking about how the day will go. How will you start? What will you say versus what will they say? Will you sell your product or service at this event? What is special about this event? Can you show customers how to do something simple with your product or service?

Here is a sample agenda for a face to face meeting. Please note that agendas for online collaborative events are more difficult. Consider how to make the event as interactive as possible when hosting online.

Sample Collaboration Agenda
Welcome / Registration / (Optional Food)
Open in prayer
Present Content – Business Collaboration Partner 1
Present Content – Business Collaboration Partner 2
Present Content – You
Panel Questions
Present Ad / Marketing – Business Collaboration Partner 1
Present Ad / Marketing – Business Collaboration Partner 2
Present Ad / Marketing – You
Optional Mingle

Will you host a collaborative marketing event? If so, then commit to a date and start planning.
Write your event date.
Write your event agenda.

Work with your collaboration event partners to determine the venue location and flow of the event.

GOD loves when we collaborate with one another. It gives us the opportunity to share our experiences so we can encourage one another toward faith in GOD. Joining with other likeminded business owners blesses more than your business.

1. **Pray first.** Let GOD lead you to the right person or people to collaborate with. Seek temporary co-branding opportunities with those who embrace your being a new creation.
2. **Plan an event together.** A collaboration event is a great way to create awareness of your product or service. Planning an event increases your reliance on GOD because of all of the moving parts. A lot can go wrong. Pray before each planning session, documenting GOD's leading along the way.
3. **Host an event together.** Communicate the event regularly prior to the event. Go to the location the day before and pray. Pray the day of the event also. Greet every attendee if possible with the excitement that only comes from GOD. Execute demonstrations, hand out samples, explain content, and be thankful all day.
4. **Follow up.** After the event, contact each attendee, preferably one on one. If the crowd is too large, send a thank you email. If the crowd is still too large, post a thank you on your website and various online outlets.

Collaboration events are strong ways to meet people, giving your attendees something they benefit from, and thus turning them into loyal customers. Whether they become customers or not, you benefit by being used by GOD to grow HIS kingdom.

"Finally, all of you, have unity of mind, sympathy, brotherly love, a tender heart and a humble mind" (1 Peter 3:8 ESV).

Local Store Marketing Approach

One approach to increase your presence is to work with other local businesses who are like minded and could benefit from selling your product or service. Work within a two to four block radius of your business location. Discuss how your product or service would benefit both parties. Mention the business you are collaborating with regularly. Hopefully, you will win many to CHRIST by working together.

Exercise 2 – Understand Content Marketing
Objective: *Choose your method of content marketing.*

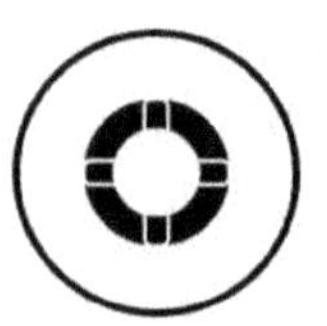

GOD says "Tell the truth."

*But this is what you must do: Tell the truth to each other.**

Content Marketing

Content marketing is a marketing technique of creating and distributing valuable, relevant and consistent content to attract and acquire a clearly defined audience – with the objective of driving profitable customer action.

Emerge DIFFERENT.

GOD made you the expert.

Build confidence in your product or service by building sound content.

This takes patience, quiet and sound thought.

You will even benefit from this.

Purposeful Life (Part 2)

Have you ever lied about your age? Did you wish you were older? Did you wish you were younger?

GOD wants you to tell the truth.

Zechariah 8:16 – *These are the things you are to do: Speak the truth to each other, and render true and sound judgment in your courts* (NIV)

> Truth takes courage and leaves your conscience clear.

Truth takes courage and leaves your conscience clear.

Read the content marketing definition from the image. Do you have a lot of money laying around to do advertising? No? Most people do not have enough money to advertise but still desire to be found. Unless your customer searches for your website name, search engines like Google, will not usually place your website on the first or second page of results.

Let's play "False or True".

Let's see if you can be found on the internet

Since I like my sentences to end with a positive message, let's play false or true."

False or true, there are over 1.75 billion websites as of May 2021.

True. According to a web search, this estimate points out that there are almost 2 billion websites in existence.

That makes it harder to find a single website.

False or true, If you build or have your site built, then people will find your business website easily.

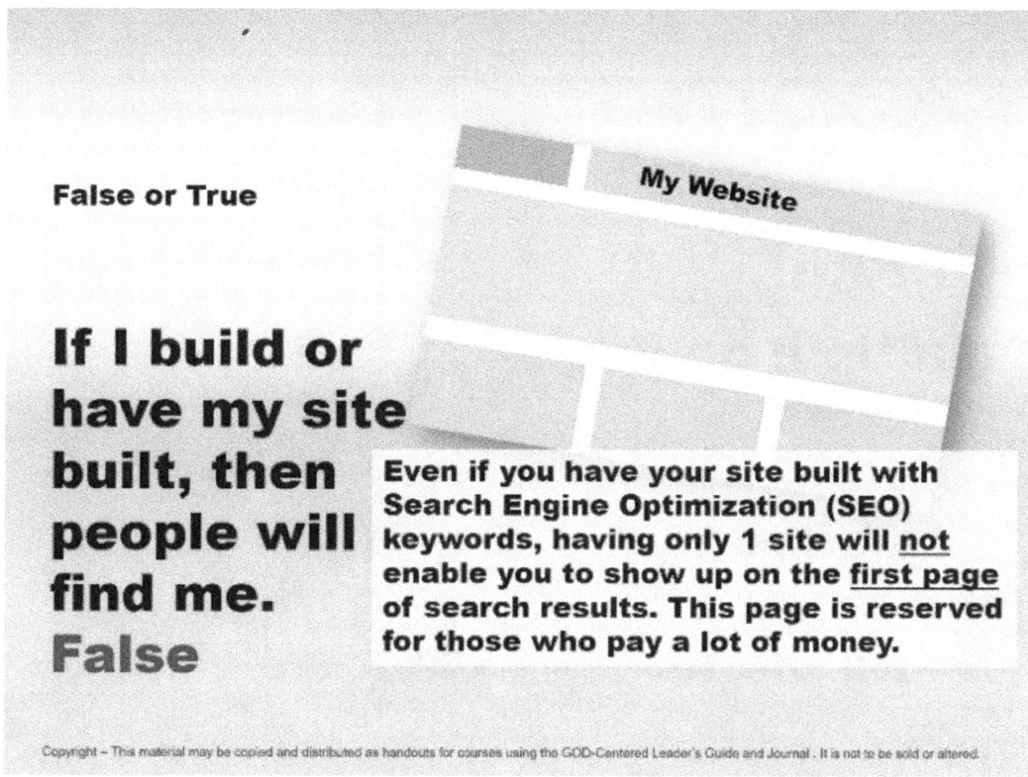

If you said false you are correct.

Even if you have your site built with Search Engine Optimization (SEO) keywords, having only 1 site will not enable you to show up on the first page of search results. This page is reserved for those who pay a lot of money.

False or true, multiple online sources, referencing my site increases my chance of being found.

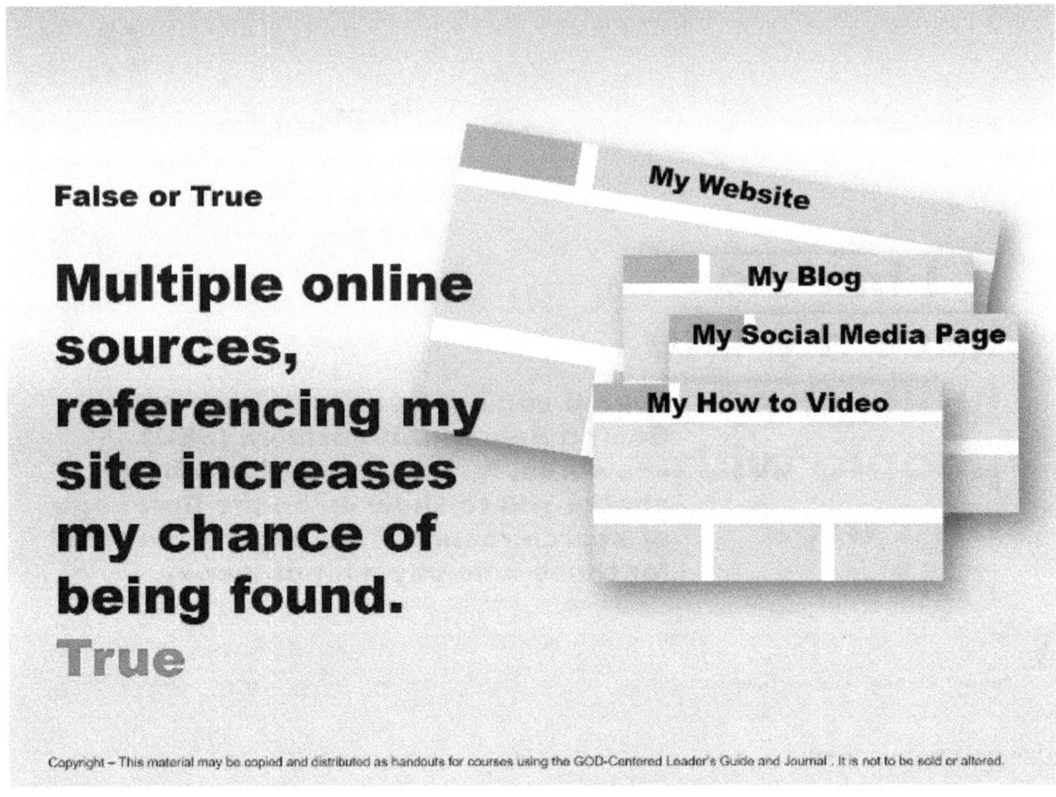

True. Referencing your website from other online locations, adds positively to your online reputation. Ideally you want a minimum of 100 references. This will take time to acquire.

False or true, Content Marketing is free.

True"
Content Marketing is free.

Free usually is not cheap. If you don't have advertising money, then you must use sweat equity to make people aware of your brand. This can be achieved by using content marketing. In other words, you may have to work a little harder to make this free marketing method, work for your business.

Let's discuss what content to create.

Exercise 3 – Develop Content Marketing Ideas

Objective: *Gain exposure to types of content that can be used to explain why you should be considered the expert, before releasing the product or service.*

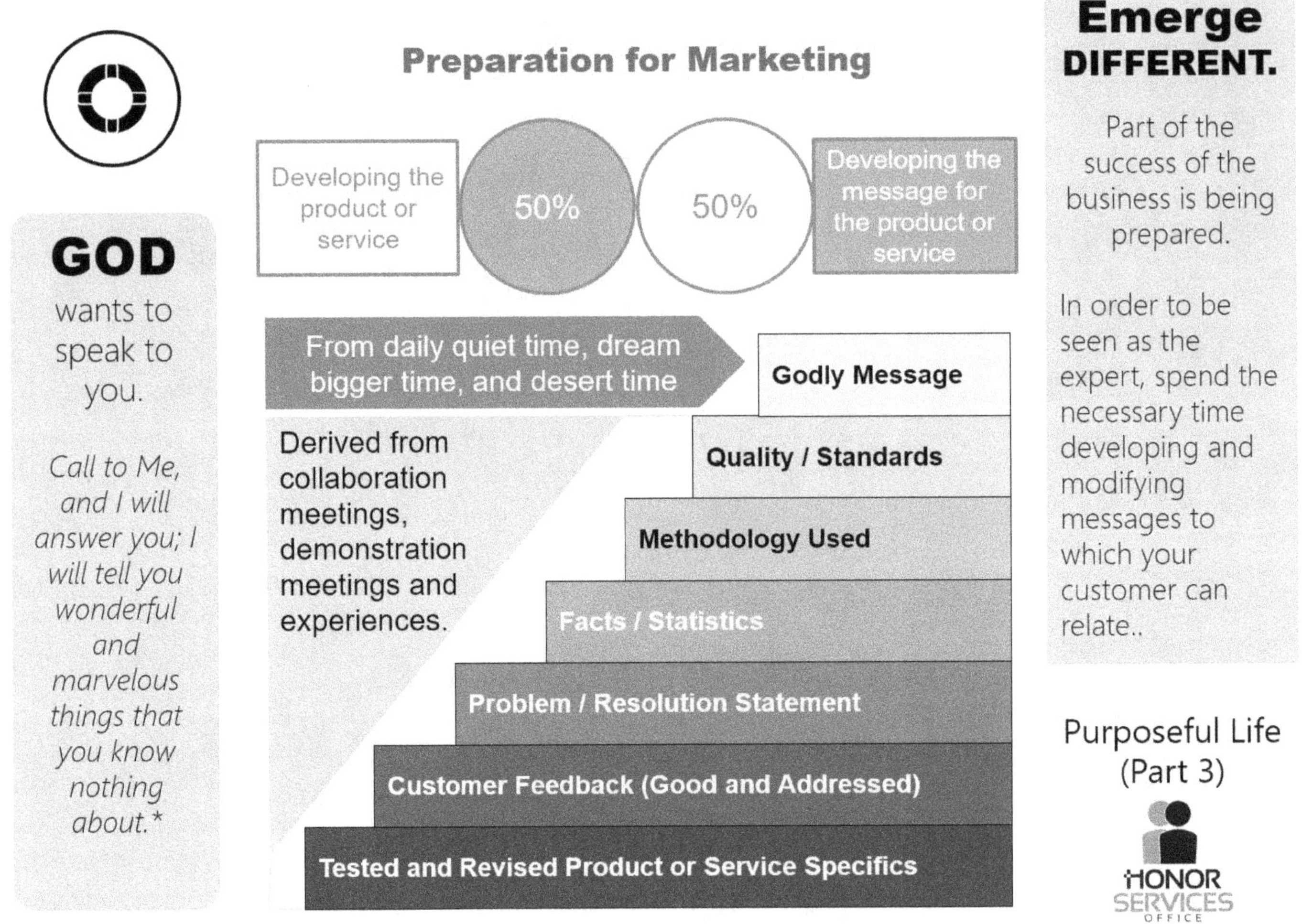

Have you ever been at a loss for words? What was the situation? Did you feel unprepared?

Be prepared and call to GOD. HE will give you the right words at the right time.

Jeremiah 33:3 – *Call to me, and I will answer you; I will tell you wonderful and marvelous things that you know nothing about.* (GNT)

When you partner with GOD HE will give you the right words to grow HIS kingdom if you have the heart for it.

Understand Expert Content

Imagine getting 50% of something when you were supposed to get 100%... Would you accept paying for a whole trip to someplace, only to discover the driver will drop you off halfway to your destination? Many entrepreneurs make the mistake of building their product or service without developing expert content that explains what the product is, why customers should buy it or the expertise behind it." Review the image above as a thought starter to developing marketing content.

This image provides some suggestions for topics you can use for your content marketing. You can write about test results or the specifics of the test.

Some people write about customer feedback or their interaction with their customers. Others write about current problems they are solving to improve the quality of their product or service.

The key is to keep your customers interested through relevant information. Let's clear up releyance. If you are a cake baking business, you may want to stay away from cat claw trimming tips, unless you can truly make them relate. Who knows, some of you may be clever enough to make them relate.

> Trust is earned, not given.

Trust is earned, not given. Help your customers overcome the trust gap. Before you do this, understand where they are. Your customer may not know about you or your products and services. The may also have needs that are not expressed.

Lastly, your customers put up guards to keep from being hurt. They may have been lied to or cheated by slick sales people.

Imagine being the customer. Now imagine their skepticism about your product or service... Okay, got that picture? Now imagine hearing "25% off" as the first words they encounter while learning about your product or service. Most people will be immediately turned off, or think they should never pay full price when purchasing from you later.

Importance of Content Marketing

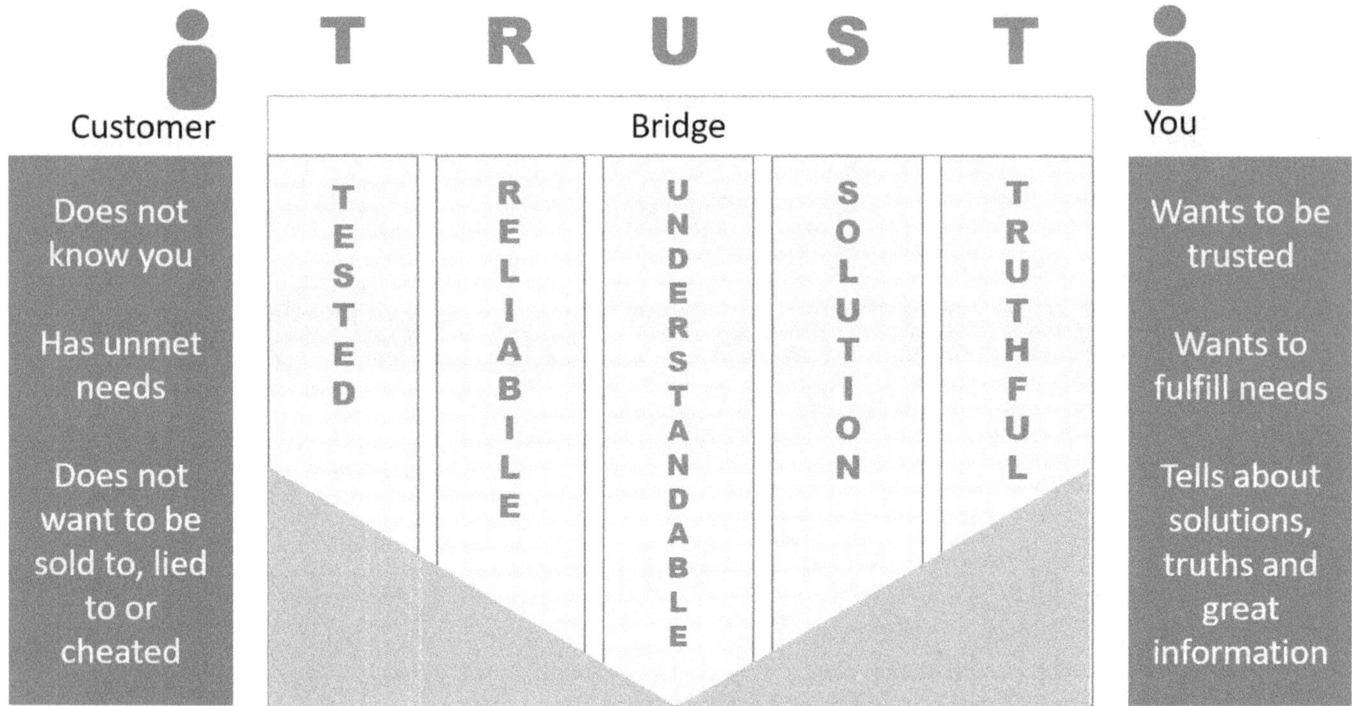

Now let's help your customer build trust. Use the TRUST bridge to help your customers understand your product or service. Steps to get over the trust bridge are small... the bigger you make the customer leap, the more scared they are to take the jump.

T is for '**Tested**.' Your customers want to know if your product or service has been tested with other people. Do you have a unique way of doing things? Is your product a new idea? By showing your test results, your customers build confidence.

R is for '**Reliable**.' Customers want to know if your product or service is reliable. Is it dependable, on-time, or strong enough to handle life's challenges?

U is for '**Understandable**.' Do your customers understand your product or service? Is it complicated and need to be explained? What assumptions are you using that need to be verified?

S is for '**Solution**.' By now you see the pattern of getting feedback from your customer. Have you met their needs with your product or service.

And finally, **T** is for '**Truthful**.' Honesty goes further than hiding. mistakes or flaws. Do you have a flaw with your product or service you can discuss?

Using the trust bridge enables the customer to come over to your side. After trust is built you can make an offer like 25% off.

What types of marketing content do you and your team produce? Video is emerging as a popular way to convey a message. Blog posts, articles and press releases are popular to build a following who craves knowledge or tips.

Please note, just because the methods are popular, does not mean they are effective. Also note, just because some are not used as much, doesn't mean they are ineffective. It may mean people don't have the means to create this type of content.

Whatever the case, many businesses are seeing the value in providing relevant content as a means of drawing awareness.

My Favorite Content

As I look at content from businesses, I quickly become bored with self-promoters. I love your smiling face and some may feel more relaxed when you show that you are a real person. But is that the extent of your content? My favorite content is how you made someone else successful. Who are you celebrating? Is your marketing saying "Look at me?" versus "Look at GOD and how HE provided for Mr. Jenkins." Mention how GOD has blessed you with your talents.

Thank GOD that HE placed you at the right place at the right time. Giving GOD credit enables HIM to bless your service more and more.

Let's start thinking of what content marketing methods you will use.

My Content Marketing

Take time to plan out your expert content. What will you write about to show you are the expert? Will you discuss the quality or the raw material you used? Will you discuss adjacent problems to the one you are solving? The possibilities are endless.

Try writing messages that do not brag about your credentials, rather on topics that interest your customer, showing you know the problems and solutions of your industry. Good content builds trust.

Fill out the table below.

Think of ideas you will use to develop your content. Imagine having a Feature of Business titled "Afterschool Program" for a childcare business. Your content idea could be to develop a blog article to address a problem of "Why kids need mentoring at young ages." The target audience of this blog article is "Parents within 123 Main Street and 345 Main Street."

Do you notice the article is related to the "Afterschool Program" feature but not directly?

This article is informative to the parent who will use the afterschool, but doesn't try to sell the reader on afterschool programs. It is content to show the breadth of expertise the childcare owner has. A cleverly placed ad, within or next to the content, will point the customer to put their child in the afterschool program.

Content Idea	Problem Addressed	Target Audience
Blog Article	**Why kids need mentoring at young ages**	**Parents within 123 Main Street and 345 Main Street**

Remember, content is 50% of your product or service. The more complex your product or service is, the more content you will need to explain it. Some restaurants not only explain their menu, but they develop content to explain the experience, safety and services.

Your expertise is needed and wanted by those GOD has given to you. Take time not only building your product or service, but also talking about the benefits your customers can expect. GOD will provide you with the confidence you need to speak or write about the passion you have for your product or service.

1. **Be truthful.** Exaggerating what your product or service does or is, will make you fail quickly. Be honest about what you provide and what the product will do. Remember, you are not only the expert, but also your expertise came as a gift from GOD. "*Truthful words are everlasting; but a lying tongue lasts only a moment*" (Proverbs 12:19 NIV).
2. **Be confident.** Speaking about your product or service is not bragging when you are stating facts. The GOD-centered business owner recognizes where the credit should go without worrying about gimmicks or salesy talk. "*But now, thus says the LORD, who created you, O Jacob, and He who formed you, O Israel: "Fear not, for I have redeemed you; I have called you by your name; You are Mine*" (Isaiah 43:1).
3. **Be thorough.** Competence can be derived from your thoroughness. Your research, processes, safety, attention to detail, and delivery strategy will say a lot to your customers. "*Through wisdom a house is built, and by understanding it is established; by knowledge the rooms are filled with all precious and pleasant riches*" (Proverbs 24:3-4).

Content is part of your product or service. Unfortunately for many, an extreme amount of time and effort are spent on developing the product or service, while little time is delegated to helping the customer understand what the product or service does.

By helping your customer understand your product or service, you will win over their confidence. But that is not the finish line. Continue with the relationship, hoping your customer will be part of GOD's family or grow in faith.

Exercise 4 – Understand the Heart behind Marketing

Objective: *Use positive words when marketing.*

You've undoubtedly seen ads where one product is negatively compared to another. How do you usually react when you see an ad like that? Positivity is a preferred method of communicating. It is needed in marketing messages. Try to speak from the positive rather than using negative words. One way to do that is to avoid negative comparison. Change *Theirs doesn't* to *Ours does.*

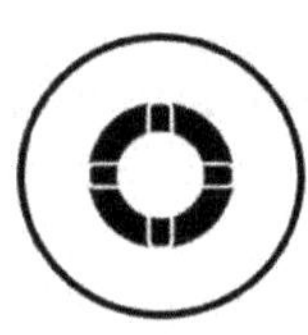

What is the "heart" behind your Marketing?

Try adding a positive spin.

GOD

says "Speak from the heart."

This people honors Me with their lips, but their heart is far from Me.

Avoid	Add
Evil thoughts	Positive thoughts
Sexual immorality	Purity
Theft	Generosity
Murder	Life (Eternal/Mortal)
Adultery	Great relationships
Coveting	Achieving
Wickedness	Love
Deceit	Truth
Sensuality	Respect
Envy	Admiration
Slander	Encouragement
Pride	Service
Foolishness	Wisdom

Emerge DIFFERENT.

Being different is not just being another type of evil.
It means standing firm on GOD's values and being confident enough to rely on them.

The HOLY SPIRIT will give you the right words at the right time because you are prepared.

Purposeful Life (Part 4)

Avoid negative words like "Can't" or "Won't".
Change "Theirs doesn't" into "Ours does."

Have you ever been around a sore winner or a sore loser? One brags about winning and the other complains about losing.

Now that GOD has cleaned your heart, speak from it.

Matthew 15:8 - *This people honors me with their lips, but their heart is far from me* (ESV)

GOD sees the heart and is willing to place HIS love in it so your words will be desirable.

Encouraging words are needed and in few supply these days. By being that light in the darkness, your customers will see something different about you and your business. Tell people they "can", by using your product or service. Avoid telling them they "can't" or "won't" or "shouldn't." Leave the audience with a positive feeling about your product or service. Avoid magic content, for example "Snake oil... It does it all!" Be courageous to say what your product or service does and solves.

My Positive Marketing Promise

Fill in your promise to use positive marketing.
My commitment to positive marketing (Be specific as you finish this sentence)

Marketing makes people aware of your product or service, but will they purchase it at the price you have set. Let's look at pricing.

Game Suggestion. Play "Price Me Right"
This game has 4 images

Suggested Script

Group Leader:
Price Me Right is a game in which I will give you the retail prices of the product and you tell me how you can sell at that price and why.

We will discuss your assumptions.

Group Leader:
I will give you the definition of the pricing you see on this image later. Each image has a price and a cost. Have your group discuss why they would use this price. The <u>penetration</u> price is $6 and it costs you $8 to make the product.

How can you sell at the price shown?

Listen to the class response.

Group Leader:
This is a marketing investment to get people to purchase your product at a much lower cost. Think of this as a sample you give to your customers to taste your product, except your customers are paying you for it.

How long should you run this price?
Not long. You still have expenses to cover.

Group Leader:
The economy price is $14 and it costs you $8 to make the product.
How can you sell at the price shown? Please provide your assumptions.

Listen to the class responses.

Group Leader:
What do you immediately notice? Was it the $6 profit?
When operating the business, focus on the "cost to make" line on a financial report more than the fictitious "profit" that you see only in your head.

We will discuss this soon.

Group Leader:
**The <u>median</u> price is $18 and it costs you $8 to make the product.
How can you sell at the price shown?
Do you notice the cost is the same as Economy Pricing?**

Listen to the class responses.

Group Leader:
One assumption is a bakery is nearby, but not in the neighborhood and they sell a similar product for a higher price. Another assumption is a second bakery is nearby, but not in the neighborhood but sells a similar product for a lower price.

This price is the <u>middle</u> between the two , <u>not</u> the average.

Group Leader:
The price is $180 and it costs you $100 to make the product.
How can you sell at the price shown?
Do you notice the cost to make has changed?
Do you notice the profit has changed?
What are your assumptions?

Listen to the class responses.

Group Leader:
More than likely the ingredients are premium. Delivery may be included in the cost.

Did anyone think about the size of the cake may be different? If the size is different, then the handling and setup may be different.

How often do you think the premium cake will be ordered? Not as often as the other cakes.

What we just saw a few examples of pricing strategies. Let's talk about those strategies.

End the game.

Exercise 5 – Choose A Pricing Strategy

Objective: *Use specific pricing strategies at the right time.*

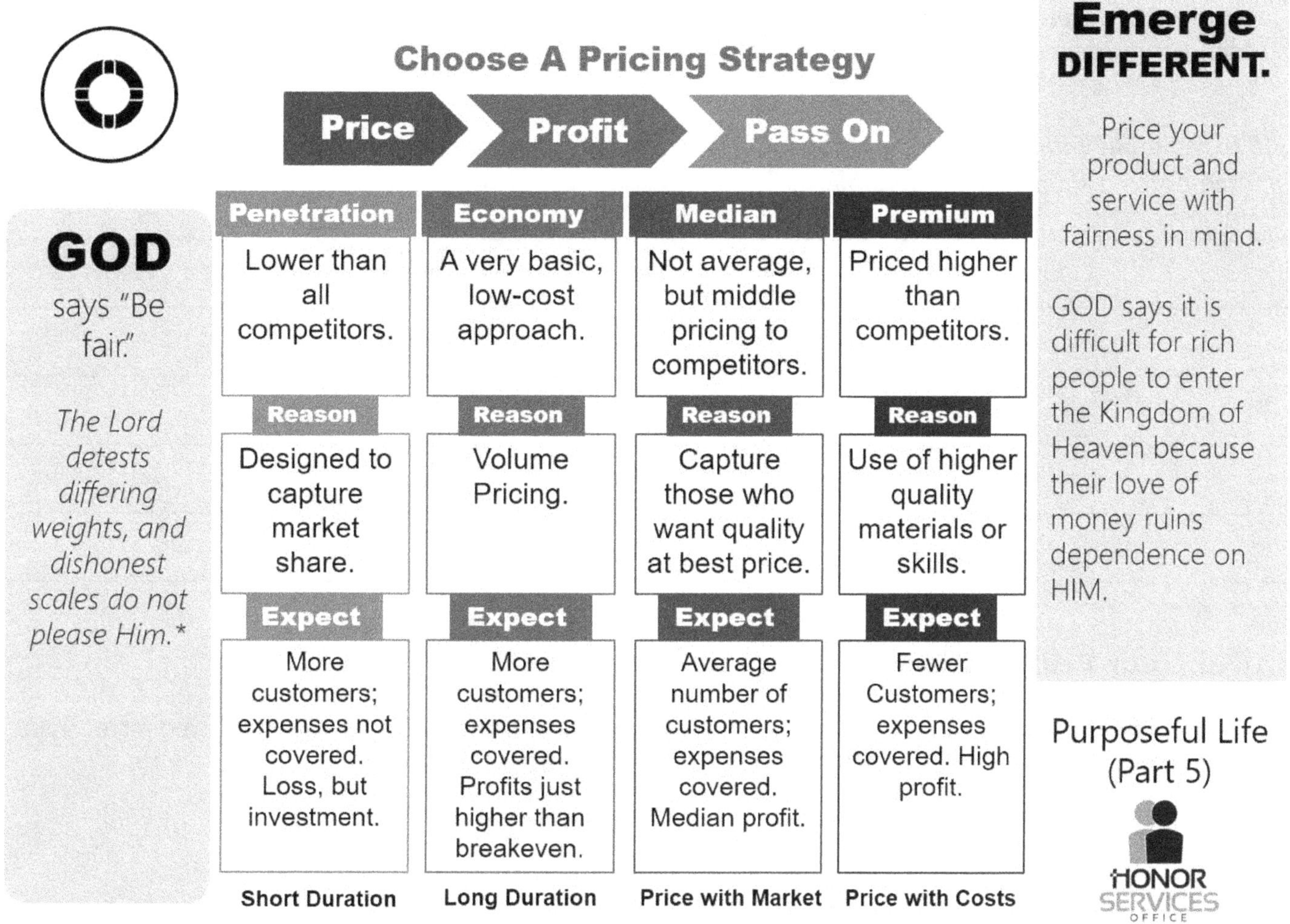

Have you ever received less than you paid for? How did you feel when you realized you paid for more and received less?

Be fair to your customers.

Proverbs 20:23 - *The LORD detests differing weights, and dishonest scales do not please him.* (NIV)

> *Group Leader:*
> *Remind the class about using **CHRIS and T** to adjust their leadership style found at the end of this book. One word of relevance to this exercise is **caring**.*

There are more than four pricing strategies. The ones displayed on this image covers a broad range of businesses. We will cover niche business pricing as well. Multiple pricing strategies can be used.

Penetration pricing is really an investment. It enables you to practically give away your product or service to gain the experience or to get noticed in a highly competitive market. This should not be done too long and you should let people know regular pricing is coming.

Economy pricing is a tier that is used for businesses that expect a large volume of purchases. In other words a **lot** of people buy a **lot** of your products and services.

Median pricing is exactly the middle price between two or more competitors. While this may work, you will be dependent on your competitors knowing what they are doing and, more importantly, that they stay in business with that price. **This strategy is high risk**.

Premium pricing is used when higher quality materials or skills are needed. Digging a hole can suddenly require premium pricing when the hole is a tunnel.

Fill in the table with your pricing strategies. You can use more than one. Consider using multiple strategies for a short time, if possible.

Pricing Strategy	Duration in months

Check Your Pricing Often

Check pricing at least once a year. For some, you should check your pricing at least once a quarter. As expenses change, so should your pricing. Pray about every price change whether up or down.

Take a moment to set a calendar date to check your pricing. Will you check in 6 months or 1 year?

Exercise 6 – Understand Pricing Factors

Objective: *Calculate expenses when considering profit margin.*

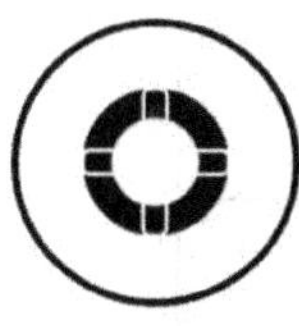

GOD

is worthy.

The workman is worthy of his wages.

Do not make your hired workers wait until the next day to receive their pay.

You

Factors in Pricing

Look at operating expenses, one time Investment costs and what the market can bear.

Expenses to Consider

Advertising
Accounting
Bank Fee
Fleet (Car maintenance and fuel)
Insurance
Labor (Salary, including your time)
Legal
Loan Payment
Material (Component or raw)
Rent(Lease + **C**ommon **A**rea **M**aintenance)
Repairs and Maintenance (Planned)
Sales tax
Supplies(Office and operating)
Telephone
Utilities (Gas/Electric)

Emerge DIFFERENT.

Making profits is essential. GOD will direct you on who to give your generosity to.

You may even be helping an angel without being aware of it. Be faithful with little and GOD will reward you to be faithful with much.

Purposeful Life (Part 6)

Have you ever felt pressured to give away your product or service to everyone for free?

You are worthy of your wages.

If so, you are not in business, rather GOD has called you to use your skill as a ministry only.

You are worthy of your wages.

1 Timothy 5:18 - *For the Scripture says, "You shall not muzzle an ox treading out grain," and, "The workman is worthy of his wages.* (BLB)

Staying in business means expenses are covered and profit is made. Let's look at your expenses before you set a price. Review the image above to identify expenses to take into consideration when determining the price of your product or service.

Fill in the blank and the table

What is your annual (or projected) sales volume? ______________________

Expense Name	Monthly Expense Amount	Annual Expense Amount

When developing your price, consider all the hard work you put into it. Some of this may be sunk costs while other costs might be recouped. Balance operating expenses versus profits. Passing on too many costs to your customers can cause them not to buy your product or service. Here are a few business costs to factor in.

Advertising fees	Accounting fees	Bank fees
Fleet car expenses	Insurance payments	Labor
Loan payments	Material	Rent + CAM
Repairs	Sales tax	Supplies
Telephone	Utilities	Other costs

Exercise 7 – Set the Price

Objective: *Set a fair price that is profitable.*

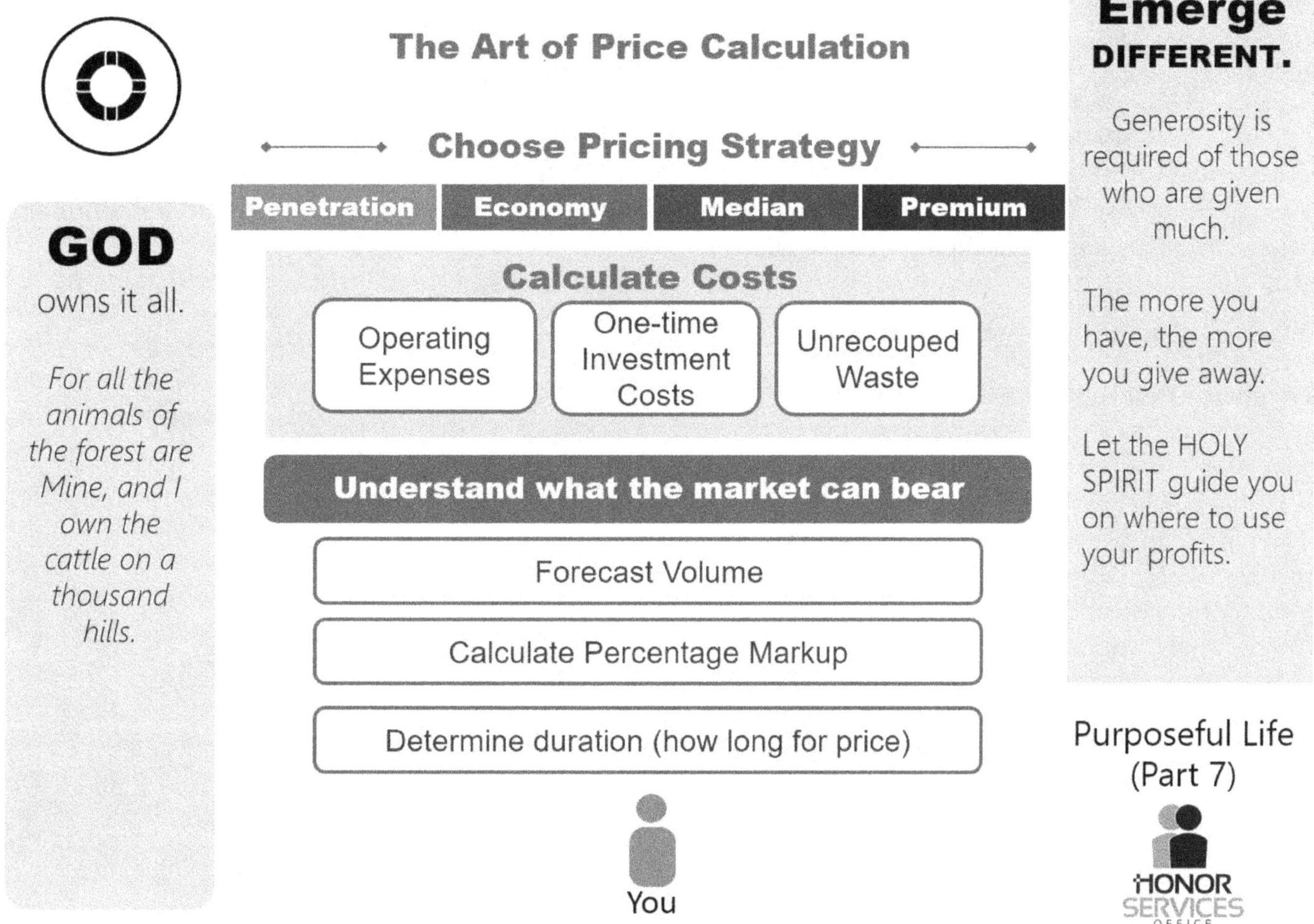

Have you ever played a game and wanted to win so badly that you cheated? What if the game was one you played by yourself like solitaire? Would you like to pay more than you should?

Everything is GOD's. Ask HIM for guidance in your pricing.

Psalm 50:10 - *For all the animals of the forest are mine, and I own the cattle on a thousand hills.* (NLT)

GOD allows us to use HIS stuff temporarily, so price HIS stuff fairly. Now it's time for you to set or adjust your price. Setting your price is an art. There are a lot of factors that goes into pricing. Be willing to research and prepare before setting your price.

1. **Choose a pricing strategy**. Refer to your choice in Exercise 5— "Choose a Pricing Strategy."
2. **Calculate the costs you want to pass on to the customer**. Not every cost can be covered. Think about the sales volume and consider spreading your cost across how many sales you bring in.
3. **Understand how much people are paying for a similar product or service.** If the product or service is new, then ask customers how much they would pay.

4. **Forecast the sales volume.** How many units of your product will be sold? If you have a service, what is the demand? Forecasting takes practice and you will become better and better at it by using at least one year of history as the basis.
5. **Calculate a percent markup.** The percent markup is after you have covered all of your costs. Pray about what is reasonable and what the market can bear. High volume businesses do not exceed a ten-percent markup while low-volume businesses can go as high as sixty percent.
6. **Determine how long this pricing model should last.** Introductory pricing should only last for a short period of time. Make sure you tell your customers this is a "limited time offer," otherwise, they will be upset when the price goes up. Other pricing models should be examined regularly and modified based on sales.

Let's look at some other ways to calculate pricing.

Keystone Pricing

The Art of Price Calculation

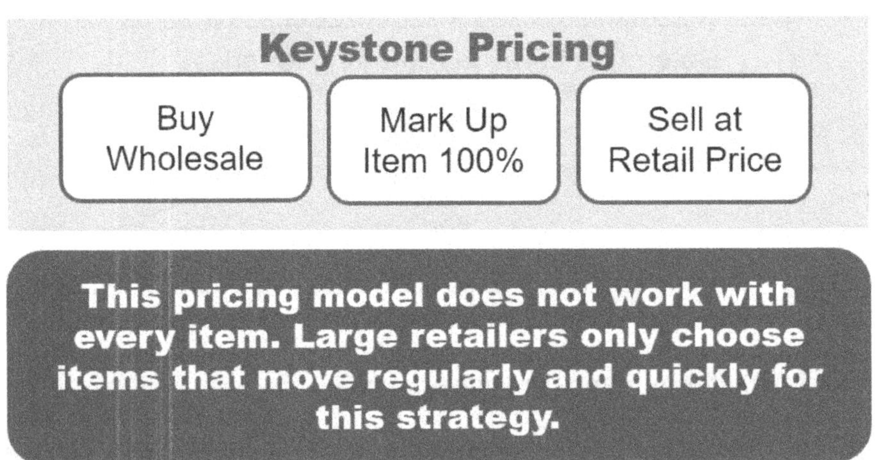

Keystone pricing is used for wholesale and retail businesses. The math is simple. Whatever it cost you to make the product, double the cost and sell it as wholesale. Whatever you buy at wholesale, double the cost and sell it retail. It is as simple as that. Retailers should limit keystone pricing as everything should not be sold using this strategy. Remember premium and economy pricing? Some items may fall into these categories so consider a mix of pricing tiers.

Hourly Pricing

The Art of Price Calculation

Choose Pricing Strategy Hourly Service

Hourly Pricing

- Calculate the Industry Standard
- Adjust for Location
- Adjust for Volume

Examine other costs. For example hourly rates do not include parts, raw material, or travel to and from the work location.

Great for:
Consulting, repair, rental, moving, cleaning, personal care, teaching or other specialized skill.

Many businesses fall into the hourly pricing category. The more specialized the skill, the higher the hourly rate. This varies by industry, however, consider the location GOD is taking you and adjust your price based on projected sales.

How many sales do you anticipate in that location?

If you have a service that takes a considerable amount of your time, is in demand and few competitors, then premium pricing may be considered. If the demand is high, but the market has plenty people with the same skill, then economy pricing should be considered.

Ready to set your prices? Not yet. Use the table below to work out your pricing.

Pricing Factor	Comment or Cost
Total Business Cost (Add up all expenses)	
Market Price (Competitor pricing)	
Minimum people have paid for this	
Maximum people have paid for this	

Forecasted Sales Volume	
Reasonable % Mark Up	

Now you are ready to set your pricing. Let's take a look at the market.

Exercise 8—Investigate the Market

Objective: *Confirm all pricing factors have been considered.*

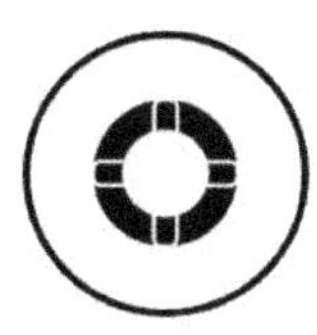

GOD

says "Be wise."

*Behold, I send you out as sheep in the midst of wolves. Therefore be wise as serpents and harmless as doves.**

Market Research

Customer **Will provide:**	Competitor **Will have:**
Issues your business can possibly solve	Price
Desires your business can possibly fulfil	Quantities
Adjustments to your current products and services	Quality
Frequency, duration, timing and size of the problem	Services offered
	Delivery model
	Other content listed on their website, ads and social media

Be thorough to supply your customer's needs. Consider praying for the success of your "competitors" as well as your success.

Emerge DIFFERENT.

Knowing people is important. GOD has opened your eyes to care with discernment. Be wise and continuously ask GOD who HE wants your business to serve. Research their needs before you research competitors.

Purposeful Life (Part 8)

Have you ever seen a sign that says "Beware of pickpockets?" Does it make you want to steal? Jokingly, if so, then revisit the Remove the Trash chapter.

Be wise.

Matthew 10:16 – *Behold, I send you out as sheep in the midst of wolves. Therefore be wise as serpents and harmless as doves.*

Understand the world's tactics, but be above them and follow GOD's ways. Now it is time to do some research. This is often the downfall of people who have been in business for a while as they only do this once and never check to see if the market has changed. Research your industry regularly and determine how you will investigate your market.

Customer Research

Know your customer and you will be able to provide a better product or service. How old are your customers? Are your customers mostly male or female? What time of day do they purchase? How often do your customers purchase? After researching, check to see if you are looking at your customers through some trash that could still be in the heart. Should you be serving another group that you have not forgiven? Ask GOD for HIS audience. HE may broaden yours. What other questions can you come up with to research your customers?

Your product or service should be built with your customers, so you should know what they desire by asking them directly.

Competitor Research

Does the GOD-centered business owner really compete? No. The GOD-centered business owner has purpose and believes that other people will work in the industry. This research is for you to look across your industry to see where your business fits. Offer what others offer and more. Learn without stealing.

Do what you do well and see what others are doing well. Be unique.

Understand what regulations you need to follow.

With that said, now look at other businesses, similar to yours. The image above will provide ideas of what to look for. GOD owns the future and gives you a gift, namely the present. You are not researching the future, but remain wise in the present.

My Market Research

Fill in this table to collect your research.

Customer Feedback

Feedback Category	Response
Problems my customers told me	
Desires my customers expressed	
Complaints my customers have expressed	
Improvement suggestions from my customers	
Frequency, duration timing and size of the problem	

Competitor Research

Research Category	Observation
Competitor Price	
Quantities sold	
Quality of service or material used	
Services Offered	
Delivery Model	
Expertise Content Marketing (Warning: do not steal)	

Exercise 9 – Develop a Content Marketing Map

Objective: *Identify locations to place well defined online content.*

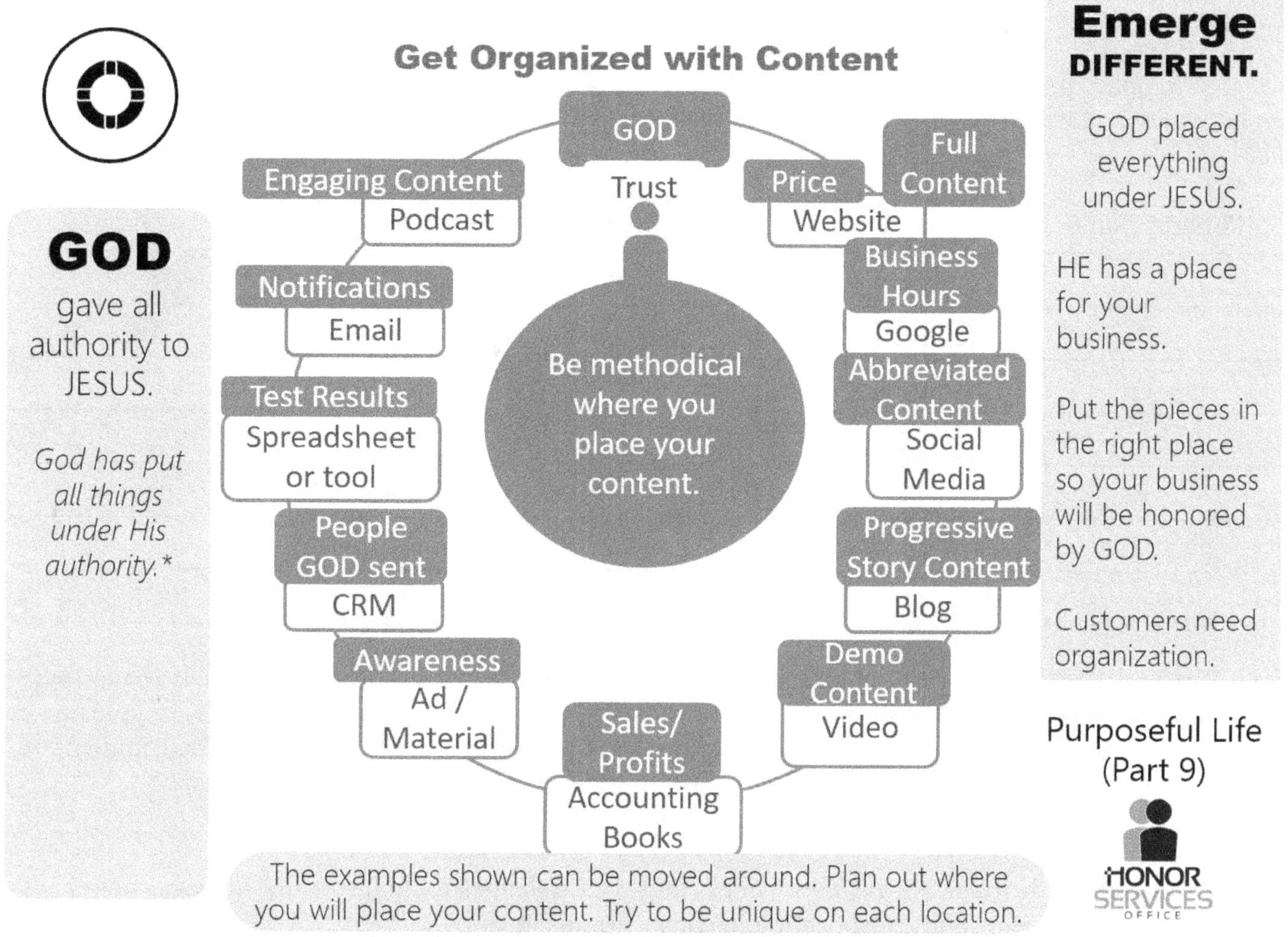

How many people lose things often? Do you put things down in a different spot every time?

GOD puts things in its place.

1 Corinthians 15:27 - *For the Scriptures say, "God has put all things under his authority." (Of course, when it says "all things are under his authority," that does not include God himself, who gave Christ his authority.)* (NLT)

GOD is orderly. HE put JESUS over all things. No one can randomly become JESUS. Your customers like order. They like to find information about your company easily.

Use the ideas you developed in exercise 3 – Develop Content Marketing Ideas of this chapter to develop your content marketing map. Try to make content as unique as possible on your various channels. See image above for marketing channel ideas.

Again, if you do not have a marketing budget, then sweat equity, hard work, must be used. Spread messages about your expertise in various forms to build up your online reputation. A good online reputation is hard to obtain and should be guarded by you. Your customers may not want controversial content, unless this is part of your business. Believe it or not, your online reputation is being watched. Any inflammatory information you write may get your site banned or restricted.

On the other hand the more positive information you write about your industry, the better your online reputation becomes. Some restaurants place cooking tips on their website to draw foodies to their site. What ideas can you come up with and where will you place it. Try to be unique as possible on various locations.

Fill in your content marketing map. Write the name of the content you are writing about. Think about where you will put it. Will the content be on your website, a blog or a small message on social media?

Content Name	Location 1	Location 2	Location 3	Location 4

While content marketing does not have to be done with a formula, it works best when you have a consistent strategy. Choose the locations you will post specific pieces of content. Try to be unique on each as much as possible. For example, post the progress you are making on a personal blog and post a limited time offer on Twitter. Each content location should demonstrate your expertise.

1. **Trust.** Place this in GOD's hands.
2. **Business hours.** Google My Business and your website should have your business hours when customers and collaboration partners can reach you.
3. **Business contact information.** Google My Business, your website, and your email signature should have all contact information. This will be how people can get in touch with you.
4. **Progress.** Blogs are great for telling your progressive story. This can show people what you are working on and how they can assist in the journey. Place a link to this on your website.
5. **Demonstrations.** Video is a great way to demonstrate small pieces of your product or service. Place this on your website.
6. **Abbreviated content.** Social media is used as a quick read. Abbreviate content as a teaser and direct readers to the full content on your website or other location.
7. **Sales and profits.** Income and expenses are content that will be shared with accountants and eventually investors if you go that route. Please note: investors will expect full disclosure and a professional-looking report.
8. **Marketing message.** Ads can be expensive, but delivering them to the right audience can produce a return on your investment. Prayerfully choose advertising that fits your budget. Be

slow to jump into this by showing self-control and patience. Place a link to the ad on your website.

9. **Potential customers.** Put notes about each potential customer/potential client, in a contact relationship management tool. These will be used for important follow-up efforts.
10. **Test results.** Document quality, strength, ease of use, regulatory requirements met, customer value achieved, aesthetics achieved, repeatable process, and how this meets GOD's vision. Each test result can become content. Even failures are noteworthy. Place this on your website.
11. **Notifications.** Leverage email to notify people about new content. Bring people to the content instead of sending it out. Place notifications on your website.
12. **Engaging content.** Use a podcast to record interviews, provide topical discussions, or explain viewpoints related to your industry. Place a link to the podcast on your website.

Once you start content marketing, do not stop. It is better to wait to do content marketing than to half-heartedly do it. Create enough topics up front then post a little at a time. Be consistent.

Does a plumber need content? Yes. Does a dog walker need content? Yes. Are there any businesses that do not need content? No. All businesses can use content to show expertise.

Exercise 10 – Leaders Get Replenished

Objective: *Develop a schedule that includes GOD and personal rejuvenation.*

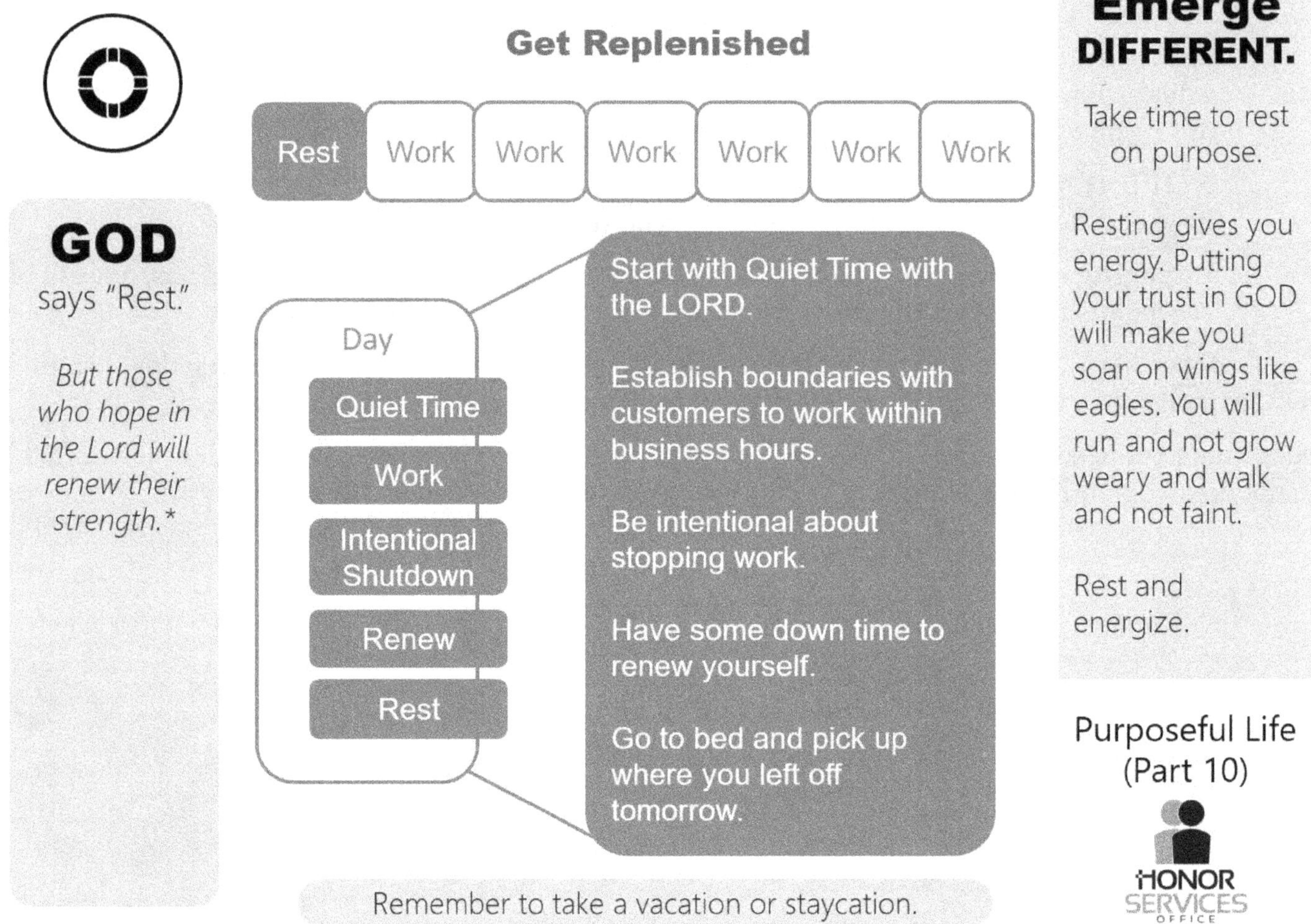

Has anyone ever done something so long you got burned out and it no longer has joy?

GOD wants you to get rest. Worry gets you nowhere but dead.

> Worry gets you nowhere but dead.

Isaiah 40:30-31 – *Even youths grow tired and weary, and young men stumble and fall; but those who hope in the LORD will renew their strength. They will soar on wings like eagles; they will run and not grow weary, they will walk and not be faint.* (NIV)

GOD wants to renew your energy daily. Remember, you are ready to emerge differently. This means you have the courage to put work down.

Leaders Take Care of Themselves

You really need to take good care of yourself. GOD needs you rested and replenished. Did you go into business to become a person no one wants to be around? Learn to shut it off. It will be there tomorrow.

Determine hours that will provide boundaries to work in for your customer, yourself, family and friends.

Let's talk about the structure of the day.

Do you spend time with GOD each day? HE wants your time. But so many people put the business before GOD and they no longer have time for HIM. Quiet time is extremely important to the GOD-centered business owner.

What are your business hours? The lack of business hours confuses your customers and they will call at all hours of the day if they do not know your hours. These should be defined and easy to find.

Will you intentionally shut down at the end of a business day? Practice stopping work. Put it down and return to it tomorrow.

What do you like to do? Do you have a hobby, sport or tv show you like? Spend some time renewing you.

Running on fumes or on empty can be devastating. The GOD-centered business owner needs to be recharged often, possibly more than those they serve. Quiet time is more important than running off and doing a lot of activity.

1. **Empty the trash again.** We are like sheep that wander off into dangerous places. Take time daily to surrender your wandering to GOD. Show GOD your confidence in HIM by listing your plans and asking, "Is this what YOU want me to do today?" Follow that question with, "Please tear down any plans I have that are not YOURS." Releasing control to GOD enables HIM to guide your day.
2. **Set family time, "me time," and business hours.** A common mistake of micro-business owners is not knowing when to stop working, or better yet, when to start their day. Get structured. Set hours for your family, yourself, and your customers. These boundaries help others understand how they can engage you consistently. Quiet down each day, then work, shut down work, spend time with family or others, renew yourself, and then rest.
3. **Be ready.** After you empty yourself, it is time to get filled up. Read GOD's word daily. Allow HIM to guide you by confirming what you should do through what you read. HIS Word breathes life and enables those who have a thirst for life to never be thirsty again. After reading, spend time reflecting and applying what you read to the direction of your business. GOD will direct you to reach out to potential clients and customers who need encouragement.
4. **Execute the vision.** GOD wants you to be focused. Stand firm to the large vision HE gave you, but be flexible to make adjustments HE gives. You may not have been ready to execute the vision HE had for you when HE first gave it to you. HE may detour you in HIS plan to develop you before returning you to HIS vision.

As you mature in your business, it will become clear what works and what doesn't. Make adjustments versus throwing everything away and starting over on a new path. This requires obedience to GOD and trust in HIS plan.

Take time to fill out a schedule for you and your business.

Category	Mon	Tue	Wed	Thu	Fri	Sat	Sun
Quiet Time							
Business Hours							
Intentional Shutdown							
Renewal Time							
Rest Time							

These hours to everyone to enable **boundaries** to complete your work. Do this with love.

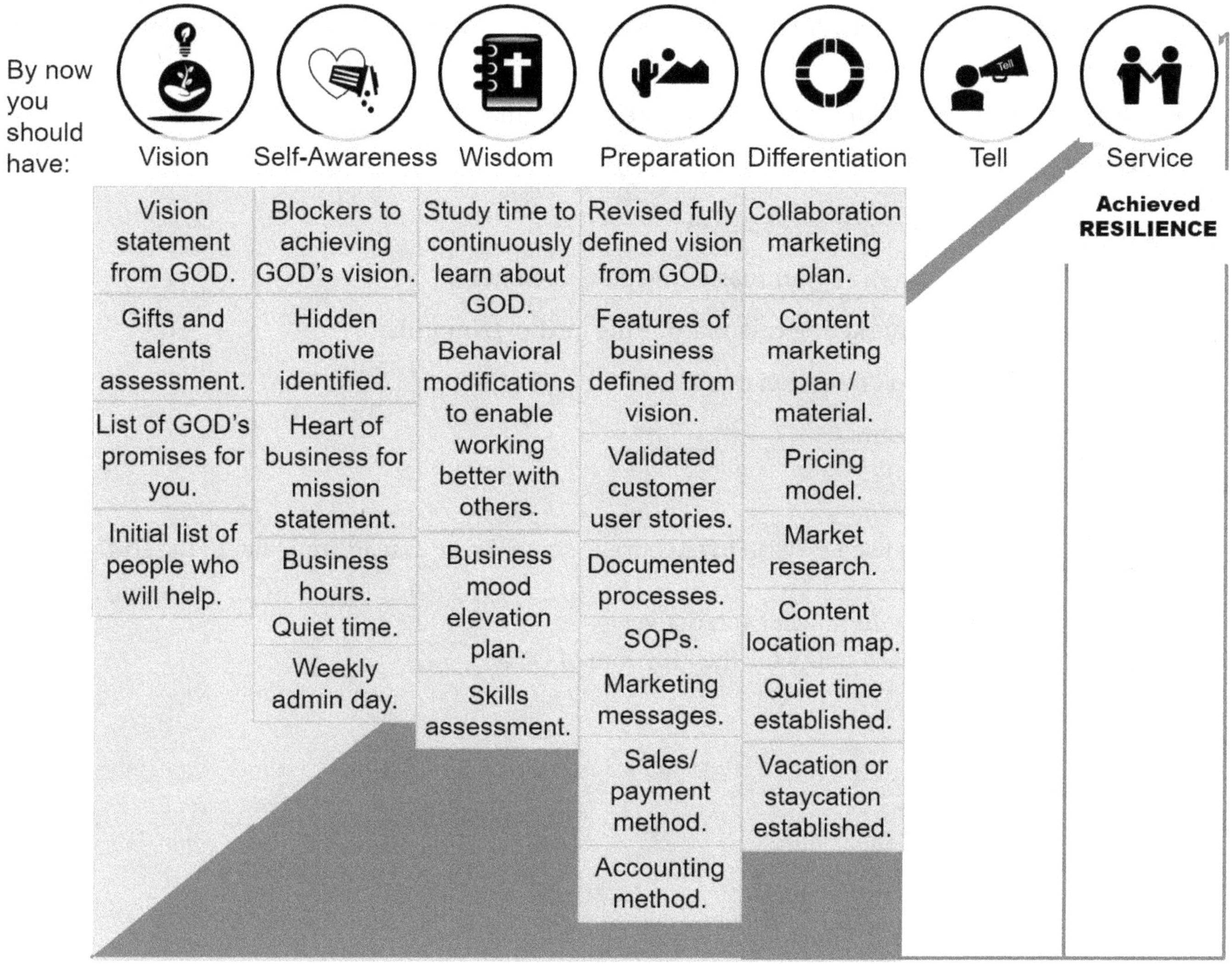

By now you should have:

Vision	Self-Awareness	Wisdom	Preparation	Differentiation	Tell	Service
Vision statement from GOD. Gifts and talents assessment. List of GOD's promises for you. Initial list of people who will help.	Blockers to achieving GOD's vision. Hidden motive identified. Heart of business for mission statement. Business hours. Quiet time. Weekly admin day.	Study time to continuously learn about GOD. Behavioral modifications to enable working better with others. Business mood elevation plan. Skills assessment.	Revised fully defined vision from GOD. Features of business defined from vision. Validated customer user stories. Documented processes. SOPs. Marketing messages. Sales/ payment method. Accounting method.	Collaboration marketing plan. Content marketing plan / material. Pricing model. Market research. Content location map. Quiet time established. Vacation or staycation established.		**Achieved RESILIENCE**

EMERGE.

Expert **M**essages **E**nrich **R**elationships **G**aining **E**vangelism

For homework, find 10 products or services that you purchased and write the reason you chose the brand. Spread this across food, personal services, electronics, cars entertainment, and doctors. Also, discuss your expertise with your thought groups.

Ask for any prayer requests and dismiss in prayer. Remember to use your personal journals found at the end of this book.

WARNING

- It's tempting for business owners to start their business, open the doors, and jump into a lot of busy work. But if they don't do the upfront planning, a lot of time and money will be wasted trying to market products the market doesn't want or need or in a way that repels rather than attracts. This can leave a business owner feeling like a failure, when in fact the only thing he or she failed to do was plan.

- Do not be afraid of committing to a budget for marketing. Many people focus all their attention on building new products, services, and ideas and forget to tell people about the benefits of the product, service, or idea.
- Understand the marketing strategies before you begin.

NEXT STEPS

- Conduct your market survey.
- Create or refine your marketing plan document.
- Create a marketing calendar for the next 6-12 months.
- Pray for collaboration events.
- Set replenishment hours.

PRAYER

- Pray to be used by GOD to encourage someone or to lead someone to the truth of salvation.
- Pray for truth in what you deliver.
- Pray to reach many for the kingdom of GOD.

Chapter 6 – Kingdom-First Mindset : Tell versus Sell

"Should you sell or pray right now?"

"Is the kingdom really first in your life?"

"Are you prepared?"

Kingdom-First Mindset preparation (Week 6)

Greet participants and remind them of the goal to track 10 products or services purchased over the past week.

If you were with us last week (or whatever your time frame),What did you purchase and why did you purchase it? What is the story behind the purchased product or service? Allow for the groups to respond.

Let's get started. Please review all documentation, content, test results and revisit Remove the Trash. Before selling your product or service, be prepared.

Introduce the Kingdom First Mindset Chapter

Explain this chapter is used to develop the message they will use to tell people about their product or service and hopefully GOD

There are 4 Sales Exercises.

Be prepared to get your solutions ready to explain to your customer.

Kingdom First Mindset Objective

We are in part 6 of the framework. This methodology teaches you what to do to prepare your business for resilience. You will learn; about your relationship with new people and your sales process.

Kingdom-First Mindset Prayer

Pray for:
GOD to adjust your leadership style to be able to work with many types of people who may come to know CHRIST.
A sales method that is not intimidating to you or the customer.
A quality relationship with many people.

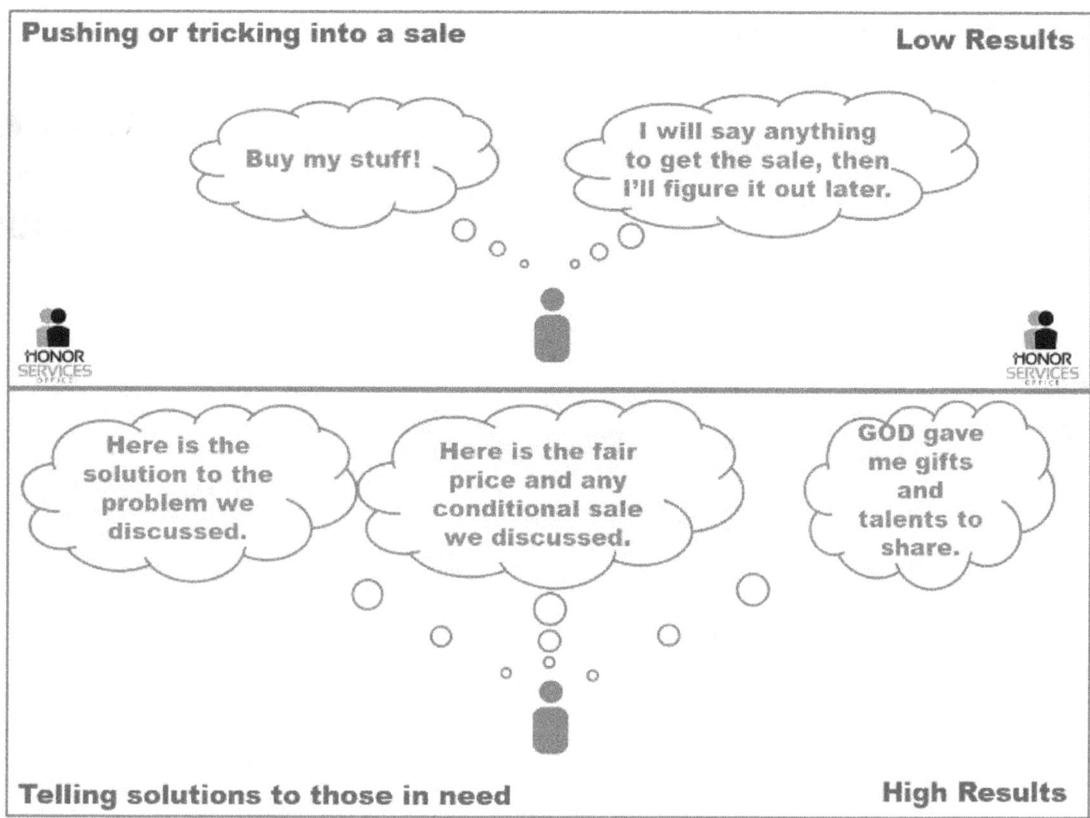

Have you ever been unemployed and wanted a job so badly that you would lie about your qualifications? Have you ever met someone who lied about their qualifications?

It is important to provide solutions to problems versus trying to push someone into purchasing unwanted or unneeded products and services.

The GOD-centered Business Owner tells the truth.

Let's prepare your sales process.

A Life with Purpose Sticks to the Plan

Objective: *Add the love of GOD as a purpose of your business.*

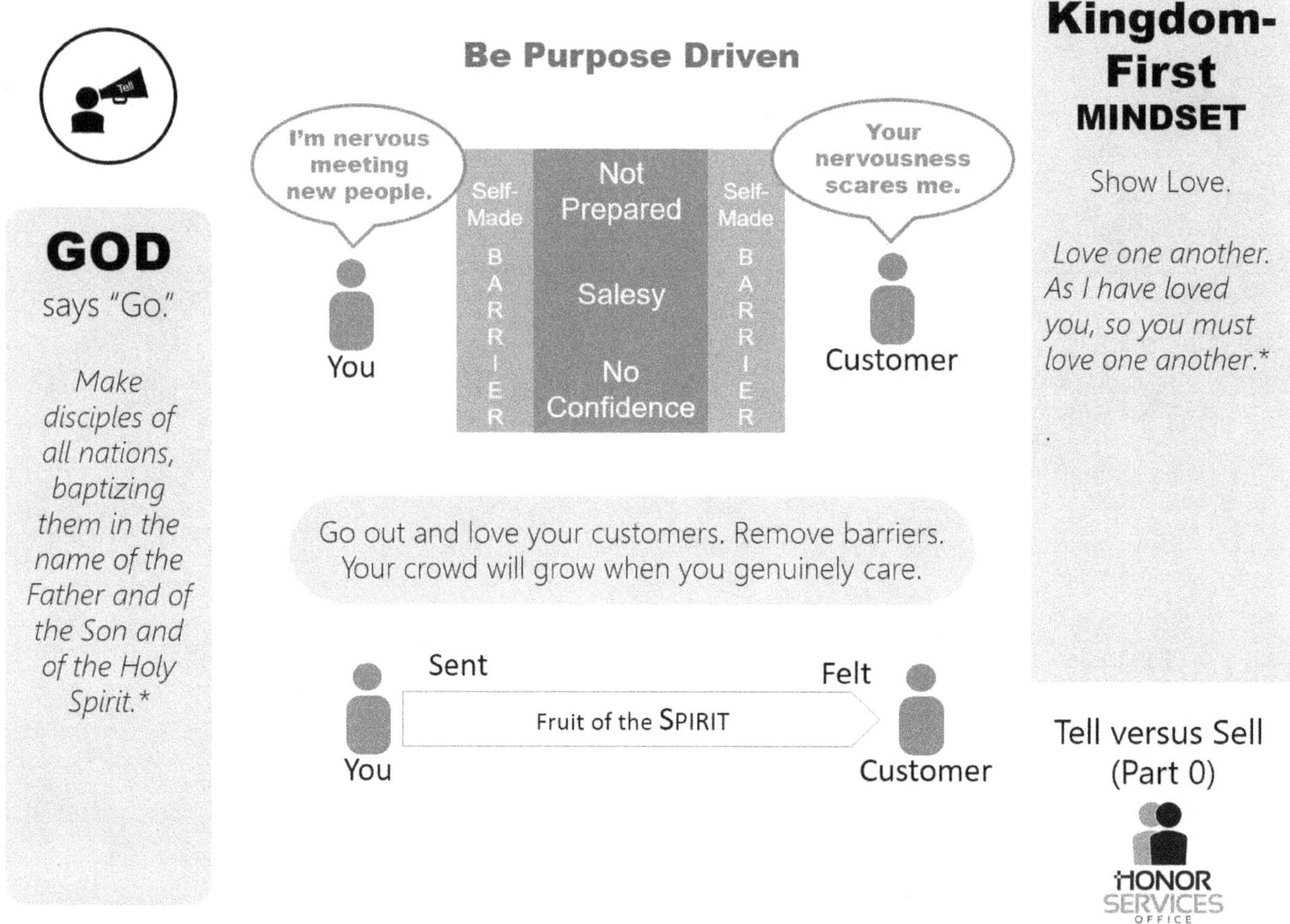

Has anyone had to go to a specialist for a medical procedure? Why do specialists exits?

Again, GOD says go. You are created by GOD. HE made you special and only you can reach specific people. No one else.

Matthew 28:19 - *Go therefore and make disciples of all the nations, baptizing them in the name of the Father and of the Son and of the Holy Spirit*

My Purpose

Businesses that have the sole purpose of making money can fail and the business owner may care, but the customers may not. The GOD-centered business owner establishes relationships that are deeper than just business. They provide purpose.

My purpose in life is (finish the sentence)

GOD's Purpose for Me

Understanding GOD's purpose for your life is important and may be different than the purpose you just listed. Some of you are prayer warriors, others like to serve silently, while others are passionate givers.

My purpose in life for GOD is (Finish the sentence)

Comfort zones vary from person to person. Some feel comfortable meeting new people in person while others would rather sit in their home speaking to an anonymous group online. Growing business should be done on purpose, but placed under GOD's Matthew 28:19 guidance.

Be sent. Meeting new people is vital for the GOD-centered business owner to help their business thrive. Getting out of the house can be intimidating or impossible for some, but GOD still needs you to meet as many people as possible. For those who cannot leave their homes, prayerfully meet people online. But go with . . .

1. **A purpose.** Confidence in your product or service is assured because you prayerfully and skillfully built it. But now it is time to tell people what you offer. GOD-centered business owners have an advantage because their goal goes beyond the sale. GOD has given you a purpose to show HIS attention to detail, HIS creativity, HIS knowledge and the type of servanthood HE wants you to show through your product or service. Living your purpose is a credit to GOD.
2. **A destination.** The community that keeps coming to your mind is where HE wants you to serve. Learn it. Study it. Pray about that group. Meet people in this community and learn their names. JESUS "had" to go to Samaria on one of HIS trips (see John 4). HE knew this destination needed HIM.
3. **Character.** Healed people heal people. As you are sent to grow GOD's kingdom through your business, integrity is important. Write down any commitment you may have made and follow up immediately. Keep all promises. Pray for every person you meet and be ready with an answer to "What is different about you?" GOD will give you the right words to speak boldly about HIM. Sometimes you may only need to share by example.

Exercise 1 – Lead with Discernment

Objective: *Use discernment to know when to tell people about your product or services versus listening to speak to them about JESUS.*

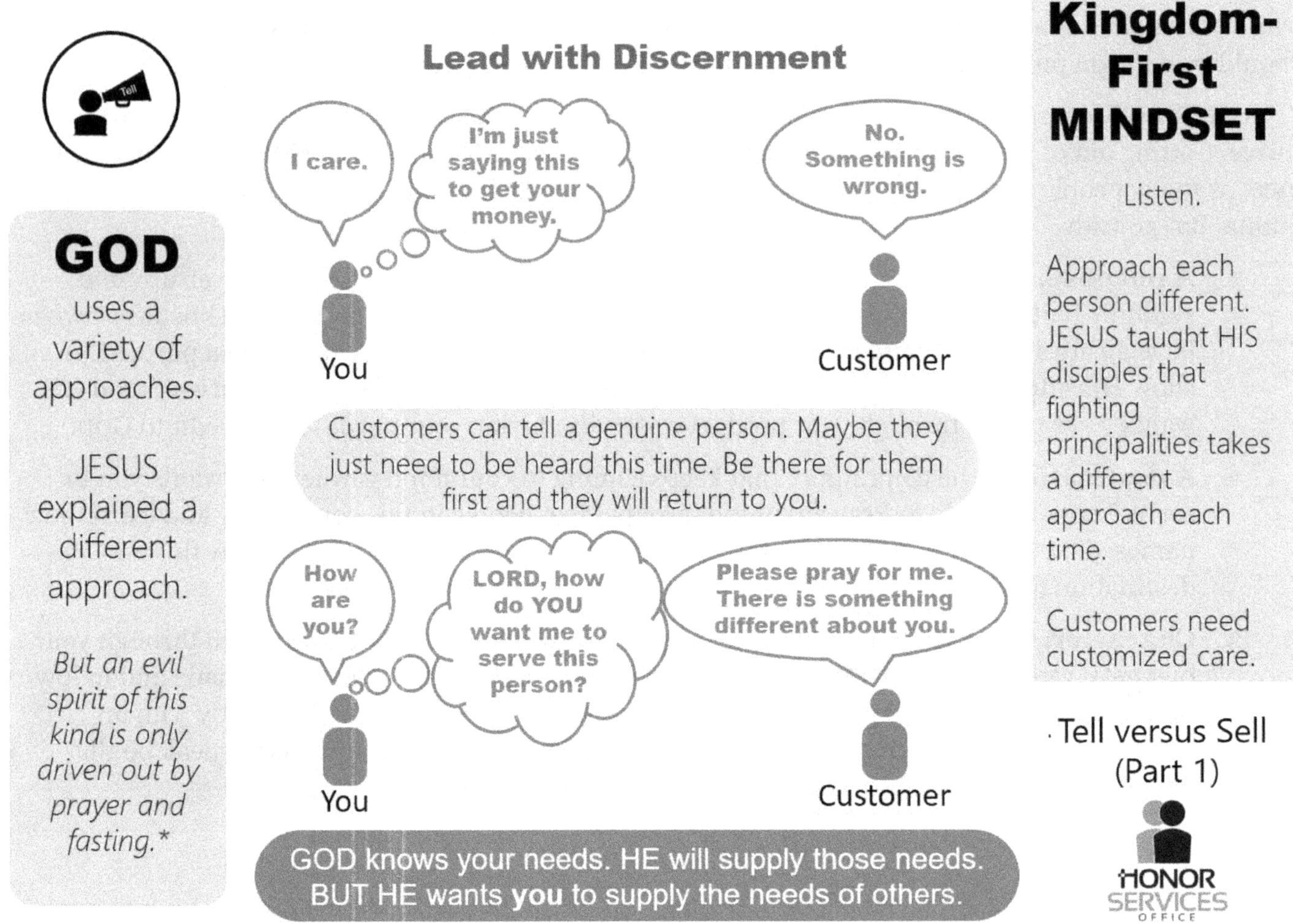

Have you ever met someone who said the right words to you at the right time? Were you feeling sad? Did the person calm you when you were angry? Did they inspire you to do something incredible?

JESUS knew there was a variety of approaches when it came to spirits.

Matthew 17:21 - *But an evil spirit of this kind is only driven out by prayer and fasting* (WNT)

JESUS also knows there is a variety of approaches when it comes to speaking with people.

Each person is different. Trying the same approach on different people will lower your conversion rate, also known as the capture rate, also known as the customers who purchase from you. Get to know your customers if you can so you can use discernment when speaking to them.

On a scale of 1 – 10 how well do you know your product or service? Be honest

Fill in the blank with your answer.________

Based on your answer, fill in the response below.

I need to get more familiar with (Finish the sentence)

Revisit your target audience in Dream Bigger to begin understanding specific needs from specific people.

> Not every person who waves money at you is your customer.

Be Prepared. Know your product or service very well. Understand what people are saying about your company and be prepared to address any issues the company may be experiencing. The GOD-centered business owner is also prepared to present the gospel of salvation at a moment's notice.

A quick overview of salvation:

GOD created humans. Satan, being a prideful angel, wanted to be GOD, but was thrown out of heaven. He decided to ruin humanity by lying to the first humans, introducing sin, causing all to fall (see Genesis 3). But GOD allowed HIS SON, who volunteered HIS life, to become a human. JESUS lived a sinless life only to be blamed for every sin people would do. HIS own creation murdered HIM on a cross, but HE was resurrected and is now alive with all authority. By believing in JESUS' power and authority to forgive, anyone can have eternal life.

Be picky. Not every person who waves money at you is your customer. Be prayerful about who to serve and be ready to stop serving people who may be harming other people or your walk with the LORD. Continue to pray favorably for people you have to cut loose.

Now let's prepare to lead with character.

Exercise 2 – Lead with Character

Objective: *Use character and bravery when speaking about your business.*

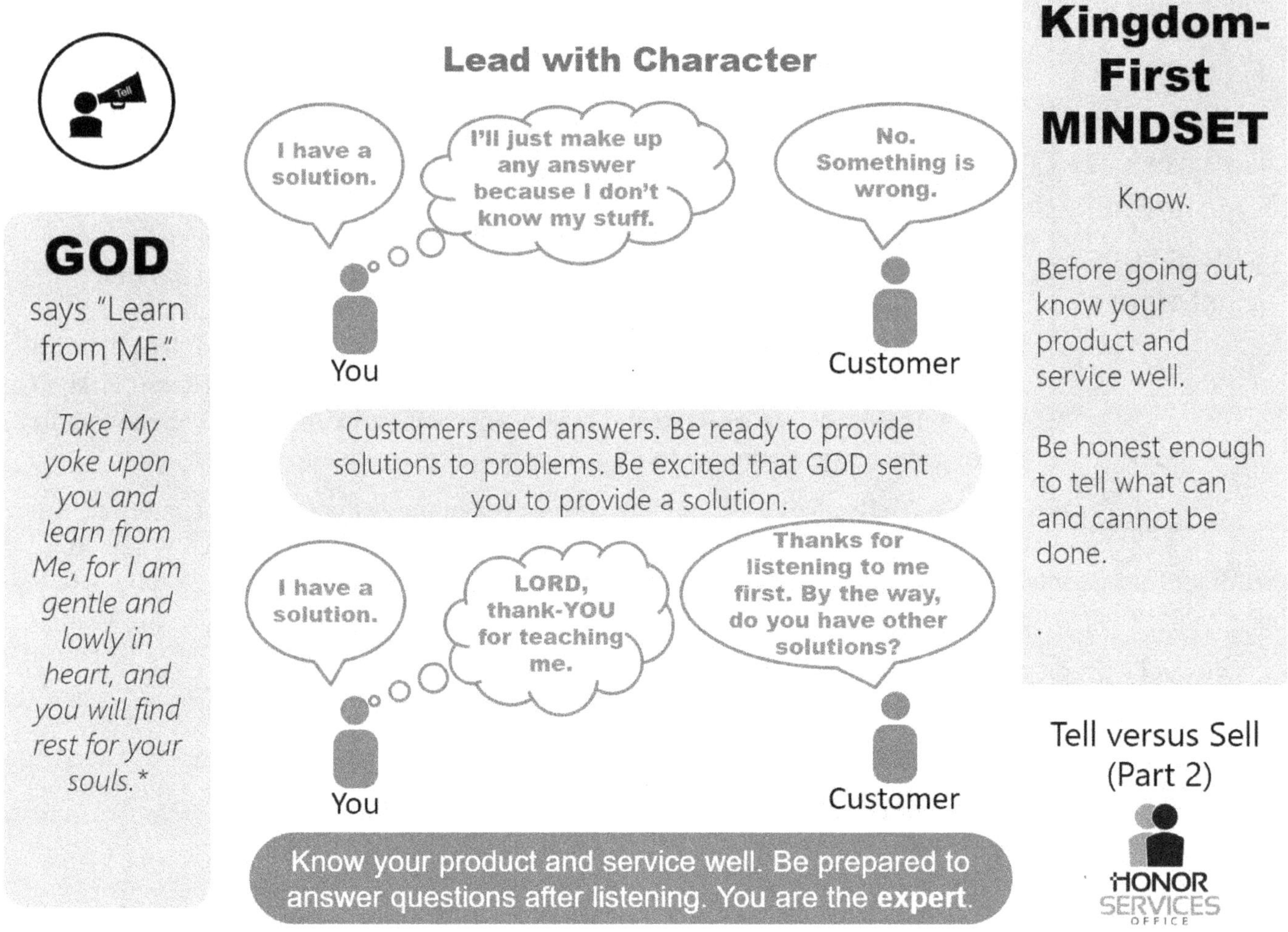

Have you ever been trained in something you have never done before? Did you feel confident doing it by yourself before you received training?

GOD will teach you.

Matthew 11:29 - *Take My yoke upon you and learn from Me, for I am gentle and lowly in heart, and you will find rest for your souls.*

> Some unconfident people like to fake it until they make it.

By connecting to GOD, you will have a constant source of knowledge.

Some unconfident people like to fake it until they make it. This is not the character GOD wants to use. If you still think you should fake your expertise or exaggerate what your product or service can do, then please revisit the Remove the Trash chapter before selling. Have confidence that GOD is with you and is willing to equip you with everything you need for a GOD-centered business.

Prepare Yourself

Character is doing the right thing when no one is looking. What prayer do you have about your character? Also, are you really prepared? Do you know your product or service well?

Before meeting people I will pray this prayer (Write out your prayer)

Be peaceful. Peaceful selling means putting someone at ease. The God-centered business owner listens to problems people have and provides real solutions. If you have a product or service that fulfills a need, be bold about providing the right information. But timing is everything. Is that person ready to hear your solution? Is he hurting and in need of an encouraging message? Read your audience and provide the peaceful option God has for you. Remember, God knows your situation and wants your total engagement.

Exercise 3—Lead with a Sales Approach

Objective: *Customize a sales approach.*

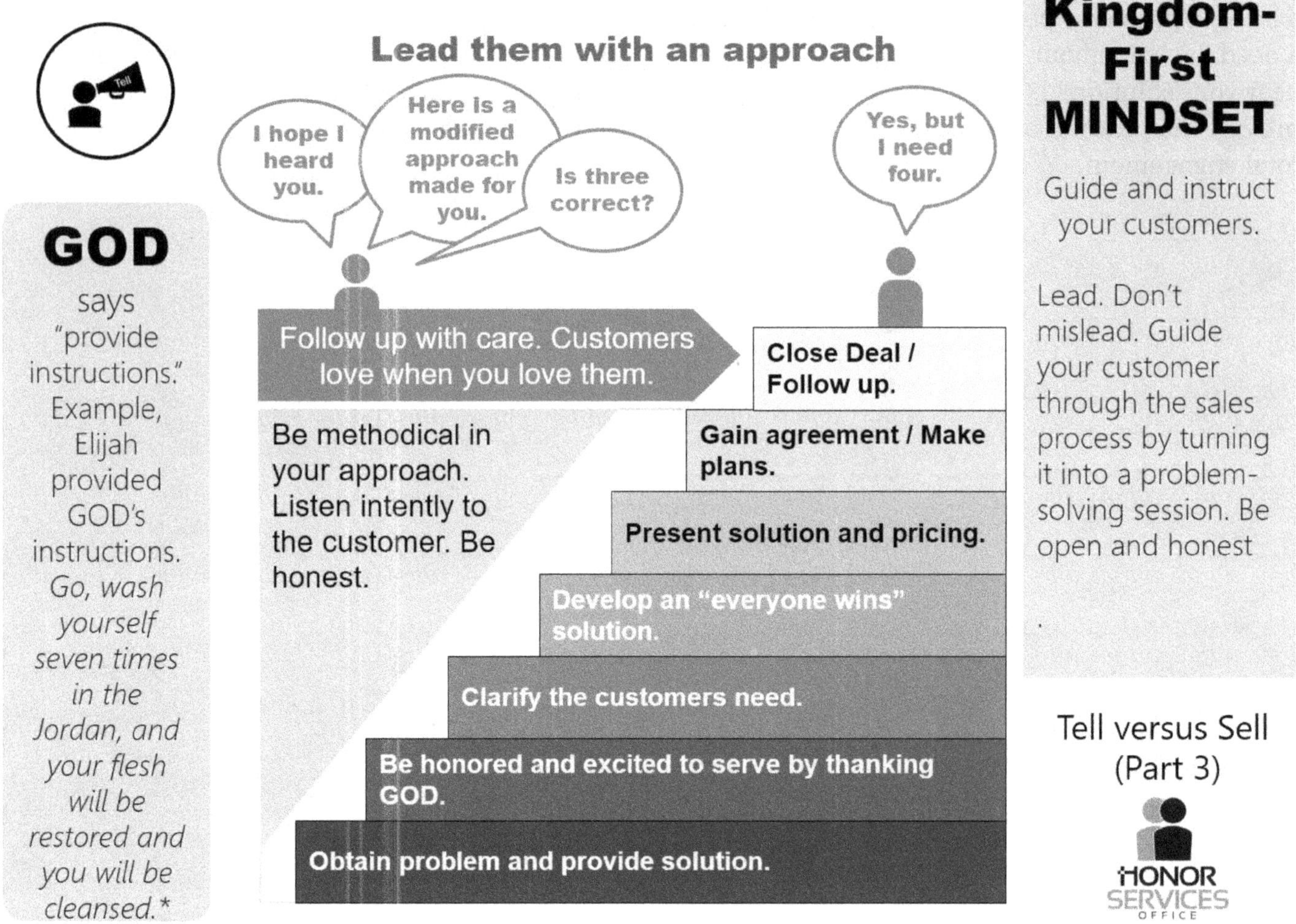

Have you ever been to a new city and wanted to know more about the city but had no guide? Have you ever been on a tour of a city and learned more about the city than the residents?

GOD provides guides who can provide instructions and standards. Elisha provided GOD's instructions.

2 Kings 5:10 – *Then Elisha sent him a messenger, who said, "Go and wash yourself seven times in the Jordan, and your flesh will be restored, and you will be clean.* (BSB)

> You are a guide. Lead the customer to your solution.

You are a guide. Lead the customer to your solution. You works hard getting it right.

First chose the audience GOD told you to serve. This is the audience you got feedback from and provided demonstrations to.

After choosing the audience, then seek their needs with sincerity. Listen to their problems, suggestions and ideas to provide a genuine solution.

How can this be beneficial to your business?

Next, be honored to serve this audience and thank GOD for meeting people. This step should always be done. Customers may say one thing but mean another. Clarify the need by repeating it in your own words.

What are some ways you can use to clarify?

Develop an "everyone wins" solution. Some professions are notorious for gouging customers or lying about an aspect of what will be delivered to maximize profits. The GOD-centered business owner is confident in the profit they have set and will stick to the price. You do not have to lose out, nor does the customer.

Is your pricing flexible enough to offer deals for a short period of time? Do you have a relationship with your customer that can show you genuinely care? After listening to the customer's response, then present him or her with the solution and provide the fair price from your market validated and adjusted prices.

Is your solution ready? Have your customers validated you have the MVP? What feedback did you get back from your thought group?

When the customer agrees, then guide him or her through the standard, validated order fulfilment and payment processes.

Will you send invoices? Will you accept payment in cash, checks, credit or debit cards? Have you tested the payment acceptance solutions? How will you fulfil the order?

Once the customer pays, the relationship begins rather than ends. Follow-up is extremely important. Make the time to ensure your customer is satisfied. Not only does this help you improve, but it builds confidence in your customer, enabling them to refer others to your product or service. It also enables you to hear about your relationship with GOD.

Do you have a follow-up methodology? Have you said "thank-you?" Did you check to make sure the customer got everything they paid for?

Now you are prepared to customize your sales approach.

Having a sales approach is imperative to enable business growth. Many people think marketing is sales and sales is marketing. These are two different, yet vital areas of your business. Let's focus on the sales process.

Chose the right audience. Guilt arises when you push a person into paying for your product or service without her needing or wanting it. There is a need for your talents and an audience who will pay what you are asking. Remember the group of people who gave you the need in the first place? Start with the group who have the same problem as those who originally expressed it to you.

Obtain the problem and provide a solution. Before you ask to buy, listen to your customer's needs, wants, and desires so you can customize a solution from your company's expertise.

Thank GOD for the honor of serving others. Thankfulness is always heard by GOD and HE blesses those who do this with sincerity. Genuine excitement for providing for the needs of your customers shines through the GOD-centered business owner. Your audience wants quality and great service.

Clarify the customer's needs. Ask clarifying questions that include the problem, solution, and expected result. Remember, you are there for your customer, not for yourself. Having a servant's heart is important.

Develop an "everyone wins" solution. You put time and quality into building your product or service and are worth your wages. Your product or service is worth being paid for. The customer should benefit from this as well. Create deals that benefit you and your customer. Think about obtaining the right amount of profit based on the pricing strategy you chose. In this strategy you also chose benefactors of your generosity.

Present the solution and pricing. Prayerfully and honestly present a solution to your customer's problem. Give that person the price you have discussed. Praise GOD for being able to present solutions.

Gain agreement and make plans. Once the customer says yes, plan for the delivery of the product or service. Explain how and when she can expect your product or service to be delivered. For more complex services, a statement of work (SOW) is drafted with deliverables, schedules, and acceptance criteria. Payment processes are presented.

Close the deal and follow up. Enable the customer to go through your payment solution to pay for your product or service. Follow up with each purchase. Be careful of putting your product or service on discount too often. It could be detrimental to your profits. Consider alternate pricing with clear criteria, so you can help those who need your services but may not be able to afford them. Send an invoice with the product or service listed, the final amount, payment terms, and dates. If you do not use invoices, make sure the payment system is clear and easy to use. Once paid, send a receipt with a thank you. Follow up with the customer to see how he enjoyed the product or service. If the customer is anonymous, then provide a way to collect feedback.

The sales cycle varies from business to business. Some are instant, some take time. Regardless, follow the sales steps with structure, leading your customers to great solutions you provide.

Meet 22 People Per Month

There are usually 22 business days in a given month. You should be meeting 1 person a day or 22 people in a month.

There are about 22 business days in a given month. You should meet at least 1 new person each day to sustain your business, let alone grow it. If you meet 5 in one day and 10 on another and 7 on another, you have met the minimum for that month.

Pray for your new contacts.
Place them in a CRM.
Follow up with them to see how they are doing.

Relationships take time. Be ready to explain your product or service without pushing your product or service. Be a problem solver.

Many times the problem is their need for an encouraging word GOD gives you.

Sell It or Tell It Exercise

Game Script

Group Leader:
Let's play Sell It or Tell It
In this game you will be the owner of various businesses. The sub-title of this game is Tell, versus sell, meaning if you have to sell someone on the idea, you may or may not be the solution for that particular person.

Let's begin.

If you have to sell it, it's bad or the answer is "No" If you can tell it, it is good or the answer is "Yes."

Any questions?

Group Leader:
In this example your business is Giraffe Grooming. You get a phone call inviting you participate as a vendor in an office furniture conference. All you have to do is pay to be part of the conference? Do you pay? Is this a good audience for your Giraffe Grooming business?

Listen for their responses.

Group Leader:
Sell it! Or No! Just because there may be a crowd doesn't mean it is your crowd. You may have a hard time finding someone who is remotely interested in Giraffe Grooming at this convention. Many conferences simply want to make money on any business willing to pay. Beware! Look at the audience GOD specified. Review the audience GOD said for you to serve.

Listen for responses. Some people may be confused over the title "Sell it or Tell it." If so, then switch to "yes" or "no" answers.

Group Leader:
In this example you sell your own brand of pet pillows. Someone approaches you and asks 'Do you mow lawns?' Do you walk away insulted? Or is this a good opportunity to identify their needs?" "Sell it or Tell it?"

Listen for their responses.

Group Leader:
Unlike the last example, this person is simply expressing a need. 'Tell it' or 'yes', is the answer. Ask what they are looking for and politely explain what you do. This conversation may lead to an opportunity to share your faith, but start with trying to help with sincerity.

Group Leader:
You are now in the business of providing advice. You have had a pretty good month in sales, so you say to yourself "My customers are so lucky to have me guiding them!" Is this a thankful attitude?

Listen for their responses.

Group Leader:
Sell it!" or "No!" It is a blessing to be in business. Thank GOD for the gifts HE has given you and be truly thankful for each customer. When GOD says, "Do not think more highly of yourself", HE was addressing attitude. Try thanking HIM for being able to be in business.

"For I say, through the grace given to me, to everyone who is among you, not to think of himself more highly than he ought to think, but to think soberly, as God has dealt to each one a measure of faith." Romans 12:3

Group Leader:
Perhaps pray for each one of your customers.

Group Leader:
Getting the hang of this? Hopefully so. Now you are a Nuts and Bolts company. A customer asks for 55 nuts and 25 bolts. You say 'Let me see if I understand... you want 55 nuts and 25 bolts for your project. May I ask what your project is?'

Is this a clarifying question? Sell it or Tell it."

Group Leader:
Tell it" or "yes!" Restating the request always helps show you heard what they said. Asking questions helps with clarification of the need. By finding out more about the customer's needs, you can clarify how you can help them.

You are doing well.

Group Leader:
Last one. Now you are a retailer with a product that is being sold at the lowest price you can offer it. A customer asks if they can have a discount on that item. You notice they are purchasing other items from you so you reply 'I can't discount that item. Can I offer you a 20% discount on another item you are purchasing?'

Is this an "everyone wins" question?

Group Leader:
Tell it" or "yes!" "You don't have to lose to have your customer win. Your customer does not have to lose top have you win. Both parties should walk away feeling blessed by the experience. You do not have to give away everything, nor does your customer have to suffer. Think of ways both can be blessed.

Hopefully these examples will help you with the next exercise.

My Sales Approach

The sales approach is customizable. Be consistent. Use the GOD-centered sales model to customize your own sales approach.

Do you know your true customer?

Business to Business versus Business to Consumer

Some businesses may sell to other businesses. This is known as "Business to Business" or B2B. Some businesses sell directly to the customer or the consumer. This is known as "Business to Consumer" or B2C.

B2B sales means you have spoken to potential customers of the product or service, done the appropriate testing and are ready for sales. Your customer, however is a business that will use your product or service to grow their business. The business that uses your business may sell your product or service or use it as a component to their business.

B2B may require more relationship building and the time it takes for the business to purchase your product or service may be longer than that of selling directly to a customer. The benefit, however, is that businesses may be more consistent purchasers.

B2C sales means your product or service is sold by your company directly to the customer, otherwise known as consumer because they may consume or use the product or service.

B2C may require less of a relationship, but still requires one. For example, a hot dog vendor may get to know regular customers by name, but first time customers are treated with respect without knowing her name, hoping to make her a regular customer. Selling directly to the customer means you are willing to talk to a lot more people than B2B. This requires more time or more money to reach the audience you anticipated.

Both B2B and B2C, needs an encouraging word to the customer.

Develop a custom approach that differentiates your product or service.

Write out your sales approach.

Choose a Customer Relationship Management (CRM) tool like Honor Services Office to keep track of your customer's needs. Visit https://www.honorservicesoffice.com. Did you see how I told you about the CRM versus trying to convince you? This CRM has all of the exercise listed in this book. I would be honored if you would choose this as your system of choice.

Exercise 4 – Getting over the Profit Conflict

Objective: *Become confident in your profit.*

Take time to pray about how you will use your profits. How much is too much?

Where is GOD leading you regarding profits? Will you keep them all for yourself? Will you give some profit to other people? Will you give your entire business over to GOD and allow HIM to grow you?

Profit Conflict

Financial gain. The difference between the amount earned and the amount spent in buying, operating, or producing something is the definition of profit. Conflict sometimes creeps in with a thought like, *How much is too much?* Profit is not the finish line for the GOD-centered business owner. GOD wants us to seek the lost, help the poor and those who are hurting. This may include giving some of your profit to them.

The GOD-centered business owner gives GOD 100% of her business versus 10%. Each piece of equipment, computer, smartphone, raw material, or documented process is HIS. By knowing what is HIS, you will be able to hear what HE wants you to do with the excess easier.

1. **Seek to give in secret.** Tax breaks are great. Give to the church or charity in a form of a payment that can be tracked and credited to your business. But what is GOD asking for? HE wants sacrificial giving as well. Giving to someone in need in secret is a delight to GOD. HE sees what you do in secret and will reward you greatly for helping HIS little ones. "*so that your giving may be in secret. Then your Father, who sees what is done in secret, will reward you*" (Matthew 10:42 NIV).
2. **Get instead of give.** Rarely is it spoken that people need to receive instead of giving. But what about those who are struggling to make the next bill payment and are on the verge of being evicted? GOD sees you too. The GOD-centered business owner is humble enough to admit

things are not going well financially and that this is a time of spiritual growth. GOD said, "*Ask, and it will be given to you; seek, and you will find; knock, and it will be opened to you*" (Matthew 7:7). Be willing and humble enough to receive help when problems arise. This shows you are human. Thank GOD when you receive help. This builds faith and trust in HIM.

3. **Expand your territory.** GOD's currency is loving people. HE wants as many people in your account as possible. This requires you to go out and seek those to whom HE sends you. Some will buy from you. If so, thank GOD for the profit. But it doesn't stop there. As you expand into other communities, GOD enables you to be there for more and more people.

By now you should have:

Vision

Self-Awareness

Wisdom

Preparation

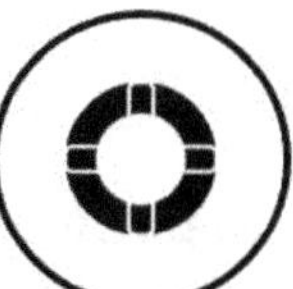
Differentiation

Tell

Service

Vision	Self-Awareness	Wisdom	Preparation	Differentiation	Tell	Service
Vision statement from GOD.	Blockers to achieving GOD's vision.	Study time to continuously learn about GOD.	Revised fully defined vision from GOD.	Collaboration marketing plan.	Adjusted leadership style.	**Achieved RESILIENCE**
Gifts and talents assessment.	Hidden motive identified.	Behavioral modifications to enable working better with others.	Features of business defined from vision.	Content marketing plan / material.	Refined product or service instructions or ingredient list.	
List of GOD's promises for you.	Heart of business for mission statement.	Business mood elevation plan.	Validated customer user stories.	Pricing model.	Refined product or service sell sheet.	
Initial list of people who will help.	Business hours.	Skills assessment.	Documented processes.	Market research.	Sales process.	
	Quiet time.		SOPs.	Content location map.	CRM established.	
	Weekly admin day.		Marketing messages.	Quiet time established.	Follow-ups scheduled.	
			Sales/ payment method.	Vacation or staycation established.		
			Accounting method.			

FIRST

Fruit of the Spirit
Inform, providing options
Repeat the need
Solve
Tell the price

For homework, listen to the needs of seven separate people (business or personal). Write their problem or need. Develop a solution, but wait to tell the person until after you clarify the problem.

Ask for any prayer requests and dismiss in prayer. Remember to use your personal journals found on at the end of this book.

WARNING

- Avoid pushy sales tactics.
- Learn how to be patient while waiting on someone to decide, but follow up to keep the process moving.
- Remember to set aside the product or service you promised to deliver in the business deal.

NEXT STEPS

- Document your sales process.
- Create a sell sheet with all of your products and services.
- Begin writing notes about potential clients in a CRM tool. Collect at least 22 potential clients per month. This equates to one per business day in a month.

PRAYER

- Pray for GOD to adjust your leadership style to be able to work with many types of people who may come to know CHRIST.
- Pray for a sales method that is not intimidating to you or the customer.
- Pray for a quality relationship with many people.

Chapter 7 – Lead to Promises: Outstanding Customer Service

"What promises did you make?"

"Did you follow up after the sale?"

"How do you keep loyalty?"

"What are GOD'S promises for your customers?"

Lead to Promises preparation (Week 7)

Greet participants and remind them of the goal of listening to the needs of seven people.

If you were with us last week (or whatever your time frame),Did you listen to the needs of people? How did it feel clarifying the problem? Allow for the groups to respond.

Review your customer list to see who you need to follow up with. This will be the beginnings of your prayer list.

Introduce the Lead to Promises Chapter

Explain this chapter is used to develop their customer service model.

There are 4 Customer Service Exercises.

Be prepared to get satisfied customers.

Lead to Promises Objective

We are in part 7, the final chapter of the framework. This methodology teaches you what to do to prepare your business for resilience. You will learn; how to follow up with your customers after the sale and how to handle complaints.

Lead to Promises Prayer

Pray for:
Your class to get new customers.
Those who helped the business owners get this far.
The expansion of their territory so HIS word can be spread to those who need it.

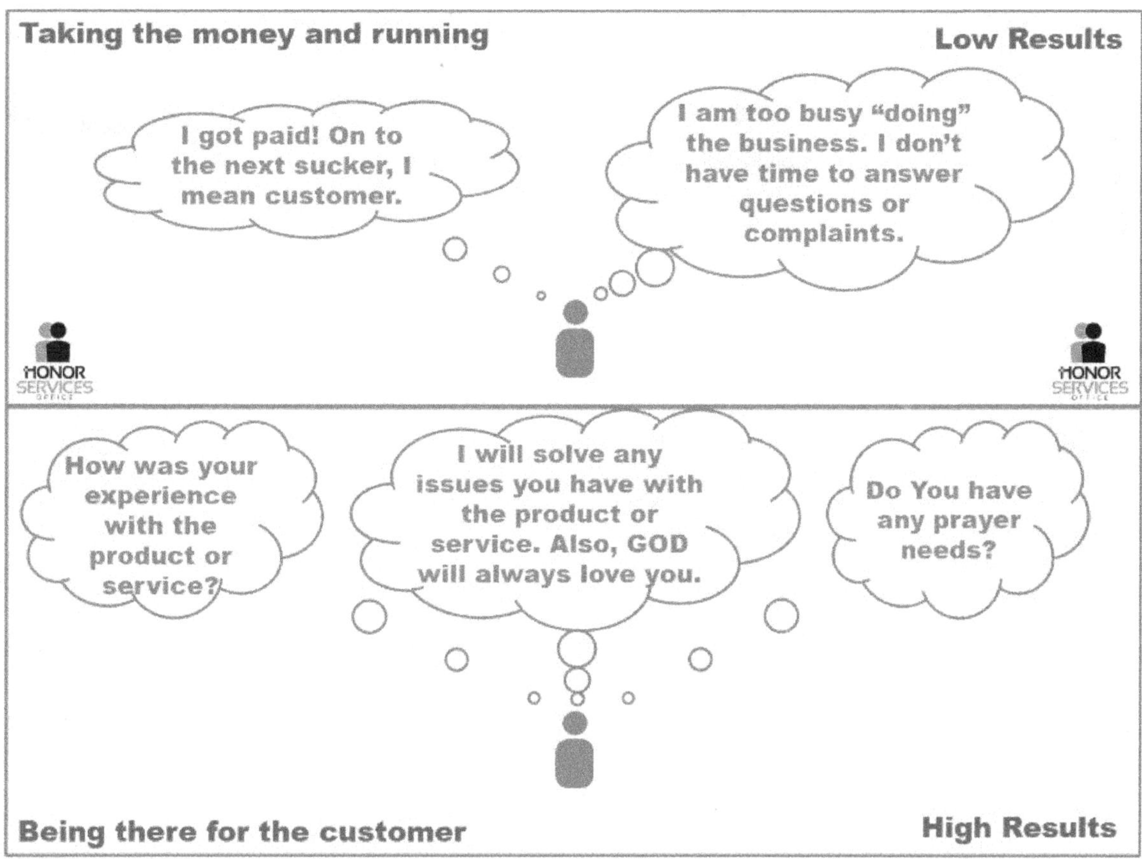

Have you ever received poor service or a broken product? What if you paid a lot of money for the product or service, would you want your money back or the problem rectified? Are your customers so happy that they are willing to refer you but you never asked for a referral?

It is important to follow up after the sale in order to show outstanding customer service. The GOD-centered Business Owner follows up with promises and provides GOD's promises.

Let's prepare outstanding customer service.

A Servant's Heart

Objective: *Use your gifts and talent to serve past and present customers.*

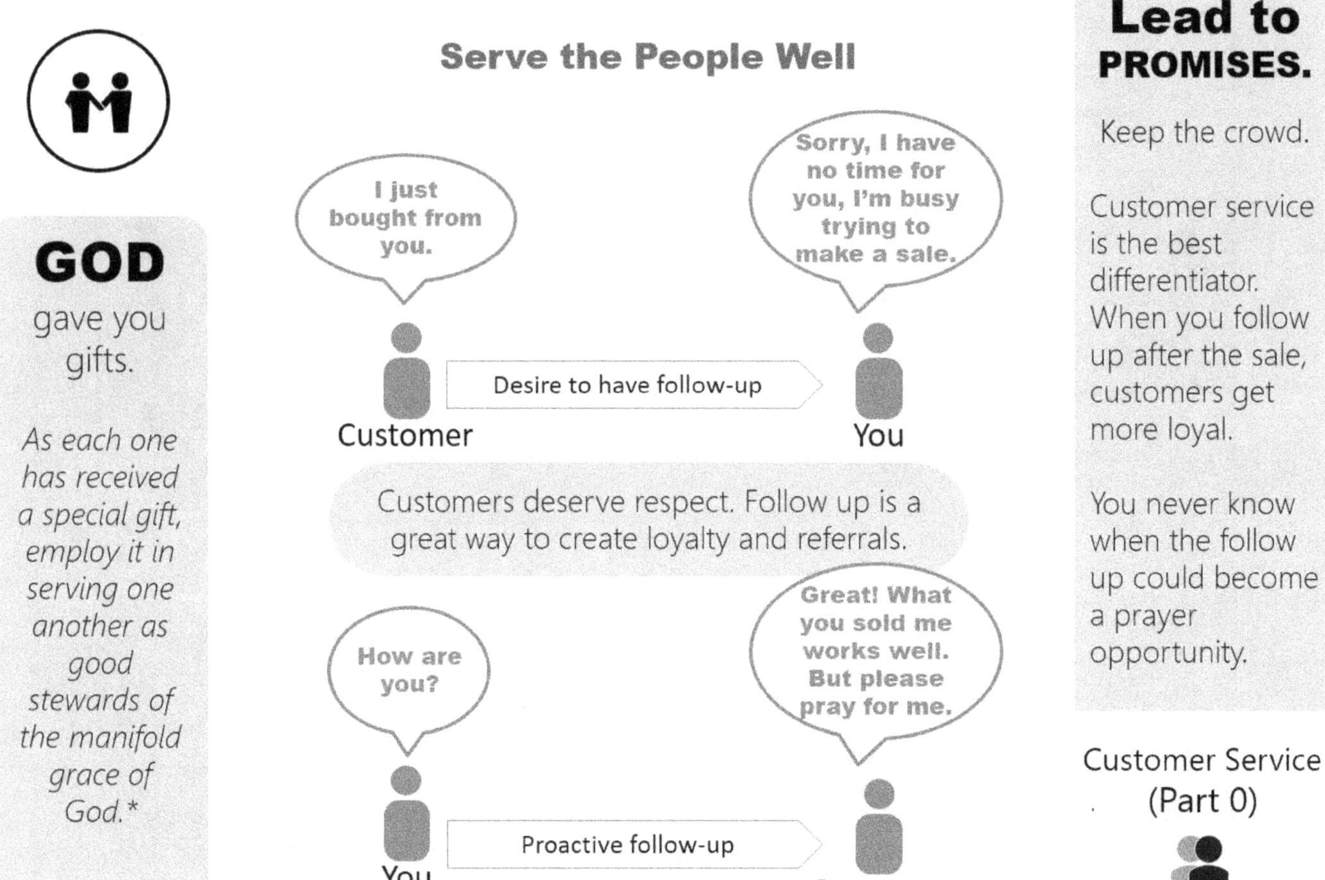

Have you ever wanted a paycheck but did not want to do the job? Have you ever disliked doing a job but only wanted a paycheck? What level of commitment did you have to that job? Were you passionate or simply paid?

GOD has given you gifts and talents and wants you to use them for HIM.

> Your talents and special abilities have been given to you to serve others.

1 Peter 4:10 – *As each one has received a special gift, employ it in serving one another as good stewards of the manifold grace of God.* (NASB)

Your talents and special abilities have been given to you to serve others.

My Service Promise

Having a servants heart is the best approach to business. Customers will see your heart that is overflowing with love and want to work exclusively with you. Even when something goes wrong, the problem will be less of a problem when you have established a relationship with your customers.

I will serve people better by (Finish the sentence)

Distinction is not always achieved by having a better product or service. More than likely, your competition is working on a bigger, stronger, faster model than the one you are selling. How can you be different? Great customer service enables that distinction.

Check in with the customer. After you have fulfilled the product or service, follow up with the customer. Take a moment to add the person to your CRM if you have not done so already. Ask, "How are you doing?"

At this point it is about maintaining a relationship. GOD said, "Be strong and of good courage, do not fear nor be afraid of them; for the LORD your God, He is the One who goes with you. He will not leave you nor forsake you" (Deuteronomy 31:6). This reassuring promise enables many people to have hope. Same with your company. Let your customer know you are loyal to him and he will be loyal to you.

Exercise 1 – Establish a Follow-Up Methodology

Objective: *Schedule time to follow up with customers and pray for them.*

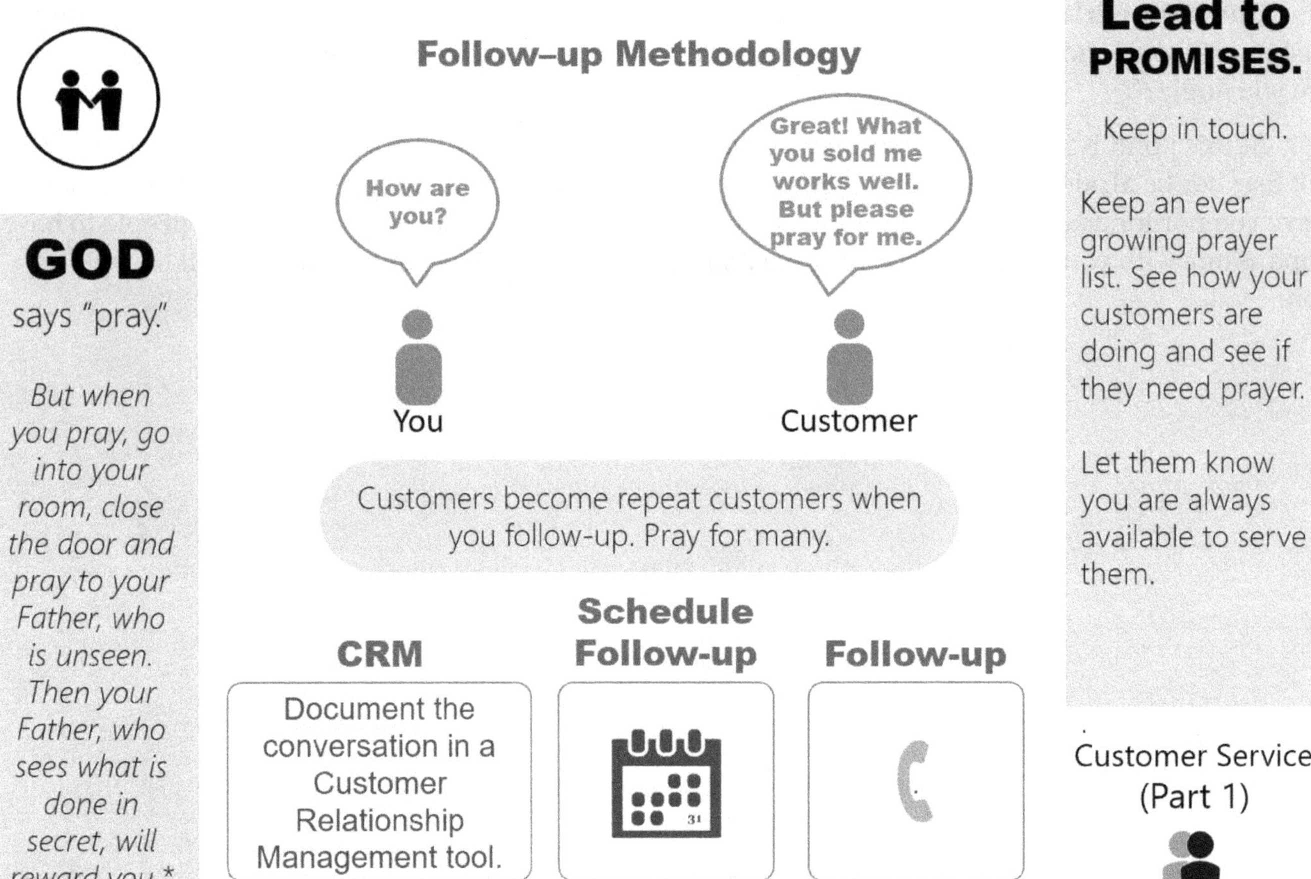

Have you ever run into a friend you have not seen in a while? As he explains what is going on in his life, you soon realize, you missed a lot. How do you feel about missing important events? How would you like it if someone checked in on you every once in a while?

> Pray for your customers regularly.

Pray for your customers regularly.

Matthew 6:6 – *But when you pray, go into your room, close the door and pray to your Father, who is unseen. Then your Father, who sees what is done in secret, will reward you.* (NIV)

The GOD-centered business owner is mature enough to set business aside for a moment to pray for the needs of their customers.

Follow up is imperative. Businesses have seen a 25% to 50% increase in sales because of timely follow-up, according to our experiences. Use your CRM to keep vital notes on each customer so your conversation can be rich.

1. **Drop a note.** Instead of an email blast, try sending a single email to the customer. Be sincere and ask, "How are you?"

2. **Make a call.** Check in on your customers if at all possible. Make the conversation about that person. See if you can pray for him in any way. Even if he says no, ask if he wouldn't minds if you pray for him, his family, or situations in general.
3. **Meet in person.** If your customer has time, why not meet in person? This will lead to a deeper, richer conversation. When you show up, care more about the person than the sale.

Walking with your customer **is** the finish line.

Walking with your customer is the finish line. Treating her with respect, praying for her, and hoping to one day see her beyond this life are the goals of the relationship. JESUS promises abundant life. Pursue each customer with HIS love in mind.

Customer Relationship Management (CRM)

A customer relationship management tool is used to keep track of the conversations you had with potential customers. Keep your promises. That is what this chapter is all about. Write in your CRM any promise you made to your customers and people you have met. This way you will not forget to follow up and keep your promises.

Follow-up Timing

Imagine being very hungry, but having no time to eat. Some may be able to miss a meal once or twice, but cannot do this for very long.

Now, imagine not getting referrals to establish new customers. Your business will not be able to sustain without other customers referring your product or service. Follow-up increases the likelihood of your customers referring your business.

The GOD-centered benefit of follow-up is you establish a relationship with your customer that enables you to pray for the customer, in hopes that they will establish a saving relationship with JESUS.

Timing is everything. Choose when you will follow up with your customers to answer their questions or meet their needs. Will you follow up within 24 hours or sometime during the week. Both are acceptable as long as you can schedule a reliable time to meet with your customer and stick to it.

Getting feedback on how well you delivered the product or service helps your business.

Do you have other messages you want to give with each follow-up? What words of encouragement can you give your customer? What promises of GOD would you like to impart?

My policy on following up with customers is (Finish the sentence)

Follow-up Method

How will you follow up? Will you use email, make a call or visit in person? Other

My follow-up method is (Finish the sentence)

Set a calendar reminder to revisit this policy 30 days from now.
Now that we have a followed up method, let's talk about customer service.

Exercise 2 – Understand Customer Service

Objective: *Implement a customer service model.*

Things don't always go as planned. When someone calls with a complaint, treat it as a gift. It is better that he called you and said what was wrong versus not calling you and telling ten people how bad your product or service was.

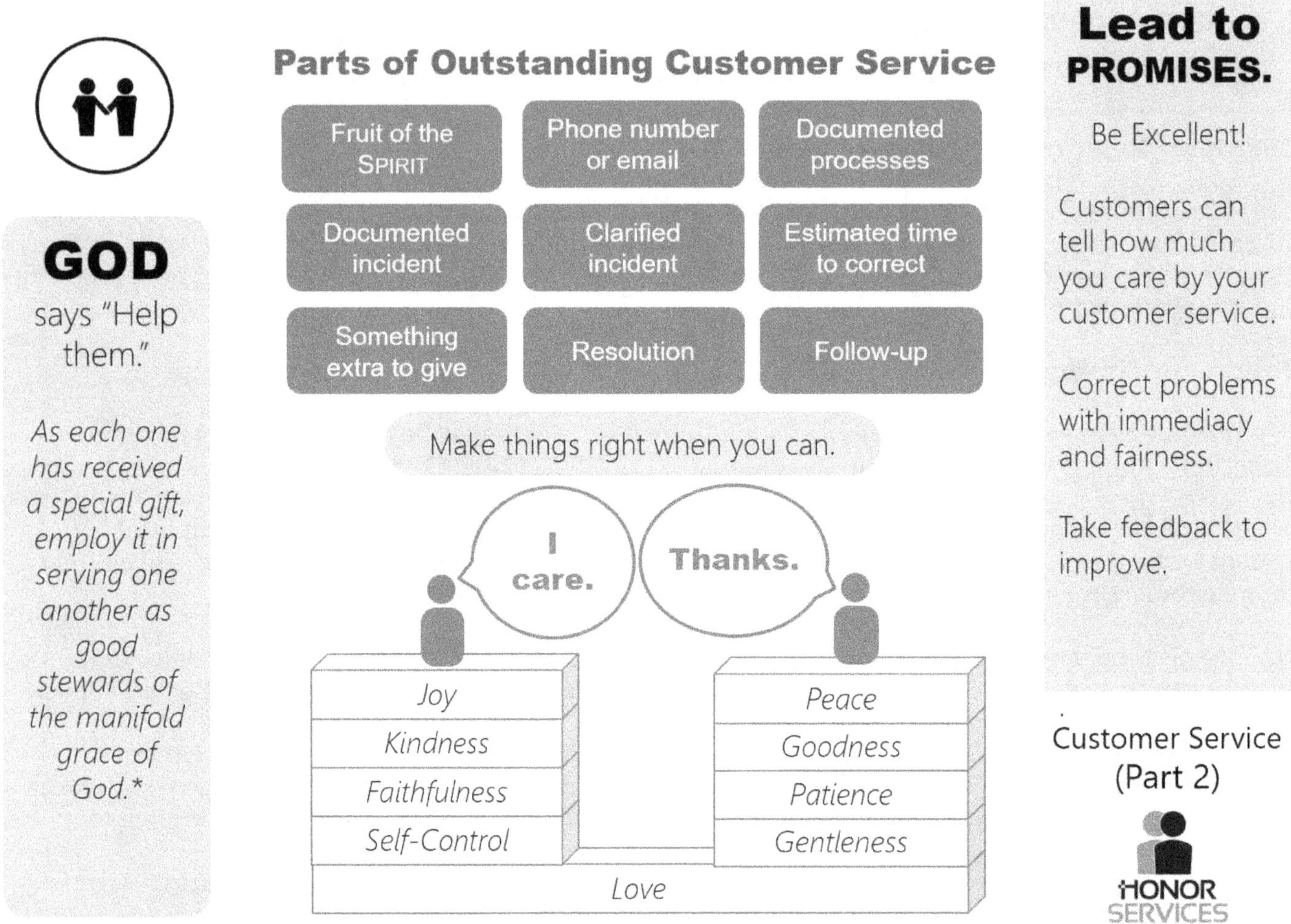

Have you ever experienced bad service? What happened? What does great customer service look like?

Serve your customers with a service model.

This was said before but it is appropriate. 1 Peter 4:10 – *As each one has received a special gift, employ it in serving one another as good stewards of the manifold grace of God.* (NASB)

A customer service model is the structure, policies and methods that you will use to answer questions, resolve issues or point to resources. A good customer service model uses your gifts and talents GOD gave you.

Have you experienced a customer service representative with a bad attitude? How did you feel?

Attitude is important. Using the fruit of the Spirit enables every interaction to remain pleasant. Whether it is simply answering a question to resolving an issue, your attitude has to be chosen rather than reactive.

Have you ever tried reaching a company to raise a concern but could not find out how to contact them?

How will customers reach you? Will you use a phone number or email chat technology? Make it clear to your customers how they can ask questions or register complaints. This shows you have confidence in your product or service.

Have you experienced a customer service representative who did not know how to solve any problem you had with the product or service?

Documented processes help you resolve issues faster. It also shows you are the expert in your field. By having documented processes, you can refer your customers to resolution faster and speak common language.

Do you believe history repeats itself?

Documenting the incident helps you identify issues that repeat. Once found, add this to your epic wish list, to resolve in an upcoming sprint.

Have you ever NERD something PLONG? Excuse me, heard something WRONG?

Clarifying the incident is important and can be done with a formal or informal script. If you use a formal script, then it will require that you write out as many possibilities of issues that you can think of. Then add the possible resolution to the issue.

This becomes a knowledge base where a customer service representative can walk the customer through a series of questions to diagnose the problem and possibly provide a solution.

An informal approach is acceptable as long as you are asking something like "Do I have this correct?" or "Have I repeated the problem correctly?'

Can you imagine doing without your phone or computer for a day? How about a week? What if you had a problem with your phone or computer and the service technician kept it for two weeks and when you called about it, he says "I don't know how long it will take to resolve this." Do you have confidence in this person?

What will be your incident resolution estimation method? Your customers expect you to be the expert so estimates to resolve the problem should be accurate as possible. How far off can the estimate be? (25% higher or lower?) For example, if you said it would take 10 hours to do something but it really took 12.5 hours, then you are 25% wrong from your estimate. Would it be better if you said it would take 12.5 hours and delivered it in 10? You are still 25% wrong but in a positive way. Under promise and over deliver.

Have you experienced a company that gave you something free or provided you with a credit of some sort because of a problem you had with the product or service?

Will you offer something extra to give to customers if you made a mistake? Remember, the goal retain customers to become repeat customers. A complaint is a gift. Customers wants "you" to succeed when they complain. Why not help "them" succeed by giving them something for their trouble.

Have you ever had to repeat the issue over and over because it seemed like no one is working on resolving the problem?

Resolve the issue. What will be your method to resolve the issue? If you are using "Root Cause" questions, then be careful of your tone as it can sound like you are blaming the customer versus trying to identify the issue. Root cause questions are simply asking "Why" five times when a customer provides a symptom.

Here is an example:
The vehicle will not start.
The mechanic may investigate by trying to identify the root cause versus fixing a symptom.
Why? – The battery is dead. (First why)
Why? – The alternator is not functioning. (Second why)
Why? – The alternator belt has broken. (Third why)
Why? – The alternator belt was well beyond its useful service life and not replaced. (Fourth why)
Why? – The vehicle was not maintained according to the recommended service schedule. (Fifth why, a root cause)

The customer is possibly frustrated and feeling inconvenienced. An approach to the five whys is to say, "I am going to ask you some root cause questions as a process to identify the problem." You can ask "Why" differently. "What do you see happening?" or "How often does it happen?" or "When does it happen?" are all questions that assist in asking "why" without making the customer feel blamed.

How do you know you are meeting or exceeding the customers' expectations when it comes to fixing a problem?

Follow-up. See if you met the customer's expectations with your service. You don't always have to survey for this. It could be a simple question after the call is finished. You can then grow to using surveys.

Review the image to customize your customer service model. Will your service model be in person, on the phone, email or other?

My Customer Service Model

My customer service model is (Complete this statement using the image at the beginning of this exercise)

Before we dive deeper into the service model, let's play "How Long or How Much?"

How Long or How Much Exercise

Let's play **How long or how much?** This is a multiple choice question game to consider your thinking behind customer service.

Let's begin.

A customer has just purchased from you. How long should you wait to follow-up?

A. Don't need to follow up.
B. Within 24 hours.
C. When I feel like it.

If you said "B" you were correct. Follow-up increases repeat business by up to 25%. Building loyalty is the goal. When you stop your service at getting the money, you miss out on building a repeat relationship that can be fruitful for GOD.

A customer was double-charged for purchasing a product or service from you and they could clearly prove it. How much should you return to them if you have a no return / no refund policy?

A. None.
B. Give all back to be nice.
C. The amount overcharged.

If you said "C" you were correct. It is your legal obligation to return the amount you overcharged. You cannot take money for a product or service you did not provide.

Your customer purchases an item from you and it arrived to them damaged. How long should it take you to get a new item to the customer?

A. Next day.
B. Ten business days.
C. It depends.

If you said "C" you were correct. It depends. Do you have a no return, no refund policy? Some food companies put policies like this in place to prevent waste. It also depends on the cost of the item. If the item is low cost and easy to ship, send it right away. If the item is more expensive and harder to ship, you may need a return before replace policy and process.

A customer started seeing excessive charges after visiting your website. Their credit card company looked into it and identified your website has vulnerabilities that could lead to stolen credit cards. How much are you liable for since it has been determined your website is the cause of the breach?

A. From $5,000 to $100,000 fine per month.
B. Twice the amount of the sale.
C. Nothing because I have a warning.

If you said "A" you were correct. In 2020, according to Payment Card Industry PCI compliance, you can be liable for as little as $5000 up to $100,000 per month until you can prove you no longer have a breach.

A second breach may increase the charges to a minimum of $10,000 and steeper high limits.

Visa, Mastercard, American Express and Discover formed a group that assesses PCI compliance. If you are out of compliance, depending on your sales volume, you can be fined somewhere in this range.

A customer leaves you a message because you were on the phone when they called. How long should you wait to return the call?

a. Immediately after you hear the message.
b. Within 24 hours.
c. Within 5 business days.

If you said "B" you were correct. A reasonable policy to put in place would be to return all calls within 24 hours of the customer leaving the message. This message can be shared with your customers to set their expectation.

This depends on your policies and promises you set with your customers. Generally, 24 hours is the minimum time to return a phone call or email. Negative reviews should be addressed as soon as possible as this could hurt your brand.

Policies are part of customer service. Policies are not just to protect you, they are to communicate what you will provide to your customers so they can have a reasonable expectation.

Let's customize your customer service model.

Exercise 3 - Establish Customer Service

Objective: *Develop a customized customer service model.*

GOD

sees your service.

*God is not unjust; he will not forget your work and the love you have shown Him as you have helped His people and continue to help them.**

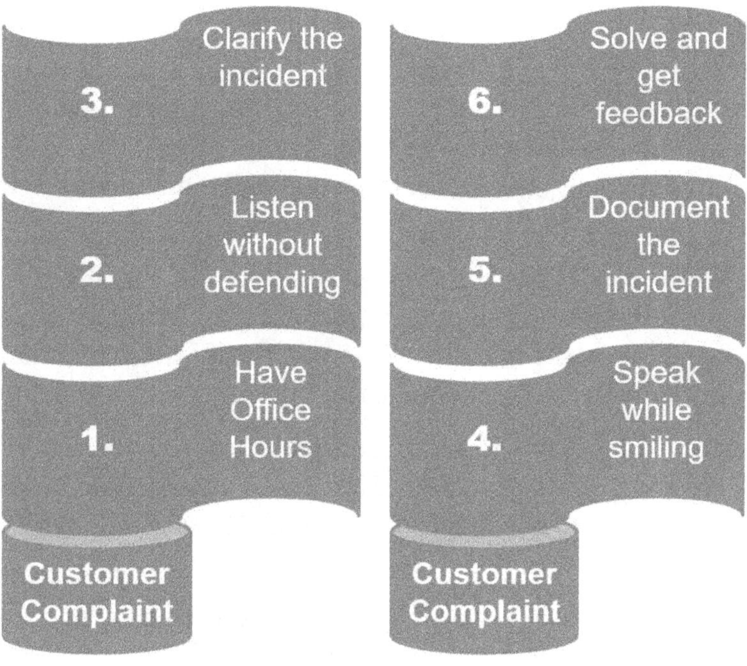

What service steps can you think of?

Lead to PROMISES.

Be courteous.

Treat a direct complaint as a gift. He/she could have used social media to complain about your product or service.

Listen and resolve as best you can.

Customer Service (Part 3)

Have you ever cleaned an area of your house or apartment and found something of value? How did it feel finding this forgotten item of value?

Be courteous. GOD sees you and loves your service.

Hebrews 6:10 – *God is not unjust; he will not forget your work and the love you have shown him as you have helped his people and continue to help them.* (NIV)

GOD remembers when you have served people with HIS motive in your heart.

Let's walk through the steps of customer service so you can customize your own model. Remember, a customer could simply be calling with a question. Some customers, however, will be calling with an issue. Your attitude towards serving your customer will show up in your sales and growth, positively or negatively.

1. **Be available during business hours.** This may seem obvious, but fight the tendency to dive into something that could take your company's time away from being available during these hours. If you are a sole-preneur, working by yourself, this is a great time to get some administrative work done while waiting on calls. When one comes in, treat it as special.
2. **Listen without defending.** When a customer calls with a complaint, the last thing she wants to hear is you defending the situation. Questions should be geared towards resolving problems,

not in trying to see if the person is lying. GOD will enable you to have discernment to identify those who are untruthful.

3. **Clarify the incident.** Repeat what the person says and use your expertise to make sure the incident is classified correctly. Root-cause type questions help. Remember, you are about to guide the person to resolution. If in fact there is an error on your part, have something to give to your customer for his inconvenience. If the customer is still dissatisfied, then consider refunding his money.
4. **Speak while smiling.** Practice smiling while talking on the phone or over your online communications. People can hear a smile. There is a tone adjustment that happens when you smile that puts people at ease. Pass this on to your employees if you have any. Take frequent breaks to ask GOD to replenish your smile, especially if the day seems to be more trying than others.
5. **Document the incident.** Transcribe the customer's name, email address, and phone number along with the name of the incident. For example: *Received product broken*. Keep track of dates and times so you can identify how to improve. Notify your customer that you are working on the incident. Check estimates or review what you promised the customer.
6. **Solve the problem and get feedback.** Continuous improvement is what the GOD-centered business owner strives for. Fix the problem. Notify when fixed. Ask the customer if you resolved the issue in a timely, knowledgeable fashion. Also ask what you could have done better.

The way you resolve issues will make or break relationships with customers. Desire what is best for them and pray favorably for each one who has a complaint.

My Office Hours

What are your office hours? You wrote these down in the Time Management section of Remove the Trash chapter. These hours should be posted as content on your website.

My office hours for my customers are (Finish the sentence)

My Calm Pledge

Some people are gifted in remaining calm, other people need practice. Not every customer, who has a complaint, will speak respectfully. The best approach is to diffuse the situation with a calm tone. How will you do this?

My pledge to remain calm when customers complain is (Finish the sentence)

My Clarity Method

Communication is a two way street. Message sent is not always message received. Repeat, in your own words, what the customer said to you, clarifying with questions along the way. Will you have a script? Will you have a conversation?

My method for clarifying the issue is (Finish the sentence)

My Service Tone

People can hear a smile over the phone. Having the right attitude makes all the different when servicing your customer. Try this for yourself... smile while explaining something. Do you notice a change in the tone of your voice?. How will you implement smiling while talking? Will you put up a sign that says "Smile before answering the phone?" Will you place a mirror next to the phone that has smile written on it?

Write your pledge to practice smiling when talking.

My Incident Documentation Method

Capturing incidents helps you prevent them in the future. By documenting the incident, you can develop a plan to keep it from happening again. How will you document the incident? Will you do this while the customer is on the phone? Will you use a spreadsheet or a Word document or a service application?

Write your incident documentation method.

My Resolution to the Incident Method

What will be your service level agreement? Will you promise to have all issues resolved within 24 hours or will it take a week. It depends on your industry.

Write how you will deliver the solution to the incident here.

Now let's get some referrals and great reviews.

Exercise 4 – Ask for a Referral or a Review

Objective: *To ask customers for referrals and ratings.*

What is the difference between a paper cup and a glass or steel cup?

The paper cup is temporary and the others are more permanent. Your GOD-centered business is expected to grow and remain a permanent part of many customer's lives. Practice asking for a referral with each customer. This will broaden your territory to serve GOD in a mighty way.

Possible Referrals

Many business owners become "too busy" to ask for a referral. This should be a standard practice, done without shame because you really desire to grow to reach people for GOD.

The following people are willing to refer me: (Write out the list)

Five Star Ratings and Reviews

Getting high reviews on Google or a similar platform is paramount. People shop based on ratings, so it is important to get some good ones up front. No matter the business make sure you have a "Google My Business Page. In 2021 it was free to sign up for a page. You will be able to add you business hours, add pictures and current posts. Sounds great? You will also be open to receive reviews, positive or negative. Address all reviews in a timely fashion.

The following people will rate my site: (Write out a list)

My References Template

Some B2B (business to business) companies may require you to provide three or more references. Many times people cannot remember what you did for them. Write out the reference for them as a thought starter so they do not have to work from a blank page. Here is a template you can use.

On _______ date you and I solved ________________ (problem).
I did 1. _______, 2. _______ and 3. ______________. The result was _________ (some positive response).
_____________ (quantifiable) was also the result.

"His lord said to him, 'Well done, good and faithful servant; you have been faithful over a few things, I will make you ruler over many things. Enter into the joy of your lord.'" Matthew 25:23

The GOD-centered business owner does not need validation from humans because GOD provides the true reward. By focusing on serving with excellence, you will receive human rewards as well.

Now that you have a referral method, let's finish up with a couple of meetings.

Retrospective Meeting

You are almost there. Now that you have gone through all of this work with your customers, developing parts of your product or service with them, it is time to determine what went well and what did not go so well.

Hold a retrospective meeting with the people who helped you build the product or service. Pray before starting the meeting, leaving blame outside the door.

Ask GOD to reveal issues and good things so you can correct the product or service or praise for a job well done.
Ask GOD for patience and strength to recognize it take time to get things right.

Do you want this process to be easier? What problems did you encounter when listening to GOD? Did you identify the correct audience HE sent you to? Did you remove all the trash out of your life? What skill gaps did you overlook? When developing your product or service, did you cut corners of forget test something important? Do you have a message that shows why your company is the expert in your industry? Do you have the right pricing? Do customers understand your sales process? And do you have customer service in place? Have you prayed for your customers and reached them with a message of JESUS as Savior?

Write what went right and what could have been done better over the past two to eight weeks.
Write how you will avoid this over the next two to eight weeks.

Are we finished? Never. Plan on doing this entire methodology over and over. Let's talk about how.

Innovation Planning

Innovation planning happens in two week increments. Here is how the entire lifecycle should go.

1. Obtain the vision from GOD and the audience HE wants you to serve.
2. Remove the things that block you from becoming the leader HE wants you to be.
3. Seek wisdom to identify the things you do not know and learn them or outsource.
4. Go to a place that you can quiet down, see a different beauty and listen to GOD to divide the vision, so you can build and validate components of your business based on customer input.
5. Emerge as a servant leader, willing to collaborate using your expert content as the way you draw people to you and GOD.
6. Keep GOD's kingdom top of mind as you meet people and tell them of your product or service.
7. Provide outstanding customer service, leading them to GOD's promises.

Now that you have done this, you are ready to plan the next lifecycle. You will add to the wish list and update definitions. Quiet down to ask GOD to guide you to the next group of people.

Two Week Innovation Agenda (Requires customers and volunteers who have time)

Innovation Meeting Day 1 (4 – 8 hours)

Round table discussions about problems your customers are facing
Summarize Issues

Innovation Meeting Day 2 (4 – 8 hours)

Solution Challenge (Divide into teams and address each issue with solutions)
Discuss the parameters of building the solution

Innovation Meeting Day 3 (4 – 8 hours)

Give each team time to develop a prototype of the issue they are working on

Innovation Meeting Day 4 (4 – 8 hours)

Give each team time to develop and finish their prototype

Innovation Meeting Day 5 (4 hours)

Have each team summarize and answer questions

Innovation Meeting Day 6 (4 hours)

Prioritize the innovations
Document dependencies (What does this depend on and what depends on it?)

Innovation Meeting Day 7 (4 hours)

Define the features (Long Definitions)

Innovation Meeting Day 8 (4 hours)

Plan the development sprint(s)
Plan the marketing sprint(s)
Plan the sales sprint(s)

Innovation Meeting Day 9 (4 hours)

Engage resources (People who will build or do the work)
Review the plan

Innovation Meeting Day 10 (4 hours)

Obtain commitment to start the first two week sprint
Plan Sprint 1 Meetings and write agendas

Not ready for this type of meeting? No worries. Work your way up to it. You will get there. "

By now you should have:

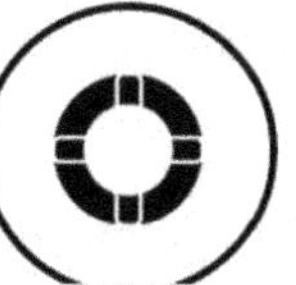

Vision	Self-Awareness	Wisdom	Preparation	Differentiation	Tell	Service
Vision statement from GOD.	Blockers to achieving GOD's vision.	Study time to continuously learn about GOD.	Revised fully defined vision from GOD.	Collaboration marketing plan.	Adjusted leadership style.	Proactive Follow-up list.
Gifts and talents assessment.	Hidden motive identified.	Behavioral modifications to enable working better with others.	Features of business defined from vision.	Content marketing plan / material.	Refined product or service instructions or ingredient list.	Prayer list.
List of GOD's promises for you.	Heart of business for mission statement.	Business mood elevation plan.	Validated customer user stories.	Pricing model.	Refined product or service sell sheet.	Customer service model.
Initial list of people who will help.	Business hours.	Skills assessment.	Documented processes.	Market research.	Sales process.	Customer service measures.
	Quiet time.		SOPs.	Content location map.	CRM established.	
	Weekly admin day.		Marketing messages.	Quiet time established.	Follow-ups scheduled.	
			Sales/ payment method.	Vacation or staycation established.		
			Accounting method.			

Achieved RESILIENCE

PROMISES.

Pleasantly
Repeat the issue
Obtaining clarity
Making a note
Identifying the root cause
Solving the problem
Expressing an apology
Smiling for feedback

Homework: Spend the next week encouraging seven people.

Now you have reached full resilience! After listening to GOD and implementing business operational components you will have a resilient business that weathers the storms. Your leadership style has now changed and you have grown to reach new customers and grow GOD's kingdom. Revisit Remove the Trash often, update your wish list in Dream Bigger, plan meetings and get feedback. Most of all, Lead them to the Promises of GOD.

Remember to use your personal journal found at the end of this book.

(Optional)Host a graduation. Since this is a methodology that will be done over and over, the GOD-centered business owner never really says "I made it." Recognition for working hard is, however, encouraged.

Understand the symptoms

Having a resilient business is important. It doesn't mean you are perfect, rather that you know how to respond to adversity through GOD's power.

Here are a few starter symptoms and areas to check when you run into them.

Symptom	Chapter	Suggested Action
Product or service not selling at all	Dream **BIGGER**	QUIET **Q**uiet down - **U**nderstand what GOD said - **I**nvestigate **E**xcellence and **T**arget the right audience.
People not calling or buying from you	Remove the **TRASH**	LOVE **L**eave **O**ld (behaviors) **V**alue **E**veryone
Product or service incomplete	**SEEK** Wisdom	ASK **A**ssess yourself - **S**eek professional help or classes - **K**now what is missing & pray
Product or service looks unprofessional or misused or misunderstood by the customer	Go to the **DESERT**	TEST Test - Every - Solution - Thoroughly with customers and employees
Reacting to every request versus being able to "respond"	**EMERGE** Different	READY **R**eliable - **E**xpert - **A**ccount for expenses - **D**ifferentiating - **Y**ou being and loving how GOD made you
People shy away from you	Kingdom-**FIRST** Mindset	PRAY **P**eople's needs met - **R**elationship strong - **A**sk to meet the need - **Y**ou Meet 22
Complaints or poor reviews.	Lead to **PROMISES**	FIX **F**ollow up to see if everything is fine - *Investigate* and resolve issues - **X**-press (express GOD's promises, your gratitude and compensation for the problem)

Believe. **I**gnite **G**OD's **G**race **E**verywhere **R**elationally!	**T**ame **R**age **A**nd **S**elfish **H**abits	**S**tudy **E**xcellent **E**nriching **K**nowledge.	**D**ivide **E**verything. **S**eek **E**xcellence. **R**evise. **T**est.	**E**xpert **M**essages **E**nrich **R**elationships, **G**aining **E**vangelism	**F**ruit of the SPIRIT **I**nform providing options **R**epeat the need **S**olve **T**ell the price	**P**leasantly **R**epeat the issue **O**btaining clarity **M**aking a note **I**dentifying the root cause **S**olving the problem **E**xpressing an apology **S**miling for feedback.

Strength and Leadership - My Personal Growth

GOD-Centered Leadership

Leaders of the world are sometimes admired by many for things GOD is not excited about. Their names are mentioned more than GOD in some circles of influence. The measure of success also is often distorted. JESUS mentioned how impossible it is for a rich person to enter heaven. HE is not saying all rich people will go to hell; rather, wealth can sometimes enable temptations to be realized and acted upon. The more sin, the deeper the blindness.

GOD-centered leadership is different. It is less "me" focused and more "you" focused.

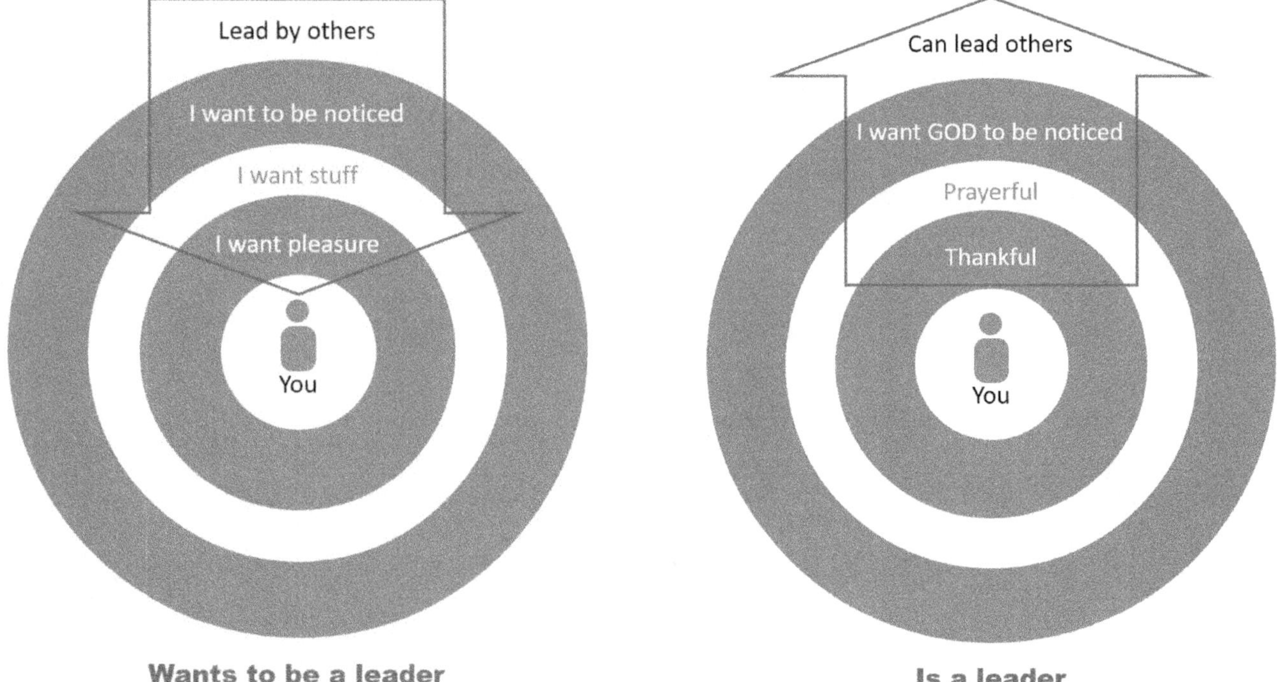

As a business owner, you automatically become a leader. As a person of GOD, HE already gave you the leadership qualities you need to lead the people only you can reach. Your confidence comes from knowing GOD and HIS abilities.

In the above images two leaders are illustrated. The first leader has the world's concerns blocking him. "For all that is in the world—the lust of the flesh, the lust of the eyes, and the pride of life—is not of the Father but is of the world" (1 John 2:16). The second leader uses the fruit of the SPIRIT to get beyond the pull of the world.

Use CHRIST to be Like CHRIST

How much would you be willing to pay if you could have just one meeting with the most influential leader in the world? Many would name an exorbitant price simply because of the value of the advice they would receive. But what if I told you that you could take not just one meeting, but thirty for free?

JESUS is the ultimate leader. While on earth, HE led by example. "But HE's GOD," you say. Yes, but HE became a human to show that the behavior HE modeled is possible for any human. With GOD, all things are possible. It is impossible to sum up HIS examples; therefore I urge you to be led by the HOLY SPIRIT as you learn about HIM. GOD reveals HIMSELF to those who earnestly seek HIM.

One way to look for CHRIST is by using the CHRIST method. This is not really an acronym; rather, words that begin with the letter ***C***, ***H***, ***R***, ***I***, ***S***, and ***T***. What follows are some examples of word studies of words related to JESUS that you can prayerfully examine and apply to your leadership style.

For the next thirty six days, you will be mentored by the Master HIMSELF. Savor time with the LORD.

C	H	R	I	S	T
Caring Compassionate	Honest Humble	Respectful Reverent	Interesting Intuitive	Saves Sent	Teachable Talented

Notes

Caring. When JESUS was on HIS way somewhere, HE always had a crowd around HIM. HE had achieved a certain status amongst the people that after a while the crowd started judging who should see HIM and who should not. HE stopped to show HE cared. Caring changes crowds. Spend the next three days examining the ways JESUS showed concern for others.

Day 1 Leadership Scripture: Mark 10:46-52

10:46 Now they came to Jericho. As He went out of Jericho with His disciples and a
great multitude, blind Bartimaeus, the son of Timaeus, sat by the road begging. 47
And when he heard that it was Jesus of Nazareth, he began to cry out and say,
"Jesus, Son of David, have mercy on me!"

48 Then many warned him to be quiet; but he cried out all the more, "Son of David, have mercy on me!"

49 So Jesus stood still and commanded him to be called.

Then they called the blind man, saying to him, "Be of good cheer. Rise, He is calling you."

50 And throwing aside his garment, he rose and came to Jesus.

51 So Jesus answered and said to him, "What do you want Me to do for you?"

The blind man said to Him, "Rabboni, that I may receive my sight."

52 Then Jesus said to him, "Go your way; your faith has made you well." And immediately he received his sight and followed Jesus on the road.

What was the initial reaction to Bartimaeus?
When JESUS stopped to show HE cared, what was the reaction of the crowd?
What did Bartimaeus do when he received sight?
Do you believe JESUS cares about you dearly? Think back to a time when you knew without a shadow of a doubt that HE cared. Who needs to hear this story? Consider who you can tell.

Notes

Day 2 Leadership Scripture: John 4:5-14 (ESV)

5 So he came to a town of Samaria called Sychar, near the field that Jacob had given to his son Joseph. 6 Jacob's well was there; so Jesus, wearied as he was from his journey, was sitting beside the well. It was about the sixth hour.

7 A woman from Samaria came to draw water. Jesus said to her, "Give me a drink." 8 (For his disciples had gone away into the city to buy food.) 9 The Samaritan woman said to him, "How is it that you, a Jew, ask for a drink from me, a woman of Samaria?" (For Jews have no dealings with Samaritans.) 10 Jesus answered her, "If you knew the gift of God, and who it is that is saying to you, 'Give me a drink,' you would have asked him, and he would have given you living water." 11 The woman said to him, "Sir, you have nothing to draw water with, and the well is deep. Where do you get that living water? 12 Are you greater than our father Jacob? He gave us the well and drank from it himself, as did his sons and his livestock." 13 Jesus said to her, "Everyone who drinks of this water will be thirsty again, 14 but whoever drinks of the water that I will give him will never be thirsty again. The water that I will give him will become in him a spring of water welling up to eternal life."

Put yourself in the woman's place. How would you have reacted to JESUS' request? Why?
How was JESUS' request a sign of HIS concern?
What's your usual approach to people of a different ethnicity? Circle the response that best fits yours below. (Be honest.)

- Caution unless they show willingness to learn about me.
- Openness. I can learn from them.
- Suspicion because of past dealings.

How can you prayerfully show concern to someone who is different from you? If doing so is difficult for you because of something that happened in the past, know that GOD is willing to heal. Talk to HIM about it. You can be honest with HIM.

Notes

Day 3 Leadership Scripture: John 4:15-26 (ESV)

15 The woman said to him, "Sir, give me this water, so that I will not be thirsty or
have to come here to draw water."
16 Jesus said to her, "Go, call your husband, and come here." 17 The woman
answered him, "I have no husband." Jesus said to her, "You are right in saying, 'I
have no husband'; 18 for you have had five husbands, and the one you now have is
not your husband. What you have said is true." 19 The woman said to him, "Sir, I
perceive that you are a prophet. 20 Our fathers worshiped on this mountain, but you say that in
Jerusalem is the place where people ought to worship." 21 Jesus said to her, "Woman, believe me, the
hour is coming when neither on this mountain nor in Jerusalem will you worship the Father. 22 You
worship what you do not know; we worship what we know, for salvation is from the Jews. 23 But the
hour is coming, and is now here, when the true worshipers will worship the Father in spirit and truth,
for the Father is seeking such people to worship him. 24 God is spirit, and those who worship him
must worship in spirit and truth." 25 The woman said to him, "I know that Messiah is coming (he who
is called Christ). When he comes, he will tell us all things." 26 Jesus said to her, "I who speak to you
am he."

What need do you think the woman had? Consider the fact that she came to the well by herself during the day when many women in this culture went to the well together toward the evening when the temperature was cooler.
How did JESUS propose to meet that need?
Observe how JESUS engaged her in conversation. How did HE show what HE knew about her? Do you think HE judged her for her situation? Why or why not?
When are the times when you're tempted to prejudge someone's situation? Does disapproval of a person's lifestyle affect whether or not you help that person? Explain why or why not.

Notes

Compassionate. JESUS not only cared, HE felt the pain of others. HE showed great compassion for all people. Spend the next three days contemplating JESUS' compassionate nature, and how HE wants to show through you.

Day 1 Leadership Scripture: Mark 1:40-44

40 Now a leper came to Him, imploring Him, kneeling down to Him and saying to
Him, "If You are willing, You can make me clean."
41 Then Jesus, moved with compassion, stretched out His hand and touched him, and
said to him, "I am willing; be cleansed." 42 As soon as He had spoken, immediately
the leprosy left him, and he was cleansed. 43 And He strictly warned him and sent
him away at once, 44 and said to him, "See that you say nothing to anyone; but go
your way, show yourself to the priest, and offer for your cleansing those things which Moses
commanded, as a testimony to them."

What do you notice about Jesus' response to the leper's request? Many times we think we have to beg God for an answer to prayer. Knowing that Jesus is compassionate, what does that encourage you to ask Him?

Have you ever wondered if Jesus would pass you by if He saw you on the street in need? Why or why not?

What needs do you notice around you? Sometimes we get busy or think that the needs of others would drain our time and energy. But God might have you respond to just one need, rather than a multitude of needs. It starts with a willingness to ask God for what He would have you do.

Notes

Day 2 Leadership Scripture: Luke 7:11-17 (NASB)

11 Soon afterwards He went to a city called Nain; and His disciples were going along with Him, accompanied by a large crowd. 12 Now as He approached the gate of the city, a dead man was being carried out, the only son of his mother, and she was a widow; and a sizeable crowd from the city was with her. 13 When the Lord saw her, He felt compassion for her, and said to her, "Do not weep." 14 And He came up and touched the coffin; and the bearers came to a halt. And He said, "Young man, I say to you, arise!" 15 The dead man sat up and began to speak. And Jesus gave him back to his mother. 16 Fear gripped them all, and they began glorifying God, saying, "A great prophet has arisen among us!" and, "God has visited His people!" 17 This report concerning Him went out all over Judea and in all the surrounding district.

JESUS was surrounded by a crowd of people. Yet HE noticed this widow. What made her stand out?

Sometimes we're afraid to approach people who are grieving, because we don't know what to say, or we think their needs are far beyond our ability to do anything about them. But helping often starts with first noticing who is grieving. Who do you know who has recently suffered a loss of some kind? What can you do to help people who are grieving a loss (a spouse, a child, a dream)?

Notes

Day 3 Leadership Scripture: Mark 5:25-34

25 Now a certain woman had a flow of blood for twelve years, 26 and had suffered many things from many physicians. She had spent all that she had and was no better, but rather grew worse. 27 When she heard about Jesus, she came behind Him *in the crowd and touched His garment. 28 For she said, "If only I may touch His clothes, I shall be made well."*

29 Immediately the fountain of her blood was dried up, and she felt in her *body that she was healed of the affliction. 30 And Jesus, immediately knowing in Himself that power had gone out of Him, turned around in the crowd and said, "Who touched My clothes?"*

31 But His disciples said to Him, "You see the multitude thronging You, and You say, 'Who touched Me?' "

32 And He looked around to see her who had done this thing. 33 But the woman, fearing and trembling, knowing what had happened to her, came and fell down before Him and told Him the whole truth. 34 And He said to her, "Daughter, your faith has made you well. Go in peace, and be healed of your affliction."

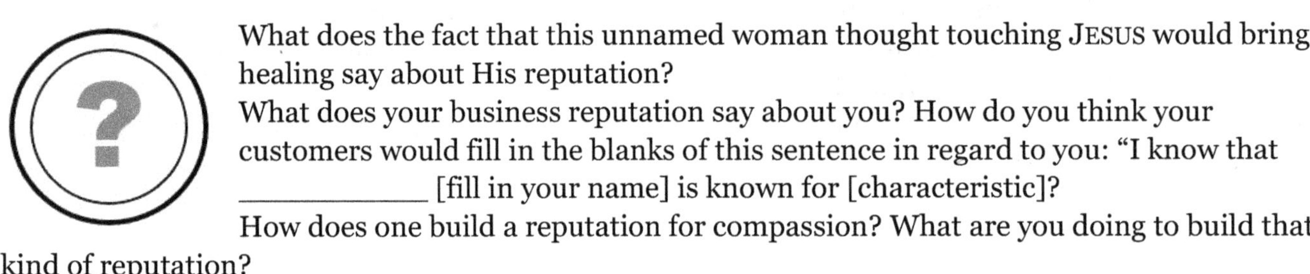

What does the fact that this unnamed woman thought touching JESUS would bring healing say about His reputation?

What does your business reputation say about you? How do you think your customers would fill in the blanks of this sentence in regard to you: "I know that ____________ [fill in your name] is known for [characteristic]?

How does one build a reputation for compassion? What are you doing to build that kind of reputation?

Notes

Honest. "I'm just being honest." When was the last time you heard someone say that? Often this statement is the conclusion to a crushing or critical remark. Truth used as a weapon. Jesus was compelled to be honest, because He is the source of all truth. While He walked the earth, He was the master of "speaking the truth in love" (Ephesians 4:15) not only to announce the kingdom but also for the betterment of people (Ephesians 4:15). For the next three days, talk with God about Jesus' example of honesty with heart.

Day 1 Leadership Scripture: John 5:24 (NLT)

I tell you the truth, those who listen to my message and believe in God who sent me have eternal life. They will never be condemned for their sins, but they have already passed from death into life.

Do you ever change the truth when you get nervous or made a mistake? Why or why not? What observations do you notice about JESUS' honesty?
Have you ever seen an advertisement for a product that made the product seem great, but after buying the product, you realized the ad wasn't exactly honest? How did that make you feel? Would you buy that product again, knowing what you know after buying it? Why or why not? What does this experience teach you about marketing your product of service?

Notes

Day 2 Leadership Scripture: John 8:26-32

26 "I have many things to say and to judge concerning you, but He who sent Me is
true; and I speak to the world those things which I heard from Him."
27 They did not understand that He spoke to them of the Father.
28 Then Jesus said to them, "When you lift up the Son of Man, then you will know
that I am He, and that I do nothing of Myself; but as My Father taught Me, I speak
these things. 29 And He who sent Me is with Me. The Father has not left Me alone, for I always do
those things that please Him." 30 As He spoke these words, many believed in Him.
31 Then Jesus said to those Jews who believed Him, "If you abide in My word, you are My disciples
indeed. 32 And you shall know the truth, and the truth shall make you free."

What does the statement, "I do nothing of Myself; but as My Father taught Me" tell you about JESUS?

Sometimes we're afraid to give credit where credit is due because we want the admiration of others.

(For example, someone who declares he or she is a "self-made success" as if he or she never received help from anyone else.) But what's your honest assessment of the purpose of your business or service? Is it to glorify GOD or yourself? Why?

How has abiding in GOD's Word helped you to honestly evaluate where you are?

Notes

Day 3 Leadership Scripture: Matthew 15:21-28 (NASB)

*21 Jesus went away from there, and withdrew into the district of Tyre
and Sidon. 22 And a Canaanite woman from that region came out and began to cry
out, saying, "Have mercy on me, Lord, Son of David; my daughter is cruelly demon-
possessed." 23 But He did not answer her a word. And His disciples came and
implored Him, saying, "Send her away, because she keeps shouting at us." 24 But He
answered and said, "I was sent only to the lost sheep of the house of Israel." 25 But
she came and began]to bow down before Him, saying, "Lord, help me!" 26 And He answered and
said, "It is not good to take the children's bread and throw it to the dogs." 27 But she said, "Yes,
Lord; but even the dogs feed on the crumbs which fall from their masters' table." 28 Then Jesus said to
her, "O woman, your faith is great; it shall be done for you as you wish." And her daughter was
healed at once.*

In this passage JESUS seems to be brutally honest. How would you have responded had HE said this to you? Why?

What JESUS' said was a common belief of the day about Gentiles. But why do you think HE said it to the woman? What do you think would have happened had the woman taken offense and stormed away? What does the woman's persistence in the face of offense tell you?

Have you ever received feedback about your product or service that was expressed in terms that were brutally honest at best or greatly offensive at worse? How did you react? What can help you focus on the need (learning from feedback in order to improve your product or service) versus expressing your displeasure over the perceived offense?

Notes

Humble. JESUS' life is a textbook example of humility. Think about it: the GOD who created the world became like one of His own creations, human. Not only that, HE came to die for the ones HE created. Yet being humble is always a tightrope walk. The moment we say, "I'm humble," it sounds like pride. Take the next three days to examine how JESUS walked the walk, rather than just talking.

Day 1 Leadership Scripture: Philippians 2:1-11

Therefore if there is any consolation in Christ, if any comfort of love, if any fellowship of the Spirit, if any affection and mercy, 2 fulfill my joy by being like-minded, having the same love, being of one accord, of one mind. 3 Let nothing be done through selfish ambition or conceit, but in lowliness of mind let each esteem others better than himself. 4 Let each of you look out not only for his own interests, but also for the interests of others.
5 Let this mind be in you which was also in Christ Jesus, 6 who, being in the form of God, did not consider it robbery to be equal with God, 7 but made Himself of no reputation, taking the form of a bondservant, and coming in the likeness of men. 8 And being found in appearance as a man, He humbled Himself and became obedient to the point of death, even the death of the cross. 9 Therefore God also has highly exalted Him and given Him the name which is above every name, 10 that at the name of Jesus every knee should bow, of those in heaven, and of those on earth, and of those under the earth, 11 and that every tongue should confess that Jesus Christ is Lord, to the glory of God the Father.

This passage was written by the apostle Paul about JESUS. What is Paul's definition of *humility*? How does JESUS' life show this?
Some people think humility equals looking down on yourself and your accomplishments—"Oh, it's nothing." Or "I'm nothing special." Would you agree? Why or why not? How would you explain humility to someone?
What are some ways you show humility in your daily practice?
JESUS was extremely popular, yet most of the time HE tried to tell people not to speak about the healing HE had just performed. How does this apply to your business?

Notes

Day 2 Leadership Scripture: John 13:3-8

3 Jesus, knowing that the Father had given all things into His hands, and that He had
come from God and was going to God, 4 rose from supper and laid aside His
garments, took a towel and girded Himself. 5 After that, He poured water into a
basin and began to wash the disciples' feet, and to wipe them *with the towel with*
which He was girded. 6 Then He came to Simon Peter. And Peter *said to Him, "Lord,*
are You washing my feet?"
7 Jesus answered and said to him, "What I am doing you do not understand now, but you will know
after this."
8 Peter said to Him, "You shall never wash my feet!"
Jesus answered him, "If I do not wash you, you have no part with Me."

Why do you think the disciples were shocked that JESUS washed their feet before they took the Passover meal?
Many people have the expectation that leaders should be served, rather than serve others. But JESUS often behaved in a way that was countercultural. What does HIS example inspire you to do?
Serving others takes humility. In what ways are you serving others?

Notes

Day 3 Leadership Scripture: Luke 14:7-11

7 So He told a parable to those who were invited, when He noted how they chose the best places, saying to them: 8 "When you are invited by anyone to a wedding feast, do not sit down in the best place, lest one more honorable than you be invited by him; 9 and he who invited you and him come and say to you, 'Give place to this man,' and then you begin with shame to take the lowest place. 10 But when you are invited, go and sit down in the lowest place, so that when he who invited you comes he may say to you, 'Friend, go up higher.' Then you will have glory in the presence of those who sit at the table with you. 11 For whoever exalts himself will be humbled, and he who humbles himself will be exalted."

Why do you think Jesus advised taking "the lowest place"? Does that fit with what you hear suggested on social media and in advertisements? Why or why not? What does taking "the lowest place" look like in your life? In your business? How will you promote the interests of others this week?

Notes

Respectful. GOD respecting someone? Absolutely! JESUS sowed respect and it was reciprocated. Take the next three days to examine the beauty and necessity of a respectful nature.

Day 1 Leadership Scripture: Matthew 8:5–13

5 Now when Jesus had entered Capernaum, a centurion came to Him, pleading with
Him, 6 saying, "Lord, my servant is lying at home paralyzed, dreadfully tormented."

7 And Jesus said to him, "I will come and heal him."

8 The centurion answered and said, "Lord, I am not worthy that You should come
under my roof. But only speak a word, and my servant will be healed. 9 For I also am a man under
authority, having soldiers under me. And I say to this one, 'Go,' and he goes; and to another, 'Come,'
and he comes; and to my servant, 'Do this,' and he does it."

10 When Jesus heard it, He marveled, and said to those who followed, "Assuredly, I say to you, I have
not found such great faith, not even in Israel!.". . . 13 Then Jesus said to the centurion, "Go your way;
and as you have believed, so let it be done for you." And his servant was healed that same hour.

How did the centurion show respect to Jesus? What was Jesus' reaction to the centurion? Keep in mind that Jesus was a Jewish man but also God and the centurion was a Gentile and also a Roman—a member of the ruling class at that time. How do respect and authority work together? How will you show the respect you have for people in your community? For people who are different from you?

Notes

Day 2 Leadership Scripture: Romans 13:1–7; Matthew 22:19-21

*13:1 Let every person be subject to the governing authorities. For there is no
authority except from God, and those that exist have been instituted by
God. 2 Therefore whoever resists the authorities resists what God has appointed, and
those who resist will incur judgment. 3 For rulers are not a terror to good conduct,
but to bad. Would you have no fear of the one who is in authority? Then do what is
good, and you will receive his approval, 4 for he is God's servant for your good. But if
you do wrong, be afraid, for he does not bear the sword in vain. For he is the servant of God, an
avenger who carries out God's wrath on the wrongdoer. 5 Therefore one must be in subjection, not
only to avoid God's wrath but also for the sake of conscience. 6 For because of this you also pay taxes,
for the authorities are ministers of God, attending to this very thing. 7 Pay to all what is owed to
them: taxes to whom taxes are owed, revenue to whom revenue is owed, respect to whom respect is
owed, honor to whom honor is owed.*

*22:19 "Show me the coin for the tax." And they brought him a denarius. 20 And Jesus said to
them, "Whose likeness and inscription is this?" 21 They said, "Caesar's." Then he said to
them, "Therefore render to Caesar the things that are Caesar's, and to God the things that are God's."*

When have you found obeying this passage in Romans most challenging?
Some have used this passage as a weapon to force others to one view or another. How can you show respect to leaders, even to those you don't agree with?
Why do you think Jesus said to "render to Caesar the things that are Caesar's" (Matthew 22:21)? How is that a way of showing respect?

Notes

Day 3 Leadership Scripture: Matthew 7:12 (NASB)

In everything, therefore, treat people the same way you want them to treat you, for this is the Law and the Prophets.

JESUS spoke these words in His most well-known sermon: the Sermon on the Mount. We know this as the Golden Rule. Why is this important?
If someone shows disrespect to you, what's your usual first reaction? Notice that JESUS didn't "Treat *only the people who show you respect* the same way you want them to treat you."
How do you treat your customers or clients "the same way you want them to treat you"?

Notes

Reverent. =JESUS, though GOD, always gave thanks to the FATHER. HE wanted to provide an example for those who followed HIM. Study HIS example over the next three days.

Day 1 Leadership Scripture: Matthew 14:13- 21 (NIV)

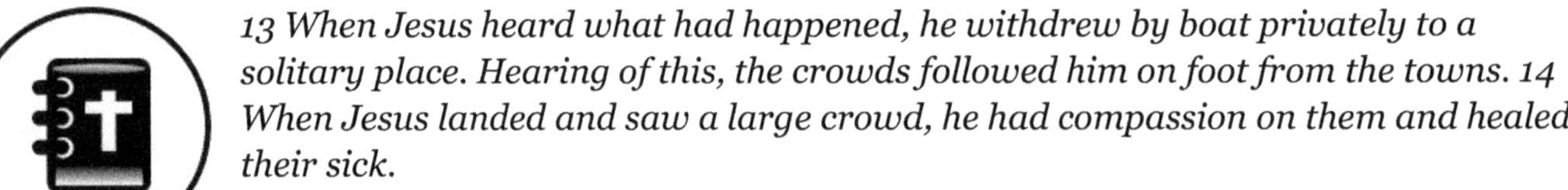

13 When Jesus heard what had happened, he withdrew by boat privately to a
solitary place. Hearing of this, the crowds followed him on foot from the towns. 14
When Jesus landed and saw a large crowd, he had compassion on them and healed
their sick.

15 As evening approached, the disciples came to him and said, "This is a remote
place, and it's already getting late. Send the crowds away, so they can go to the villages and buy
themselves some food."

16 Jesus replied, "They do not need to go away. You give them something to eat."

17 "We have here only five loaves of bread and two fish," they answered.

18 "Bring them here to me," he said. 19 And he directed the people to sit down on the grass. Taking the
five loaves and the two fish and looking up to heaven, he gave thanks and broke the loaves. Then he
gave them to the disciples, and the disciples gave them to the people. 20 They all ate and were
satisfied, and the disciples picked up twelve basketfuls of broken pieces that were left over. 21 The
number of those who ate was about five thousand men, besides women and children.

This familiar story is known as the "Feeding of the Five Thousand." What was the first thing JESUS did before passing out the food? Why do you think this was important to JESUS?

JESUS is also GOD. Yet HE modeled a reverent attitude toward HIS Father. HOW do you show this attitude toward GOD? How can you give GOD more credit for the things that happen in your day?

Notes

Day 2 Leadership Scripture: Luke 11:1-2 (NLT)

11:1 Once Jesus was in a certain place praying. As he finished, one of his disciples came to him and said, "Lord, teach us to pray, just as John taught his disciples."

2 Jesus said, "This is how you should pray:

"Father, may your name be kept holy.
May your Kingdom come soon.

How do you usually start a prayer? Most of us, if we're honest, will admit we jump right into asking for what we want. Why do you think JESUS suggested starting this way?.
How does prayer change when we start by focusing on GOD and what honors HIM? How can you honor HIM through your business?

Notes

Day 3 Leadership Scripture: Luke 18:1-8 (NIV)

18:1 Then Jesus told his disciples a parable to show them that they should always pray and not give up. 2 He said: "In a certain town there was a judge who neither feared God nor cared what people thought. 3 And there was a widow in that town who kept coming to him with the plea, 'Grant me justice against my adversary.'

4 "For some time he refused. But finally he said to himself, 'Even though I don't fear God or care what people think, 5 yet because this widow keeps bothering me, I will see that she gets justice, so that she won't eventually come and attack me!'"

6 And the Lord said, "Listen to what the unjust judge says. 7 And will not God bring about justice for his chosen ones, who cry out to him day and night? Will he keep putting them off? 8 I tell you, he will see that they get justice, and quickly. However, when the Son of Man comes, will he find faith on the earth?"

What do you think it means to "fear GOD"?
Who have you met who had the attitude of this judge? What would you say to this person to convince him or her of the need to fear GOD? Why?
Whether or not we fear GOD is connected to our perspective of HIM. What's your honest perspective? Is HE big? Small? How do you think that affects the way you do business?
Our perspective of GOD doesn't change the reality of GOD. Instead, our perspective often changes as we stay connected to Him. As JESUS said in John 15: 1 (NIV): "I am the vine; you are the branches. If you remain in me and I in you, you will bear much fruit; apart from me you can do nothing." How will you stay connected this week?

Notes

Interesting. JESUS always kept things interesting. Even as a child, JESUS captivated audiences with HIS wisdom. Those who heard HIM were interested in what HE had to say. And there was never a dull moment when JESUS was around. HIS disciples never knew what to expect! But you can expect a blessing these next three days as you think about JESUS and the interest HE inspired.

Day 1 Leadership Scripture: Luke 2:41- 52 (NIV)

2:41 Every year Jesus' parents went to Jerusalem for the Festival of the Passover. 42
When he was twelve years old, they went up to the festival, according to the custom.
43 After the festival was over, while his parents were returning home, the boy Jesus
stayed behind in Jerusalem, but they were unaware of it. 44 Thinking he was in their
company, they traveled on for a day. Then they began looking for him among their
relatives and friends. 45 When they did not find him, they went back to Jerusalem to
look for him. 46 After three days they found him in the temple courts, sitting among the teachers,
listening to them and asking them questions. 47 Everyone who heard him was amazed at his
understanding and his answers. 48 When his parents saw him, they were astonished. His mother said
to him, "Son, why have you treated us like this? Your father and I have been anxiously searching for
you."

49 "Why were you searching for me?" he asked. "Didn't you know I had to be in my Father's house?"
50 But they did not understand what he was saying to them.

51 Then he went down to Nazareth with them and was obedient to them. But his mother treasured all
these things in her heart. 52 And Jesus grew in wisdom and stature, and in favor with God and man.

What do you observe about JESUS' curiosity? What was the reaction to HIS curiosity?
What was JESUS' reaction to HIS parents when they questioned HIM?
How would you have reacted, had you been JESUS' parents?
Many adults overlook children (other than their own), because they don't think they have anything interesting to say simply because they are children. Or, they tire of the endless, curious questions. But JESUS showed an amazing wisdom, even though HE was only twelve. Later, in Matthew 19:13-15, we see how HE welcomed children to come into HIS presence. Even if your business doesn't cater to the needs of children, how can you be welcoming to children?
What do you do to show your interest in people of all ages?

Notes

Day 2 Leadership Scripture: Matthew 17:1-8

17:1 Now after six days Jesus took Peter, James, and John his brother, led them up on a high mountain by themselves; 2 and He was transfigured before them. His face shone like the sun, and His clothes became as white as the light. 3 And behold, Moses and Elijah appeared to them, talking with Him. 4 Then Peter answered and said to Jesus, "Lord, it is good for us to be here; if You wish, let us make here three tabernacles: one for You, one for Moses, and one for Elijah."

5 While he was still speaking, behold, a bright cloud overshadowed them; and suddenly a voice came out of the cloud, saying, "This is My beloved Son, in whom I am well pleased. Hear Him!" 6 And when the disciples heard it, *they fell on their faces and were greatly afraid. 7 But Jesus came and touched them and said, "Arise, and do not be afraid." 8 When they had lifted up their eyes, they saw no one but Jesus only.*

Life with JESUS just became more interesting! How would you have reacted had you been the disciples?

Why do you think JESUS allowed them to see not only HIMSELF in a glorified way, but also to see past leaders like Moses and Elijah?

The disciples saw JESUS as HE truly was. How do people see you? What do you do to show people who you are? Why?

Notes

Day 3 Leadership Scripture: Luke 5:1-8

5:1 So it was, as the multitude pressed about Him to hear the word of God, that He stood by the Lake of Gennesaret, 2 and saw two boats standing by the lake; but the fishermen had gone from them and were washing their *nets. 3 Then He got into one of the boats, which was Simon's, and asked him to put out a little from the land. And He sat down and taught the multitudes from the boat.*

4 When He had stopped speaking, He said to Simon, "Launch out into the deep and let down your nets for a catch."

5 But Simon answered and said to Him, "Master, we have toiled all night and caught nothing; nevertheless at Your word I will let down the net." 6 And when they had done this, they caught a great number of fish, and their net was breaking. 7 So they signaled to their *partners in the other boat to come and help them. And they came and filled both the boats, so that they began to sink. 8 When Simon Peter saw* it, *he fell down at Jesus' knees, saying, "Depart from me, for I am a sinful man, O Lord!"*

A typical fishing day became infinitely more interesting. After the frustration of no results, how would you have felt had you experienced the abundance Peter and his partners faced?

If you are a believer, how has your life changed with Jesus? Does it have to be problem free to be considered "good"? Why or why not?

How will you be a fisher of people?

Notes

Intuitive. JESUS sensed what the crowd was thinking and knew how to adjust. Spend the next three days observing how GOD wants you to filter your instincts through HIM.

Day 1 Leadership Scripture: Matthew 12:22-30

12:22 Then one was brought to Him who was demon-possessed, blind and mute; and
He healed him, so that the blind and mute man both spoke and saw. 23 And all the
multitudes were amazed and said, "Could this be the Son of David?"

24 Now when the Pharisees heard it they said, "This fellow does not cast out demons
except by Beelzebub, the ruler of the demons."

25 But Jesus knew their thoughts, and said to them: "Every kingdom divided against itself is brought
to desolation, and every city or house divided against itself will not stand. 26 If Satan casts out Satan,
he is divided against himself. How then will his kingdom stand? 27 And if I cast out demons by
Beelzebub, by whom do your sons cast them out? Therefore they shall be your judges. 28 But if I cast
out demons by the Spirit of God, surely the kingdom of God has come upon you. 29 Or how can one
enter a strong man's house and plunder his goods, unless he first binds the strong man? And then he
will plunder his house. 30 He who is not with Me is against Me, and he who does not gather with Me
scatters abroad."

What does JESUS mean when HE says, "He who is not with Me is against Me, and he who does not gather with Me scatters abroad?"
What is JESUS' reaction to the Pharisee?
As an expert in your field, how important is intuition to problems? Why?

Notes

Day 2 Leadership Scripture: Mark 2:1-12

2:1 A few days later, when Jesus again entered Capernaum, the people heard that he had come home. 2 They gathered in such large numbers that there was no room left, not even outside the door, and he preached the word to them. 3 Some men came, bringing to him a paralyzed man, carried by four of them. 4 Since they could not get him to Jesus because of the crowd, they made an opening in the roof above Jesus by digging through it and then lowered the mat the man was lying on. 5 When Jesus saw their faith, he said to the paralyzed man, "Son, your sins are forgiven."

6 Now some teachers of the law were sitting there, thinking to themselves, 7 "Why does this fellow talk like that? He's blaspheming! Who can forgive sins but God alone?"

8 Immediately Jesus knew in his spirit that this was what they were thinking in their hearts, and he said to them, "Why are you thinking these things? 9 Which is easier: to say to this paralyzed man, 'Your sins are forgiven,' or to say, 'Get up, take your mat and walk'? 10 But I want you to know that the Son of Man has authority on earth to forgive sins." So he said to the man, 11 "I tell you, get up, take your mat and go home." 12 He got up, took his mat and walked out in full view of them all. This amazed everyone and they praised God, saying, "We have never seen anything like this!"

None of us can read minds. But we can read the body language of others to intuit what they're thinking but not saying. JESUS, however, actually knew what people were thinking and wasn't afraid to confront attitudes. Have you ever confronted someone, based on a "gut feeling"? What was the result?

JESUS was always accurate in regard to what HE gleaned about the thoughts of others. HE was also intentional about what HE shared concerning the thoughts of others. Have you ever confronted someone only to realize your intuition was way off base? What happened?

What is your usual first step after you get a hunch about something? (Circle the answer that best fits.)
Do you . . .
Act on it immediately without verifying?
Talk to GOD about it?
Talk to a spouse, friend, or other family member?

Explain why you answered the way you did.

Notes

Day 3 Leadership Scripture: John 8:2-11 (NIV)

2 At dawn he appeared again in the temple courts, where all the people gathered around him, and he sat down to teach them. 3 The teachers of the law and the Pharisees brought in a woman caught in adultery. They made her stand before the group 4 and said to Jesus, "Teacher, this woman was caught in the act of adultery. 5 In the Law Moses commanded us to stone such women. Now what do you say?" 6 They were using this question as a trap, in order to have a basis for accusing him.
But Jesus bent down and started to write on the ground with his finger. 7 When they kept on
questioning him, he straightened up and said to them, "Let any one of you who is without sin be the first to throw a stone at her." 8 Again he stooped down and wrote on the ground.
9 At this, those who heard began to go away one at a time, the older ones first, until only Jesus was left, with the woman still standing there. 10 Jesus straightened up and asked her, "Woman, where are they? Has no one condemned you?"
11 "No one, sir," she said.
"Then neither do I condemn you," Jesus declared. "Go now and leave your life of sin."

Many times, when JESUS was about HIS mission, the Pharisees tried to stop HIM. This time they used the law of Moses to trap HIM. How do you deal with someone who is determined to put you down or work against you?

What do you notice about JESUS' strategy for handling the accusation? Even if you don't face this kind of situation, how can JESUS' method of handling opponents help you in your business or day-to-day confrontations?

What do you notice about the way JESUS handled the woman being accused? How can you mirror that when you have to deal with someone who has been caught in a wrongful act?

Notes

Saves. This is the ultimate task in JESUS' job description. HE is called the Savior because that is what HE came to do. While HE's most known for HIS saving work on the cross, JESUS also saved people from other situations. Sometimes, HE simply saved people from the embarrassment they would have faced. For the next three days, examine the ways JESUS saved people. HE continues to save today.

Day 1 Leadership Scripture: John 2:1-11

2 On the third day there was a wedding in Cana of Galilee, and the mother of Jesus
was there. 2 Now both Jesus and His disciples were invited to the wedding. 3 And
when they ran out of wine, the mother of Jesus said to Him, "They have no wine."
4 Jesus said to her, "Woman, what does your concern have to do with Me? My hour
has not yet come."
5 His mother said to the servants, "Whatever He says to you, do it."
6 Now there were set there six waterpots of stone, according to the manner of purification of the Jews,
containing twenty or thirty gallons apiece. 7 Jesus said to them, "Fill the waterpots with water." And
they filled them up to the brim. 8 And He said to them, "Draw some out now, and take it to the master
of the feast." And they took it. 9 When the master of the feast had tasted the water that was made
wine, and did not know where it came from (but the servants who had drawn the water knew), the
master of the feast called the bridegroom. 10 And he said to him, "Every man at the beginning sets out
the good wine, and when the guests have well drunk, then the inferior. You have kept the good wine
until now!"
."

This was JESUS' first miracle. Running out of wine was considered a huge embarrassment for a host in this culture. But HE did it after HIS mother brought it to HIS attention. What needs have been brought to your attention? In what small ways can you save someone embarrassment or trouble?

In what way(s) has GOD (directly or through someone you know) saved you from embarrassment in the past?

Many times we think GOD is only concerned with "big" things—the needs versus the wants. What does this miracle suggest to you about what GOD is willing to do about your needs and your wants?

Notes

Day 2 Leadership Scripture: Matthew 14:25-33

*25 Now in the fourth watch of the night Jesus went to them, walking on the
sea. 26 And when the disciples saw Him walking on the sea, they were troubled,
saying, "It is a ghost!" And they cried out for fear.
27 But immediately Jesus spoke to them, saying, "Be of good cheer! It is I; do not be
afraid."
28 And Peter answered Him and said, "Lord, if it is You, command me to come to You
on the water."
29 So He said, "Come." And when Peter had come down out of the boat, he walked on the water to go
to Jesus. 30 But when he saw that the wind* was *boisterous, he was afraid; and beginning to sink he
cried out, saying, "Lord, save me!"
31 And immediately Jesus stretched out* His *hand and caught him, and said to him, "O you of little
faith, why did you doubt?" 32 And when they got into the boat, the wind ceased.
33 Then those who were in the boat came and worshiped Him, saying, "Truly You are the Son of God."*

Many people tend to focus on what Peter stopped doing—walking on water—than on what JESUS did: save him. We often complicate things, based on our own expectations, of what's necessary to be saved/rescued from anything, whether from drowning, poverty, or other life circumstances. For example, you have to get your life together first; you have to be a good person; you have to "deserve it." What did Peter have to do to get JESUS to save him?

Have you ever rescued someone? What happened as a result?

In what way(s) does your business or service help rescue people? How can you connect that to what GOD does on a spiritual basis: rescue us from sin?

Notes

Day 3 Leadership Scripture: John 19:28-30

28 After this, Jesus, knowing that all things were now accomplished, that the Scripture might be fulfilled, said, "I thirst!" 29 Now a vessel full of sour wine was sitting there; and they filled a sponge with sour wine, put it on hyssop, and put it to His mouth. 30 So when Jesus had received the sour wine, He said, "It is finished!" And bowing His head, He gave up His spirit.

JESUS did what HE came to do: save people from sin through HIS death on the cross. You can read the whole experience on the cross in John 19 and the other three Gospels. Why do you think it was important for JESUS to fulfill what was then known as the law of Moses as well as all of the prophecies about the Messiah in the Old Testament?

Who will you tell about what JESUS did for you and for all people?

How does your business or the service you offer reflect your belief in JESUS?

Notes

Sent. Live life with purpose is a strong message from JESUS. Throughout HIS ministry, HE sent small and large groups of disciples to proclaim the kingdom of GOD. HE provided a clear message for them to proclaim. As you study HIS example over the next three days, consider the ways GOD sends you today.

Day 1 Leadership Scripture: Mark 6:7-11 (ESV)

6:7 And he called the twelve and began to send them out two by two, and gave them authority over the unclean spirits. 8 He charged them to take nothing for their journey except a staff—no bread, no bag, no money in their belts— 9 but to wear sandals and not put on two tunics. 10 And he said to them, "Whenever you enter a house, stay there until you depart from there. 11 And if any place will not receive you and they will not listen to you, when you leave, shake off the dust that is on your feet as a testimony against them."

Why do you think JESUS told HIS disciples "to take nothing for [the] journey" (Mark 6:8)?

How do you prepare when you start the business day? Is prayer part of your preparation? Why or why not? If you knew that GOD was sending you as HIS representative, how would that affect your prep time?

What do you usually do when someone ignores or speaks negatively about your product or service? What do you think GOD would want you to do?

Notes

Day 2 Leadership Scripture: Luke 10:1-6

10:1 After these things the Lord appointed seventy others also, and sent them two by two before His face into every city and place where He Himself was about to go. 2 Then He said to them, "The harvest truly is great, but the laborers are few; therefore pray the Lord of the harvest to send out laborers into His harvest. 3 Go your way; behold, I send you out as lambs among wolves. 4 Carry neither money bag, knapsack, nor sandals; and greet no one along the road. 5 But whatever house you enter, first say, 'Peace to this house.' 6 And if a son of peace is there, your peace will rest on it; if not, it will return to you."

This passage shows that JESUS had more than twelve people to send with the message of GOD's kingdom. Would you have preferred to be with the twelve or among the seventy, though with both groups people were sent in pairs? Why?
What does it mean to you to be a "lamb among wolves"? Why?
Who would you send to help spread the word about your business or service? Prayerfully consider who you would send. How does the message of your business or service fit the message of GOD's kingdom?

Notes

Day 3 Leadership Scripture: Matthew 28:16-20 (NIV)

28:16 Then the eleven disciples went to Galilee, to the mountain where Jesus had told them to go. 17 When they saw him, they worshiped him; but some doubted. 18 Then Jesus came to them and said, "All authority in heaven and on earth has been given to me. 19 Therefore go and make disciples of all nations, baptizing them in the name of the Father and of the Son and of the Holy Spirit, 20 and teaching them to obey everything I have commanded you. And surely I am with you always, to the very end of the age."

This passage is known as the Great Commission, where JESUS gives HIS disciples their marching orders. Note in verse 16 the phrase, "they worshiped him; but some doubted." When you think about this act of JESUS and what HE told HIS disciples to do, which group are you in (be honest): (1) the worshipers—totally ready to do whatever JESUS says or (2) the doubters—still not sure about GOD? Why?

What do you consider to be your purpose in life? Why? Where does the Great Commission fit in that plan?

What are you prompted to do?

Notes

Teachable. JESUS chose people with everyday professions—fishermen, tax collectors, etc.—to be HIS disciples and learn from HIM. They weren't trained rabbis or lawyers. But they were what HE looked for: teachable. For the next three days you can show your teachability as you examine how JESUS interacted with those who were teachable.

Day 1 Leadership Scripture: Matthew 11:25-30 (ESV)

25 At that time Jesus declared, "I thank you, Father, Lord of heaven and earth, that
you have hidden these things from the wise and understanding and revealed them to
little children; 26 yes, Father, for such was your gracious will. 27 All things have been
handed over to me by my Father, and no one knows the Son except the Father, and no
one knows the Father except the Son and anyone to whom the Son chooses to reveal
him. 28 Come to me, all who labor and are heavy laden, and I will give you rest. 29
Take my yoke upon you, and learn from me, for I am gentle and lowly in heart, and you will find rest
for your souls. 30 For my yoke is easy, and my burden is light."

Under what circumstances are you most resistant to being taught? Why?
What is GOD teaching you? Are you open to HIM making changes in your life? Why or why not?
Ever have a teacher who seemed reluctant to teach? What does JESUS' invitation tell you about HIS willingness to help you learn from HIM?

Notes

Day 2 Leadership Scripture: John 3:1-8

3:1 There was a man of the Pharisees named Nicodemus, a ruler of the Jews. 2 This
man came to Jesus by night and said to Him, "Rabbi, we know that You are a teacher
come from God; for no one can do these signs that You do unless God is with him."
3 Jesus answered and said to him, "Most assuredly, I say to you, unless one is
born again, he cannot see the kingdom of God."
4 Nicodemus said to Him, "How can a man be born when he is old? Can he enter a
second time into his mother's womb and be born?"
5 Jesus answered, "Most assuredly, I say to you, unless one is born of water and the Spirit, he cannot
enter the kingdom of God. 6 That which is born of the flesh is flesh, and that which is born of the Spirit
is spirit. 7 Do not marvel that I said to you, 'You must be born again.' 8 The wind blows where it
wishes, and you hear the sound of it, but cannot tell where it comes from and where it goes. So is
everyone who is born of the Spirit."

Nicodemus was a member of the Jewish council. Many of the council members resented JESUS for HIS authority though HE was not trained under a well-known rabbi like they were. How is Nicodemus's attitude different here?

Nicodemus took a risk to seek Jesus. What are you willing to risk for the sake of learning about JESUS?

Are you worried about anything? If so, what?

Are you born of the SPIRIT? How do you know?

Notes

Day 3 Leadership Scripture: Luke 19:1-10 (NIV)

19:1 Jesus entered Jericho and was passing through. 2 A man was there by the name
of Zacchaeus; he was a chief tax collector and was wealthy. 3 He wanted to see who
Jesus was, but because he was short he could not see over the crowd. 4 So he ran
ahead and climbed a sycamore-fig tree to see him, since Jesus was coming that way.
5 When Jesus reached the spot, he looked up and said to him, "Zacchaeus, come down
immediately. I must stay at your house today." 6 So he came down at once and
welcomed him gladly.
7 All the people saw this and began to mutter, "He has gone to be the guest of a sinner."
8 But Zacchaeus stood up and said to the Lord, "Look, Lord! Here and now I give half of my
possessions to the poor, and if I have cheated anybody out of anything, I will pay back four times the
amount."
9 Jesus said to him, "Today salvation has come to this house, because this man, too, is a son of
Abraham. 10 For the Son of Man came to seek and to save the lost."

How did JESUS set the stage for Zacchaeus to learn from HIM?
How did Zacchaeus show that he was teachable?
Had you been present, what would you have done to meet JESUS? What do you do in our time to get together with JESUS?

Notes

Talented. Many celebrities are fawned over because of their talents, while others are worshiped simply because they are famous. Gifts and talents are special to JESUS because HE gave them to each person. However, HE is always interested in what each person does with what was given to him or her. Spend the next three days considering JESUS' advice for those who are talented.

Day 1 Leadership Scripture: Matthew 25:14-30

14 "For the kingdom of heaven is like a man traveling to a far country, who called his own servants and delivered his goods to them. 15 And to one he gave five talents, to another two, and to another one, to each according to his own ability; and immediately he went on a journey. 16 Then he who had received the five talents went and traded with them, and made another five talents. 17 And likewise he who had received two gained two more also. 18 But he who had received one went and dug in the ground, and hid his lord's money. 19 After a long time the lord of those servants came and settled accounts with them.

20 "So he who had received five talents came and brought five other talents, saying, 'Lord, you delivered to me five talents; look, I have gained five more talents besides them.' 21 His lord said to him, 'Well done, good and faithful servant; you were faithful over a few things, I will make you ruler over many things. Enter into the joy of your lord.' 22 He also who had received two talents came and said, 'Lord, you delivered to me two talents; look, I have gained two more talents besides them.' 23 His lord said to him, 'Well done, good and faithful servant; you have been faithful over a few things, I will make you ruler over many things. Enter into the joy of your lord.'

24 "Then he who had received the one talent came and said, 'Lord, I knew you to be a hard man, reaping where you have not sown, and gathering where you have not scattered seed. 25 And I was afraid, and went and hid your talent in the ground. Look, there you have what is yours.'

26 "But his lord answered and said to him, 'You wicked and lazy servant, you knew that I reap where I have not sown, and gather where I have not scattered seed. 27 So you ought to have deposited my money with the bankers, and at my coming I would have received back my own with interest. 28 So take the talent from him, and give it to him who has ten talents.

29 'For to everyone who has, more will be given, and he will have abundance; but from him who does not have, even what he has will be taken away. 30 And cast the unprofitable servant into the outer darkness. There will be weeping and gnashing of teeth.'

Which of these individuals do you most identify? Why?
What are your talents? How are you using the talents GOD has given you? How can you use more of your talents for HIS purpose?

Notes

Day 2 Leadership Scripture: Mark 10:17-22 (NIV)

17 As Jesus started on his way, a man ran up to him and fell on his knees before him.
"Good teacher," he asked, "what must I do to inherit eternal life?"
18 "Why do you call me good?" Jesus answered. "No one is good—except God
alone. 19 You know the commandments: 'You shall not murder, you shall not commit
adultery, you shall not steal, you shall not give false testimony, you shall not defraud,
honor your father and mother.'"
20 "Teacher," he declared, "all these I have kept since I was a boy."
21 Jesus looked at him and loved him. "One thing you lack," he said. "Go, sell everything you have and
give to the poor, and you will have treasure in heaven. Then come, follow me."
22 At this the man's face fell. He went away sad, because he had great wealth.

Many talented individuals often talk about those who mentored them. Why do you think this man, who is known as the rich young ruler, sought JESUS? Was he looking for a mentor? Why or why not?

Why do you think JESUS told him to get rid of all that he owned? What would you have done?

Do you think money or talent is enough for success? Why or why not?

Notes

Day 3 Leadership Scripture: John 16:12-15 (NIV)

12 "I have much more to say to you, more than you can now bear. 13 But when he, the Spirit of truth, comes, he will guide you into all the truth. He will not speak on his own; he will speak only what he hears, and he will tell you what is yet to come. 14 He will glorify me because it is from me that he will receive what he will make known to you. 15 All that belongs to the Father is mine. That is why I said the Spirit will receive from me what he will make known to you."

What did you have to do to gain the talent you have?
During the last supper, JESUS talked about the HOLY SPIRIT. What do you think JESUS meant when HE said the HOLY SPIRIT "will guide you into all the truth"? How is that a help to your honing your talent?
How do you "glorify" JESUS with your talent?

Notes

About the Author

Stan Washington accepted the LORD at the age of 12. He walked away from serving GOD in college and pursued fulfilling his own desires. His pursuit led him to barely finish college. He became a programmer but wanted to get into learning about the business world. Still empty, he returned to the LORD wanting to get his life in order. He took many continuing education classes at a Bible Institute.

Later, he joined the largest quick service restaurant and became a McDonald's executive over Operations and Technology. After many years he turned to entrepreneurism and became the founder and president of Honor Services Office, a software company that helps small businesses grow in CHRIST as they grow their business. He is ready to share the tips he learned from his experiences while enabling a community of prayer to truly follow JESUS. Stan is the author of GOD-Centered Business: A Foundational Framework to Grow with Resilience and also is the co-author of Plans to Prosper: Strategies, Systems and Tools for Small Business Marketing Success and Peaceful Selling: Easy Sales Techniques to Grow Your Small Business.

He is married and has two children. He has traveled to Zimbabwe, China, Mexico, and many places in the United States to spread the great news about JESUS.

Contact us:

Facebook: @HonorServicesOffice and GOD-Centered Business: Global People of All Colors

LinkedIn: Honor Services GOD Centered Business

Instagram : @HonorServicesOffice

https://www.HonorServicesOffice.com

Author's Daily Devotional (This is my quiet time)

https://www.facebook.com/groups/honordevotional

https://honordevotional.blogspot.com

Other Do it Yourself Resources

Here are some other resources you can leverage to help grow your business:

Business Foundation

This study guide includes visioning, resilience testing, marketing, sales and customer service tips and a 36-day devotional.

GOD-Centered Business: A Foundational Framework to Grow with Resilience Copyright 2020 ISBN: ***978-0-9909831-6-3***

GOD-Centered Business Presentation

There is also a presentation that goes with the class. The presentation is for use with the GOD-centered Business class and can be downloaded from www.honorservices office.com. Feel free to use this in print or presentation format.

Marketing Growth Tools

Plans to Prosper: Strategies, Systems and Tools for Small Business Marketing Success (Victoria Cook and Stan Washington) Copyright 2015 ISBN: 978-0-9909831-0-1

Business Management Software

Honor Services Office is a small business management tool that provides an easy to use CRM, Online invoice / Bookkeeping System and Content Marketing system.

Visit https://www.HonorServicesOffice.com

www.ingramcontent.com/pod-product-compliance
Lightning Source LLC
Chambersburg PA
CBHW080659110426
42739CB00034B/3328
* 9 7 8 0 9 9 0 9 8 3 1 6 3 *